THE STORY 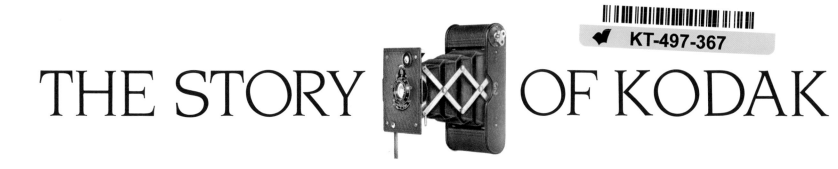 OF KODAK

HARRY N. ABRAMS, INC.,
PUBLISHERS, NEW YORK

DOUGLAS COLLINS

THE STORY OF KODAK

CONTENTS

THE KODAK CAMERA

YOU
PRESS
THE
BUTTON
WE
DO THE
REST.

AN APPROPRIATE WEDDING PRESENT

THE EASTMAN CO.
ROCHESTER·N·Y·

"IT WORKS LIKE A KODAK."

hoolboy or girl c   one of the

Eastman

ROWN   AS.

e instruments have f   hutter for snap=
time exposures—the   ous Bullet and
Kodaks. They have   ne for upright
and one for horizontal exposur   led fittings, are
covered with imitation leather,   lges and

LOAD

No. 2 Brownie Camera,
Transparent Film Cartr

$2.00
.20

*Brownie Book and Kodak Catalogue
free at the dealers or by mail.*

chester, N. Y.

$4,000.00 in Prizes fo

THEY *ALL* REMEMBERED THE

KODAK

A vacation *without* a Kodak is a vacation wasted. A Kodak
doubles the value of every journey and adds to the pleasure,
present and future, of every outing. Take a Kodak with you.
Kodaks, $5.00 to $100.00 ; Brownie Cameras. They work like
Kodaks, $1.00 to $12.00.

EASTMAN KODAK COMPANY,
ROCHESTER, N. Y., The Kodak City.

· Pictures.

KODAK

Put a
Kodak
in <u>your</u>
Pocket.

Take a
KODAK *camera*
with you

By the
KODAK
system

Pocket
Photography

The Picture From Home

Project Director and Editor: Charles Miers
Designer: Bob McKee
Rights, Reproductions, and Photo Research: John K. Crowley, Maxwell Silverman, and
Johanna Cypis

The Publisher wishes to acknowledge the cooperation of the International Museum of
Photography at George Eastman House in providing illustrations for this volume.

Publisher's Note:

Before modern trademark laws developed, many companies, including the Eastman
Kodak Company, used trademarks and names creatively but not necessarily wisely. At
the time, usage such as "Take a Kodak with you" or "Kodak as you go" was permitted
in advertisements and marketing releases. Some examples of this usage are mentioned
in this book for historical reference only.

As correct usage legally became clearer, the Eastman Kodak Company moved to
protect its trademarks vigorously and without loss of its rights. All Kodak trademarks
are now managed with great care and guarded with the appropriate attention.

Library of Congress Cataloging-in-Publication Data

Collins, Douglas, 1945–
    The story of Kodak / Douglas Collins.
        p.   cm.
    ISBN 0–8109–1222–8
    1. Eastman Kodak Company — History. 2. Photographic industry — United States —
History. 3. Photographic film industry — United States — History. 4. Camera industry —
United States — History.
I. Title.
HD9708.U64E273   1990
338.7'681418'0973 — dc20   90–364
                                                                                        CIP

FOREWORD

The story of Kodak seemed worth telling. It was long and complex enough to be described as epic. The cast of characters contained major figures in the worlds of business, politics, science, and art. It was episodic. Each era in the company's history quite naturally took on the color and temper of the times. It could easily be illustrated. In fact, much of the narrative was wordless, told purely by pictures. Above all, it was a good story, absorbing, dramatic, interesting—and it had never been told.

In other words, it was irresistible, particularly in view of the fact that the art of photography was just then celebrating its one-hundred-and-fiftieth anniversary. By 1989 the medium rightly deserved all the congratulatory messages written on its behalf. The record of photography's achievements was plain to see. Exhibition after exhibition of the great works of the great photographers were mounted, some, indeed, cosponsored by the Eastman Kodak Company. For the most part, however, these sesquicentennial shows limited themselves to a single segment of the photographic world. They were art shows, anthologies of excellence, masterpiece showcases.

As satisfying as these exhibitions were, however, they said only one thing about photography: that it was capable of great sensitivity and artistic achievement. But was that all there was to the medium? It seemed not. From its first days photography had lent itself to low as well as to high mimetic applications. Indeed, the overwhelming majority of photos taken during the past century and a half are not masterpieces. Far from it. Most are rather simple pictures, just snapshots. Though the power of these photos is usually privately held, how could a history of the medium ignore their attractions?

Most conspicuously absent from the celebrations were moving pictures. The miracle of photography is perhaps nowhere more evident than in the sequential projection of still photographs. Though movies did not come along until almost fifty years after the invention of photography, a good

Joseph DiNunzio. George Eastman. ca. 1914. Two-color Kodachrome film.

case can be made that they are its single most persuasive genre. Then there are the purely factual images, X rays, for instance, microfilmed documents, or those used for scientific measurements. Few of these could be considered artistic uses of photography, but without them photography would be a slimmer and poorer discipline.

With all this in mind Charles Miers, senior editor at Harry N. Abrams, Inc., with Robert Morton, director of special projects at Abrams, approached the Eastman Kodak Company with an idea. Kodak had been for over a hundred years the most important photographic firm in the world. There was no questioning the company's influence. Its founder, George Eastman, had with his 1888 Kodak complete system invented popular photography. The Eastman Kodak Company had also been primarily responsible for the development of color photography, most stocks used in the production of Hollywood movies, high-speed film for press photography, amateur cinematography, scientific plates and films, materials for aerial photography, and dozens of other specialized photo supplies.

Would Kodak agree to cooperate in the telling of this story? Like most large corporations the Eastman Kodak Company has traditionally claimed the right to manage its own image. Certainly it has never been reluctant to list its accomplishments. And its difficulties have been hard to hide. All the same, the goodwill it has accrued in the past one hundred and ten years is to Kodak a valuable commodity. But recognizing that its history is the basis of that goodwill, the company agreed to cooperate with the telling of this story.

This then is the story of a single company's effect upon the world of photography. But it is not only about Kodak. It is a history of photography as seen through the thousands of inventions that followed the introduction of George Eastman's first photographic products. It is also a political, scientific, and commercial story, one that cannot help but reflect the spread of photography into all sectors of modern society. In that sense, it is a narrative of the times as they have been preserved on film.

Most of all, however, it is simply a good story, and that, ultimately, is what makes it worth telling.

—Philadelphia

March 1990

ACKNOWLEDGMENTS

The year I spent working on this book was quickened by the lively conversation of all those who, when asked for help, generously offered their expertise, intelligence, and good judgment. I was responsible for the questions, however curious and unremitting; they for the patient and time-consuming effort to come up with the answers.

I am grateful, in particular, to those Eastman Kodak Company employees whose interest in this project matched my own. Michael More, director of Editorial Services, has, from the beginning, been there when I needed his intelligence, taste, and way with words of counsel. It is to his credit that this book was done at all. Members of the Editorial Services staff, Wayne J. Andrews, Rick Brunelle, Barbara Spanfelner, Michael Baziw, David Harney, and Cindi Koch, were remarkable for the speed and efficiency with which they answered requests. Wayne and Barbara, in particular, made things work — not always an easy task.

Lois Gauch, director of the Business Information Center, guided me carefully through the thousands of pages of information and the over five thousand historical photographs in the Kodak historical archives (before this collection was donated to the International Museum of Photography at George Eastman House). For that and for her sensitivity during a difficult time I am unable to thank Lois enough. The staff of the Business Information Center, Andrea Imburgia, Barbara Ann Smith, and Hildegarde Tomasino, were unfailingly cheerful even when my requests interfered with other jobs. The cooperation of David J. Metz, Kodak vice-president and director, Communications and Public Affairs, throughout this project is much appreciated, as is the time spent carefully reading the manuscript for historical references to trademark uses put in by Ronald S. Kareken, director, Trademark and Copyright Legal Staff.

Charles Styles, coordinator of Publications, Communications Licensing, was also a pleasure to work with. After Charlie's initial work was finished, he remained in disposition and interest a friend of this enterprise. David Gibson, who was about to retire as director of the Kodak Patent Museum, gave me more of his time and effort than could be expected. Ed Fortuna, imaging editor of Kodak's Image Center, the keeper of its fifty-five thousand photographs, not only shepherded me through this mass of visual information, but sent me off in other directions when necessary. Edward Howell of the Motion Pictures and Audiovisual Products Division provided me with movie information otherwise unobtainable.

At the Kodak Research Laboratories, Murray Pierson, research archivist, was my principal guide before her retirement. Despite the fact that the archival files were in the process of being moved, Murray always led me to the correct box whenever I asked to see just another photo or another piece of paper. Timothy Hughes, coordinator of Research Communications, generously provided me with some of the texts being gathered for a history of the Kodak Research Laboratories. These scientific papers and historical reminisences, written by past and present members of the lab, were a rare sort of resource.

Many of the photographs included in the final chapter of this book were made possible through the efforts of Raymond DeMoulin, vice-president and general manager of the Professional Photography Division. DeMoulin's consistent and attentive support of professional photographers of all sorts has resulted in high-quality images being made on the latest Kodak films by many of the world's best photographers. I am grateful to DeMoulin and members of his staff, C. Douglas Putnam, director, Worldwide Marketing, Professional Photography Division, and Ann Moscicki, manager, Special Projects, Professional Photography Division, for their help in obtaining such photographs for this book.

Three people at Kodak were kind enough to read the manuscript and offer suggestions, both factual and interpretive: Lois Gauch who offered her historical expertise; retired Kodak chemist Dr. T. H. James, a scholar in his own right, who with patience and meticulous care taught me much science; and David Gibson, whose mastery of the history of Kodak cameras seems to me unsurpassed. Whatever mistakes I made along the way were purely my own. Much of what I got right was due to their help.

I am also indebted to the efforts of Kodak employees overseas. Chris Roberts, head of Specialist Information Services at Harrow, provided me with much of my information about the early days of Kodak Limited. Chris's knowledge of photography and sophistication in visual matters were often of great help. Dr. Karl Steinorth of Kodak A.G. in Germany provided photographs otherwise unobtainable. Gilbert Delahaye of Kodak-Pathé in Paris sent along valuable information about the history of that Kodak subsidiary.

Finally there are those many Kodak retirees, people such as Bob Brown, John Faber, and the dozens of others who told me a story or provided information. In this category I include Brian Coe, former curator of the Kodak Museum at Kodak Limited, whose books have been a mine of information, and the late Wyatt Brummitt, who researched the history of Kodak with the knowledge of an insider and the thoroughness of a historian. Without the work of these and the countless others who over the years gathered the historical records contained in the Kodak archives, much of the company's history would be irretrievably lost.

Many of the photographs reproduced in this book were chosen from the vast photographic collection at the International Museum of Photography at George Eastman House in Rochester. David Wooters, GEH's print archivist, and his assistants Janice Madhu and Joe Struble spent innumerable hours gathering the photographs I requested. David, who also offered suggestions to the manuscript, is one of the most patient, knowledgeable, and considerate researchers I have ever worked with. Robin Blair Bolger of the GEH film department, who diligently pulled movie stills from the museum's collection, answered every question I asked with an unmistakable scholarly delight. To Philip Condax, GEH's technology curator, I owe much for his hours of discussion and for the use of dye-transfer images made by his father, Louis Condax. Also at GEH Michael Hager and David Gibney helped me track down many of the color photographs in this book. I would also like to thank James Conlin, GEH's assistant registrar, for searching out early George Eastman photo albums. To Patricia Musolf and Barbara Galasso, who, under a tight time schedule, obtained for us images for this book, much thanks. James Enyeart, Eastman House's director, also gave us his support. Similar thanks must be given to Frances Diamond of the Royal Archives at Windsor Castle for her help with the photographs taken by Queen Alexandra and to the print researchers at the Kodak Museum in Bradford, England, for locating turn-of-the-century Kodak photographs.

At Abrams, Charles Miers, senior editor, stands as the instigator and the most ardent, enthusiastic, and hard-working supporter of this book. It was Charles who shared my satisfaction as month after month the story of Kodak began to come together in words and pictures. For this rapport and, indeed, for his relentless curiosity and rigorous trailing of material, I thank Charles. Robert Morton, director of Special Projects, was instrumental with Charles in supporting the idea and in presenting it to Kodak. Abrams designer Bob McKee, whose quick eye and good hand are responsible for the layout of this book, was also a good companion. In Rochester, looking at the literally thousands of pictures spread before him, Bob was faced with the formidable task of seeing how the final selections might make syntactical sense on the page. That this book looks good is Bob's work. I would also like to thank Abrams picture researchers John Crowley, Johanna Cypis, and Maxwell Silverman for their help in locating some of the seldom published photos included here; Ellen Rosefsky for her patient editorial assistance; and Suzanne Cohn for expediting business matters.

Finally there are important words of debt directed to two very important people: Raymond D. Collins, pax, and Kristine F. Collins, felix.

As so often happens, not much besides a single photo is left to tell the story. True, there are a few stray historical facts, and they help. We know that the name of the little boy who stares expectantly at the viewer is George Eastman. We are also told that when this tintype was taken he was three years old. We can thus figure by simple arithmetic that the photo must have been made sometime in 1857, three years after Eastman's birth on July 12, 1854. But for the moment, that's about all there is in this slim historical file.

All, of course, except for the most important piece of information, the photograph; but at first even it seems fairly commonplace, one of the thousands of inexpensive tintypes taken of small children during the nineteenth century, not really all that important. However, like all continuous-tone photographs, this one is dense with historical data. Each of its thousands of grains of light-sensitive silver halides is like a piece of a puzzle. When drawn into a startlingly lifelike pattern by the magical actinic agency of ordinary light, these specks of silver suddenly begin to narrate an intricate and surprisingly expansive tale. In this single uninspired picture, as in many photographs, there is art, industry, social history, science, some luck, and, not surprisingly, a small amount of inexpertise.

But first the photo. If truth be told, the boy does not look awfully comfortable. Perhaps it is the parade-ground posture, the struggle against slouch. The young Eastman seems ill at ease. And indeed, why not? In the mid-nineteenth century having one's picture taken was not an everyday event. Photography had not as yet outspread the realm of the special.

It is possible that one day the wagon of an itinerant tintypist showed up in Eastman's rural hometown and people lined up as they would at a country fair. Perhaps the occasion was more formal. By the mid-1850s most good-sized towns and cities registered at least one portrait studio on their commercial rolls, so it is reasonable to suppose that for the express purpose of having his picture taken the boy was dressed in his Sunday clothes and driven up the plank road to the city of Utica, New York, twenty miles to the north.

In a larger city such as New York, he and his parents might have been ushered into a tastefully decorated parlor, its carpeted lobby decorated with brocade sitting chairs, carved-oak side tables, and oriental carpets. Looking around, the customers would have seen framed examples of the operator's work hung on the walls. Here and there, well-arranged display cases would contain frames, cases, and all the other peripherals that went along with the purchase of a picture.

Probably not in Utica, though. More likely, this studio would be a salon in name only, not much more than a single large room with a plank floor, an open window catching the light, and a low ceiling rigged with some sort of crudely constructed skylight. Its most conspicuous—and maybe its only—furnishings would be a large camera on a tripod, an ordinary kitchen chair, and a muslin curtain hanging from the ceiling.

Inauspicious surroundings for such a magical operation. But after about twenty minutes the customer would walk out with a lifelike image in his hand, and what could be more curious, illogical, enigmatic, and miraculous? That a plain wooden box with a protruding brass tube could be capable of manufacturing an image of a human being would seem to make precious little sense, especially to a three-year-old child. Exposure times in those days could last anywhere between two and twenty seconds, and it was not uncommon for children to be gently but firmly strapped in the posing chair and told not to move; under no circumstances to move until the busy man in the black coat behind the camera said so. The boy in the picture sits very still — waiting.

There are two other immediately striking facts about this picture. The first is the disconcerting streak of dark shadow about the face. The shape of the head is alright, but Eastman's eyes are very dark and deep set, unusual in a child of that age. What's more, dingy gray middle tones almost entirely cover the lower half of his face. In fact, it appears as if the prominent cleft in Eastman's chin, so noticeable in pictures made of him as a grown man, is comically hidden beneath a five-o'clock shadow of fine backyard dust. The boy's hair also seems a little peculiar. On one side of his head it is fair and relatively thin; on the other it is bushy and well-defined. As a whole, the surface texture of the entire picture is soft, unfocused, and creamy, except that is, along the right-hand side of the profile, where the contrast is razor sharp.

Perhaps this is the result of poor posing and misdirected light. The two major errors of portrait photography, one tintype handbook of the time stated, are the wedgelike appearance called "hatchet" face, caused by too strong a stream of harsh window light, and "the shadow under the chin assuming the shape of a beard," created by an equally intense burst of light from above. Here the camera operator has bungled on both counts. The boy's face looks in need of a good washing, and a cap of trimmed and combed hair leans lopsidedly across the top of his head.

The harsh, direct light has also made the boy's clothing look unaccountably old and threadbare. The collar of his shirt is a drab, chalky white; the dark woolen jacket lackluster and shapeless. It is hard to imagine the boy not being dressed in his best clothes that day, but that's not what we see. The monochromatic background does not help much either. Behind the boy hangs a curtain of featureless white space without depth or texture. In effect, the figure looks as if it was crudely scissored out of another photograph and pasted onto a piece of off-white bond paper.

By modern pictorial standards, actually by any gauge, this tintype is a pretty bad picture. The noted photographic historian Helmut Gernsheim called tintypes "these hideous looking cheap pictures," and the writer and curator John Szarkowski has described a similar photographic technology, the ambrotype, as "scrofulous." In truth, even at the height of its popularity the tintype had a reputation for poor quality. Whatever its genesis or literal meaning, the nineteenth-century expression "not on your tintype" was probably not intended as flattery. And later, around the turn of the century, Broadway theatrical producers latched on to the term, dismissing the newly popular art of moving pictures as nothing but "galloping tintypes."

Whatever the quality of the final product, at least the whole thing was over quickly and it didn't cost too much. By the time the boy was settled into the posing chair, the tintypist had already materialized from behind a black curtain carefully carrying between the pads of his fingers a plate holder containing a thin wet piece of flat black iron. A practiced flip of the box's lid and the plate holder was slipped between a set of vertical wooden slats inside the back of the camera. (This was the wet-collodion method of picture taking, but such technical details were certainly beyond the understanding of the average customer.)

The camera itself looked plain enough. Just a box. It is unlikely that the tintypist's instrument came equipped with even a simple shutter mechanism, so, after cautioning the boy, the photographer reached around the front of the box, removed a brass cap from the tube, held it in his palm for a few seconds, and then, with a sigh of relief, stuck it back on the lens tube. The picture taken, and that part of the job finished, the operator reversed his movements, removing the plate with great care and disappearing behind the curtain.

If the customer had been allowed to follow the photographer into his makeshift darkroom, it would have taken a while to get used to the orangey yellow light, an effect produced by a makeshift masking over a small window with colored glass. (The light-sensitive solution spread across the plate was red blind; but that also would probably be beyond the customer's comprehension.)

Once inside his small dark closet, the photographer cradled the plate over some sort of hastily outfitted sink with one hand and, after adroitly grabbing a bottle with the other, poured an ounce or so of its ferrous sulfate-alcohol-water solution over the front of the still black plate. Within seconds, a creamy white deposit of silver would begin trailing across the plate. As the eyes adjusted to this change, the outline of a picture appeared, seemingly etched by the dark lines left between the irregular patches of silver.

When a tolerable likeness materialized, the tintypist immersed the entire picture in another pan of fluid for a few seconds, shook off the excess, and gently rinsed the whole plate in a bowl of the purest, cleanest water he could come up with. In a few minutes the plate was dry and could be handed to the customer with the admonishment to be careful. If the tintypist was a good businessman, he probably then directed the buyer to a small display of Ferro mounts and holders, or maybe he offered for a few cents extra to coat the front of the photo with a special rock-hard varnish.

And that was it: easy, economical, and fast. Not as simple as stepping in and out of a coin-operated photo booth, but close. If the operator was swift of hand, he could move customers in and out in a matter of minutes and after a day's work take enough pictures to make it financially worth his while. The exact price of this particular picture is hard to come by, but in those days a good quality half-plate (4¼ x 5½ inches) daguerreotype could be bought for as little as a dollar. This tintype is a one-ninth plate (2¾ x 3¼ inches) and probably cost about a quarter. Of course, if the customer was willing to throw in a few cents extra, the picture could be gussied up by the purchase of a little daguerreotype frame.

And a frame made a considerable difference. Frames of the sort that Eastman's parents bought, along with the small ornate picture boxes popularly called "Union cases," were also relatively cheap. Molded from a mixture of shellac and sawdust, they came in hundreds of off-the-shelf designs. Certainly, the fake carving and intricately interwoven tendrils around the borders of these mass-produced thermoplastic frames almost comically overpower the unassuming little pictures. But a molded frame was low cost, readily available, and at least looked like the real thing. Enhanced by its elaborate frame or case and propped up on the family mantelpiece, the tintype was, if not a thing of artistic beauty, at least an article of genuine family value.

Not that the tintype had any particular artistic pretensions. No doubt if a portrait of the boy had been taken by a skilled operator, exposing a glass-plate negative by means of the latest wet-plate technology and then reproducing the picture on low-gloss albumen paper, the print quality of this little portrait would have been considerably higher. But that sort of picture was not universally available. In New York, Philadelphia, Washington, and other large metropolitan centers, spacious, ornate portrait galleries, such as that owned by Mathew Brady, were putting out what we now consider museum-quality images. In Paris, a commercial photographer who called himself Nadar was initiating a series of psychologically acute portraits of men and women of the day that even a hundred years later would be avidly collected by museums. And in England in the early 1860s, to cite another example, a gifted amateur named Julia Margaret Cameron had begun making remarkable art-inspired portraits heavy with the windswept spirit of Pre-Raphaelite painting. There is little doubt, though, that anyone unable to visit studios of this caliber (and that included most of the photographic public) would have a chance to see anything approaching the best photographic work of the time.

By the end of the century this would change in unexpected ways. As a matter of fact, in 1890 George Eastman would have his picture taken by Paul Nadar, the photographer's son, and would reciprocate by taking a portrait of that photographer himself. By then both pictures, surprisingly enough, were taken on film bearing the Eastman brand name. But that was a photographic revolution away.

In 1857, however, the tintype was a transitional photographic technology. It was a single-copy, direct-positive, metal-plate picture, and each of those characteristics looked back to the beginnings of the medium. Yet its light-sensitive silver salts were suspended in a wet-collodion solution, a process that dominated photography for the next twenty-five years.

At the time, a tintype such as this was good enough. Actually more than good enough. No doubt all who saw it thought the likeness uncannily accurate. No one who knew him would have trouble recognizing the boy. At least that part of photography was to change very little.

When the young George Eastman had his picture taken, photography had been around for less than twenty years, considerably less than a generation. Hardly time for the world to become used to it, much less to grasp or understand its magic. However, then as now, for most consumers of the medium a detailed knowledge of photographic technology was not important. By the middle of the nineteenth century, the consumer demand for pictures of all kinds, especially portraits, had become part of the economics of picture making. People wanted photos; the easier, quicker, and cheaper the better.

The Eastman family was perhaps typical of this phenomenon. Roger Eastman and Thomas Kilborne, the paternal and maternal progenitors of Eastman's father and mother, had emigrated to Massachusetts and Connecticut from England in the mid-1600s. In the early 1800s descendants of each family had moved westward to upstate New York. At that time, the natural pastures and wooded hills of Oneida County, just south of the Adirondack Mountains, was still wild, scrubby country with a few dirt roads running between isolated villages.

In mid-century the railroad and the Erie Canal would change that. By the time George Washington Eastman, Sr., was an adult, the westward expansion movement had begun. In 1842 Eastman left his hometown of Waterville, New York, a village of several hundred hops farmers and small tradesmen, for Rochester, a commercial and industrial city about a hundred miles to the west. It is not clear where he acquired his business training and expertise, but in Rochester he founded a college: The Eastman Commercial College, a business school that offered courses in the study of commercial penmanship, double-entry bookkeeping, and even spelling, a linguistic discipline that had only recently become regularized by Noah Webster's new American dictionary.

The Eastman Commercial College was soon successfully established. By 1854, when his son was born, the elder Eastman was able to move his academy to the fourth floor of one of Rochester's most prominent buildings and, according to his catalog, was charging "for Teacher's course, including Ornamental Penmanship in all the Ancient and Modern Hands: $30. For Collegiate Course and Diploma: $25. For a Course of Lessons in Book-keeping alone: $10. For 24 lessons in Penmanship: $5."

By all accounts Eastman the business educator was a fiscal conservative. He believed in the security of hard coin in the hand, no doubt a sensible economic persuasion in the years following the panics, depressions, and market fluctuations of the late 1840s and early 1850s. In light of this principle, Eastman's school advertised that it was "the first training college in the country to introduce actual business transactions in its course of studies."

Students were issued printed paper currency drawn on Eastman's College Bank, and in the course of their studies they made transactions in "Wholesale, Retail, Commission, Manufacturing, Shipping and Steamboating, Individual Partnership and Compound Companies." A bad investment and the student found himself cash poor. Apparently Eastman presumed that an empty pocketbook, albeit only short of the college's paper currency, tutored the student in the grim realities that lay just behind the unbalanced debit column.

Eastman also wrote a textbook on formal handwriting entitled *Chirographic Charts.* A kind of McGuffey's reader for penmanship, it preached as the pupil practiced. Students were asked to copy short sayings of "proverbial philosophy" of "very general application":

> *My boy, be cool*
> *Do things by rule,*
> *And then you'll do them right.*

Not the best piece of poetry around, but unavoidably direct in its compact single couplet and horatory dactylic summation.

In 1844, two years after the founding of his college, Eastman went back to Waterville and married Maria Kilbourn. It is hard to say what financial anxieties beset Eastman, but for the next few years his family remained in Waterville and he regularly commuted the hundred miles between work and home. In that time, three children were born, first two daughters, Ellen and Emma, and then in 1854, a son, George. Given the difficulties and expense of transportation, weeks probably went by between Eastman's trips home. Sometime in the late 1840s, if we can correctly guess their ages from the two undated images, both Eastman parents sat before the daguerreotype camera. Maybe the two pictures were wedding photos or perhaps they were simply emblems of Eastman's growing good fortune.

The craft of daguerreotypy, the chemistry of which had been first described in France in 1839, was a relatively simple piece of work. Just about anyone handy and smart enough to follow instructions could produce a passable image. Many a small-town commercial photographer, such as Holgrave, the daguerreotypist in Nathaniel Hawthorne's *House of the Seven Gables*, was more tradesman than artist, having wandered into the occupation from any one of a number of skilled or semiskilled jobs. "Today you will find the Yankee," Hawthorne noted, "taking daguerreotypes, tomorrow he has turned painter, the third day he is tending grocery, dealing out candy to babies for one cent a stick."

The sales and service sides of daguerreotypy, however, were sometimes less easy to manage. More than one customer complained that his daguerreotype portrait was unflattering, even ugly. One trouble was that the cold and indifferent eye of the camera lacked the soft stroke of the painter's brush. Daguerreotype pictures were indiscriminate when it came to the duplication of detail. Though the sitter may not have been happy with the result, it often turned out that people with oversized features were the most graphically photogenic. In fact, one of the first how-to books on photography, the American Henry Hunt Snelling's 1849 *History and Practice of the Art of Photography*, begrudgingly admitted that sometimes "the most homely faces make the handsomest pictures."

Time and discomfort also conspired to disrupt the production of pleasing and attractive portraits. Daguerreotypy required a well-lighted studio and a closet full of noxious and sometimes dangerous chemicals. And it was a slow process. Well into the mid-1840s, even after significant improvements in the procedure, portrait photography still required exposure times of somewhere between ten and forty seconds. To sit still this long was no easy task, even with an iron brace called an appui-tête pressing against the subject's spine and his hands gripping a chair arm for dear life.

No doubt the grim, operatic dyspepsia we spy on many of the faces peering out of daguerreotype frames is the result of the slow, choking off of oxygen that stiffened muscle after muscle during the interminable half a minute the person was warned to hold still. So, as astonishing an invention as daguerreotypy was, in its beginning days it was often a rough, unpolished business. Its potential was apparent; its successes problematic.

The formal announcement of the invention of photography in January 1839 had a nearly instantaneous impact upon the public — particularly in America. Just a few short months after the notice of the Daguerrean procedure was published in Paris, curious and inventive Americans were eager to try out this new thing.

Samuel F. B. Morse, the inventor of the electric telegraph, bought a copy of Daguerre's manual, had a manufacturer of scientific instruments named George Prosch rig up a camera, and succeeded in October 1839 in making one of the first American photographs, a picture of Boston's city hall. The next month, November, Robert Cornelius, a Philadelphia jack-of-all-trades is reported to have taken a tin box, fixed it up with a two-inch lens from a pair of ordinary opera glasses, and by following Daguerre's procedure made the earliest surviving portrait of a human being. Some scholars have doubted Cornelius's word and accorded this honor to Morse and a photographer named John Draper; but whomever the first portraitist, capturing a living likeness, considering the necessity of a long exposure time even in bright sunlight, was a remarkable feat. (One claimant to the award of first portraitist, Alfred Donne, was discovered to have avoided the problem of movement by taking a picture of a dead man.)

By the late 1840s, daguerreotypy was fully qualified to be called a craze. At first, the exposure time required for a daguerreotype portrait was too long for this genre to be commercially practical. But with the introduction of the Petzval lens, which admitted twenty times more light than the lenses used by Daguerre, and the addition of a bromine accelerator ("quickstuff") to the plate's coating, exposure times were reduced to one minute.

In America, the commercial possibilities of daguerreotypy were also stimulated by improved methods of manufacturing and merchandising. A few large supply houses, primarily the Scovill Company of Waterbury, Connecticut, and the Anthony Company of New York City, sold mechanically buffed and electroplated daguerreotype plates and high-quality cameras and chemicals. In some cities there were huge daguerreotype galleries, and even a few organized daguerreotype retail chains, such as John Plumbe's. For the most part, however, the thriving American daguerreotype industry was made up of thousands of single-proprietor shops advertised only by a sign out front. And it was into one of these that Eastman's parents, George W. Eastman and Maria Kilbourn Eastman, had, like thousands of others, entered and sat for formal portraits.

George and Maria assumed almost exactly the same pose, seated with the right shoulder half turned toward the camera, left arm propped on a small inconspicuous side table. In all fairness, it should be noted that these two pictures are absolutely routine and prosaic. Their quality is acceptable, but just so. As one early photographer commented about similar daguerreotypes, "Some magnificent portraits were taken, which were perfect likenesses, in which only one thing was wanting — expression." While all old photographs are predestined to date themselves (articles of clothing, furniture, even the pose inevitably carry tags of their times), daguerreotypes seem the most timebound of all. Jackets and dresses contain their occupants like molded plastic; arms are held stiffly like crooks of wood. Most people seem to be stoically struggling against the taut pull of a backstage puppeteer's strings.

But for all their deficiencies, the pictures are uncommonly handsome in their range and depth of detail. Modern photomechanical reproductions of daguerreotypes are slightly deceiving. Most daguerreotypes were, as John Szarkowski has written, "generally smaller than the palm of one's

Shortly after George Eastman, Sr., and Maria Kilbourn were married, the two had daguerreotype portraits taken. Daguerreotype exposure times were still measured in seconds, and though the subjects strained to keep still, the often unintended consequences of this tenacious effort were the oddly wooden gestures and arrested expressions that we now associate with the early days of portrait photography.

hand," and "should be looked at with [their cases] not fully opened, preferably in private and by lamplight, as one would approach a secret." When these images are examined under a magnifying glass, an almost microscopic world of exquisite lines and shades appears. The phrase that has become synonymous with daguerreotypes is in all senses exact; each seems to be a "mirror with a memory."

Thus even if the Eastmans' daguerreotypes lack liveliness and animation, each is an individual portrait produced quickly by pure chemical and mechanical means, and to a world unaccustomed to such a luxury that single fact more than accounts for the great popularity of the daguerreotype. In the hands of skilled operators such as the American masters Albert Southworth and Josiah Hawes or the equally distinguished French portraitist Antoine-Samuel Adam-Salomon, the daguerreotype image has an odd though quite particular beauty. Despite the rigidity and stillness of most daguerreotypes made during the classical era of this technology, nothing like its graphic quality existed before, or since.

The daguerreotype's pioneers, two clever and enterprising Frenchman, Joseph Nicéphore Nièpce and Louis-Jacques-Mandé Daguerre had, after much trial and error, succeeded where numbers of others had failed. Together, they had come up with a permanent chemical and mechanical method of image making. Before the daguerreotype, portraits were painted, drawn, or etched by those lucky enough to be gifted with artistic ability. There were a few ways to get around a lack of talent, of course, but none of them was particularly satisfying. Silhouettes could be made by positioning a subject between a bright light and a paper background and then tracing the outline on the paper. However, these looked like what they were: monochromatic cutouts.

There was also the physiontrace, an eighteenth-century pantographlike device that hooked a tracing pencil by means of a Rube Goldberg series of levers and linkages to a hard-pointed etching stylus. The physiontrace had this advantage over the silhouette: if the pieces of linkage connecting the two drawing points were cleverly constructed, a life-sized silhouette could be reduced or enlarged at will. Another of these copying devices was the camera obscura, the most faithful and accurate of all these mechanical techniques. In a certain sense, it was also the most photographic. Historians dispute the date of the camera obscura's invention, but at least since Aristotle in the fourth century B.C. its optical principles had been noticed.

Reflected light, which allows us to see the objects of the world, glances off objects in an infinite number of directions. Like rubber balls thrown against a wall, each ray of light comes from one direction and bounces in another. Thus two people standing a couple of feet apart will both be able to see the same object, one by means of one set of reflected rays, the other by a wholly different group. Additionally, and even more importantly, each of these infinite number of light rays travels in an apparently straight path, so straight that Isaac Newton believed that light was made up of tiny bulletlike corpuscles traveling at incredible speeds. (Later it was discovered that Newton was wrong, that light moves in waves, but for the purposes of early photography this was not important.) Out of a legion of reflected rays only a single discrete set enters a pair of human eyes. Otherwise, instead of a sharply composed single image, we might see millions of images, perhaps just a halo of light—a dizzying prospect.

These simple optical laws have had a profound effect upon photography. Without them the daguerreotype process loses a crucial ingredient: the camera. First described in 1568 by an Italian professor, Daniello Barbaro, the early camera obscura (literally "dark chamber") was nothing more complex than a box with a small lens in one end and a piece of unpolished ground glass at the other. It captured and retained images in much the same way that a common telescope does. Since the hole in the camera obscura was quite small, smaller than the eye in fact, only a very few of the infinite number of rays reflecting back from an object were allowed to enter the dark box. The rest bounced off the front of the box or missed it entirely. When these few rays were viewed through the ground glass at the back of the box, they formed an image in some ways similar to the image focused on the human retina.

In the case of the camera obscura, however, the viewing glass was large enough so that if a piece of transparent tracing paper was placed over it, the luminous image in front of the eyes could be traced. In other words, an image could be copied directly and accurately from nature. However, if the small opening in the box, its aperture, was covered, the image disappeared. This not inconsiderable obstacle had to be overcome. At first Nièpce and Daguerre both worked on the problem independently and for different reasons. Nièpce was a free-lance inventor who at some point became interested in lithography, the technique of printing multiple images by using a wet stone to retain greasy pencil markings.

The technique worked fine; but Nièpce couldn't draw. To get around this not uncommon lack of expertise, he decided that a way ought to be found to leave the haplessly untalented person out of the process, to put some sort of mechanical device between nature and the finished image. Nièpce knew that certain chemicals change color when placed in sunlight. After a number of trial-and-error failures with various compounds, he dissolved a natural asphalt called bitumen of Judea in a liquid mixture known as Dippel's oil and spread the concoction over a polished pewter plate. He then placed a translucent paper engraving over the sensitized plate and exposed the plate, chemicals, and paper to the light.

A remarkable thing happened. After the paper was removed and the coated plate washed with lavender oil, each minute line of the engraving appeared etched on the surface. This result was easy to explain. Bitumen of Judea hardens when exposed to light. Where the light was blocked by the black engraved lines of the picture, the asphalt remained soft. The lavender oil floated away these canals of soft asphalt, leaving the pewter plate looking as if it had been finely etched. Which in one way it had; and in one way it had not. Nièpce, who had no skill with the pencil or stylus, also had no hand in the drawing. It was the catalytic properties of light—simple, direct sunlight—that had succeeded in scratching the lines into what is now known as photosensitive material.

Nièpce then met another Frenchman also interested in photochemical reproduction. Daguerre was at the time a Parisian theatrical producer; the owner, operator, and principal artist of an illusionistic stage display known as the Diorama. By a series of manipulations of projected light upon painted theatrical gauze, the Diorama produced an effect we might now call cinematic. When the theatrical scrim was manipulated within the beams of these primitive floodlights, Daugerre's painted images moved, danced, and shimmered. But Daguerre was not satisfied with the slow and sometimes tedious process of hand painting each piece of theatrical gauze. All along he had sometimes made use of the camera obscura to expedite the drawing process.

Daguerre had been working with various light-sensitive substances when he and Nièpce began corresponding. Nièpce had experimented with iodized silver plates but had been unable to fix his images. It is unclear exactly which ideas Nièpce gave Daguerre, but Daguerre was encouraged by their correspondence and continued to work on photochemical methods of image making after Nièpce's death in 1833. Four years later Daguerre succeeded in taking and fixing an image, and in January 1839 François Arago, the director of the Paris Observatory, to whom Daguerre had shown his pictures, recommended in a lecture to the Academy of Sciences that the French government purchase the invention. In return, Daguerre was asked to describe publicly his picture-making procedure.

Thus on August 19, 1839, the French Academy of Sciences and Academy of Fine Arts jointly made the formal announcement of the invention of photography. Nièpce had died six years earlier, but his son Isadore and Daguerre were granted lifetime annuities by the French government: Daguerre of six thousand francs and Nièpce of four thousand francs.

When the procedure was first described, the bitumen of Judea lithographic technique had been eliminated. In its place was a version of the light-sensitive silver-salt process that today we call photography. Daguerre had coated a copper plate with silver and then polished the shiny surface by lightly buffing it with very fine pumice powder. That step completed, he washed the plate and put it in a light-proof box with its silver side facedown over a saucer of iodine. When the iodine fumes hit the plate, the molecular dance known as a chemical reaction occurred and the heretofore unattached silver and iodine paired to form silver iodide.

The plate was then inserted into a camera obscura, the lens of which had been focused. The lens was uncapped and light was allowed to strike the silver iodide. After five to forty minutes, depending on the brightness of the sun, the plate was removed, looking slightly frosty but not significantly different than it had looked before the exposure. The silver-iodide copper plate was then placed over a pan of heated mercury. Fumes from the mercury rose, again causing a chemical change of partners. This time, the mercury was absorbed where the plate had been exposed to light, leaving a bright silver amalgam image that mimicked every minute intensity of the light that had found its way through the lens of the camera. The image was rinsed with hydrosulfite of soda, which washed away the unaffected silver iodide, in effect fixing the picture.

Today we would say that the mercury vapor developed the latent image produced by the reaction of the sun's rays with silver iodide compound. The subatomic intricacies of that chemical reaction would not be understood for almost a hundred years, but at the time that did not matter. It was the picture that counted, an image etched by nothing more than the sun, a primitive camera, and a few chemicals.

Initially the commercial possibilities of the invention were hard to gauge. Daguerre patented the process in England, and in 1838 he and Isadore Nièpce tried unsuccessfully to find commercial backers. In 1841 one observer dismissed this earliest version of photography as "a beautiful but almost useless thing—a philosophic toy, which lent a little assistance to the cultivation of taste, but afforded none to the economy of manufacture."

During the next few years, however, exposure times were shortened, and development techniques improved. The "useless" little scientific amusement produced lifelike pictures, and no matter what the deficiencies of product or production, people wanted these pictures.

From 1841 until the late 1850s, particularly in America, where the mechanics of the process were improved, daguerreotype technology caught society's imagination. Portraiture was the genre most in demand, and business was brisk. By the early 1850s competition and greater efficiency had driven the price of a high-quality, one-sixth plate picture down from five dollars to two dollars and fifty cents. In many markets, in fact, a small daguerreotype could be had for a dollar.

The daguerreotype business was not limited solely to portraiture. The Langenheim brothers of Philadelphia were among the first to begin marketing souvenir travel pictures. Niagara Falls, a hundred miles to the west of the Eastman home in Rochester, was a particularly popular subject. The Langenheims traveled to the falls, daguerreotyped a series of majestic views, and sent off matched sets of these pictures to the crowned heads of Europe. The Niagara Falls pictures were applauded, admired, but, to the Langenheim's disappointment, went unsold.

A few daguerreotypists also seemed to be intrigued by the yet unnamed idea of photojournalism. In 1853, about fifty miles north of the Eastman home, a large mill on the Oswego River caught fire. A daguerreotypist named George N. Barnard operated a studio nearby. While the mill was burning intensely, Barnard took on-the-spot pictures of the disaster from just across the river. His daguerreotype plates had a very difficult time stopping action, of course. Even with hand coloring the flames are little more than a spreading glow, and the clouds of smoke swirl upward like slowly waving sheets.

After having mastered the wet-collodion method of photography in 1852, Gaspard Félix Tournachon, who called himself "Nadar," spent much of the next two decades taking portraits of the most celebrated Parisian celebrities and boulevardiers of the day. Many of Nadar's three-quarter-length character studies, such as this portrait of the architect Viollet-le-Duc, were in the late 1870s printed by the gelatin-relief Woodbury process and published in an edition of 241 portraits entitled Galerie Contemporaine.

Though the daguerreotype technology, with its long exposure times, was ill-equipped to capture events as they unfolded, in 1853 George Barnard set up his daguerreotype camera on a bank of the Oswego River and took pictures of a fire destroying a complex of wooden mill buildings a few hundred yards in the distance. The movement of the firefighters is blurred, and even after hand coloring the smoke and flames melt into a waving mass, but at the very least the picture prefigures the camera's future role in purely reportorial news coverage.

*The introduction of albumen paper en-
abled photographers, as never before, to
manipulate the quality of their final prints.
Gustav Le Gray, one of the first to sensitize
plates with wet collodion, was also a master of the albumen printing process. Since
his plates were overly sensitive to the blue
end of the photographic spectrum, he was
unable to capture sea and sky in a single
shot. To create this image Le Gray took
two separate exposures and assembled
them in a combination albumen print.*

As pioneering as these pictures were, the daguerreotype had a number of defects. The
coating was, at the time, relatively insensitive, but another problem was the support, the silver-
coated copper sheet upon which the chemicals were coated. Like today's instant pictures,
daguerreotypes are one of a kind; the image is permanently attached to the support. At first this
seemed acceptable, but when in response to the development of other photographic processes
the public began to demand multiple copies of an image, the daguerreotype could not respond.
The only way to reproduce a daguerreotype was to daguerreotype it. The daguerreotype also
had a related problem. The silvered copper plate was relatively strong, but the delicate deposit
of mercury amalgam on its surface was not. To protect the picture a piece of glass needed to be
placed over it, and glass was breakable. For photography to be efficient and workable, the
balance between light-sensitive coating and support had to be absolutely steady, a fact made
more than clear by the fate of photography's acknowledged co-inventor, the British amateur
scientist William Henry Fox Talbot.

It is one of the curiosities of scientific history that the world will wait hundreds of years for a
single invention only to have two or more experimenters come up with the same idea almost
precisely at the same time. In 1839, coincidentally but on different sides of the English Channel,
both Daguerre and Talbot demonstrated the magical combination of camera and light-sensitive
silver salts. Talbot's method, however, differed from Daguerre's in two significant ways: Talbot's
photographic support was paper, and his image was produced by the negative-to-positive
process.

In place of Daguerre's polished and silvered plate, Talbot placed high-quality writing paper
behind the camera's lens. After long exposure and mercury fuming, the light that had struck the
silver iodide on Daguerre's polished pewter plate built up a reflective deposit of mercury silver
amalgam. Talbot discovered that by bathing his paper in successive solutions of silver nitrate

and potassium iodide and washing it in another solution called gallo-nitrate of silver, an extremely light-sensitive coating was created.

After being photographically exposed, the paper was then rewashed (developed) in the gallo-nitrate. Where light had hit the light-sensitive silver salts it left an invisible latent image on Talbot's paper negative. Chemical development made the image visible. (This discovery considerably shortened exposure times.) Where light had struck the paper the chemicals now turned the silver black. In fact, the more intense the light the blacker the deposits of silver. The brightest highlights came out pitch black, and the deepest areas of dark shadow were as white as the hue of the negative paper allowed. Talbot's friend Sir John Herschel came up with precisely the right word to describe this curious effect. The Talbot paper picture was, he said, a negative.

This negative image, Talbot soon realized, could be reversed by shining light once again through the paper, projecting the image onto another sheet of similarly light-sensitized paper and thereby transposing and correcting the tones. The black areas blocked the light and the white areas allowed it through. Furthermore, as Talbot also soon discovered, this apparent defect had an unexpected advantage. Once the photographer had a fixed negative in hand, he could repeat this printing process as often as he liked. One Talbot negative could conceivably generate hundreds of absolutely identical positive prints.

However, to many viewers, Talbot's prints, which he called calotypes, lacked the detail of the daguerreotype. What one hand gave, the other took away. The weave of the paper negative blocked so much light that it looked as if a sheet of gauze had been placed between camera and scene. Even Herschel, one of Talbot's strongest supporters, commented that "compared to the masterful daguerreotype, Talbot produces nothing but mistiness."

In the hands of accomplished calotypists such as the Scottish photographers David Octavius Hill and Robert Adamson, who made hundreds of portraits in the 1840s, the Talbot process

The British photographers David Octavius Hill and Robert Adamson were the most famous and successful practitioners of William Fox Talbot's paper-negative to paper-positive method of photography. Though the diffuse print quality of their portraits lacked the fine detail of daguerreotypes, the two capitalized on the defects of Talbot's calotypy by artfully arranging the soft textures and tones of their pictures around well-composed central figures.

Almost from its first days, photography has attempted to satisfy the viewing public's affinity for the exotic. Travel views of the Middle East were eagerly sought after, as were photos of the even more distant Far East. For those who were unable to visit Japan, pictures of this sort, lushly hand tinted, brought back visual proof of the texture of life in foreign and unfamiliar lands.

produced subtle and beautiful prints. But though Hill once cleverly argued that the calotype revealed "the imperfect work of man—and not the much diminished perfect work of God," by and large the photographic public did not buy this argument.

The calotype also suffered from distribution problems. Talbot had not only patented his process, but he also charged quite large fees for its use. In America, the Langenheims attempted to interest the public in the procedure, paying Talbot one thousand pounds for the rights to the process and advertising calotype prints as "devoid of all metallic glare." But they and other American commercial calotypists had very little success, and except for isolated uses the paper support was never popular.

By 1857, when the tintype of young George Eastman was taken, the photographic marketplace was beginning to respond to public demand for images that were sturdier and more cheaply produced than daguerreotypes. The tintype had been introduced and patented only a year earlier by Hamilton Smith, a Kenyon College professor of chemistry. For a twenty-dollar fee, Smith and his associate Peter Neff, a seminary student at the same school, would reveal the

secrets of the process to any and all enterprising tintypists. Armed with this knowledge, a supply of chemicals, and a batch of photographic plates, the newly licensed tintypist then set off to sell pictures.

The clever technical trick behind the tintype had been around at least since Sir John Herschel had noticed that a slightly underexposed photographic negative would look like a positive when viewed against a black background. In 1854 an American photographer named James Cutting had capitalized on this idea and patented what he called the "ambrotype." Cutting's ambrotype utilized the newly invented wet-collodion, glass-plate process. He sensitized a glass plate with silver halides suspended in a collodion binder, then exposed and fixed the glass plate. However, instead of printing the photograph on paper, he brushed a coat of black paint on the back of the glass plate and glued a protective piece of glass to the dark side with a gummy, transparent cement called fir balsam. Smith and Neff had a better idea. They got rid of the painting and pasting stages by simply spreading a light-sensitive emulsion on a piece of dull japanned black iron. The inventors called their products melanotypes, combining the Greek root words for black (*melan*-) and impression (*typos*).

This large-format documentary photo of British soldiers stationed in Egypt was taken by L. Fiorillo in 1882. Fiorillo carefully framed his record of the scene to encompass as much information as possible. Soldiers and civilians sit in rows, pyramids rise behind dunes, and the sky hangs just above the sandy desert.

But as businessmen Smith and Neff ran into a good deal of bad luck. In their first year of operation their Ohio japanning factory burned down and they found themselves in competition with another Ohio inventor, Victor Moreau Griswold, who modified the process and called his products "ferrotypes." (The commonly used term "tintype" did not accurately describe either process, since the plates did not contain tin.)

In 1857 both Smith and Griswold, with tintypes in hand, began to merchandise their newly introduced products. It would not stretch the imagination much to visualize a representative of one of these companies, with barely a few weeks of photographic training, showing up one day in upstate New York promising sturdy, quick pictures at indisputably cheap prices. The name of the young Eastman's photographer and even the location of his studio have not been identified. What we can guess with some certainty, however, is that the picture was taken in summer, when the sun was reliably bright. In fact, since Eastman's birthday was in early July, just the right season, it is not unlikely that his mother had this picture made to commemorate that occasion. The time was right, the price was reasonable, and even if the picture was not great, it at least succeeded, as one tintype enthusiast argued, in satisfying "the craving to possess some memento of the passing moment in this world of change."

In 1860, with the growth and success of the Eastman Commercial College, the entire Eastman family had moved to Rochester. At the time, Rochester was a city of over fifty thousand inhabitants, many of whom had been drawn there by its propitious location a few miles south of Lake Ontario, at the intersection of the Erie Canal and the Genesee River. Mid-nineteenth-century Rochester was a fairly prosperous town of small factories and flour mills. It had ready access to the New York Central Railroad, which ran East-West through the city, and it was growing. Seven hundred streetlights illuminated downtown avenues, and almost three thousand homes and businesses were brightened at night by gas.

News of the approaching civil war reached Rochester one evening in 1859, when New York Senator William Seward predicted to an assembly of Rochester citizens that in the future an "irrepressible conflict between opposing and enduring forces" would soon break out. In 1861, when the inaugural train of the newly elected President Abraham Lincoln stopped at the Rochester depot, Lincoln expressed surprise at "this vast number of faces at this hour of the morning." Four years later, at about three in the morning, the Lincoln funeral train passed through Rochester. There are reports of thousands lining the tracks holding burning torches.

While the town and the country were straining between economic prosperity and the devastating civil war, the Eastman family was facing more private concerns. In 1862, two years after settling his family in its new home, George Eastman, Sr., died, apparently unexpectedly. Probably never actually poor, the family's standard of living was nonetheless considerably lowered. Mrs. Eastman took in borders, one of whom, Henry Alvah Strong, would soon play a significant role in Eastman's life.

Some have speculated that these early financial worries and a lifelong fear of poverty would follow Eastman into business, but that sort of inference seems difficult to prove. On the other hand, the stories of his hard work and his equally hard eye for the budgetary bottom line indisputably point toward the future.

At fourteen, Eastman had already made five dollars' profit from the sale of "sawed" bookshelf brackets that he "cut out of black walnut in filigree design." He banked the money. He also quit school and got a job that year, being hired to work in an insurance office for three dollars a week. At the end of the year, by Eastman's own "recapitulation," he had received $131 in wages, and spent $92 on clothes, board, sundries, shoes, underclothes, and hats. That left $39, which on top of the $5 already on deposit equaled a total savings account of $44. But significantly, Eastman's personal balance sheet did not record the figure that way. Rather than adding the two figures and totaling, he subtracted his original $5 balance from that year's deposits of $39 and recorded $34, the amount of increase. Clearly he saw equity as a function of growth.

By 1871 Eastman had done moderately well for himself. On January 1, squaring away his books, he recorded $3,600 in cash and investments over and above expenses. In 1874, at age twenty, he left the insurance office to become a junior bookkeeper at the Rochester Savings Bank. By then he had taken on all financial responsibilities for the Eastman household, budgeted vacations to Maine and Niagara Falls, bought tools (and his first razor), and purchased a flute—though oddly enough for a man who would later fund orchestras and music programs, Eastman had such difficulty with the instrument that after practicing "Annie Laurie" for two years he was unable to recognize the tune when he heard someone else play it.

One other item that showed up here and there on Eastman's list of expenditures was photography. In 1869 he had recorded the purchase of a framed photograph, apparently his first, as a present for a teacher. Later that year, he bought some more photographs and a stereoscopic viewer. Similar photographic acquisitions appear on Eastman's personal books through November 1877, when he entered his most significant outlay, $94.36 for photographic "sundries and lenses." At the time, Eastman was receiving $1,400 a year in wages. An investment of $100 was almost a month's wages.

Photographic views of the natural wonders of the world were much in demand during the nineteenth century. Niagara Falls, one hundred miles west of Rochester, was one of the most often photographed scenes. This wet-plate collodion photograph, taken by an unidentified photographer, records the ice-encrusted falls in the middle of an upstate New York winter.

Between 1857, when the Eastman tintype had been taken, and 1877, the daguerreotype and calotype technologies had given way to a number of new print and plate techniques. When Eastman began buying photos, all of his purchases probably had been taken on collodion-sensitized glass plates and printed on albumen paper. Both glass plates and sensitized paper had been in use for almost thirty years, at least in nascent forms. In 1847 Abel Nièpce de St. Victor, a cousin of Nièpce's, had announced a method of coating a mixture of sensitized silver iodide and ordinary egg white on glass plates. Several years later another French photographer, Louis Blanquart-Evart, coated paper with a similar albumen solution and produced positive prints on paper.

The major breakthrough in plate coating occurred in 1851, when Frederick Scott Archer, an Englishman, published in a British journal of chemistry the details of what is now known as the wet-collodion process. Collodion, a chemical compound formed by dissolving an explosive substance known as guncotton in alcohol and ether, is a viscid, sticky fluid. Collodion had first been discovered in 1847 but had been used mainly as a surgical dressing.

Archer had a better idea. He mixed collodion with potassium iodide and spread it on a glass plate. The mixture adhered beautifully. (Collodion makes use of the Greek root for *adhere*.) Archer then bathed the plate with silver nitrate, thus attaching a gummy, light-sensitive mixture of silver iodide and transparent collodion to the top of the transparent glass plate. Placed still wet in a camera, exposed to light, and chemically developed, the wet-collodion negative plates turned out to be faster and more light sensitive than any photographic material yet invented.

At first Archer considered drying the collodion, stripping the dry collodion off the plate, and printing it. But that proved too difficult a process. (A kink that Eastman also would face and never solve with his own 1888 stripping film.) In spite of this failure, the glass was the most effective support to date. The only major drawback of the process was that the plate had to be exposed and developed while still wet, otherwise the unchanged bits of silver nitrate inevitably left floating in the emulsion would foul the process, either making the negative almost totally insensitive or crystallizing in weblike patterns across its surface.

Together with the second great photographic invention of the 1850s, albumen paper, the wet-collodion process dominated photography for thirty or more years. Unlike the wet negative plates, which were an involved chore to coat and use, the preparation and printing of images on albumen paper was relatively simple. Common household egg whites were usually mixed with sodium chloride and spread evenly across high-quality writing paper. Once dried, the egg white gave the paper a semigloss finish. In the beginning the photographer performed this process himself, but by the mid-1850s ready-made albumenized paper had become commercially available.

In fact, the commercial manufacture of albumen paper prints soon became big business. *The British Quarterly Review* reported that in the 1860s about six million egg whites were used each year in English albumen paper plants, and the Dresden Albumenizing Company in Germany is said to have consumed sixty thousand eggs a day. Oliver Wendell Holmes, who at about this time became interested in photography, wrote in *The Atlantic Monthly* that every year ten thousand hens were "cackling over the promise of their inchoate offspring, doomed to perish unfeathered, before fate has decided whether they shall cluck or crow, for the sole purpose of the minions of the sun."

When he was ready to print, the photographer floated the prepared paper in a tray of silver-nitrate solution, thus sensitizing it to light. Once dry, the developed collodion glass negative and the sensitized paper were clamped together and set out in the sun. In time (usually about ten minutes in strong sun), light shining through the negative produced a positive picture on the sensitized albumen paper. When the image had come up to the satisfaction of the photographer, he rinsed the paper in water, toned it with a solution of gold chloride, fixed it with sodium thiosulfate, rewashed it, dried it, and had a print ready for mounting or framing.

The ambrotype, a wet-collodion negative,
was viewed as a positive by painting its re-
verse side a dark color. Where light had
struck the collodion, an off-white color
was created. Areas in shadow, more or less
transparent, revealed the dark back-
ground. This ambrotype was made by the
Civil War photographer Mathew Brady be-
fore his adoption of wet-collodion negative
plates and albumen printing paper.

In America, the merchandising of such photographs was brisk, but often inconsistent.
Mathew Brady, for instance, had entered the commercial photography business in 1844 as a
maker of miniature daguerreotype cases. Later that year he opened a New York City
Daguerrean gallery. In 1845 Brady, who was always eagerly looking for a good business
proposition, came up with the idea of selling daguerreotype portraits of the most famous,
distinguished, or otherwise notable men of the era. John Quincy Adams, Millard Fillmore,
Andrew Jackson, and John J. Audubon were just a few of the illustrious Americans
"photographed by Brady." In 1855, as one of the first to grasp the potential of the new
technique, Brady gave up daguerreotypy and began working in wet collodion. Then came the
Civil War.

The story has been told many times, but it bears repeating. Just before the first battle of Bull
Run, Brady "felt," as he wrote, "that I had to go. A spirit in my feet said go, and I went." Not
only did Brady himself go, but throughout the next four war years, Brady employees went
wherever an important battle or political event seemed worth documenting. Operating out of a
Washington, D. C., gallery, Brady and company combined the framing and printing business of
a contemporary gallery with the photographic news-gathering operations of a latter-day
Associated Press. Brady's gallery distributed its Civil War scenes through the Anthony
Company, which in the late 1850s had added prints to its line of photographic sundries and
listed almost six hundred Brady pictures in its 1862 catalog.

Despite the apparent public interest in these Civil War scenes, it is not clear how many were
actually sold. By all accounts Brady was never very good with the books. His expenses were
high, and when, after the cessation of hostilities, the demand for war images disappeared
almost entirely, Brady's business was close to bankruptcy. In 1869 he compiled a book of war
pictures and "portraits of eminent men and women of the whole country," but few were
interested. By 1874, he could not scrape up enough money to pay for the storage of his
thousands of negatives, so he sold the whole lot to the war department for $2,840. (Luckily,

through the intervention of Congressman James Garfield, Brady was given $25,000 for the collection.)

A few years earlier, one of Brady's most accomplished employees, Alexander Gardner, had run into similar financial difficulties. After spending the early war years driving a Brady photographic wagon from battlefield to battlefield, Gardner left Brady in 1863 to set up his own business. In 1866 Gardner published a volume of pictures entitled *Photographic Sketckbook of the War*. Since mechanical reproduction of pictures by the halftone process was not yet available, the *Sketchbook* contained albumen photographs, carefully printed and pasted onto the book's pages. But like Brady, Gardner found very little public interest in his project. Few copies were sold, and a year later Gardner closed his Washington gallery and headed West, hiring on as a field photographer to document the construction of the Eastern Division of the Union Pacific Railroad.

During the middle and late 1870s the practically uninhabited mountain and desert territories spanning the Great Divide were roamed by a remarkably talented group of men who today are considered among the masters of nineteenth-century American photography. In the Far West, California-based photographers Carleton Watkins and Eadweard Muybridge traveled into the Sierra Nevada Mountains, bringing back detailed wet-plate pictures of the recently explored Yosemite region of California. Timothy O'Sullivan, who had also worked for Brady and Gardner, accompanied the government-sponsored Clarence King survey of the fortieth parallel, and produced equally remarkable pictures.

William Henry Jackson, another wet-plate photographer first signed on with a Rocky Mountain survey expedition, a year later joining A.J. Russell in the employ of the Union Pacific Railroad. On May 10, 1869, Russell was in Promontory, Utah, when the last spike was driven in, uniting the Union Pacific and Central Pacific railroads.

These photographers worked under conditions so burdensome and exacting that it is a wonder any pictures were taken at all. Wet-plate photography necessitated sensitizing, exposing, and developing the glass-plate negative all within minutes. And that meant equipment, lots of it. Jackson, for instance, took with him during the 1870 Hayden survey of the Oregon Trail at least three cameras (5 x 8, 11 x 14, and a small stereo), assorted lenses, a tripod, a darkroom tent, ten pounds of collodion, two quarts of alcohol, one and a half pounds of potassium cyanide, thirty-six ounces of silver nitrate, six ounces of nitric acid, a quart of varnish, a dozen and a half chemical bottles, an assortment of developing and fixing trays, a set of chemical scales, and three hundred to four hundred glass plates.

On his 1875 trip to the San Juan Mountains of Colorado, Jackson carried a huge, 20 x 24-inch camera. One can only imagine the difficulty involved in transporting, manipulating, and preserving glass plates of that size while climbing precipitous Rocky Mountain gorges; or of working with wet-collodion chemicals in regions with atmospheric conditions as demanding and varied as Yosemite or Death Valley.

Most of Jackson's large-format photographs were either included in unpublished government or company reports or served as the model for engravings. Occasionally pictures were bound together in limited-edition private albums. There were a number of more profitable commercial alternatives available to the professional photographer, however; chief among them, the lowly stereographic set of prints. To pick up a few bucks above their normal paycheck, almost all the photographers of the American West carried at least one stereo camera and either marketed these pictures themselves or sold the negatives to companies specializing in the manufacture and distribution of these immensely popular prints.

The delight in the visual illusion created by stereography is not hard to understand, nor is the principle behind its effect. In 1838 the English inventor Sir Charles Wheatstone had built a viewing instrument called the stereoscope, which utilized the optical principle that each human

In 1865 Alexander Gardner set up his wet-plate camera atop a wall of a Washington, D.C., armory and documented the execution by hanging of four of those convicted of conspiring to kill President Abraham Lincoln. Though this image was repro-duced only in wood engravings, it represents the final chapter in the photographic history of the American Civil War, the first conflict to be covered in its entirety by the camera.

Just after the American Civil War ended, William Henry Jackson accompanied a number of mapping and survey expeditions to the American West as their official photographer. Encumbered by a wet-plate camera and all the plates and chemicals necessary for wet-collodion photography, Jackson nonetheless managed to document the landscape vistas of the American West with an eye for their overwhelming size, unusual beauty, and the often strange scenic changes caused by the coming of industrial civilization.

Later, Jackson would write of the easy-to-use paper-negative system manufactured by Eastman, "Our labors are made sport."

eye, being separated by a couple of inches of skin and bone, sees from a slightly different angle. Two drawings of a scene were made, one reproducing the right eye's view, the other that of the left. Wheatstone's stereoscope positioned each picture directly in front of the appropriate eye, and the result was a somewhat remarkable illusion of relief and perspective. For a few years no good commercial use for the Wheatstone instrument was found. Some early photographers tried to produce double-image daguerreotypes, but with their shiny surfaces and odd viewing angles they were difficult to see in stereoscopes. When the wet-plate/albumen-print process was developed, stereo enthusiasts discovered paper prints were perfect for stereo viewing and could be reproduced in multiple editions.

By the late 1850s a number of companies were satisfying the demand for stereos. In America the ever-ambitious Langenheim brothers patented a glass stereograph process they called the "Hyalotype." The Langenheims sold their pictures in sets, advertising trips through the White Mountains, the cities of Baltimore, Washington, and Philadelphia, or the "Beauties of the Hudson River." They also imported many views, most notably the British photographer Francis Frith's photographs of the ruins of ancient Egypt.

In New York City, the Anthony Company, which for the next forty years would be the most important photographic concern in the country, marketed thousands of albumen-paper stereos of all types, the most significant perhaps being Brady and Gardner's views of the Civil War. In fact, when Brady fell into financial troubles after the war, a complete set of Brady negatives was given to Anthony's in lieu of payment for supplies advanced the photographer. (Shortly thereafter, when interest in these photographs waned, Anthony's put them into storage, where they were forgotten until their rediscovery in 1904.) Anthony's and many others also sold stereos of the American West. In fact, though very few people saw the large-format photos of Watkins, Gardner, O'Sullivan, and other photographers of the Far West, thousands bought and collected their pictures in the stereo format.

During the latter half of the nineteenth century, stereo photography was so popular that few family parlors were without a stereo-viewing device and a stack of stereo cards. Many local professional photographers, recognizing the popularity of the medium, added regional views to their picture inventory. One of George Eastman's first photographic purchases was a stereoscope. It is now impossible to say which images Eastman purchased to go with his viewer, but by chance a fellow worker at the Rochester Savings Bank had in 1871 accompanied the John Wesley Powell survey of the Colorado River, and it is likely that this acquaintance sparked Eastman's interest in western views.

Eastman probably also bought local views. In 1865 a Rochester photographer named C.W. Woodward had taken stereos of that year's great flood of the Genesee River. Unlike the typical wet-plate camera, the small-format stereo camera had a fairly short focal length. And as photographers had long understood, the shorter the focal length, the less light was needed to produce a sharp image. (Having less distance to travel between the lens and the film, light rays describe smaller, seemingly unfocused circles of confusion.) Photographs of moving objects taken with long-lens, large-format cameras were often blurred; stereos, to some extent, stopped action. Even loaded with wet-collodion plates, stereoscope cameras were very "fast," meaning that a shorter exposure time was necessary to produce a sharp photograph. As early as 1855 the Anthony Company was advertising "instantaneous views."

It is not clear how often photographers made use of this newfound ability, but at least a few candid, outdoor scenes, featuring people moving about naturally, were available in stereo format. Rochester photographer George Monroe, who was later to teach wet-plate photography to Eastman, had a few prototypical candid scenes on sale at his studio.

The other popular photographic format of the time was the cabinet card. These 5½ × 4-inch albumen prints (mounted on slightly larger cardboard backings) had evolved from the earlier and equally popular cartes de visite, which had been patented in France in 1854 by André-

The distance between the lens and the photographic plate in a typical stereoscopic camera was unusually short. Since light being bent by the lens had less distance to travel before hitting the focal plane, movement of a subject was consequently less critical. Thus stereo views were often called "instantaneous," and on-the-spot photos of momentous events and disasters of the time, such as this view of a flood in Rochester in 1865, were often circulated in the stereo format.

Adolphe-Eugène Disdéri. Disdéri made use of a special wet-plate camera with four lenses and a plate holder that could be shifted from side to side. On a single plate, eight exposures could be made by uncapping each lens, one at a time, on the first half of the plate, sliding the fresh unexposed half in place and exposing four more. Once developed and printed on albumen paper, these eight images could be scissored apart and individually mounted. If the tintype had been the poor man's portrait, the higher quality carte de visite was everyman's. Family, friends, the famous—everyone posed for carte de visites, and by 1860 albums with pockets matching the uniform 4 x 2½-inch size of these little pictures began showing up on the market.

But cartes de visite were a little on the small side, and when the bigger cabinet card was introduced in 1867, the sale of these larger pictures boomed. Cabinet cards were often mass printed on silver chloride "printing-out" paper in large sunny penthouse lofts. So many cabinet card studios opened that today almost any antique shop will have a couple of boxes full of these pictures, each bearing in flowing script the name of some long forgotten photographer and most containing the images of some equally unremembered star, political notable, or unidentified private individual.

In 1877 Eastman's growing interest in photography turned from picture buying to picture making, at the time, not an inconsiderable undertaking. Producing photographic images wasn't all that arcane a process; it was, as skills go, fairly easy to learn—at least in the most basic, bare-bones sense. There were, of course, a few amateurs who took up the photographic sciences purely for personal pleasure, but in the 1870s that huge section of the photographic public known today as amateurs, whether serious or otherwise, was quite small. The whole thing, from plate preparation to print production, was just too much trouble.

In addition, photography was fairly expensive. When Eastman purchased his first photographic kit in 1877, he paid almost one hundred dollars for "sundries and lenses," and that figure did not include lessons with local photographer George Monroe or the price of technical journals. Eastman had learned French and German in order to read European technical journals, and together with the important British magazines these publications brought him the latest information on emulsions, plates, papers, cameras, and all the rest of the data needed to attempt photography seriously.

Even if the amateur was able to afford all this, the fun was tempered by the oppressive and taxing work involved. Years later, in what has become a classic description of the rigors of wet-plate photography, Eastman wrote:

In those days one did not "take" a camera; one accompanied the outfit of which the camera was only a part.

My layout, which included only the essentials, had in it a camera about the size of a soapbox, a tripod, which was strong and heavy enough to support a bungalow, a big plate-holder, a dark tent, a nitrate bath, and a container for water.

The glass plates were not, as now, in the holder ready for use; they were what is known as "wet plates"—that is, glass which had to be coated with collodion and then sensitized with nitrates of silver just before exposure.

Hence the nitrate of silver was something that always had to go along and it was perhaps the most awkward companion imaginable on a journey. Being corrosive, the container had to be of glass and the cover tight—for silver nitrate is not a liquid to get intimate with. The first time that I took a silver bath with me, I wrapped it with exceeding great care and put it in my trunk. The cover leaked, the nitrate got out and stained most of my clothing.

But Eastman persisted, despite the bulk of the equipment and the difficulty in storing and transporting the necessary chemicals. He also began to think about the commercial possibilities of the craft. At the time, the Grant administration was discussing the purchase of the Carribean island of Santo Domingo, and Eastman's photographer friend at the bank suggested that he vacation there, take pictures, and sell them upon his return. Eastman eventually decided against the trip, but as he once said, "That did not matter so much because, in making ready, I had become wholly absorbed in photography."

As would become obvious in later years, Eastman possessed two of the qualities most necessary to the amateur photographer: persistence and a love of tinkering with mechanical and chemical processes. He also had an unflagging sense of economy, both financial and photographic. It soon became clear to him that there had to be a better way. And that better way, he discovered in an article in the *Almanac of the British Journal of Photography*, was a new process known as gelatin dry-plate photography.

The acknowledged inventor of this new process, British amateur photographer Dr. R. L. Maddox, had added silver nitrate to a slightly acidic solution of gelatin and bromide. (Photographic gelatin, much like common kitchen gelatin, is made from clippings of a calf's ear and cheek.) This combination produced a milky substance made up of light-sensitive silver bromide suspended in gelatin. After Maddox coated this mix on a glass plate, he discovered that, unlike wet collodion, the gelatin emulsion remained sensitive for weeks, even months, after it had dried. At first, Maddox's dry plates were "slow"; indeed, much less light-sensitive than the average wet plate. But because of its obvious advantages—the main one being that once the plate was prepared photographic chemicals need not accompany the photographer to the field—the dry-plate method would in a few years supersede wet-collodion photography.

Eastman began seeing dry-plate formulas show up in the photographic journals, most notably *The British Journal of Photography*, which in the spring of 1878 ran a series of articles discussing the possibilities of dry-plate photography. A few companies, including the British firms of Charles Bennett, Mawson and Swan, and Wratten and Wainwright, had already begun marketing these new plates. In America, however, photographers were slow to adopt the new

The cabinet card, a 5¹/₂ × 4-inch albumen print mounted on a slightly larger 6¹/₂ × 4¹/₂-inch cardboard backing, was one of the most popular nineteenth-century photographic genres. Many of the most renowned personalities of the day posed in elaborately decorated studio settings. These stylish portraits were mass-produced and sold as across-the-counter celebrity shots. Napoleon Sarony, William Kurtz, and José Maria Mora were among the most prestigious cabinet-card photographers, and often the average man or woman entered their studios to have portraits made that simulated some of the celebrity flair and fashion.

process. By 1880 only a few U.S. companies manufactured dry plates, the most well-known being the Anthony Company's Defiance Plate.

It is not clear how soon Eastman became aware of the commercial possibilities of this process, but there's no doubt that Eastman, always a man who liked the neatness of fine economical methods, quickly saw dry plates as the technology of the future. Setting up a makeshift chemical lab in the kitchen of his mother's house, Eastman became an emulsion maker. In light of the careful scientific methods that would years later become the rule in photochemical laboratories, Eastman's work over the sink now seems more closely aligned to cooking than to chemical experimentation. In the letters column of the July 1878 *The British Journal of Photography* there appears a note from "G. E. (Rochester, N.Y.)" asking technical questions such as "How do you treat the emulsion after precipitation?" and "Have you tried the plan, recommended a short time back, of coating the glass with a very porous collodion previous to the application of the gelatin?"

On another occasion, answering the inquiry of a fellow amateur, Eastman sent along a home recipe that called for 40 grams of gelatin, 23½ grams of bromide, 40 grams of silver and 1¼ ounces of water, prepared as follows:

Raise temperature of solution to 150 degrees fahr & unite slowly, shaking between additions of silver. Then place in the bath and keep at 100 degree five days. Then precip. with 2 oz. 95% alcohol or wash in any desired way. Add ¾ dr. alcohol and 10 m. of 8 gr. sol. chr. alum, filter and coat. Two days in bath gives about wet plate rapidity. Some kept 7 days was about five times as rapid.

After a number of these washpan and drainboard experiments, Eastman came up with an emulsion that worked pretty well; so well, in fact, that he decided to manufacture and sell the product of his labors.

Just how or when the shift from amateur Sunday photographer to commercial manufacturer of photographic supplies took place is open to speculation. But the list of men from Isaac Singer to Elisha Otis, F. W. Woolworth, Richard Sears, and Alvah Roebuck who suddenly appeared out of nineteenth-century rural America with an idea for commercial enterprise is too long not to suggest that the times were ripe for the encouragement of individual genius.

After some success with his dry-plate experimentation Eastman decided that he was ready to go into the dry-plate business and wrote to his Uncle Horace asking for a loan. But Uncle Horace was a prudent man and a few days later replied in what must be one of the models of misplaced wariness, "I could not keep faith with others by becoming a party to any agreement the future fulfillment of which could in the slightest degree be uncertain or doubtful or depend on future contingency."

Eastman was apparently undaunted by the refusal. He continued making dry plates, even going as far as supplying his former teacher George Monroe with a few to try out. Monroe was impressed, writing that "I averaged 95 percent good negatives, although the plates were brought home for development."

By mid-1879, only a little more than two years since he had first touched photographic equipment, Eastman not only was manufacturing his own plates but had invented a mechanical coating machine to replace the old honey-stick method of smearing emulsion upon glass.

In July 1879 Eastman withdrew money from his savings account, booked passage to England, applied for a patent on his emulsion-coating device, and met with various British photographic manufacturers. In September he submitted a U.S. patent application for the same machine. By October the British rights were transferred to Mawson and Swan for five hundred pounds. The

GEORGE EASTMAN AND THE
ROYAL ROAD TO DRAWING

In 1877 George Eastman purchased a wet-plate photography kit and began carrying all its cumbersome equipment, including the camera, chemicals, plates, and a portable darkroom tent, on picture-taking jaunts around Rochester. This is one of his earliest surviving wet-plate pictures, taken from the banks of the Genesee River a few blocks from the center of downtown Rochester.

One principal virtue of the dry-emulsion technology, unlike the messy and time-consuming method of wet-plate preparation, was that photographic plates could be factory sensitized and shipped to customers ready for immediate use. This simplified the photographer's work. All the purchaser of a packet of Eastman dry plates needed to do was to insert one in his camera and take a picture.

next summer, while on a photographic trip to the Thousand Islands, Monroe ran into Edward Anthony of the Anthony Company. Anthony was impressed by the quality of the Eastman dry plates Monroe was using and wrote to Eastman inquiring about a possible business relationship between the two.

Until 1880 all the capital needed to begin his dry-plate business came from Eastman's own pocket. That year, however, Henry Strong, who had lodged with the Eastmans in the 1860s and was now a successful Rochester buggy-whip manufacturer, decided to become a partner. At the time Strong knew practically nothing about photography, but Eastman trusted his friend's business expertise. Strong invested a thousand dollars in Eastman's company late in 1880 and then another five thousand dollars in 1881.

In the small photographic world, word of Eastman's new emulsion got around quickly. In the fall of 1881 a columnist for *The Philadelphia Photographer* chanced to see some of Monroe's work and wrote: "The plates I saw, negatives of both summer and winter scenes, were characterized by great delicacy of detail in either lights or shadows. This I considered a most difficult test."

Other photographers agreed. One reported "great success for interiors and all other occasions where long exposures are necessary." After trying out Eastman dry plates, William Kurtz, one of the most famous producers of cabinet cards, was said to "use nothing else." And, in a comment that would be more prophetic than he knew, a commercial photographer commented that "it was a wonderful thing for babies at five o'clock in the afternoon."

Along with the increase in exposure speed of the new dry-plate emulsion came the necessity for new camera designs. Exposure times for wet-collodion plates were often measured in the seconds. The photographer simply uncapped the lens and counted. The speed of the new dry plate, on the other hand, was measured in fractions of a second, and to match this speed cameras now came equipped with mechanically operated shutters. At the time, Eastman's small company, consisting of Eastman and a single helper, was exclusively in the dry-plate business, but the world of photography was on the verge of expanding, and it would not be long before Eastman also became interested in camera technology.

Despite all the signs of impending business success, Eastman held on to his job at the bank, working days as a clerk and nights as an emulsion maker. Not until September 1881, after the incorporation of the Eastman Dry Plate Company, three successive moves to ever-larger manufacturing facilities, and a monthly volume in dry-plate sales of four thousand dollars did Eastman resign his position at the bank and begin working full time in the photography business.

Early in the spring of 1882, however, the company ran into deep trouble. Eastman Dry Plates, the quality of which had in a very short time become well known and respected in the photographic community, suddenly began to be returned. Photographers complained that rather than being uncommonly fast and sensitive, the Eastman plates were almost completely useless. Upon examination Eastman agreed, remarking disgustedly that the new plates might just as well have been pure, uncoated window glass.

At first Eastman suspected that the problem lay in the age of the plates. Photography at the time was a seasonal business, and some plates had been stored on dealer's shelves for almost a year. So he replaced all the defective plates with new ones. But these too were bad. Eastman reworked the emulsion, carrying out just under five hundred painstaking experiments, but nothing worked. Once he thought he had come up with a workable emulsion, but the bottle was tipped over and the experimental solution lost.

In March, having failed in his efforts, Eastman and his partner of a year, Henry Strong, sailed to England. After talking to the British manufacturers Mawson and Swan and reexamining the plates, it was discovered that it was the gelatin not the emulsion that was at fault. Not until

Negative by
MR. J. H. KENT,
Rochester, N. Y.

ON EASTMAN'S
SPECIAL DRY PLATE.

Printed by
B. F. EDSALL, New York.
On Hall Columbia Paper.

Eastman dry plates were advertised to the professional trade as being perfect for portraiture. Display photos, such as this 1882 portrait taken by Rochester photographer J. H. Kent, were shown by traveling Eastman demonstrators as proof of that claim.

years later did scientists at Eastman's own laboratories come up with a satisfactory explanation of the part gelatin plays in the photographic process. They discovered, as some even in 1882 had suspected, that impurities in the gelatin itself can either promote increased sensitization or even complete desensitization. Apparently the latter had been the case with this 1881–1882 batch of gelatin.

Eastman and Strong sailed home and started afresh with a new shipment of gelatin. Production was resumed, and sales once again increased. Business was so good, in fact, that the company constructed a three-story factory and ended the year with close to fifteen thousand dollars in profit.

The Eastman Dry Plate Company had succeeded in becoming one of the best-known producers of gelatin dry plates. But in many ways, this achievement marked the end rather than the beginning of an era. Although glass plates would continue to be used for many more years and methods of preparing light-sensitive coatings would not fundamentally change, in the planning stages was a revolution in photographic supports. A new word was about to enter photography's vocabulary. And that word was *film*.

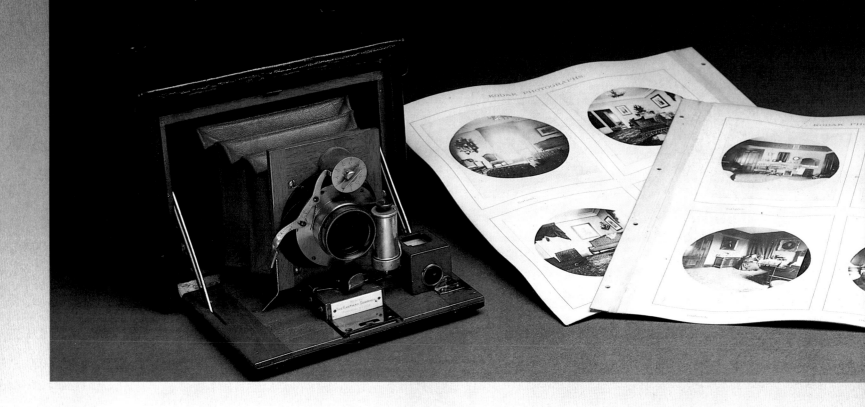

DO THE REST

One of the first Kodak camera advertisements appeared in the September 29, 1888, issue of Scientific American. *The copy underneath a line drawing of two hands holding a Kodak camera read, "The Kodak Camera—100 Instantaneous Pictures—Anybody can use it—No knowledge of photography is necessary—The latest and best outfit for amateurs—Send for descriptive circular—Price $25." In later advertisements, such as this, all that was necessary was the camera and the slogan.*

Preceding pages:
Though capturing the world on the screen of a camera lucida was not the royal road to drawing, a British artist once wrote, it "at least succeeded in macadamizing the way." The development of inexpensive hand-held Kodak cameras such as (left to right) the 1892 No. 4 Folding Kodak camera, the original 1888 Kodak camera, and the 1897 Folding Pocket Kodak camera opened this image-making avenue to additional traffic. Anyone could make photographs with the Kodak cameras. Many thousands did, taking photographs that they placed in family snapshot albums.

Opposite:
On February 18, 1884, George Eastman had his picture taken on an experimental version of American film, a paper-backed negative film from which the layer of light-sensitive gelatin emulsion was stripped and developed after exposure. This stripping operation was too difficult for most amateurs to perform. When factory processing of American film was offered to buyers of the Kodak camera the first large-scale photofinishing service was created.

It is sometimes axiomatic that the more ideas you get, the more ideas you get. Call it luck, creative fervor, or just plain inspiration; whatever the term, it is clear that by the end of 1883 George Eastman had a number of intuitions about the future of photography that in less than twenty years would utterly change the world of photochemical image making.

The first of Eastman's insights grew out of the success of his dry-plate business. For a young firm, the Eastman Dry Plate Company was doing as well as could be expected. After moving from one rented loft to another, Eastman and Henry Strong had in 1883 built a four-story factory about three-quarters of a mile north of the commercial center of Rochester.

In the three years since its incorporation in 1881, the Eastman Dry Plate Company had built its reputation on the quality of its product and the fairness of its dealings with consumers. During the great emulsion debacle of 1882 Eastman had won the respect of photographers, professional and amateur alike, by quickly replacing insensitive plates. Word had spread through the photographic community that this small upstate New York firm produced top-shelf emulsions and plates, and that, in the often chaotically competitive photography industry, the Eastman Dry Plate Company could be counted upon for quality and consistency of product.

But Eastman was not satisfied. A tenacious man when it came to the caliber of his goods, he seems to have instinctively known that establishing an absolutely uniform manufacturing standard was the key to success in the photographic marketplace; but he was also a canny, ambitious businessman. And that separated him from many of his equally ambitious, but more shortsighted competitors.

When Eastman entered the market in the 1880s photographic supplies were merchandised by large jobbing houses such as the Anthony Company of New York City and the Scovill Company of Massachusetts. For the most part, these firms were organized like photographic department stores. Some photographic goods were manufactured in-house and carried the company's name. Other products were sold through sole-agency agreements with dozens of small photographic factories. This clever and ultimately safe business strategy, as the historian Reese Jenkins has observed, "externalized the risk of innovation." The jobber simply stood as a middleman between the free-lance photographic inventor, who lacked the marketing apparatus of the big houses, and the customer, who relied on the large photographic houses for easy access to supplies and service. The chief problem with this commercial network, as Eastman saw it, was its unpredictable pace of growth. In particular, he seems from the beginning to have understood that the conservative tactics of the jobbers had to be replaced with a unified strategic vision that would draw new customers.

At the time, however, the relatively small size of the aggregate market for photographic supplies stood in Eastman's way. In the early 1880s *The Photographic Times*, a popular amateur journal, announced to its readers that "amateur photographers are counted by the thousands, and in different cities are organized into flourishing and growing societies." Though thousands seemed a surprisingly large number for such an intricate and expensive hobby, Eastman believed that figure would have to increase considerably for the photographic market to grow much beyond its present level.

Even in its vastly simplified dry-plate form, photography, whether amateur or professional, was still a skilled craft; a matter of training, expertise, and manual dexterity. Those in the trades of photography, the working commercial photographers, understood the complexity of photography to be just part of the job. Their livelihood depended upon competence, know-how, and a high level of workmanship. Part-time amateur photographers also used the same tools as the pros, and many took to their hobby with an earnestness that exceeded that of their

Made on paper
with a soluble sub-
stratum developed
after transferring

The Eastman-Walker roll holder, a mahogany frame and metal dowel mechanism designed to hold and advance flexible roll film, was built to be attached to a standard dry-plate camera. Fitted to the back of the camera, it replaced the usual single-exposure glass plate with up to forty-eight separate paper-backed negatives.

In the late 1880s, when this advertisement for the Eastman-Walker roll holder was published, few photographers had ever used flexible roll film. The loading of paper-negative material is illustrated in the first seven drawings. Figure 10 depicts the use of Eastman's patented "Translucene," a hot castor-oil treatment used to make the coarsely woven paper negatives transparent.

accomplished colleagues. Amateurs were by necessity very serious; the craft of photography was just too arduous an activity to be taken casually.

As long as photographic image making remained only in the hands of those few with enough interest and skill to learn its secrets, the business of supplying photographic goods would for all intents and purposes stand still. Thus to expand his commercial horizons Eastman had to find a way to simplify and demystify the photochemical process. According to his 1932 authorized biography, Eastman formulated four policy guidelines in the early 1880s:

1. *Production in large quantities by machinery*
2. *Low prices to increase the usefulness of products*
3. *Foreign as well as domestic distribution*
4. *Extensive advertising as well as selling by demonstration.*

Whether Eastman actually created out of whole cloth such a pat set of operating procedures is beside the point. It is more important to notice that while all four principles formed an astute and coherent business philosophy, it is item No. 1 upon which the other three are entirely dependent. Without mass production, prices would remain high, distribution would be limited, and advertising unnecessary.

Later in the century, the photographer Alfred Stieglitz would complain that after Eastman's invention of popular photography, the amateur sector had come to be divided between the "dress suits" and the "democrats." By that he meant while some (the "dress suits") still considered photography an art to be practiced with individual skill and sensitivity, others (the

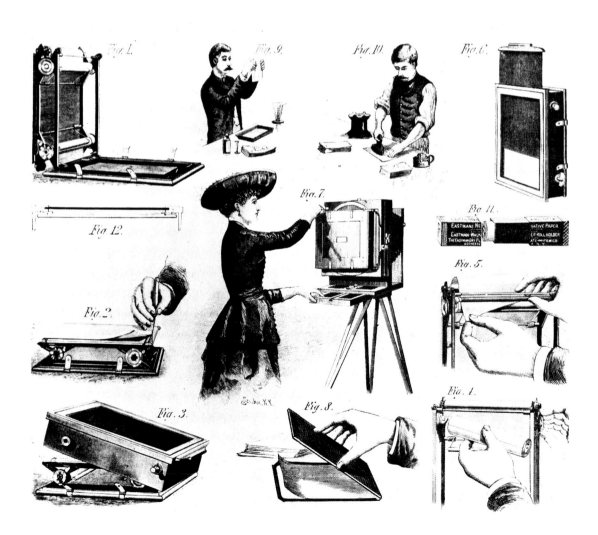

"democrats") were content to let their photos drift down the Eastman assembly line. Serious amateurs, free of the financial restraints of commercial photography, were the "dress suits"— dignified, patient, aesthetically demanding. Photographic artists.

Many amateur photographic artists such as Stieglitz thought this new class of amateurs, those only interested in the mass production of images, consisted of plebeian interlopers. Photography to them was not artistry. It was only an easy mechanical way of making mimetic, serendipitous pictures. It was not serious. But Stieglitz, whose pronouncements often displayed a struggle between pinched aesthetic stuffiness and genuine avant-garde creativity, failed at the time to understand that the future of photography depended precisely upon its democratization.

As fervently as Stieglitz may have wished to insulate art photography from popular photography, the boundaries between the two genres would often blur. Photography was unavoidably a mechanical method of image making, and as both an everyday experience and artistic endeavor many of photography's advances would in the end depend precisely upon what he dismissed as "Eastman's methods of mass manufacture."

In the mid-1880s the expansion of the amateur market seemed to Eastman the only way for his business to grow. Eastman was at the time busy with the gelatin dry-plate business, but during the next several years, with the ideas of large quantity, low price, and worldwide marketing in mind, he began item by item to redesign each piece of equipment in the nineteenth-century photographic kit bag. He started with the glass-plate negative.

In the thirty years since the invention of photography, high-quality transparent glass had proved to have so many advantages as a carrier of light-sensitive silver salts that for all practical purposes it had outmoded every other support. After a few short years of popularity, Daguerre's metal plates had been rejected as commercially limiting, and Talbot's paper negatives, despite their flexibility, light weight, and durability, yielded such unsatisfactory print quality that hardly anyone used them. But glass was also clearly not the perfect support. It was heavy; a single plate could weigh a pound or more. It was also expensive to manufacture. Most important, for all its obvious advantages, it lacked tensile strength. When mishandled, glass broke.

There were so few options to any of these materials, however, and cheap, sturdy paper was such an attractive alternative to glass, that Eastman refused to give up on it. Eastman as yet had no organized experimental laboratory, but in his spare time he began to test different sorts of paper-negative processes. After a number of failures, he came up with a paper-coating technique that worked moderately well. He first covered high-quality rag bond stock with a light-sensitive silver-bromide emulsion. After exposure and development the negative paper was then "greased" with hot castor oil. Other photographic experimenters had tested similar materials, wax for instance, but Eastman's hot-oil method of coating over the paper's fibers at least minimized the grain problem, and for a while Eastman sold presensitized paper-negative material along with a bottle of treatment oil called "Translucene."

Though the quality of prints produced by paper negatives could not match those made with glass negatives, Eastman had enough faith in the future of a flexible support that in October 1884 the word *film* was added to the company's name. The term has a complex etymological history and would be used popularly to describe all flexible negative material, but at the time *film* referred only to the gelatin coating upon the paper.

Later that same year Eastman placed advertisements in the leading photographic journals announcing the introduction of what he called "paper dry plates." "Shortly after January 1st, 1885," the part announcement, part pronouncement read, "The Eastman Dry Plate and Film Company will introduce a new sensitive film which it is believed will prove an economical and convenient substitute for glass dry plates both for outdoor and studio work."

While replacing heavy, breakable glass with lightweight, flexible paper in a typical plate camera seemed, on the face of it, a promising idea, some sort of device was needed to hold the flexible paper steady in the camera's focal plane. Fortunately for Eastman the solution to that problem came in the person of William Walker, a clever but only moderately successful camera builder who had recently moved his business to Rochester.

In the early 1880s Walker had designed and manufactured a small wooden box camera that made single 2¾ x 3¼-inch dry-plate exposures. The Walker camera was a smartly built little machine engineered to be factory made with interchangeable parts. The camera could be mass produced, and its individual parts were easily replaced. In addition, Walker's hand-held camera was marketed as a complete outfit, containing camera, plates, chemicals, printing paper, instruction manual, and all the peripheral darkroom tools and picture-mounting supplies.

This was not a new idea; similar setups had been sold even in the wet-plate days. The difference was that the Walker camera, small, compact, and practical, was clearly intended to simplify the amateur photographer's task and to lighten his load. But as tidy and functional as the camera kit was, it still required its user to possess enough knowledge and expertise to expose, develop, and print dry-plate negatives. It had refashioned amateur photography somewhat, but it had not significantly altered its chores.

Walker advertised his invention as widely as he could, even placing notices in popular magazines such as *Century*. However, few bought his camera outfit. But Walker was a skilled mechanic, his camera was evidence of that. When he and Eastman met, the two collaborated on a new product, a camera attachment designed to eliminate entirely the burdensome glass-plate negative.

It is now hard to say which came first, the Eastman greased-paper negative film or the Eastman-Walker paper roll holder, though clearly one had no reason to exist without the other. In August 1884 Eastman and Walker applied for a patent on this new device, and about a year later, in June 1885, with patents granted and production problems solved, both roll holder and roll film were put on the market.

The roll holder was an ingenious add-on apparatus meant to replace the glass-plate holder at the back of a typical dry-plate view camera. Manufactured in a variety of standard dry-plate camera sizes, the roll holder was not much more than a mahogany frame outfitted with two metal dowels, one of which was wound with paper-negative film, while the other functioned as a take-up spool. The strip of paper-negative film contained between twelve and twenty-four exposures, thus unburdening the photographer of his ever-present wooden case of glass plates. The roll holder also considerably speeded up picture taking; to ready the camera for a new exposure, the photographer simply turned a fresh piece of film into the focal plane with a twist of the knob. After the end of the roll was reached, the camera was taken to the darkroom and unloaded. The unrolled film was then cut into individual negatives, developed, oiled with Translucene, and printed in the usual way.

In truth, the Eastman-Walker roll holder was not an altogether new invention. A camera with a similar built-in roller device had been marketed in England in the 1870s by Leon Warnerke, and a few photographers, including William Henry Jackson, had tried out the system. But the Warnerke outfit was awkward to use and its collodion-coated, tissue-paper negatives were unreliable. Jackson had taken this sort of camera on a Far West expedition, hoping that the paper-negative system would lighten his baggage, but not a single one of the four hundred negatives taken on that trip was printable.

If not exactly pioneering, the Eastman-Walker–designed roll holder was certainly the first to work with fair reliability. Though many photographers were suspicious of its claims, the roll holder won a number of international design awards, and several photographic journals, including *The British Journal of Photography*, suggested "a personal examination of the ingenious mechanism." "For general outdoor work, but especially for tourist use," the journal's

reviewer commented, "the roll holder will be preferred, at least, when the prejudice existing against such innovations has been removed."

Removing that prejudice proved to be a difficult task. Most photographers were content with their glass plates, which, though clumsy to use, still produced better-quality images than Eastman paper-negative film. It is not known exactly how many took to the roll-holder system, but not as many as the two designers had expected. With roll holder working in tandem with roll film Eastman had hoped "to popularize photography to an extent as yet scarcely dreamed of." But that had not happened.

Discussing the public response to the roll holder, a spring 1886 article in *The American Journal of Photography*, observed:

The melancholy fact remains, however, that instead of trying the new invention, which could be done at a very small cost, the average amateur begins at once to pick it to pieces without knowing anything whatever about the process. He talks learnedly about the subject, insists that the grain will show; that the paper will rot in time from the use of oil; that re-oiling is necessary every time the negative is printed, or that the odor of castor oil is disagreeable to his aristocratic nose. All these objections I have heard, and upon asking: "Have you given the negatives a fair trial?" the answer has generally been: Nope; but so-and-so has, and he don't appear to think much of them"—or something to that effect.

Though many professional photographers considered the multiple steps involved in stripping, squeegeeing, and printing American film unnecessarily onerous, Eastman encouraged a few to try it out. This 1886 shot taken from the shores of Switzerland's Lake Lucerne is credited to the commercial photographer William Rau and was used by the Eastman Company to point out the ease and versatility of the roll-film system of photography.

In spite of considerable resistance to the roll-holder idea, however, Eastman was convinced that it augured the future of photography. To one correspondent he wrote, accurately, though a little testily, "You have been compelled to accept the dry plate, and when we get ready we will force you to accept films or you will be driven from your present outdoor business by those who are willing to progress with their art."

Eventually Eastman was proved right, at least if judged by one of the roll holder's most notable success stories. In 1886 Paul Nadar, the son of the well-known Parisian society photographer who went by the name Nadar, was asked by the editors of *Le Journal Illustré* to commemorate the one-hundredth birthday of the chemist Michel Chevreul by taking photographs of the venerable scientist. Paul Nadar, who by then had become an Eastman representative, attached a roll holder to one of his cameras and took over a hundred pictures of Chevreul in conversation with Nadar's father. This protocinematic sequence of photographs, snapped off quickly with the roll-holder-equipped camera, is generally known as the world's first photographic interview.

Another testimonial came from William Henry Jackson, who after being supplied with an Eastman-Walker roll holder, wrote to Eastman: "I am a thousand times obliged to you for the beautiful holder sent me, but more for the new power placed in our hands whereby our labors are made sport. Truly our day of deliverance has come." Too few, however, followed Jackson's example, particularly in the amateur community.

In fact, Eastman agreed with one of the most common complaints about the roll-holder system. It was only as strong as its weakest link, and that was the film. Even oiled, Eastman's "Negative Paper" could not match the sharpness, resolution, and tonal range of the typical glass-plate negative. No matter how well coated, paper negatives had not managed to overcome the grain problem that had limited the use of this type of photography since Talbot's days.

All along, however, Eastman had been working to perfect an alternative. Almost a year earlier, in March 1884, he had patented another and much more complicated type of negative support. This was the three-layered strippable negative he called "American film." The trick of stripping an exposed emulsion away from its support was also not innovative. During the Franco-Prussian War in the early 1870s, photographic copies of military dispatches were transported across battle zones by this method. First the messages were photographed on glass plates. The thin skin of collodion emulsion then was carefully peeled off the plate, rolled into a tight tube, inserted into a piece of quill, and attached to a pigeon's tail for delivery. After arriving at military headquarters behind the lines, the negatives were developed, placed in a projector, and enlarged upon a screen.

Eastman's American film borrowed the trick of film stripping and applied it to more routine circumstances. American film was a three-ply film, consisting of an ordinary paper support and a layer of gelatin emulsion, which were separated by a middle layer of water-soluble gelatin. After the film was photographically exposed, the negative was taken from the camera and placed emulsion-side down upon a glass plate. Hot water was poured over the film, which melted and dissolved the inner layer of soluble gelatin. Paper and soluble gelatin were then carefully stripped away, leaving only the thin layer of exposed gelatin emulsion on top of the glass plate. Once the film had been peeled down to its thin emulsion layer, another piece of wet, sticky transparent gelatin was squeegeed on top of the emulsion. After this double layer had dried, the emulsion skin could be lifted from the glass and printed in the usual way. It was a delicate operation, but if carried out with care, it produced a print entirely free of paper grain.

American film, like Eastman paper-negative film, still had obvious drawbacks. Most amateurs could easily handle the printing of paper-negative film. Despite the difference in material, the procedure was similar to that of plate-glass negative printing. But the three-step melting, stripping, and thickening procedure demanded by American film was beyond the capabilities of most amateur photographers.

Nevertheless, Eastman persisted, and by the end of 1886 The Eastman Dry Plate and Film Company was selling a variety of photographic materials and apparatus for both plate and roll-film photography. However, despite some notable successes, such as the Nadar and Jackson testimonials, neither the roll holder nor the two types of roll film had come close to replacing the older system of glass-plate photography. As compelling as both new products seemed to Eastman, they had failed to attract significant numbers of new photographic consumers.

As had been his business practice, Eastman had simultaneously patented both product and process. The carpentry and metalwork involved in the manufacture of roll holders was jobbed out, but for the coating of what Eastman hoped would be huge amounts of flexible paper film, an efficient roller, trough, and drying machine was installed in his Rochester factory to move hundreds of yards of paper along in one continuous assembly-line operation.

"This machine," Eastman commented in an interview years later, "was so satisfactory that the machinery has never been changed except in detail, since." In fact, Eastman added, the paper-negative coating process "worked so well that we immediately decided to put out bromide paper, the manufacture of which we had abandoned."

Gelatin bromide paper is a "developing-out" paper. Unlike albumen-coated silver chloride "printing-out" paper, which was clamped together with a negative and placed in the sun for the few minutes it took for an image to appear, bromide-coated paper made use of the principle of latent image formation. The paper was exposed to light through the negative for a fairly short period of time and then taken to a darkroom. There, chemical developers, rather than reexposure to light, brought up the photographic image.

One of the apparent advantages of bromide printing paper was the speed at which it operated. Unlike the slow pace of the printing-out paper process, which depended on the strength of the sun, and even on the sunniest days normally took some minutes, chemical development of bromide paper could produce an image in seconds. In fact, gelatin bromide developing-out paper was so quick that it necessitated a fine eye and fast hand, and that apparently bothered photographers accustomed to the almost mistake-proof luxury of the slow printing-out papers.

Though bromide developing-out paper would not become universally popular until after the turn of the century, for Eastman it had a more immediate use. Chloride papers, which were printed by placing the sheet in contact with the original negative, made enlargement of an original negative impossible. Bromide papers, on the other hand, which made use of the latent image, could be placed on an enlarging easel, imprinted with a latent image, and then chemically developed.

Soon after bromide paper went into production, the company added to its other business lines a portrait-enlarging service. Professional photographers could simplify their work by sending negatives to the Rochester factory, where they could be blown up into prints any size from 3½ x 4½ inches to 25 x 30 inches. By the time the American Photographer's Association assembled for their annual convention in 1887, the Eastman factory enlargement techniques had become so skilled that huge photographs hung on the walls of the company's display booth: ten photographs measuring 54 x 90 inches, six or eight 54 x 70 inches, as well as a few smaller enlargements.

Thus, by the end of the year 1886 the Eastman Dry Plate and Film Company listed among its products and services: roll holders in a variety of sizes designed to fit existing dry-plate view cameras; two types of flexible film, the old Negative Paper, and the new American film; a developing-out paper known as "Permanent Bromide"; and a photofinishing service designed to create enlargements in a variety of heretofore unobtainable sizes. What the company did not market was a camera. Early in 1887 a couple of Eastman dry-plate cameras (whose plate sizes were 6½ x 8½ inches and 8 x 10 inches) were produced, and they apparently sold well enough, but Eastman had in mind the manufacture of a simpler sort of apparatus: the detective camera.

Detective cameras, so named because they could be concealed about the photographer's person, were usually about eight inches long and weighed four or five pounds. Also called "hand cameras," they were designed to be loaded with small, relatively fast gelatin-emulsion glass plates. Detective cameras were manufactured in a number of sizes and shapes. One of the most famous and striking of these designs was the round, canteen-shaped "Stirn's secret camera," designed to be worn under a coat with its lens stuck through a buttonhole.

Most detective cameras, however, were simply small, inconspicuous boxes, loaded with gelatin-emulsion glass plates and equipped with improved light-gathering lenses and mechanical shutters. Though large-format cameras sometimes also made use of these lens and shutter improvements, their sheer bulk usually limited them to landscape or portrait work. In addition, since almost all printing was done by contact, most amateur artists considered the size of the detective cameras' glass plates too small to produce presentable images. Nevertheless, when these relatively inconspicuous hand-held cameras were used by someone as accomplished as the British photographer Paul Martin or the San Franciscan Arnold Genthe, they often succeeded in candidly capturing the commotion and excitement of street and market life.

Eastman thought that a lightweight detective camera would be the perfect vehicle for his newly invented roll-film system. William Walker had already gone to London to open the first Eastman overseas wholesale establishment, so Eastman and a new employee, Franklin Cossitt, worked together to design the camera. The finished camera differed very little from the average hand-held plate camera. It was roll-holder adaptable, of course, but so were many other such cameras.

Eastman manufactured fifty of these detective cameras, but they hardly sold. The shutter mechanism produced too much shock and, as Eastman said, "was difficult to keep in repair." After a year he remaindered them to a Philadelphia dealer. The project was a disappointment. Eastman had thought that the roll-film detective camera could have been "put on the market at such a low price that it would be a leading card for us."

Eastman had not yet found this "leading card," but no doubt the inventions of Eastman and company had simplified photography. At least in that aspect, the roll-film system was clearly superior to any that had preceded it. And the potential for mass production of photographic supplies and apparatus was promising. Roll holders with interchangeable parts were being put together on a primitive assembly line. Film- and paper-coating machines were running smoothly. And some sort of small hand-held camera, though one as yet not perfected, still seemed to Eastman a product with market potential.

What was most conspicuously missing was a market. The merits of the roll-holder, roll-film system seemed to be lost on the small group of men and women who constituted the amateur and professional worlds of photography. "When we started out with our scheme of film photography," Eastman wrote, "we expected that everybody that used glass plates would take up films, but we found that in order to make a large business we would have to reach the general public and create a new class of patrons."

It would take a completely new system of photographic image making, radically different than anything yet seen in photography, to conjure up that new class of consumers.

In September 1888 Eastman formally registered his coined word *Kodak* as a trademark. Some such combination of letters had been rolling around in Eastman's mind during the past year or so, when he had been trying to come up with a suitable name for a "little roll-holder breast camera" he was designing to replace the failed Eastman detective camera.

In his application to the comptroller of the British patent office, who required a full disclosure of the meaning and derivation of the name, Eastman wrote:

"Kodak," This is not a foreign name or word; it was constructed by me to serve a definite purpose. It has the following merits as a trade-mark word:
First.   It is short.
Second.   It is not capable of mispronunciation.
Third.   It does not resemble anything in the art and cannot be associated with anything in the art except the Kodak.

Eastman did not mention that K was his favorite letter (it was the first letter of his mother's maiden name), but that detail didn't matter. The "K" camera he had been referring to in letters and conversation officially became the Kodak camera.

At first the very strangeness of the word attracted attention. In the September 14, 1888, issue of *The British Journal of Photography*, a writer asked, "What in the name of all that is photographic is the Kodak, and from what source is the term derived? Failing to discover its origins in either the dead or living languages.... we conceive it to be a technical term in Volapuk, its significance being a small and easily worked camera of the genus disguised."

The camera this word described was as simple as its name, if not more elegant. In basic size and shape, the Kodak camera was not substantially different from all the detective cameras that had preceded it. The little leather-covered wooden box weighed twenty-two ounces and measured 6½ x 3¼ x 3¾ inches, about half the size of an ordinary shoebox. At first glance, the box hardly resembled a camera. Besides a small button on the side and a string, metal dial, and clock key on the top, there was little about the Kodak camera to suggest how it worked.

Fully enclosed in the rear section of the camera was a specially designed roll holder, which was prewound with American film. To bring a fresh piece of film into the camera's focal plane, the key on top of the camera was turned until the small circular dial indicated that the camera was ready. There was no exposure counter, but to remedy that situation a small notebook, its pages numbered to record each exposure, was included in the purchase price.

Covered in black morocco leather, the wooden case of the Kodak camera contained a simple roller mechanism wound with a fifty-foot length of film seventy millimeters wide. The camera's cylindrical shutter was cocked by pulling a string on the top of the box. Exposures were made by pushing a side button. Fresh film was then brought into the focal plane by twisting a clock key.

The Kodak camera system promised a division of photographic labors. After considering a number of paragraph-length ways to explain this idea, George Eastman finally cut out everything else but: Kodak cameras. You Press the button—We do the rest.

Centered in the front of the camera was a fixed, unadjustable, two-element lens, hidden behind a rather ingenious barrel shutter. The shutter was not much more than a piece of metal pipe a couple of inches long, the sides of which had been sliced out to form light-admitting slits. This cylindrical shutter was cocked by means of a tensed spring. Between exposures the solid section of the pipe shutter blocked light from the reaching the lens, in effect doing double duty as a lens cap.

To take a picture, the photographer simply pressed a button on the side of the camera, thus releasing the spring and allowing the slit in the cylindrical shutter to make a quick drop past the front of the lens. A pull of the string recocked the shutter; another turn of the take-up key brought fresh film into the focal plane, and the camera was ready for another shot. The lens behind this shutter was simply two pieces of glass. For the most part, the lens worked well, but when it was discovered that light scattered around the edges of the frame, a 2½-inch circular mask was placed in front of the film plane. Later models contained lenses that corrected these aberrations, but for the first year all Kodak snapshots were round.

The Kodak, like most detective cameras, lacked a viewfinder, having only a V-shaped set of lines engraved on the top of the camera to help with sighting. The photographer held the camera at waist level with both hands and pointed as best he could. But despite an occasional odd tilt of the box, framing seemed to be not much of a problem. The camera's eye encompassed a fairly forgiving 60-degree line of sight, and, to judge by many of the photos taken with the first Kodak cameras, pointing was a skill quickly learned.

With a fairly fast shutter speed (1/25 of a second) and a short fixed focal length that produced an acceptably sharp depth of field from about four feet on, the Kodak camera was easy to operate and required hardly any training or expertise. But as simple as the camera was to operate, that was not its most important distinction. After much experience with the difficulty amateurs (and indeed most professionals) had encountered with the processing of American film, Eastman decided not to bother the consumer with this chore. All Kodak camera film could be developed at the Rochester factory, where Eastman employees had both the equipment and the expertise to handle this tricky job.

The twenty-five–dollar Kodak camera came loaded with enough film to make one hundred exposures. When the photographer had finished shooting his pictures, he simply boxed up the camera and mailed it back to the factory. For ten dollars the film was developed and printed, the camera reloaded with another one-hundred-exposure roll of film, and prints, film, and camera were shipped back to the customer. All along Eastman had considered "a complete system of photography" to be the only way to attract new members into the small fraternity of amateur photographers. And now, after a couple of years of near successes and partial failures he had created that whole system practically overnight.

In a sense he had all the parts of the system on hand; roll film, roll holder, photoprocessing facilities, and even a detective camera. The genius was in the interconnecting of the pieces. The roll holder was redesigned to be an integral part of a small camera. Roll film, which many amateurs had refused to try, was offered to a brand new audience. This fresh group of amateur photographers, unsophisticated in the ways of plate photography and unaware of its conventions, had no reason to distrust the product. Did it work? That's all they seemed to be interested in.

And because Eastman had combined American film, always difficult for photographers to handle, with his in-house photoprocessing capabilities, there was no need for the newcomer to photography to worry about film development. The Eastman photofinishing service could relieve the photographer of that burden. The old fussy set of rules, formulas, and instructions that were part and parcel of all picture taking had been reduced to an economical, eight-word sentence.

"As you are aware," Eastman wrote to a friend about the origin of the now-famous Kodak slogan, "there were a number of ideas sent me for adoption. They were all in effect that the button should be pressed, and that we would do the balance of the work. I finally cut out everything else but 'Kodak Cameras. You press the button—We do the rest.' I can only add that no man was more astonished to find the phrase so universally popular."

The only difficulty left, as Eastman saw it, was to get his camera into the hands of this new class of photographers. Previously Eastman had limited his advertising to the specialized photographic journals. Ads for "the Kodak," however, which were intended to appeal to those outside the small fraternity of amateur photographers, were placed in mass-market publications such as *Lippincott's Monthly* and *Youth's Companion*. Photomechanical reproduction of photographs was then still a rarity, so to illustrate the range of his product Eastman hired an artist to produce line drawings showing "camera in use on the pier, in the sailboat, on the ocean steamer, in the canoe, on the bicycle, on the hotel piazza, on the beach, father

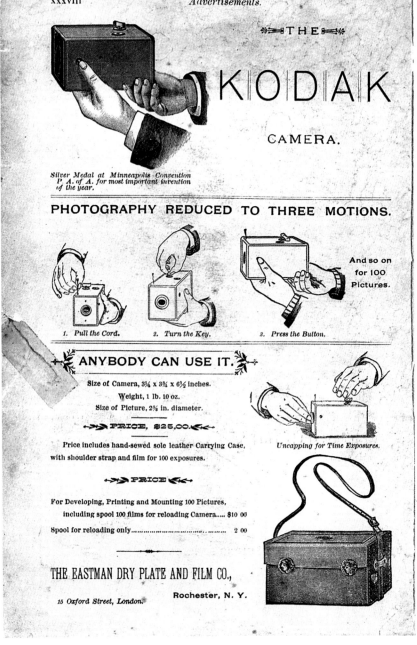

The Kodak camera reduced picture making to three simple, easily explained steps: pull the cord to cock the camera, turn the key to bring fresh film into the focal plane, and press the button.

The fashionable woman of the late nine-
teenth century, this 1889 advertising
photo suggests, could carry a Kodak cam-
era without the least bit of bother or em-
barrassment. With its leather carrying
case strung over the shoulder, the Kodak
camera was stylish, portable, and conve-
niently available whenever the occasion
called for a picture.

photographing child, father photographing children, father photographing bay, man photographing dog, man photographing pal."

At first most cameras were sold in photography stock shops. But soon after the introduction of the Kodak camera, Eastman salesmen began placing the product in drugstores. Most pharmacies at the time sold over-the-counter chemicals, and photographic supplies, falling roughly into that category, seemed a perfect product for these establishments to merchandise.

The Kodak complete system of practical photography was an almost instant success. In late July 1888 the cameras were available for sale. A month later, in late August and early September, the first cameras were returned for film processing and reloading. By the end of the year twenty-five hundred had been sold.

Eastman, who wrote much of the advertising copy for "the Kodak" and in less than five hours composed the instruction booklet that accompanied the camera, knew exactly how revolutionary his invention was. In the preface to *The Kodak Primer*, Eastman briefly summarized the history of photography before and after the invention of the Kodak camera:

The march of improvement in any given field is always marked by periods of inactivity and then by sudden bursts of energy which revolutionize existing methods sometimes in a day.

For twenty years the art of photography stood still, then a great discovery opened a new channel for improvement, and for the last ten years the art has been in a state of rapid revolution.

Ten years ago every photographer had to sensitize his own plates and develop and finish his negatives on the spot where the picture was taken.

Four years ago the amateur photographer was confined to heavy glass plates for making his negatives, and the number of pictures he could make on a journey was limited by his capacity as a pack horse.

Yesterday the photographer, whether he used glass plates or films, must have a dark room and know all about focusing, relation of lens apertures to light and spend days and weeks learning

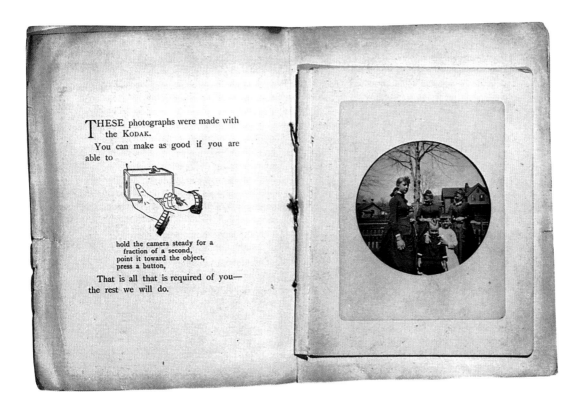

Included in the purchase of each Kodak camera was a simple instructional booklet entitled The Kodak Primer. *The first of these manuals was written by George Eastman after the New York advertising man hired to draft the first copy, had, in Eastman's words, "utterly ignored" the simplicity of the camera's operations and uses.*

developing, fixing, intensifying, printing, toning and mounting before he could show good results from his labors.

Today photography has been reduced to a cycle of three operations:

1: Pull the String   2: Turn the Key   3: Press the Button

The Kodak camera system was so compact, economical, and deceptively simple that it absolutely delighted the average consumer. There are not many of these near-perfect products in the history of mechanical innovation. And of those, not many last more than a season or two. But it was as much the Kodak idea as the Kodak camera that made this product so distinctive. Once the man in the street discovered the absolutely compelling idea of no-fuss, no-fault picture taking, the Kodak camera began selling in numbers unmatched in the history of photography.

"The craze," *The Chicago Tribune* wrote in 1889, "is spreading fearfully.... Chicago has had many fads whose careers have been brilliant but brief. But when amateur photography came, it came to stay."

Within a year or two of its introduction, the demand for cameras and film had grown so far beyond expectation that even Eastman, who had predicated his business philosophy on "production in large quantities by machinery," was writing that "if this thing keeps up we are afraid that we will be mobbed."

A good deal of this excitement was the work of Eastman's always astute marketing policy. From the very beginning, Eastman knew that the cardinal virtue of his "complete system of practical photography" was its radical departure from the often esoteric ways of nineteenth-century plate, chemical, and darkroom photography. It was not exactly true that the Kodak system took the mystery out of photochemical reproduction. The intriguing but scientifically complex explanation of the way that light acts upon chemically sensitized material to produce a lifelike picture of the world remained, as it does today, beyond the knowledge of the average amateur photographer.

What the Kodak system did was unburden the average photographer of the necessity to know any of this. As Eastman observed, "The Kodak Camera renders possible the Kodak system whereby the mere mechanical act of taking a picture, which anybody can perform, is divorced from all the chemical manipulations of preparing and finishing pictures which only experts can perform. There is no jugglery about it; photography has simply been brought down to a point where the mechanical work can be entirely separated from the chemical work." In other words, the phrase "you press the button, we do the rest" promised the nineteenth-century man a bit of twentieth-century luxury.

In a very short time, the Kodak advertising tag line rose to a rank somewhere between cliché and proverbial status. The periodical press seemed never to be in short supply of Kodak camera anecdotes and punch lines. For instance, *The New York Sun* reported that Thomas Edison, a man who soon was to have more than a passing relationship to the Eastman Company, checked into a rural hotel one Sunday morning and ordered a hot scotch. The clerk said he was sorry, but being Sunday, no spiritous beverages were available. Edison, angry, persisted. He was cold and wet and needed a drink. There was one thing he could do, the clerk answered. What's that, Edison said? Well, we can give you a Kodak, was the response. A Kodak? What's a Kodak?, Edison asked. You just go up to your room and press the button, the clerk replied. We do the rest.

Another story, perhaps less apocryphal, concerned the New York City politician Chaucey Depew, who finished a chamber of commerce after-dinner speech by announcing, "As merchants, as bankers and businessmen, we say to congress, in the language which advertises that most universal and productive of our institutions, the Kodak, 'You Press the button and we will do the rest!'"

In the early days after the introduction of
the Kodak camera, the average amateur
photographer usually took typical snapshots. Landscape photography of a purely
interpretive nature seemed of secondary
importance. This snapshot is an exception,
a winter scene photographed simply for its
beauty.

In 1890, on one of his many transatlantic trips, George Eastman went out on the deck of the U.S.S. Gallia to take a picture with a Kodak box camera. A shipboard companion had the same idea and snapped a photograph of Eastman taking a photograph.

Depew had the slogan a little wrong, but that apparently didn't bother Eastman, who immediately wrote to the politician:

The Eastman Company has taken the liberty of sending you a Kodak for Mrs. Depew. I hope that you will accept it as a slight acknowledgement of a high compliment which you recently paid the Kodak. If Mrs. Depew will press the button of the little instrument when she sees anything interesting on her travels, we will try to convince her that the doing of the rest is not a vain promise on our part.

In short order Depew responded:

I am in receipt of your letter of the 22nd announcing that you have sent a Kodak to Mrs. Depew. I know that she will be immensely delighted, but that her pleasure can by no means equal that which "Buster" [Depew's son] will have in using the instrument. I have been the victim of your invention about a million times and in all possible situations and conditions, and I know of no better way of getting even than by giving it the national advertisement which I did in my chamber of commerce speech.

Besides the acknowledgment of his camera's success, Eastman certainly would not have failed to notice two other important implications contained in Depew's note. The first was that even

children could operate the camera. Later the Brownie camera would be designed for all the Busters of the world.

The second was that the Kodak camera had already found a potential place in the journalism profession. That prospect was clearly described in another recommendation, which came from Walter Wellman, the Washington author of a nationally syndicated article entitled "Caught with a Kodak." Back in the days when he was strenuously, and pretty much vainly, trying to sell the idea of the Eastman-Walker roll-holder system, Eastman had argued that "the camera is getting to be as necessary to the newspaper correspondent as his pen."

But except in isolated cases, such as that of the great New York newspaperman and reformer Jacob Riis, who in the years just preceding the invention of the Kodak camera had photographed New York's Lower East Side slums with a plate camera and a homemade flash pan, the art of investigatory photojournalism was as yet unborn. Wellman, however, quickly figured out what this simple little gadget could accomplish. If Wellman was perhaps not as intense and perceptive a photojournalist as Riis, it is nonetheless true that his photographic jaunt down Washington's streets and boulevards at least took the camera out into the open air. And out among the crowds the camera's wide-eyed empirical glance took in more than he first expected:

I bought a kodak [sic] last week, and, like any other boy with a new toy, started out bright and early to see what I could do with it. In Lafayette Square I caught a glimpse of Mr. [James G.]

Paul Nadar, the son of the well-known Parisian photographer Nadar, was the Eastman Company's first French representative. On a trip to Paris in 1890 Eastman posed for a formal portrait in the photographer's studio. After the sitting, both men went out to the street, where Eastman snapped off this Kodak camera picture of Nadar in a sunny Parisian plaza.

YOU PRESS THE BUTTON,
WE DO THE REST

The metal parts needed for early Eastman cameras were tooled by the Rochester firm of Yawman and Erbe. When the first Kodak camera was being tested, Yawman and Erbe left work for a few moments and posed on the steps outside their shop for what is the earliest surviving picture taken with this new camera.

Blaine, walking with his head down, evidently in a brown study, and with his derby hat pulled pretty well down over his eyes. This is one of Mr. Blaine's little pecularities, and it matters not what sort of a hat he is wearing either.

At the Capitol the industrious little Kodak found many scenes meat, and fit for its devouring, but most of those shall be saved for a future letter. The Kodak is no respecter of persons, and in good time it will have some interesting stories to tell of its espionage of the great men who meet every day in the big state house.

As the rage spread, Eastman began collecting and publishing similar testimonials. Many, of course, were gathered and reprinted for advertising purposes, but others, it is clear, served as signposts pointing to the variety of uses, both amateur and professional, that seemed intrinsic to the Kodak camera, film, and processing system.

Some recommendations came from the very famous. "I am amazed at the excellence of the little Kodak's work," wrote Rudyard Kipling. But most, like that of the Joilet, Illinois, warden who found the 100-shot camera perfect for making assembly-line mug shots of convicts, came from the less well known.

A long and laudatory 1886 *Chicago Tribune* article cataloged example after example of the amateur camera's range of skills. A Professor S.W. Burnham of Chicago's Lick Observatory was reported to have taken an instantaneous Kodak photo of a cat leaping after a bird, which won him a prize at a Paris exhibition. At a Chicago medical school, a Professor Bartlett used amateur photography as a visual aid in his chemistry lectures. Another photographer, Mrs. Shears, the wife of a doctor, is said to have "taken interior views of an unusual nature....":

In order to assist her husband in surgical work she photographs tumors, cancers, and other cheerful things of like character. She has "taken" a man before, during, and after an epileptic fit. Her views are of great value to the medical profession and are copied widely.

"Another amateur," *The Tribune* continued, "is Mrs N. Gray Bartlett. Professionals and amateurs unite in praise of her exquisite work. She has an inexhaustible fund of original ideas in posing. Within the last three months her pictures have been published in Wide Awake, St. Nicholas, Outing and Scribners."

Less than a year after its introduction, over thirteen thousand cameras had been sold, and the company was processing sixty to seventy rolls of film a day. *Wilson's Photographic Magazine* sent a correspondent to Rochester to visit the Eastman factory. After watching the Eastman machines coat about six thousand feet of negative film a day and then climbing to the "airy" printing room on the rooftop of the factory, the writer speculated:

In the short period of its astonishing existence, this little black box has persuaded thousands to the pursuit of photography, and its name has become a household word. It is the pioneer of a new type of camera, the creator of a new class of photographers, and has brought all the pleasures of the art-science within the reach of those who never thought they should enjoy them before it came upon their view; it has added largely to the ranks and considerably changed the methods of amateur photographers.

But while the Kodak roll-film revolution of 1888 was changing forever the nature of photography, another photographic product, perhaps equally important, was in the early stages of development. And that was transparent film base made of nitrocellulose — the cellulose, among other things, of the celluloid screen.

By no stretch of the imagination could George Eastman be called a trained chemist. True, like many photographic innovators (Daguerre and Talbot come immediately to mind), Eastman had the patience to run thousands of improvisational chemical experiments. In the days when he had begun working on dry-plate emulsions, all that was needed to be successful in such a venture were a few chemicals, a set of reliable measuring devices, and a place to work.

Eastman had a friend, though, who was a university-educated chemist. Professor S. A. Lattimore had joined the University of Rochester in the early 1870s, and by the time Eastman met him, perhaps through an old friend at the Rochester Savings Bank who contributed the funds necessary to outfit the university's chemical laboratory, Lattimore was chairman of the chemistry department and had achieved a national reputation for his experimental work.

Just prior to its commercial introduction, Eastman had given Lattimore one of his first roll holders. According to Eastman, the well-educated chemist was a representative amateur. "The holder we sent out with Dr. Lattimore," Eastman commented at the time, "was simply an experiment to find out how the instrument would work in the hands of an inexperienced person. As Dr. L. lives here and would send his exposures to us to develop, it was a good opportunity to determine whether any weak points in the apparatus would be developed."

There is no record of Lattimore's response, but clearly Eastman's interest and respect for the chemist went considerably beyond the merely mundane purposes of product testing. Eastman, who had very little formal schooling as a young man and sometimes downgraded its importance, knew that if his photochemical business was to make the next technological leap, scientific knowledge and organized experimental techniques were necessary. In particular, that meant that a scientist must be hired. Eastman asked Lattimore to recommend someone qualified, and in August 1886 an "ingenious, quick-witted fellow" named Henry Reichenbach joined the company as its first full-time chemist.

At the time, Eastman was already marketing and manufacturing three sorts of emulsion-support combinations: Eastman dry plates, Eastman negative paper, and American film. With the possible exception of the negative paper, the production of which was gradually discontinued, all three were still part of the Eastman inventory in 1888 when the Kodak camera was introduced. But even as early as 1886, Eastman knew that emulsions must be improved and

Sometime in the early 1890s the Raymond K. Albright family of Buffalo, New York, took a tour of Europe and the Middle East. During their travels the family shot four rolls of one-hundred-exposure Kodak film, one of which they had printed in Paris by the Eastman representative Paul Nadar.

Each of the Albright photos is numbered, and on its cardboard back is written a short description of the picture. Arranged in sequential order the photos narrate a place-by-place itinerary of the travels: where the Albrights went, what they saw, and who was along on the trip. Conspicuously missing, however, is the father—apparently the man responsible for the family photographs.

that the paper-backed films were the least efficient link in the roll-film camera system. American film, in particular, the complicated nature of which had necessitated factory development of each Kodak roll, would eventually have to be replaced by something better.

Eastman assigned Reichenbach two separate chores: to upgrade wherever possible the speed and sensitivity of gelatin emulsions and to develop a strong, stable, flexible transparent film base upon which these new emulsions could be coated. This was a little like asking an automotive engineer to design both engine and fuel, but Reichenbach, who at the time knew practically nothing about photography, took on the project with enthusiasm and skill.

Reichenbach began experimenting with various varnishes, hoping to create a tough, yet flexible film skin. Neither the varnishes nor any other of the hardening solutions that he tried worked; they were either too thin, too pitted, or too slick to be coated with emulsion. About ten years earlier, however, another upstate New York inventor named John Wesley Hyatt, while looking for a material to replace ivory in billiard balls, had come up with a method of hardening nitrocellulose. Hyatt called this product "celluloid." In 1884 the Philadelphia photographer John Carbutt had asked Hyatt to slice off 1/100-inch-thick sheets of celluloid for coating with photographic emulsions. Carbutt sold such thick and fairly inflexible sheets of film under his own imprint, but he did not patent the product.

Eastman had asked his chemist to create a flexible transparent film base that could be adapted to the methods of factory production, and late in 1888 Reichenbach mixed up a batch of nitrocellulose solution in wood alcohol, which when poured upon glass, produced a smooth, glascine film. The nitrocellulose skin, however, was not very strong and Reichenbach, still working by trial and error, added a little camphor to the mixture. The result was a fairly strong and flexible film, but one that still showed annoying spots of crystallization. Finally, and one can only imagine Reichenbach's surprise and relief, he added a solution of fusel oil and amyl nitrate to the camphor, and when the nitrocellulose skin was heated and dried, a workable, spot-free transparent film was formed.

Eastman and Reichenbach were elated. A patent on the new process was applied for in April 1889. However, after the patent examiner looked over the Reichenbach application, he declared

that it interfered with another cellulose film application first received in the summer of 1877. That year the Reverend Hannibal Goodwin, an amateur photographer, had devised a similar transparent film base, but his patent had been rejected by the examiner as too broad to qualify as a valid invention and had remained unissued for the next twelve years. In December 1889 the patent examiner compared the Goodwin and Reichenbach formulas and decided, apparently on the basis of Reichenbach's specific combinations of chemicals, to issue the patent in his name.

Goodwin protested, and for the next twenty-five years the issue of which chemical formula preceded the other bounced from courtroom to courtroom. Expert witnesses were called and the case ground on through fifty-four hundred pages of testimony; Goodwin's contention being that shortly after the film went into production, the formulas contained in the original Reichenbach application had been adjusted.

In 1889 the question of just who put what chemical into the formula at which stage seemed to Eastman a knotty but in some ways inconsequential problem. At the time, nitrocellulose difficulties were more of a production than a legal nature. Previously, each new Eastman negative support had been designed with a machine for its manufacture in mind. The old roller-and-trough dry-plate coating mechanism, which was, in fact, still in operation, had enabled the company to put out large, consistent quantities of product. The same was true of the continuous paper coater then used for negative films and printing papers.

However, neither machine could handle the nitrocellulose "dope" that formed the transparent base of this new film. There were two problems associated with the new material: the dope had to be spread on a perfectly smooth surface and, to allow the manufacture of sizable batches of film, that surface had to be fairly large. Perhaps with the American film system in mind, Eastman initially considered producing long strips of wax from which the dried and hardened dope could be stripped. But the tedious and tricky nature of this sort of operation was precisely what he hoped to avoid.

Eastman began studying the idea of using glass and made inquiries about the maximum lengths and widths then available. Finding that he could order fairly large sheets, the first glass

coating tables were soon constructed by cementing 3½-foot-wide sheets of glass together to form continuous 80-foot tables. The joints were then ground and polished to create a silky smooth surface.

A hopper was suspended over the tables, which, as it rode along a conveyor belt, released a thin stream of nitrocellulose dope. As soon as the dope had been spread along the entire length of the table, wooden boxes were lowered to form a duct through which warm air was forced to speed up the drying of the solution. The next morning, after the dope had hardened, the lights were turned off and a light-sensitive emulsion was spread over the entire 80 x 3½-foot sheet of hardened nitrocellulose. This top layer was again dried with warm air, and by early afternoon the film was ready to be stripped from the table, sliced into strips, and individually rolled for insertion into a camera.

Despite the facts that the film sometimes curled and frilled as it was stripped from the table and that airborne dirt and grime, some from the nearby railroad line, often fouled the emulsion, by midsummer 1889 the first batches of transparent film were coming out of the factory. "This new film," Eastman wrote to Walker, "is the 'slickest' product that we ever tried to make and the method of manufacture will eliminate all of the defects hitherto experienced in film manufacture. The field for it is immense...."

The prospects for flexible transparent film were soon to be increased by the sudden appearance of a new, almost entirely unsuspected use for strips of nitrocellulose film. In May

1889, a month or so before the introduction of the new transparent film, Thomas Edison had written the Eastman Company and ordered a Kodak camera. Edison and Eastman had not met, though from the very early days Eastman factories had been equipped with electric lights and one acquaintance recalls an Edison gramophone sitting in Eastman's parlor.

Throughout 1888 Edison and his assistant William Kennedy Laurie Dickson had been working on the optical equivalent of the gramophone. Edison had met Eadweard Muybridge in January of that year and was apparently interested in the photographer's experiment with the projection of sequential photographs. In 1878 Muybridge had been asked by the former governor of California Leland Stanford to prove photographically that at some point a trotting horse simultaneously lifted all four of its feet off the ground. The photographer set up twelve wet-plate cameras along the edge of a race track, the shutters of which were attached to thin threads stretched across the track. As the horse ran past the cameras, its hooves consecutively snapped each thread, thus exposing a series of pictures.

Muybridge's photos proved that Stanford was correct. At first the photographer displayed pictures of this sort as a series of stills, but then realizing that if the pictures were viewed successively they would give the illusion of movement, he constructed a revolving glass plate projector that he called a "Zoopraxiscope." In 1881, while on a European tour, Muybridge met Etienne-Jules Marey, a French scientist interested in the physiology of animal movement. Marey was impressed with Muybridge's photographs and in 1882 designed a photographic "rifle" in order to take sequential pictures of birds in flight. The barrel of Marey's "chronophotographic gun" contained the camera's lens, behind which glass plates were arranged along the edge of a revolving metal disc. With his gun loaded with relatively fast gelatin dry plates Marey was able to make twelve exposures per second.

At the time Edison was attempting to engineer a system to synchronize the sound produced by his phonograph with pictures. Though Edison had filed three preparatory caveats with the U.S. patent office, his system of taking moving pictures on a revolving cylindrical surface never worked well enough to be marketed. It is not known what Edison and Dickson intended to do with the Kodak camera and film, though it is possible that the two had either seen or heard about earlier motion-picture experiments making use of strips of Eastman paper negatives.

In January 1888 the French inventor Louis Le Prince had applied for an English patent on a motion-picture camera in which, the application read, "Sensitive film for the negatives may be an endless sheet of insoluble gelatin coated with bromide emulsion or any convenient ready-made quick-acting film such as Eastman's paper film." Le Prince had exposed a number of rolls of this film in his camera (one sequence recorded a street scene in Leeds), and it is perhaps justifiable to name him as the first actually to make use of flexible film in motion-picture work. However, those few experimental films were the extent of Le Prince's contributions to film. In September 1890 he boarded a train in Dijon, disappeared, and was never heard from again.

The same month that Le Prince applied for his patent, Marey suggested in a lecture to the French Academy of Sciences that 22-foot-long by 2¾-inch-wide strips of Kodak camera stripping film could be used to replace the dry plates in a motion-picture camera. Later that fall, Marey managed to work out the mechanics of the process and recorded a sequence showing waves beating upon the seashore.

Other motion-picture pioneers had similar ideas for the use of film. In Britain, William Friese Greene had been experimenting with "photographic sensitized films," but it is unclear whether he ever successfully showed moving pictures. Another English inventor, Wordsworth Donisthorpe, had designed a motion-picture camera that used the new flexible Kodak film. From the surviving example of Donisthorpe's work, a strip of circular pictures 2½ inches in diameter of Trafalgar Square in London, it appears that the inventor simply unloaded a Kodak camera and ran the film as is through his camera.

In 1890 the British inventor Wordsworth
Donisthorpe loaded what appears to be a
strip of film from the first Kodak camera
into an experimental movie camera and
recorded the movement of carriages and
pedestrians in London's Trafalgar Square.
But Donisthorpe was unable to find financial backers for his Kinesigraph, and work
on the project was halted.

A few months after Edison wrote ordering a single Kodak camera, he visited Marey in Paris, where he may have seen examples of motion pictures exposed on flexible film. Back at his laboratory that fall, he and Dickson continued working on their own version of the flexible film movie apparatus. In the meantime, while Edison was out of the country, the Eastman Company had formally introduced its new transparent nitrocellulose film. On July 30 a demonstration of the film was presented before the New York Society of Amateur Photographers, and legend has it that in attendance that night was none other than Edison's assistant W. K. L. Dickson. The story continues that once shown a piece of this new transparent film, Edison said, "That's it—we've got it—now work like hell." But whatever the accuracy of the story, in early September Dickson wrote to the Eastman Company:

Dear Sirs:
Enclosed please find sum of $2.50 P.O.O. due you for one roll Kodak film for which please accept thanks—I shall try same to-day & report—it looks splendid—I never succeeded in getting this substance in such straight & long pieces—

Sincerely yrs.
W. K. L. Dickson

A couple of weeks later, Dickson ordered six more rolls, but then apparently, activity on their "Kinetoscope" ceased for some time. About a year and a half later, however, Eastman wrote to Reichenbach:

Enclosed is a small fragment of film furnished Edison for his phonograph arrangement. He perforates it on both edges and delivers it by means of cog wheels. The film has to move 40 times a second and the movement has to be made in 1/10 of the time. The trouble with the film we have sent him is that the cogs tear the films slightly, as you can see by the enclosed, and gives blurred images. I gave the Edison representative a sample of the double coated film made last August and told him if heavy enough we could furnish him that if he would take a whole table at a time in 41 inch strips.

In 1882, as part of his continuing study of animal locomotion, the French scientist Etienne-Jules Marey used a photographic "gun" to expose small glass plates at a rate of twelve per second. In 1889 Marey loaded flexible Kodak camera film into a primitive motion-picture camera and was able to expose upwards of one hundred pictures per second.

In November 1891, the Edison factory was back at work on the moving-picture problem. Another order was placed, this time for twenty-seven rolls 50 feet long, 1½ inches wide, and 1/500 of an inch thick. This film was apparently to be used for the exhibition of motion pictures. Edison had already applied for patents on a "Kinetograph" camera and had shown an experimental film on what he called a "Kinetoscope viewer."

This viewer was a wooden box with a small magnifying glass inserted in a peephole cut in its top. Inside the box a continuous loop of film was wound around a series of spools. As a person squinted through the viewer, film was advanced past his eye by an electric motor at a speed of about forty-six frames a second. A simple rotary shutter opened and closed as each frame passed. Illuminated from behind by an electric light bulb, the flickering images gave the illusion of movement.

For the next few years Edison and Dickson prepared for the commercial introduction of their system. When a design had been settled upon, the film gate of the standard Edison camera was built to use film 1⅜ inches wide (35mm) and almost 50 feet long. Lore has it that Edison decided on this film width by holding his thumb and forefinger apart and saying, "About this wide." But the fact that 35 millimeters is exactly half the width of the 70-millimeter film designed for the Kodak camera, and that 50 feet is about twice the length needed for one hundred exposures, suggests that in their early experiments with camera, lens, and gate size, Edison and Dickson simply slit a roll of film down the middle and then cemented the two pieces together end to end.

At the time, neither Eastman nor Edison was aware that these few years of work would turn out to have almost as powerful an effect upon the world of photography as the original Kodak camera. When Eastman and Reichenbach began experimenting with transparent nitrocellulose film, this slick new invention was intended to simplify the production of film for the expanding amateur market. Few knew, however, that celluloid film would soon be ordered by the table, and that not too many years in the future movie producers would purchase film by the millions of feet.

In May 1892, at the end of an incredibly active and successful decade of business, the Eastman Dry Plate and Film Company formally changed its name to the Eastman Kodak Company.

The "K" word, as Eastman had called it in the days before the camera's introduction, was first used by him as an adjective (the Kodak camera). Within a very few years, however, many misused it as a verb. People carried "Kodaks" around and "Kodaked" everything in sight. A few years earlier Sir John Herschel, from whose fruitful imagination had come the terms negative and positive, had also used the word "snapshot," a British hunting term, to describe "the possibility of securing a picture in a tenth of a second." Eventually that word would come to signify any photograph taken quickly and casually.

By the mid-1890s one hundred thousand Kodak snapshot cameras had been manufactured, and the craze showed no signs of abating. With this inconspicuous small camera in hand, snapshooters were seemingly everywhere. Its ease, speed, and simplicity were inspiring everything from candid portraiture to bad poetry.

The camera's ability to seize the moment, seemed to poet J. H. Steadman, its prime virtue and brought forth a paean to the camera he entitled "Kodaktyl":

> *The kodak lately caught a fish*
> *And if the truth be told*
> *It will catch anything you wish*
> *Except, it won't catch cold.*

It will take everything you see
Yes! Quicker than a wind;
A pretty girl, earth, sky and sea,
But it won't take a drink.

In Thomas Edison's Kinetoscope, successive images photographed on fifty-foot lengths of Eastman film were passed at approximately forty-six images per second past the viewer's eye. As each frame appeared a light flashed, illuminating the picture long enough so that each image persisted for a fraction of a second. Seen rapidly one after another these images produced the illusion of movement.

In Britain, where "Kodaks" were marketed through a small Soho Square office, the camera inspired song. In the Gilbert and Sullivan comic opera *Utopia Limited*, two "modest maidens," stepping out of a chorus of camera-carrying "Kodakers," sang to the audience "a sprightly stanza" that went:

If evidence you would possess
Of what is maiden bashfulness
You only need a button press—
And we will do the rest.

Good fun, apparently, but as one reviewer wrote:

That the song and chorus is charming goes without saying. The names of Gilbert and Sullivan are a sufficient guarantee of that. But have the managers stopped to consider what the effect is to be on the front rows? Think of a bald-headed man—and most likely married too—looking into a battery of fifty kodaks [sic]. The kodak buttons click in unison. Too late, the horrible idea comes to him that fifty witnesses to his frivolity are contained in those fifty little black boxes.

His hard old heart beats wildly and a sea of crimson rushes up to his massive forehead, across the broad expanse of unadorned cranium, and disappears in the row of fringe on the back of his neck. With a wild rush he leaves the theater, and hastening home, he pens with trembling hand, the check that is to buy for his unsuspecting spouse the sealskin coat that has long been her earthly ambition.

Others warned that even more dire consequences would come to those who skulked about snapping photos of the unaware and unprepared. One English editorialist wrote in 1893: "Several decent young men, I hear, are forming a Vigilance Association for the purpose of thrashing the cads with cameras who go about at seaside places taking snapshot at ladies emerging from the deep in the mournful garments peculiar to the British female bather."

Most "Kodakers" apparently found much less aggressive uses for the camera. Eastman had proposed that the Kodak camera could be used by travelers, tourists, bicyclists, engineers, architects, artists, parents, surgeons, sportsmen, campers, and lovers of fine animals. "Anybody can use it," he concluded. "Everybody will use it." Judging by the subject matter of the many early Kodak snaps still in existence, that's exactly what happened.

In fact, despite the enormous improvements in camera design and emulsion sensitivity, snapshot content has changed very little since the introduction of the first Kodak. Travel was, then as now, perhaps the most important occasion requiring the presence of a camera. No matter what the length of the trip, around the world or just across the state, the amateur camera went along to record landscapes, prominent buildings, noteworthy events, and most importantly, the travelers themselves—usually posed in front of an easily identifiable landmark; sometimes just standing arm in arm with friends and families.

Above:

Beaches, with their bright sunshine and constant activity, were very often the favorite places to take a family's box camera. The best pictures taken at the beach, such as this, included sea, sand, and people in one well-composed photograph.

Opposite:

In July 1889 a snapshot album of Kodak photographs recording the "Sea journey of His Majesty the Emperor and King Wilhelm II to Norway" was compiled from pictures taken by two friends, Dr. Güssfeldt and the German marine painter Salzmann. The album, now part of the Lebeck Collection in Hamburg, Germany, affords an uncommon glimpse into the private lives of European royalty.

(top to bottom)

Kaiser Wilhelm on board the yacht Hohenzollern in the harbor of Bodö.

Left to right: Messrs. Scholl, Wedel, Captain Lieutenant Gretz, and Count von Waldersee, chief of staff.

Breakfast onshore. The emperor is sitting in the foreground.

Dr. Güssfeldt with a tripod camera on the deck of the Hohenzollern.

Closer to home, of course, the camera began to be used to record all the family events that heretofore had been only registered in the mind's eye or the family Bible. Birthdays, christenings, reunions with relatives, Fourth of July picnics, even the family's favorite dog or horse or goat, became the subjects of both posed and candid photographs.

Although at least one commentator had called the camera "an instrument of torture," the dominant mood caught in most snapshots plainly contradicts that statement. For some reason, many who found themselves standing in the line of sight of a snapshot camera were seized by a sudden impulse for foolery. In the days of daguerreotype, wet-plate, and dry-plate photography, picture taking had sometimes been touched with an explicable but disconcerting dourness. The slow speed of older technologies, particularly the daguerreotype and wet-collodion techniques, had in some ways encouraged rigid poses, as had photography's attempt to mimic the hierarchical carriage of the body in the typical painted portrait. But the new technology does not fully explain the change in poses that followed the introduction of the Kodak camera.

Though the Kodak camera's shutter and film speed were fast, both of these features were available to professional and serious amateur photographers. More likely this liberation of the comic and serendipitous is simply a function of the popular photographer's sense that picture taking could, indeed, be fun. In every group of a dozen or so typical snapshot portraits or landscapes there is a picture of someone milking a horse or a group posing backside to the camera or just someone looking goofily at the camera. Nineteenth-century photography, for all its accomplishments, artistic and technological alike, had seldom been playful. "Kodaking" was fun.

The apparently never-ending appetite for film and cameras often threatened to strain the manufacturing resources of the Eastman Kodak Company. Between 1881 and 1889 the company had continually moved to new and larger quarters, but about 1890 it was decided that a new manufacturing facility was needed, and a parcel of land was bought three miles away from the original State Street building in the center of Rochester. To design and operate this facility, which initially was meant to contain a powerhouse, film factory, and bromide paper plant, Eastman hired Darragh Delancey, a young mechanical engineer who had just graduated from the Massachusetts Institute of Technology. Less than a year later, this factory complex, named Kodak Park, began operation.

From the first days of his interest in cameras, Eastman, apparently wanting to concentrate his energies upon the production of emulsion products, had jobbed out most mechanical work. Metal parts were manufactured by the Rochester firm of Yawman and Erbe, lenses came from the Bausch & Lomb optical factory, and woodworking tasks were assigned to Frank Brownell, a local camera builder. But it was Brownell, whom Eastman once called "the greatest camera designer the world has known," whose work contributed most to the huge expansion and improvement of the Eastman camera inventory.

In the early days, Kodak cameras were manufactured in Brownell's factory and then shipped across town in horse-drawn carts to be loaded with film at Eastman's State Street plant. In 1892, however, Eastman built a factory next door to his own, which was called the "Camera Works" and rented it to Brownell. Between 1885, when Brownell began manufacturing the Eastman-Walker roll holder and 1902, when he retired from the business, more than sixty new models and camera designs came out of the Camera Works. By 1889 the original Kodak camera, had been succeeded by the No. 1 and No. 2 Kodak cameras. (The No. 1 differed from the original Kodak camera mainly in its shutter design; a simpler sector shutter had replaced the cylindrical shutter, which was difficult to manufacture. The No. 2 produced a picture one inch larger in diameter.)

The No. 3, introduced in 1890, featured rack-and-pinion focusing, had two reflecting viewfinders, and contained a sophisticated Bausch & Lomb lens. It was the first to produce a

Casual photos of children became possible with the introduction of the Kodak snapshot cameras. This little girl, outfitted in a long white dress and high shoes for an 1890 Fourth of July celebration, is seen adjusting her hat. Her candidly captured expression, though unsuitable for a formal portrait, is in every way representative of the new snapshot portraiture genre.

rectangular negative. That same year Brownell designed his first folding camera, called simply enough the "Folding Kodak." The next year Brownell designed three cameras that used film cartridges that could be loaded and unloaded in subdued daylight. Film was fed out of a light-proof spool carton by means of a black cloth leader and threaded into the camera. The end of the film also had a leader that protected the exposed film when the camera was unloaded.

Daylight loading had another important effect upon the photography business. Now that customers need not send the entire camera back to Kodak for processing, a few independent photofinishing shops were opened. Not until after the turn of the century did this industry begin to grow significantly, but its impact upon the average consumer was beginning to be felt. Brownell's 1895 camera, the "Pocket Kodak," created even more public interest. This small box camera made fairly small pictures (1½ x 2 inches). But it was easy to carry, its light-proof cartridges of film fast to load, and, with a little red window that displayed the exposure number printed on the paper-backed film, it was easy to operate.

The Pocket Kodak camera was so popular that Brownell was asked to step up his production to five hundred units per day, and by the end of the year one hundred thousand of these cameras had been sold. (Perhaps significantly, 1890 was also the year that manufacture of the No. 1 Kodak camera was discontinued. A little over ten thousand of these cameras had been built; about one tenth as many as the 1895 Pocket Kodak camera.)

Over the years Brownell had come up with a half a dozen or so folding cameras but the aluminum "Folding Pocket Kodak" was the first that caught on with the consumer market. Unlike the Pocket Kodak, which was in truth a little large for the average pocket, this camera could actually be folded and slipped away in one's coat. Eastman, with his penchant for the "K" sound, was ready to name this camera "The Collapsing Kodak," until one of his advertising men suggested that the public might misinterpret and imagine "the whole thing falling to pieces."

There are no accurate figures of the number of cameras sold during the first forty years following the invention of photography. But certainly that number came nowhere close to the million and half Kodak cameras sold by the middle of photography's sixth decade. As the nineteenth century neared its end, this phenomenal pace of growth showed no signs of slowing.

The great Chicago World's Fair of 1893 opened to large and enthusiastic crowds, despite a financial panic earlier in May of that year that sent fifteen thousand commercial institutions into bankruptcy. A reported four hundred and ninety-one banks also failed, one of which was owned by George Eastman's partner, Henry Strong. At the time Strong and Eastman were the principal owners of the photography company, though a few Rochester friends had bought stock and were minority shareholders. The Eastman Kodak Company, despite the tightness of money, planned an impressive exhibit for the Columbian anniversary.

The Chicago fair had been intended as a celebration of American culture, ingenuity, and expertise. Even Henry Adams was fascinated, staying there "a fortnight absorbed in it." "Since Noah's Ark," Adams wrote, "no such Babel of loose and ill-joined, such vague and ill-defined and unrelated thoughts and half-thoughts and experimental outcries as the Exposition, had ever ruffled the surface of the Lakes."

The fair was a chance for the country as a whole to ask, Adams ruminated, "Whether the American people knew where they were driving." Though Adams continued to brood over that question for the rest of his life, the answer was probably there right before his eyes. Like all

Kodak cameras were advertised as being easy even for children to handle. The boy in this advertising photo has taken his camera along on a hike and is making a record of that outing by taking a picture of his two companions perched on a fence rail.

Before the introduction of the Kodak home camera, the hiring of a professional photographer to record parties, celebrations, or simply family get-togethers was not financially feasible for most people. When snapshot cameras became a common household item, hardly one of these occasions went by unrecorded on film. This is a typical example of the genre, the long shadow of the photographer, who was instructed to stand with his or her back to the sun, falling conspicuously across the foreground of the photo.

World's Fairs to follow, the attractions that filled the grounds and buildings of the exposition ranged from the spectacular, to the titillating to the merely amazing.

In the "Egyptian Village," a suitably clad dancer called "Little Egypt" swayed and bumped to the beat of a faux Middle Eastern number described as the "hootchy-koochy." On the midway, George Washington Gale Ferris's 250-foot amusement wheel was said to rival Gustave Eiffel's tower in technological ingenuity.

Hundreds of commercial firms sent representatives to display their latest and most eye-catching products, Kodak among them. Robert Peary had recently returned from his expedition to "Greenland's Icy Mountains" with two thousand Kodak snaps of the trip. Peary's testimonial on behalf of the camera was widely advertised, as was a "round-the-world" bicycle trip, also documented with a Kodak camera.

In addition, the Eastman Kodak Company advertised a specially designed commemorative camera, appropriately called (and spelled) the "Kolumbus Kodak." In fact, by 1893, the company listed nineteen camera models in its catalog. For the fair, the company also published an illustrated souvenir booklet, and not the least of the Chicago exposition's distinctions is that it was certainly the first national event on record to have its attractions captured on film by the general public.

For this privilege, strangely enough, each camera-carrying patron was assessed a two-dollar surcharge. Perhaps the fair's organizers saw this as a chance to make a few more dollars, or maybe the fee was intended to discourage competition with the fair's official photographers. At any rate, Kodak responded by setting up film-changing and developing darkrooms that could be used free of charge by amateurs.

Adams was probably right in his suspicion that the course of the twentieth century would depend on the future of many of the fair's "experimental outcries." These were the exhibits that the gloomy but always perceptive historian, "jostled by these hopes and doubts," turned to "for help," and which he did not find. For instance, Thomas Edison had hoped to exhibit his first motion-picture machine, the Kinetoscope, at the fair. The Eastman-produced film worked well enough, and Edison employee Fred Ott had, after repeated failures, finally been induced to sneeze on camera with the help of an office boy and a box of pepper. But the Kinetoscope viewing boxes were not ready, and in place of a flexible-film motion picture, fairgoers had to content themselves with Eadweard Muybridge's justly famous series of sequential photographs. These glass-plate pictures projected by his Zoopraxiscope device, gave the illusion of movement. But they were not movies.

Mass-market photojournalism also missed the fair. Those not having the opportunity to travel to Chicago had to be content with newspaper and magazine lithographs depicting its beaux arts buildings, huge reflecting pools, and rows of exhibits. Photography may have been at the fair in

Sometimes called the world's first screen personality, Fred Ott, a machinist working for Thomas Edison, was asked to repeat one of his apparently infamous sneezes before the Kinetoscope motion-picture camera. Ott tried to sneeze on cue but nothing happened until an office boy snuck up behind him and sprinkled pepper in the air. The resulting few frames are considered to be the first moving-picture close-up.

the hands of snapshot camera owners, but for all practical purposes photojournalists were nowhere to be seen. When "Little Egypt" danced, no one was around with a camera to try to prove one critic's contention that she "was really a corn-fed American girl with dark eyes and a little special training."

Yet for all his worries and doubts, Adams was right about one thing: the Columbian Exposition endorsed "industrial and speculative growth." But if many were unsure about where all this growth would lead, Eastman had no doubts. Writing to Henry Strong, Eastman outlined his business philosophy with absolute clarity:

The manifest destiny of the Eastman Kodak Company is to be the largest manufacturer of photographic materials in the world, or else go pot. As long as we can pay for all our improvements and also some dividends I think we can keep on the upper road. We have never yet started a new department that we have not made it pay for itself very quickly.

At the time, these departments did not really exist. For the most part, the company produced only snapshot cameras and film. But Eastman had a fearsome ability to concentrate on all aspects of the photographic world at once, and throughout the remaining years of the nineteenth century the company continued to expand and departmentalize a number of new product lines.

Robert E. Peary documented his five trips to Greenland in the 1890s on Kodak film. These roll-film photographs, taken during his successful 1909 polar expedition, were widely advertised as proving that Kodak photographic supplies were reliable even in the most severe Arctic conditions.

(Indeed, in 1930 photographs on Eastman film taken after the crash of Andree's polar balloon flight, which had laid next to the bodies of the explorers for thirty-three years, were discovered and developed, providing documentary evidence of the expedition's fate.)

Permanent Bromide print paper had been manufactured since the early 1880s, and the
company continued to sell this developing-out paper and to operate an in-house enlarging
service. In the early 1890s, after the introduction of the daylight-loading system, Eastman
realized that many photographers would then want to print their own work, and the company
introduced a gelatin printing-out paper called "Solio."

Solio paper, which as its name suggests, is printed by placing negative and paper in the sun,
was a low-gloss paper that displayed warm purple brown hues. Color photography, of course,
was not yet a practical commercial possibility, but much of what we now consider to be the
flavor of nineteenth-century snapshots is the direct result of the ability of different sorts of
photographic paper to color an image with warm, cozy sepia tones.

In 1894 Eastman added collodion printing-out paper to the line by purchasing the Western
Collodion Company and moving its operations to Rochester from Cedar Rapids, Iowa.
Collodion paper was fairly glossy and, like gelatin printing-out papers, produced warm tones,
though collodion prints were perhaps slightly more purple than those made on Solio paper.

In 1899, with the acquisition of the American Aristo Company, the Nepera Company, and a
number of other paper-manufacturing firms, the General Aristo Company was created as a
subsidiary of the Eastman Kodak Company. And with the further addition of Nepera's Velox
paper, a slow developing-out paper that could be effectively handled in a room illuminated with
the subdued tones of gaslight, Eastman, who had already signed contracts with leading
European paper manufacturers, was able to offer almost the entire spectrum of currently
available printing papers.

When General Aristo was formed, a San Francisco newspaper predicted that it would signal
the beginning of "the greatest rate war in photographic supplies that ever has been inaugurated
in this country and there is no telling where it is going to end." A trust, the article argued, "will
be formed that will force the price of amateur photographic supplies up to a figure where the
pastime will become one of the greatest luxuries in the country."

Eastman thought that this attack missed the point entirely. He responded that the "reporter
may not be able to grasp the idea, but for the future growth of our business and profit we do
not look for a 'forcing up of prices,' but rather such a reduction as shall enable us to make
Kodakers of every school boy and girl and every wage-earning man and woman the world
over."

It was the expansion of the parameters of photography that made sense to Eastman, and
each time the possibility of a new use for the medium came along, as it did in 1896 when

Wilhelm Roentgen discovered that X rays would expose photographic plates, Eastman was quick to see the possibilities. An employee was assigned to examine the X-ray process, and a short time later the company began manufacturing X-ray plates and had come up with a version of the small cardboard-backed packet films that are today still used for dental purposes.

By the late 1890s, Eastman had opened a European factory in Harrow, a suburb of London, and was selling photographic material in Eastman shops from Australia to Russia. In the 1880s Eastman had sold his products through "sole agencies," independent proprietor-owned shops that stocked Eastman products. This arrangement changed in the 1890s when subsidiary corporations were formed, each owned by the Kodak company but administratively operated as a discrete unit. Subsidiaries such as Kodak S.A.F. in Paris and Eastman Kodak GMBH in Berlin had retail as well as wholesale responsibilities. Each of these companies carried the Kodak name and thus encouraged the spread and acceptance of the Kodak brand of photography.

Above, opposite, and overleaf:
*Many private soldiers brought Kodak cam-
eras along when they were to fight in the
Boer War of 1899–1902. With these small
hand-held cameras, they documented
camp life, troop movements, and occasionally scenes on the battlefront. Their candid
record of war as it was unfolding added a
new dimension to the snapshot genre.*

To celebrate and advertise this worldwide success, in 1897 Kodak sponsored an amateur photography competition open to anyone using Kodak cameras and supplies, and within weeks had been deluged by over twenty-five thousand entries. In London, a nineteen-day exhibition of competition winners was mounted by the company's British subsidiary, Eastman Photographic Materials Ltd. The show was housed in a gallery designed for the occasion by the Scottish architect George W. Walton, and in its short run drew thousands of visitors.

In a review of the show the London *Daily Telegraph* commented that "some of the competing pictures are gems ... but the striking thing is the high average of merit, which means that hand camera photography is far removed from toy-work, and that its influence in training the eye to appreciate points of beauty is greater than those who have never followed it would really appreciate."

To counter the perception that Kodak cameras and supplies were only good for snapshooting, Eastman commissioned some of England's leading art photographers, among them Henry Peach Robinson, Andrew Pringle, and George Davison, to take photos using Kodak supplies, and he published a small illustrated volume of the resulting photographs.

But what Alfred Stieglitz had described as the war between the "dress suits" and the "democrats" continued unabated. Eastman was able to convince the average man that fine photographs could be taken with his hand-held roll-film camera, but for the most part the often conservative community of professional and serious amateur photographers continued to use large-format, glass-plate cameras.

In fact, when wars broke out at the end of the century, many photographers covering the conflicts still lugged along their oversized plate cameras. Sent by William Randolph Hearst to record the Spanish-American War, the photojournalist J.C. Hemment carried three glass-plate cameras (a 12 x 20, an 11 x 14, and a 6 x 10) that were not significantly different in size than the equipment used by Mathew Brady during the Civil War forty years earlier. To develop his · photographer's plates, Hearst outfitted a "spacious second-cabin dining room" on one of his yachts as a darkroom. More comfortable perhaps than Brady's photographic wagon, but still a long way from the world of twentieth-century photojournalism.

Later Hemment wrote that "the future photographing of war scenes will be done with cameras quite different from those I used in this campaign," and suggested that "a camera not larger than five by seven is the most convenient to use." Ironically, Hemment's boss, William Randolph Hearst, had such a camera, a simple hand-held box camera, and posed on the deck of his yacht taking pictures of Santiago harbor with it.

Although professional photojournalists had not yet accepted the roll-film system and generally only succeeded in producing posed behind-the-lines shots, at least a few common soldiers brought their Kodak cameras along to the front. When the Boer War broke out in South Africa, so many Kodak cameras were present that for the first time a candid history of army camp life and even a few battle scenes were captured by amateur hand-held cameras.

By the late 1890s, however, the world of photojournalism had also been expanded by the introduction of the newsreel motion-picture camera. The new roll-film technology may have been lost on one group of photoreporters, but a new class, the movie cameramen, quickly saw its potential. Since the introduction in the early 1890s of Edison's peepshow Kinetoscope, the moving-picture business had changed dramatically. In May 1895, Major Woodville Latham, an American entrepreneur and inventor, had projected light through an exposed strip of film and cast a moving image onto a screen. In France, the Lumière brothers, Auguste and Louis, were also experimenting with screen projection. One of their first publicly shown films featured delegates to the Lyons Photographic Congress, including, coincidentally, the early experimenter Etienne-Jules Marey walking down the gangplank of a ship.

With all this new interest in movie photography, Eastman stepped up experiments in the production of movie film. The Eastman Kodak Company had been selling a slightly thicker version of its film to Edison, and by 1896 Edison and other movie producers began ordering

entire 200-foot tables of this new movie stock. But as more movies began to be projected in more showings the need arose for an even thicker stock. Kodak film was alright for one-time use in a movie camera, but when the film was developed into a positive and repeatedly projected, the edge perforations would tear and rip.

In June 1896 this problem was remedied by the experimental production of a heftier film stock designed specifically for projection. This particular 19-foot strip of heavy gauge film was the first motion-picture positive film to be manufactured, and within a couple of years movie producers were ordering it by the thousands of feet for use as release prints.

To Eastman the financial prospects of movie film were only dampened by the production problems. In Rochester, Henry Strong, who was administering sales of what was then called "Cine" film, warned, "If the disease breaks out seriously, I think we will have no surplus film, as this trade will keep up, I judge, through the winter." The disease did indeed outlast that winter. Soon Strong was writing to Eastman, then in London, "You may have taken some large order for Cine film, but I propose to knock you silly. I spent all of yesterday forenoon negotiating a contract for 300,000 feet of 2½-inch film to be taken within six months...."

A few weeks later Strong wrote again: "We have just booked a standing order for 20,000 feet every Saturday for five weeks. The large order which I wrote you about some time since which was to be used in the Corbett-Fitzsimmons fight has not yet materialized."

On March 17, 1897, that fight did in fact take place. The fourteen-round match, which ended when Fitzsimmons knocked out Corbett, was photographed by three movie cameras, which between them consumed eleven thousand feet of film, apparently the largest single amount of footage used for a single event until that point. When the film was shown in theaters that summer it drew three-quarters of a million dollars in ticket sales.

Since film emulsions, whether for snapshots or movie film, were at the time relatively insensitive, most motion pictures were shot outdoors with the benefit of bright sunlight. In fact, Edison's first studio, called the "Black Maria" after the nickname of a paddy wagon, was little more than a tarpaper shack with a removable roof built on a turntable so that the entire building could be swung around to follow the light. Edison staged a few events on this primitive movie stage, most notably a fight for the lightweight title between Michael Leonard and Jack Cushing, but other competing moviemakers simply took to the street and shot events as they were happening.

Cameraman Billy Bitzer, who would later be director D. W. Griffith's closest collaborator, was sent by the Biograph Company to Canton, Ohio, to photograph William McKinley at home shortly before the 1896 presidential election. When the film was shown in a small New York City theater the public response to this candid and casual view of the future president was wild and enthusiastic. In its review of the film *The New York Herald Tribune* reported:

The biggest part of the enthusiasm began when a view of a McKinley and Hobart parade in Canton was shown. The cheering was incessant as long as the line was passing across the screen, and it grew much greater when the title of the next picture appeared: "Major McKinley at Home." Major McKinley was seen to come down the steps of his house with his secretary. The secretary handed him a paper which he opened and read. Then he took off his hat and advanced to meet a visiting delegation.

By the late 1890s the Lumière brothers, who called their newsreels *"actualités,"* were sending cameramen around the world to film such events as the coronation of Czar Nicholas II in Moscow and McKinley's presidential inaugurations in Washington, D.C. The demand for these sorts of films became so great, in fact, that when footage of historical events was unavailable, as in the case of the Battle of Santiago Bay, enterprising moviemakers just faked it.

During the Spanish-American War William Randolph Hearst outfitted a yacht with the darkroom facilities necessary for the development of the large glass-plate negatives then still used by most of the photojournalists he had hired to cover the conflict. Hearst himself documented Santiago's harbor from the deck of the yacht with a hand-held Kodak box camera.

Brown Brothers

Prizefights were among the most popular subjects of early Kinetoscope films. Since the film loop was seldom more than fifty feet long, viewers sometimes watched the first round in one machine, moved to the next for the second round, and so on down the line.

Two clever Vitagraph Motion-Picture Production Company filmmakers, Albert Smith and J. Stuart Blackton, made small ships out of cardboard, turned a kitchen table upside down, filled it with water, and filmed the ships maneuvering around each other amid a gunpowder haze produced by an office boy puffing on a large cigar. The film was well received (and apparently believed) though it is hard to say whether this was the result of good filmmaking or simply a gullible audience.

Although these nonfiction films were at first the most popular movie genre, Edison, in particular, was building up a catalog of short adventure and comic films. His 50-to-75-foot-long story films were often not much more than a single, extended slapstick gag. The plot summary, for instance, of one early Edison film, *Happy Hooligan Has Troubles with the Cook*, begins: "Mr. Hooligan introduces himself to the audience and also to a large juicy apple pie which rests temptingly on the window sill," and ends with his housewife adversary "promptly" dousing "poor Mr. Hooligan with water."

Happy Hooligan, shot with only a single stationary camera and lasting only several minutes, was hardly a Hollywood feature film. But it was a film, and like X rays, snapshots, news photos, all the other images that made use of celluloid film coated with a sensitive photographic emulsion, it significantly altered the nineteenth century's style of photography.

Eastman had begun with a plan to create a huge market for his complete system of photography, but even he, astute, ambitious, and always ready to follow wherever film markets led, had not anticipated all the courses the roll-film revolution would take.

The Edison catalog of Kinetoscope films included many one-scene comic stories. Kinetoscope patrons wanted action above all, and the pillow fight enacted in this frame from Seminary Girls, *no matter how short, was at least robust and animated.*

Preceding pages:
Some early twentieth-century Kodak snapshot cameras, such as the 1917 Stereo Kodak camera (left), which made twin pictures for stereo viewing, and the 1914 Autographic camera (center), a camera with a small door on its back that enabled picture takers to make notes on the negative, were more sophisticated than models introduced in the late nineteenth century. Others, such as the one-dollar Brownie camera (right), were easily operated, reliable, and very inexpensive.

Opposite:
At the turn of the century the word Kodak *began appearing on shop exteriors in cities as far apart as Cairo and Melbourne. The principal mission of these company-owned retail and wholesale establishments was to spur the Kodak idea across international boundaries. The deluxe and smartly laid-out interiors of company stores, some designed by the British Arts and Crafts architect George W. Walton, signaled to the discriminating buyer that Kodak stood for quality, accountability, and reliability.*

In 1896 Henry Strong began to worry about the size and scope of the Eastman Kodak Company. Strong was a holder of a large block of the company's stock and his net profits, even with the Eastman policy of continual reinvestment, were substantial. The average shareholder, the 1898 treasurer's report estimated, would in a period of fourteen years have earned a twenty-five-to-one return on his money. Still, Strong was concerned about the rate of growth.

"Paralyzing" was the word that came to his mind. There were simply too many photographic projects in the works. Eastman's response to Strong was, "My desires are only limited by my imagination." Strong, who had trusted Eastman this far, was apparently at least placated. "I know full well his persistence," he said at the time, "and that his indomitable will must result in success." Indeed, thus far, there was no question about the financial good fortune and commercial prosperity of the company.

Kodak had just recorded its one-hundred-thousandth camera sale. The monthly demand for transparent celluloid film had risen to three hundred or four hundred miles. New patents were being examined for possible purchase. Two hundred Eastman demonstrators and salesmen were on the road. Entire companies were being bought outright and transferred to Rochester: the American Camera Company in 1898, the Blair Company in early 1899, and then later that year the Aristo and Nepera paper companies.

William Walker, who with Strong was one of the original holders of company stock, had in 1885 moved to England to supervise the overseas operations of Eastman Photographic Materials Ltd. In all aspects of photography, manufacturing, research, and artistic achievement, London was the acknowledged world center of photography, and Eastman regarded the aggressive management of the British subsidiary to be crucial to the success of his plans for the international acceptance of the Kodak system. Walker's management style, however, was anything but vigorous.

A *British Journal of Photography* reporter visited the new Eastman Photographic Materials Soho Square office in 1889, just prior to its opening, and wrote of Walker: "It was the speaker's great good fortune to join him before even the fittings were complete, and he could picture him now as he then first saw him. He was sitting in a chair very much tilted back, with a cigar in his mouth, his feet on the table, superintending the fitting up of the office and endeavoring to instill into the workmen some of his own great energy."

Worse to Eastman's mind was Walker's suggestion that the value of Eastman stock be inflated and all partners sell out while the price was good. Eastman dismissed this idea as ridiculously shortsighted. Thus far the company had profited by its energetic creation of new markets, and Eastman thought that leadership in the industry would likewise depend "greatly upon a rapid succession of changes and improvements." "If we," he wrote Strong, "can get out improved goods every year nobody will be able to follow us and compete with us." In 1892 Walker resigned.

Another American, George Dickman, was appointed managing director in Walker's place, and shortly thereafter the overseas ventures of Eastman Photographic Materials began to prosper. By the late 1890s several more London shops, designed and outfitted by G. W. Walton, had been opened. What was lacking was an administrative unit that effectively consolidated these and other worldwide enterprises. In 1898 the British Eastman Photographic Materials and the American Eastman Kodak Company, both of which had been until this time privately held, were reorganized into a single worldwide holding company, Kodak Limited, which also directed the subsidiaries. Eastman decided that incorporating his business in London would both increase its stature and help to raise the necessary funds for further expansion. At first British investment bankers were skeptical, some even outraged by the impudence of this American upstart, but finally the deal was set, and, in fact, when stock went on sale it was almost immediately oversubscribed. Eastman gave up some of his own shares to meet the demand.

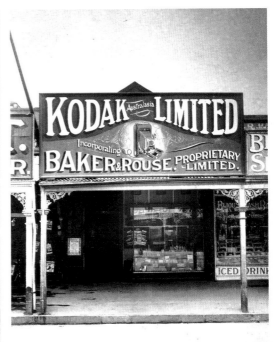

Capitalized at a million and a half pounds, Kodak Limited continued its expansion, by 1902 opening retail and wholesale outlets in Belgium, Holland, Austria, and Hungary.

However, a few months before the complex financial negotiations that preceded the formation of this global company were complete, the new managing director, George Dickman, died. After a year-long search, George Davison was appointed to take Dickman's place. Davison was best known as a founding member of the Linked Ring, a league of British pictorial photographers at odds with what they considered to be the stodgy conservatism of the Royal Photographic Society. One discontented photographer summed up his dissatisfaction with the society in a single sentence. "Like the Bourbons," he wrote, "it learns nothing and forgets nothing."

The putative voice of the Linked Ring was Peter Henry Emerson, whose 1889 book *Naturalistic Photography* had dismissed as quaint and outdated such elaborately staged studio scenes as Oscar Reijlander's allegorical *The Two Ways of Life* and Henry Peach Robinson's languid bedroom death scene, *Fading Away*. Many of these compositions attempted to imitate popular salon paintings of the era. Emerson described such photography as "the quintessence of literary fallacies and art anachronisms." But as much as Emerson disliked the stiff poses and sweeping pathos of such photographs, he objected even more strenuously to their crisp and unrelenting sharpness of focus.

Emerson argued that it was impossible for the human eye to record the world with such unfailingly acute eyesight. "Nothing in nature," Emerson wrote, "has a hard outline." In reality, he continued, "When human beings fix their eyes upon a particular scene, everything besides the primary object in view appears in soft focus." Robinson, speaking for the society's

Kodak Panorams, swiveling lens cameras that took rectangular photos ranging from two to three inches high to seven to twelve inches long, were often used during the first two decades of the twentieth century to record scenes that stretched beyond the reach of the normal snapshot camera's viewfinder. Landscapes, beach fronts, and urban sights, such as this panoramic picture of a London square taken about 1905, were the locales most favored by owners of these wide-format cameras.

photographers, replied testily that "healthy human eyes never saw any part of a scene out of focus."

For a while, the hard/soft-focus dispute was debated monthly in the letter pages of British photographic journals. Joseph Gale, a partisan of the sharp-focus school, thought that the eyesight of the Emerson school appeared to have "suddenly become deranged." One critic singled out Davison's 1890 pictorial landscape *The Onion Field* as looking as if it had been taken with a primitive pinhole camera. Davison, who was one of the noisier members of the naturalistic faction, responded to the critics of this type of photography that one "would imagine that all want of focus was hateful and unnatural."

At some point in the middle of this controversy Emerson had a change of heart. In 1890 he wrote a "Renunciation," dismissing photography as a purely mechanical operation, not an art: "I, saner than ever, renounce and abjure all theories, teachings, and views on art written, and first promulgated by me. . . . I cast them upon the dust heap."

In spite of the loss of Emerson's leadership and continued attacks upon the Linked Ring photographers as "fuzzyites" and "neuropaths," Davison argued that he trusted no serious photographer reading Emerson would "be deluded by such cheap trash as this pamphlet contains," and suggested that Emerson take up a hobby "more suited to his abilities—a humorous friend of mine suggests fretwork." This rancorous quarrel continued without resolution throughout the late nineteenth century.

In light of his views on photography, Davison hardly seemed the right man to manage the spread of Eastman Kodak Company consumer products in Europe. Indeed, even after he was in a position of authority at Kodak he lost none of his fractiousness. His contentious espousal of

aesthetic standards was matched by his equally combative political ideas. Davison was an anarchist. While still a member of the Kodak board of directors, he astonished fellow workers by leading a parade of anarchists past the company's Kingsway building carrying a sign that read "Down with Capitalism."

Eventually, Eastman had enough. After reading a copy of Davison's paper "The Anarchist," which had been printed in the Kodak Glasgow offices, Eastman wrote to its author: "I do feel that if you are lending aid to an advocate of anarchy you are not a useful or suitable member of our board of directors and I think you ought to resign. . . . I am not too intolerant to view with great interest the tendency of a man of your stamp toward anarchy and would not have a word to say against it if I did not think it was inconsistent with you holding a position of director in our companies." In 1915, Davison, who had become very wealthy through the purchase of Kodak stock, retired to the south of France and founded a school for the education of destitute children.

In 1900, the year of Davison's appointment, Kodak had introduced a piece of equipment that sidestepped the aesthetic war zones and created a new army of photographers who had practically no interest, or indeed knowledge of such internecine artistic squabbling. A year or so earlier Eastman had asked Frank Brownell to build a camera that was cheaper and easier to operate than any yet listed in the Kodak catalog.

On February 1, 1900, the first shipments of this new small box camera were sent to Kodak dealers. At the time, this date, just a month into the twentieth century, doesn't seem to have been thought of as epochal. Each year more cameras had been added to the company's trade catalog, and few at the time knew how symbolic this particular product would become.

This new camera was the "Brownie," a camera so popular that in one form or other it remained in production for almost eighty years, its name becoming emblematic of an entire genre of photography. The original Kodak camera had quite literally liberated photographers from the darkrooms of the nineteenth century and enabled people to step outside and casually take pictures. It democratized the craft of photography. Anyone, the first Eastman advertisements promised, could operate a Kodak camera.

The Brownie expanded even that large group; everyone, it was claimed, could take good pictures with a Brownie, even children. Particularly children. When the camera appeared on dealers' shelves its box was decorated with drawings of Brownies, "imaginary little sprites," created by the very popular Canadian illustrator Palmer Cox, and the camera cost only one dollar. Many had called the original Kodak camera a toy; and what could be more playlike than a one-dollar camera? But that was precisely the Brownies' appeal. The first batch of five thousand sent to dealers was bought almost immediately, and by the next year, when the original Brownie was superseded by the No. 1 Brownie, just under a quarter of a million had been sold.

Advertisements for the Brownie were primarily directed at the children's market. Brownie camera clubs were organized by Kodak. Competitions specifically aimed at adolescent Brownie users were staged. Included with the camera was a fifty-four-page booklet that provided children with simple directions for posing, picture taking, film developing, and print making. The Brownie Boy, a cute, good-natured kid who loved photography, began appearing in print advertisements.

The simpler the idea, however, the more sophisticated the engineering; following that rule, the Brownie was something of a design masterpiece. Built of jute board and wood, the camera was equipped with an inexpensive two-piece glass lens and a mechanically uncomplicated rotary shutter. It came loaded with a six-exposure cartridge of Kodak roll film. The camera was designed to take what we now think of as typical snapshots: individual or group portraits, pictures of pets, vacations scenes. And in all those situations it worked perfectly. When used in

Opposite:
Picture taking with a Kodak camera was promoted in advertising photos as a genteel pastime able to be practiced with so little fuss or bother that anyone, even a woman in full afternoon dress, could unfold a camera and effortlessly take a photograph.

strong sunlight, the camera's relatively small lens opening (its aperture was approximately f/14) admitted enough light to expose film adequately and yet had a deep enough depth of field that everything from a few feet to infinity was in acceptable focus. With a shutter speed of approximately 1/50 of a second, the photographer need not even worry about small amounts of movement.

The first Brownie cameras contained only enough film for six 2½-inch-square exposures. These could be developed, printed, and mounted for forty cents, and a new roll of celluloid film could be purchased for an additional fifteen cents. In time, the Brownie camera became more costly. The No. 2 Brownie, introduced in 1901, took a slightly larger picture (2¼ x 3¼), had two reflecting viewfinders, an adjustable lens, and cost two dollars. But even at that price the idea remained the same. It was a low-cost amateur camera that anyone could use with unfailing reliability. The artistry of the Brownie was in all senses a function of its downright commonness: it averaged out the difficulties of photography and fabricated a tolerant piece of equipment out of the sum of those figures.

In 1902 another piece of photographic apparatus of almost equal simplicity and elegance was added to the Kodak line. Early that year, A. W. McCurdy, a free-lance inventor, had walked into Eastman's office with a small oblong metal-lined box that he said would completely eliminate the photographic darkroom. McCurdy showed Eastman how a strip of film could be spooled inside the box by means of a celluloid leader and, after the addition of a chemical solution, developed by hand cranking the film through the tank.

That day McCurdy's demonstration was not a complete success. Some of the negatives were streaked. Eastman had to tell McCurdy, "For a picture that had been perfectly exposed your developer is all right, but for the average amateur it will never work." McCurdy left with his machine under his arm but a few days later reappeared, having discovered that washing the film with water between the developing and fixing stages eliminated the problem. Eastman

then purchased the rights to the McCurdy device on a royalty basis, and by the end of the year the Kodak developing machine went into production.

Eastman was elated. He wrote to Strong:

It looks as if it [the McCurdy device] will give photography another lift, bigger than the Pocket Kodak. These machines will enable us to advertise "To Hell with the Darkroom," and our traveling men, nerved by this inspiring but gently and refined tocsin, will carry the good word into the utmost regions of the earth; yea, into even the Sunday Schools and Kindergartens, until it shall finally come to pass that children will be taught to develop before they learn to walk, and grown-up people—instead of trying word painting—will merely hand out a photograph and language will become obsolete.

Neither Eastman's scheme for a universal photographic language nor, indeed, the home-developing tank, were finally as successful as he wished. Many amateurs, it seems, did not want to bother with printing or development and continued to send their film back to the Kodak factory or to have it processed by one of the private photofinishers who had gone into business to take advantage of the growth of amateur picture taking.

The developing tank, however, did have a significant impact on early twentieth-century photojournalism. When the Russo-Japanese War broke out in 1905, press photographer Jimmy Hare took a portable developing tank along with him to the front and was able to rush developed negatives back to *Collier's* magazine for quick printing and publication. In the introduction to his collection of Russo-Japanese war photos, Hare wrote that "under adverse conditions in the field," he and his small corps of press photographers were "greatly facilitated by the use of the films and developing machine of the Eastman Kodak Company." Within months, that endorsement appeared in Eastman advertisements.

In 1905 the Kodak exhibition, which had traveled from town to town in England the previous year, was shipped to America. The show was intended to extol the varied applications of Kodak materials: photojournalism, travel pictures, nature studies, "the home side" snapshots. Two of the photographs exhibited on a panel entitled "With the Children" were by soon-to-be-famous photographers: "Lady and Child" by Edward Steichen (above) and "Soap Bubbles" by Alfred Stieglitz (opposite). Both photographers, who would go on to become famous for pictures in other modes and genres, had been award winners in that year's Kodak competition.

Along with the yearly introduction of improved and simplified snapshot cameras and the new Kodak developing machine, there were also advances in film and film supports. In 1903 N.C. film, a noncurling film that was backcoated to prevent its edges from twisting inward, and Kodoid film, a cardboard-backed film cut in conventional sizes for use in plate cameras, were announced. Although N. C. roll film would remain the standard Kodak film for many years, Kodoid cut film, which was recommended for its light weight and durability, did not catch on in the professional market.

Despite small improvements in speed and latitude, film emulsions remained about the same. The silver salts suspended in the original Kodak film's gelatin emulsion had been sensitive mainly to the blue and violet end of the chromatic spectrum. In fact, blue colors, like those of the sky for instance, so strongly affected the film that a clear summer sky would print bright white. In 1873 the German chemist Hermann Wilhelm Vogel had discovered that adding dyes to the emulsion would increase chromatic sensitization, but chemists had succeeded only in extending the range of the negative's sensitivity as far as the spectrum's blue green bands. On this new film, which was called orthochromatic, predominantly red objects, such as flowers, autumn leaves, and even lips, sometimes appeared black on the print. As emulsion research at the time was mostly a matter of trial and error, fully panchromatic film, sensitive to the entire visible spectrum, would not be widely available until after World War I.

In 1904, to advertise the company's entire line of products, Kodak Limited sponsored a spectacular traveling photographic show. *The Grand Kodak Exhibition*, which was trucked from town to town across Britain, was as successful a single advertising venture as the company had ever undertaken. In Croydon, one newspaper reported, "The doors had to be locked, so great was the crush, while at St. Leonards the great hall, capable of seating, 1,500 people, was found too small, and the people had to be turned away."

The display consisted of forty-one panels, divided between prints and enlargements (thirty-eight) and technical exhibits (three). Dr. Dixon, a favorite public speaker, was engaged to travel with the show to extol the virtues and felicities of popular photography. There was even a cine-film shown that illustrated various techniques and technologies. A widely read British magazine, *The Amateur Photographer*, reported that "the Kodak traveling Exhibition seems to be stirring up the country like a revolutionary banner...creating a yearning for camera and lens in others in whom heretofore the wish was dormant."

The waving of the "revolutionary banner" of amateur photography was certainly one of the purposes of the exhibition. The show featured the work of many who had won prizes in the previous year's "$1,000 Competition," a Kodak-sponsored international contest open to amateur photographers. In fact, when the show traveled to America in 1905, it featured the work of two aspiring amateur photographers, Edward Steichen and Alfred Stieglitz, whose pictures had won first and third places in the previous year's competition and were now displayed on a panel entitled "With the Children."

Another famous photographer, perhaps the most well-known in England, whose work was exhibited in the traveling show was Her Majesty Queen Alexandra. The royal family had long been interested in photography, and as early as the 1890s the Eastman Company had presented photographic equipment to family members. Princess Alexandra in particular, an enthusiastic and talented snapshooter, appears to have exclusively used Kodak equipment. In 1897 the company had presented her with a purple leather-bound No. 4 "Bull's-Eye Special" camera, and in 1902, after she became queen, Alexandra granted George Eastman a royal warrant as purveyor of photographic materials to the royal family.

That year Alexandra and other royal photographers agreed to take part in exhibitions at Kodak's Strand and Oxford Street galleries, and thousands lined up to see for the first time

Queen Alexandra, wife of King Edward VII of England, was an enthusiastic amateur photographer who exclusively used Kodak cameras and who in July 1901 prepared a Royal Warrant appointing Mr. George Eastman "purveyor of photographic apparatus" to her majesty. A selection of Alexandra's photos was included in a Kodak-sponsored exhibition in 1897, and another group was published in a 1908 volume en-titled Queen Alexandra's Christmas Gift Book. *The book's announcement stated that these rare pictures of the royal family were "simply snapshots—informal, unof-ficial, everyday, human snapshots."*

(Opposite left) Alexandra, then Prin-cess of Wales, with her Kodak box camera in 1889.

(Opposite above) A panoramic photo-graph taken aboard the yacht Reval in 1908 during a visit by the Russian royal family. In the center, from left to right: Queen Al-exandra, Tsar Nicholas II of Russia, King Edward VII, Grand Duchess Olga, Prin-cess Victoria, and Grand Duke Michael of Russia.

(Above) A snapshot of Alice, Princess Alexandra of Teck, with her children, Prin-cess May and Prince Rupert of Teck, taken at the royal country retreat in Balmoral, Scotland in 1898.

casual snapshot pictures of the royal family and their residences. In the traveling show of 1904, eleven of Alexandra's photos, including shots of the king at home, the royal yacht, and life at Sandringham, were exhibited. Few had ever been privileged to see the royal family in such informal settings. But many of Alexandra's snaps, despite the high station of their subjects, hardly differed in content from those taken by the average amateur photographer. At family events, kings, queens, princes, princesses, and all sorts of imperial relatives, were glimpsed leaning together in typical poses. These people were, of course, special, and then as now that

increased the public's appetite for candid glimpses into the private lives of the privileged and celebrated.

There were also a number of screens in the 1904 exhibition that displayed the work of other well-known British amateur photographers, including Andrew Pringle, J. Craig Annan, George Davison, A. Horsley Hinton, and Frank Sutcliffe. Since the 1890s many of these photographers had maintained a working arrangement with Kodak; the company supplied cameras and film and in return was allowed to use copies of the photographs taken for advertising purposes.

Sutcliffe, who had become famous for his large-format, plate-camera photographs of the Yorkshire town of Whitby and its harbor, was one of the most enthusiastic of these Kodak camera users. Having lugged around a heavy plate camera since the 1870s, Sutcliffe was pleased both by the Kodak's portability and its ability to get the work "so quickly done that there is no time wasted." Sutcliffe wrote that the Kodak "has freshened my interest in outdoor photography"—in fact, his friends wondered whether he always kept "that thing" under his arm.

Sutcliffe also remarked upon the possibilities of this camera for photojournalistic work. But though Sutcliffe, as he said himself, "was unfortunately born forty years too soon," others in the show were already exploring the commercial and artistic possibilities of on-the-spot picture taking. In addition to a series of photos taken during the Boer War, the exhibition included five panels of pictures from the Russo-Japanese War taken by Percival Phillips, war correspondent to *The Daily Express*.

When the Kodak exhibition was taken to America in 1905, the photojournalism displayed a distinctly American cast. The show now included Jimmy Hare's Russo-Japanese War photos, a few pictures of Theodore Roosevelt, panoramic views of sledge teams used on Ziegler's polar exploration expeditions, photos from the American West by Sumner Matteson (and George Eastman), and even shots of an auto race taken with the "Graflex," a high-speed camera manufactured by the firm of Folmer and Schwing, which had recently been acquired by Kodak.

By the early 1900s, the list of photographic supplies advertised in the exhibition's catalog included the Brownie Kodak, Folding Brownie, Folding Pocket Kodak, Cartridge Kodak, a variety of glass plates, N. C. film, Kodoid plates, the Premo film pack (a cut film for glass-plate cameras), Solio paper, self-toning Solio paper, Kodak bromide papers for printing by artificial light, Kodak C.C. (collodion-chloride) paper, self-toning Aristo (pure collodion) paper, and Kodak Platinum paper (a high-quality printing paper for art photographers).

The length and breadth of the diverse Eastman line, which had worried Strong, now stretched from amateur to professional film, from films for landscape, portraiture, and snapshot genres to the new craft of press photography and from high-speed specialized cameras to inexpensive outfits able to be used by children.

During these years Eastman spent much of his time in Britain and on the Continent. By 1905 the Harrow plant was coating photographic papers, preparing light-sensitive emulsions, and operating a very busy photofinishing service. Yet in spite of advances in manufacturing methods, the overwhelming demand for photographic supplies forced Eastman to look for new ways to speed up the work.

In 1905 Kodak engaged a number of the most well-known illustrators of the day to depict the use of its cameras in diverse circumstances: at parties, on trips, while hunting. One of Frederic Remington's contributions to the series was this drawing of a war correspondent, notebook in one hand and Kodak camera slung over his shoulder, ready to record all the graphic details of a faraway battlefront. Remington's relationship with the Kodak advertising department continued throughout the early part of the century.

Opposite:
One of the best-known large-format plate photographers in the late nineteenth century, Frank Sutcliffe also took hundreds of snapshots with a hand-held Kodak camera. "In this hurried age," he once wrote, "there are certain things which have a delightful precision or snap about them, combinations of natural forms which arrange themselves in a certain way for an instant or two, and then alter entirely." This Kodak camera snapshot taken in Whitby, Yorkshire, where Sutcliffe lived, and printed on Solio paper records one of those occasions.

The three-mile ride from downtown Rochester to work at Kodak Park in 1904 took a half hour or so, providing the employee chose to ride the Lake Avenue trolley to its last stop and walk the last quarter mile down the cinder path that led to the factory gates. Each morning about a thousand workers, both men and women, clocked in at one of the thirty buildings of various sizes, shapes, and heights clustered together behind the combination iron-and-wood picket fence that surrounded this industrial complex.

Summer Matteson was an itinerant commercial photographer who traveled the American West between 1898 and 1908 with two Kodak cameras, a No.3 Folding Pocket Kodak and a No.5 Cartridge Kodak. The portability of these small cameras and the fact that he was able to produce Solio paper prints in the field allowed Matteson quickly and often inconspicu-

ously to record pictorial scenes of the passing of Western culture.

(Top) Freight outfit moving across the prairie near Malta, Montana.

(Above) Plowing in Last Mountain Valley, Canada.

(Right) Sunrise procession of flute ceremony at Walpi, Arizona.

Returning to his studio on the morning after the 1906 San Francisco earthquake, professional photographer Arnold Genthe discovered that his large-format cameras had been destroyed. Borrowing a Kodak 3-A Special from a nearby dealer, Genthe spent the following weeks wandering the city and taking pictures with the Kodak hand camera. Some of these dramatic documentary photographs were published in the weeks after the disaster by The San Francisco Examiner.

Most were skilled workers, though their skills, emulsion making, paper coating, film spooling, were of a very specialized nature, only marketable in a town such as Rochester, home to the world's largest manufacturer of photographic supplies.

Closer to the center of town, the company maintained two more production facilities. On State Street, next door to the original site of the Eastman Dry Plate Company plant, Frank Brownell's Camera Works factory employed about another thousand people. A few other photographic sundries, including roll-film spools and certain chemicals were still being produced at the old State Street address, but that building was slowly being made over into the administrative center of the company's operations.

Across the river and back toward the center of town, the Court Street plant, which since 1890 had housed the long glass coating tables used to make nitrocellulose transparent film base, had been shut down and its production chores moved to Kodak Park. Left in the area, however, were a few buildings that had been used to house one or more of the photographic firms acquired by the Eastman Kodak Company over the past twenty years. The original "Photo Materials" building, for instance, had been renamed the Blair Building after the acquisition of the Blair Camera Company in 1899. In a few years its occupants would begin producing lenses and metal parts, and the building would be called the Hawk-Eye Works, after the popular Hawk-Eye camera.

Each of these plants had its place in the scheme of production, as did the Eastman overseas factory in Harrow, just outside London. But it was Kodak Park that grew the fastest and was clearly the center of Eastman's intertwined web of factories, laboratories, and distribution facilities.

Once inside the gates, workers would walk several hundred yards along a winding path through carefully maintained beds of shrubbery, flowers, and small trees. It is perhaps not far from the mark to visualize many nineteenth-century factories, especially those in the inner cities of America and Europe, as poorly maintained, grimy, utilitarian places, but Kodak Park was an exception, and for a few very good reasons. The field of industrial relations had not yet been formally organized, but Eastman seems instinctively to have understood the benefits of good labor relations, particularly in the manufacturing of photographic supplies. A finger smudge, an inaccurate measurement of chemicals, a door left open in a darkened emulsion room, any of these slipups would ruin a piece of film.

Eastman, who in the first days of the company cooked emulsions and coated plates himself, also seems never to have forgotten that the smartest ideas for production improvements often come from the shop floor. Though by the late 1890s he was for the most part preoccupied by financial issues, a number of Kodak memoirs mention "Mr. Eastman" wandering around one factory building or another talking to workers and tinkering with machinery. By 1898 the purpose of these trips was formalized into the suggestion system, whereby workers were given bonuses ranging from twenty dollars to five dollars for production-enhancing recommendations.

Eastman also seems to have believed that his employees were as entitled to the fruits of the company's success as its stockholders. In 1899, after making a sizable personal profit when the company went public, Eastman decided to share some of the money with those who had made the success possible. Eastman called it the "divvy," and one payday each employee received an extra check and the following note in his or her pay envelope:

I have the pleasure to inform you that Mr. Eastman has set aside to commemorate the recent combination of the Kodak business a sum for distribution among the employees of various Kodak companies, to be apportioned according to their time of service, present rate of pay, and the kind of employment. The amount apportioned to you in accordance with the above is $ . . . . which *please find enclosed herewith.*

This is a personal matter with Mr. Eastman and he requests that you will not consider it as a gift, but as extra pay for extra good work.

One hundred and seventy-eight thousand dollars was distributed among Kodak's three thousand workers, and though the 1899 "divvy" was not to be institutionalized into the wage-dividend system until 1912, among workers even in 1904 there "was some speculation whether this idea might be repeated." So those workers who walked each morning through the carefully maintained Kodak Park gardens had good reason to believe that the smooth-running factory system was in their best interests.

They also realized, and this came in the form of constant reminders, that next to efficiency and orderliness, cleanliness was perhaps the most important single commandment of a photographic facility. Film-production facilities had been moved away from downtown Rochester for precisely this reason. Rochester was probably no dustier or dirtier than any other small city, but any amount of airborne contaminant was too much.

Every day the factory's macadam and brick walks were carefully broomed clean by a crew of men who then trucked off the dangerous dust and grime in wheelbarrows. In the summer, the roads both inside and outside the plant's gate were wetted down by horse-drawn sprinkling wagons. And in the slack periods during the winter, when film production slowed down, those currently out of work shoveled snow and operated horse-drawn plows.

Each building in Kodak Park, then as now, was numbered. On the left, as one walked into the complex, was Building No. 12. Entering this long, narrow single-story structure, employees passed through heavy blue duck curtains that were hung as a light lock. Once inside, in the subdued red light, workers could be seen spooling and slitting film and attaching squares of the newly developed Kodoid cut-sheet film to cardboard backings.

Since all film was orthochromatic and thus practically insensitive to the red end of the color spectrum, it was perfectly safe to handle new film in rooms dimly lit with red-coated light bulbs. Across the yard, in Building No. 2, workers had it a little easier. In the Solio papermaking half of that building, which produced "slow" daylight printing-out paper, all work proceeded under white lamps. In the other half of Building No. 2, the Velox paper department, where gaslight developing-out papers were made, hooded electric lamps cast a safe amber-colored illumination.

Behind Building No. 12 were a couple of sheds where the very inflammable powder then being manufactured for Kodak flash pans was made. Working with large quantities of flash powder, which was used for indoor shooting in the days prior to the invention of the flashbulb, was a fairly perilous business, and for this reason the building sat close to the edge of the factory's fence. Next door was the much safer paper-emulsion building.

By the early part of the century Kodak was producing an extensive and varied line of printing papers: Velox, Permanent Bromide, Azo, Solio. Here, in Building No. 3, the light-sensitive emulsion for each of the papers was mixed, poured into sealed earthenware jars, and then trundled across the lot on two wheeled pushcarts to the coating room in Building No. 2.

Plate and film emulsions were prepared in an entirely separate facility halfway across the yard. Once a week or so, high-quality bar silver, 99.96 percent pure, was delivered by a horse-drawn wagon whose driver was armed with a shotgun. The silver was then dissolved in a solution of nitric acid (nitrated) and taken to Building No. 14 to be added to the gelatin emulsion.

In 1904 emulsion-quality gelatin was purchased from an out-of-town dealer, shipped to the park, where in large squares it was hoisted by block and tackle up to the second-floor emulsion-mixing room. Only those who had business in this building were admitted, and even of those who were, hardly any knew the entire gelatin silver-nitrate formula. Indeed, emulsion formulas were such closely guarded trade secrets that when mailed to the English plant at Harrow, the written formula was torn in half and each part sent under separate cover. Scattered here and there between the larger buildings were a few fairly specialized shops. On the far south end of the park there was the baryta-coating building. Using a conveyor machine not significantly different than those that had first been installed twenty years earlier, baryta, a smooth paper coating, was applied by the roller-and-trough method to raw stock. After coating, the paper was strung out in huge looping festoons to dry. In another small shop, the new Platinum paper, a very high-quality printing product intended for fine arts photographers, was being coated, though not in the same quantities as Solio or Velox or any of the other mass-market papers.

There were, of course, various tool and machine shops around Kodak Park, but the acknowledged heart of all this sort of support work was centered in Building No. 1, the first to be constructed when Kodak Park was opened in 1891. This was the engine, dynamo, refrigeration, and boiler building. The air in the boiler building, to which fifty tons of coal was delivered each day, was almost tropical, and though the practice had been discontinued by 1904, in the park's early years Maria Kilbourn Eastman, George Eastman's mother, had tended a forest of rubber plants that thrived in the hot, damp air around the five boilers.

Other buildings, or floors of buildings, housed packing and shipping, box-making, product-testing, silver recovery, and paper-coating departments. There was even a very small two-story laboratory, which also served as a lunch kitchen and a meeting room just big enough for a table and twelve chairs.

The most technologically advanced of the park's facilities, however, were the adjoining buildings, Nos. 13, 19, and 20. These were the nitrocellulose "dope" buildings. For use in the transparent film base, cotton was washed and nitrated across the yard and then brought to the dope department. There it was mixed with the semisecret solvents in large copper tanks on an upper balcony and funneled downstairs through brass tubes into one of a series of large white storage barrels.

Building No. 19, just next door, contained the most impressive and revolutionary machines in the park. By 1899, with the demand for transparent film (still and cine) increasing almost daily, Eastman began looking for a method of film coating that would replace the old, sometimes inefficient two-hundred-foot coating table. The answer to this problem seemed to be some sort of continuous casting device that would spill out dope in a slow, steady sheet. A number of engineering concepts were tried out, including a system that flowed dope out of a wooden trough that had a narrow slot in the bottom of a sheet of tinned copper. Unfortunately, as one of the designers said, "A very imperfect sheet of support was obtained in this manner."

In 1900 a method of dripping the dope off huge wheels had been perfected. The cast surfaces of the wheels had to be perfectly smooth and the rate of transfer had to be figured to the one-hundredth of an inch, but these engineering problems were worked out, and in a year or two seven huge wheels were flowing out two-feet-wide ribbons of dope at a rate of one hundred and fifty feet an hour.

Building No. 20 was the largest in the complex, over three hundred feet long. Dope that was mixed in Building No. 3 was piped into Building No. 19, where it was spun off the enormous continuous-coating wheels. The transparent dope was dried and hardened, then it traveled into Building No. 20, where fresh emulsion was spread upon it by long-loop coating machines. The demand for film was so great that a few years after the wheels' introduction the work of making transparent film went on twenty-four hours a day, seven days a week.

The continuous-coating method affected all areas of the film market. Moviemakers now could order film in much larger quantities than in the old coating table days, and as the demand for snapshot cameras continued to increase in exponential proportions, Kodak Park was able to keep up with the huge requirement for film.

In fact, by 1904 the production lines at Kodak Park were running so efficiently that the normal working day was reduced from ten to nine hours—without a reduction in pay.

"The ideal large corporation," George Eastman once wrote, "is the one that makes the best use of the brains within it." While in London in 1886, Eastman met and hired a man who would for the next thirty-four years travel the world for the Eastman Company with a single assignment: to use his brains.

When Eastman first met him, Joseph Thacher Clarke was marketing a small box camera called the "Frena," which he had designed to be fitted with a film magazine that held forty 3¼ x 4¼-inch sheets of celluloid-based film. Photography, however, was only one of Clarke's interests. The son of a Boston physician, Clarke had been educated in Germany, spoke German, French, and Italian fluently, played the cello, and had as a young man sailed to Asia Minor to join an archaeological expedition at Assos, near the site of ancient Troy. Clarke had taken a glass-plate camera on the expedition and made photographic records of the excavations near the temple at Assos. Back in London after his trip he decided that the large-format plate camera was too bulky to be carried about efficiently and went to work designing a smaller apparatus that incorporated the use of lightweight celluloid film.

The manufacturer of the Frena, R. and J. Beck, advertised that "anyone who can ring an electric bell and turn a key can take pictures with this apparatus." Eastman admired the camera's simplicity—and, no doubt, the general drift of its slogan. But even though roll rather than sheet film seemed to Eastman the technology of the future, he and Clarke hit it off, and when Eastman offered him the position of roving technical expert, Clarke, intrigued by the idea, accepted.

In 1889 Clarke's job at Eastman Photographic Materials Ltd. was listed in personnel records as "In Charge of Patent Matters." For the next few years Eastman periodically received long letters mailed from various locations on the European continent describing in voluminous detail new products and currently pending photographic patents. Clarke was particularly interested in

Equipped with a Kodak No.4 Bull's-Eye Special, Frances Benjamin Johnston was present when President William McKinley left in his carriage to attend the opening of the Pan-American Exposition. Benjamin's photograph of McKinley, the last before he was assassinated on September 6, 1901, was widely circulated during the days after the president's death. Finding that this famous photograph was taken with a Kodak camera, George Eastman included it in Kodak advertising. Johnston was later admired for her pictures of Hampton Institute and Tuskegee Institute, colleges heavily endowed by George Eastman.

the latest experimental efforts to introduce a commercially marketable technique for color photography. As was Eastman, who in 1904 wrote to Clarke, "If we could achieve a practical color process, it might have quite a vogue." The phrase "quite a vogue" now seems to be a masterpiece of understatement, but at the time none of the currently available color technologies was well-suited to the commercial mass market.

The scientific principles behind the production of color photographs had been known at least since 1861, when the Scottish physicist James Clerk Maxwell demonstrated photographically that all colors seen by the human eye can be matched by mixing in proper proportions the so-called primary colors, red, green, and blue, and that a multihued picture could be produced by mixing transmitted beams of these "additive" primary colors.

The principles of additive color had been explained early in the nineteenth century by two scientists, Thomas Young and Hermann von Helmholtz. Both knew, as Isaac Newton had discovered in 1666, that when white light was split apart by a prism it separated into all the colors of the visible spectrum. This is known as the physical theory of color. The physiological explanation of how human beings perceive colors, however, is another matter entirely. Young and Von Helmholtz speculated that the color cones of the eye are receptive to only three colors (red, green, and blue) and that the ability of the eye to perceive a multitude of colors must therefore be the result of a physiological mixture of these three primaries.

One afternoon in 1910 as Brown Brothers' picture-agency photograher Barney Roos was leaving New Haven, Connecticut, after an unsuccessful attempt to photograph the Yale graduation of President Taft's son Robert, he heard the town's fire-bell ring. As Roos loaded a glass plate into his Kodak-manufactured 5x7-inch Graflex press camera, a fire engine rounded the corner, its horses in full gallop. Roos exposed the plate, capturing the scene—and, coincidentally, the cap-and-gowned Taft, who just then happened to be crossing the street.

In 1861 Maxwell illustrated this theory by photographic methods. The scientist made three wet-collodion black-and-white negatives of a multicolored tartan ribbon, one shot through a red filter, one through green, and one through blue. The three negatives were developed to positives. Lantern slides were then made of the black-and-white positives, and when these slides were projected in register, each through its original filter, the beams of colored light overlapped on the screen to produce an acceptably realistic color image.

Maxwell's technique is known as the additive method; the three transmitted primary colors being added together in different proportions to create color pictures. This experiment proved that color photography was possible. There was, however, an alternative to Maxwell's additive technique. In 1868, a few years after Maxwell's demonstration, a French inventor patented an entirely different method of making color photographs. In that patent and in his 1869 book *Les Couleurs en photographie, solution du probleme*, Louis Ducos du Hauron described what is now known as the subtractive method. Instead of mixing beams of colored light together to create a color image, du Hauron simply subtracted the colors he did not want from white light.

Like Maxwell, du Hauron first exposed three negatives through three filters: orange red, green, and violet blue, the colors he thought closest to the three primaries. He then developed the negatives into positives. However, rather than reprojecting black-and-white records of the primary colors through the appropriate filter, du Hauron printed each of his positives on a piece of semitransparent paper dyed a color blend that was reciprocal, or complementary, to the original filtered color.

In other words, each positive was dyed a new color obtained by blending together the two primary colors not recorded by that particular negative. The negative exposed through the orange filter, for instance, was printed as a positive on paper colored by taking the two remaining primaries, blue and green, mixing them together, and coming up with a bluish green color called cyan. Similarly the positive of the green negative was dyed blue red (magenta) and that of the violet exposure dyed red green (yellow).

Thus, when Eastman and Clarke began their search for a practical system of color photography there were two basic processes of color production, the additive and subtractive, and two potential methods by which to view that color, either by transmitted or reflected light. Some combination of these, they thought would yield a commercially workable system.

In 1904 Clarke thought he had solved the problem. Kodak had just begun manufacturing the Premo film pack, a cut-film packet that enabled photographers to bring a fresh negative into the camera's film plane by pulling the sheet of exposed film over a small metal bar and stashing it at the rear of the film pack. Three successive shots, each exposed through the appropriate colored filter, could thus be taken quickly, producing the three separate color records necessary for color photography. But as logical as the system seemed, manufacturing problems kept appearing, and after much experimentation the idea was dropped.

That same year Eastman was visited by a representative of the American inventors John Powrie and Florence Warner. The two had, it was argued, perfected the additive line-screen method of photography that had been another of du Hauron's color suggestions. Du Hauron had pointed out that if a single glass plate was made that had very fine alternating lines of the three primary colors printed or etched on its surface, each would allow only one color to pass through. If this screen was placed in front of a color-sensitive black-and-white photographic plate in a camera and exposed, each line would act as a filter. For instance, where red light was allowed to pass through to the plate, only red light would be recorded, and so on for each of the other two colors. The negative would thus consist of thousands of minute lines, some exposed, some not.

The black-and-white plate was then developed to a positive (exposed areas would now be clear and unexposed areas opaque), rebound in exact register with the screen plate and the two plates held with the original screen facing the viewer. If this combination of plates was viewed as a transparency, the white light shining through the minute transparent lines of the positive would pass once again through the appropriate filter and be seen by the viewer in color.

If the colored lines were close enough together, du Hauron observed, and if the resulting transparency were viewed from an appropriate distance, the lines of color would meld together enough to provide a satisfactory color picture. (A version of the line method is used in the production of color television pictures. Dots of transmitted color blend together to create colored images.)

In 1894 John Joly, a Dubliner, made an acceptable color transparency using this screen-line method. Joly ruled his alternating lines of color across a gelatin-covered plate with drawing pens that inscribed lines less than 1/225 of an inch wide. The Joly process was put on the market, but at the time most photographic plates were still orthochromatic, lacking the ability to record the red end of the spectrums, and the transparencies were not commercially successful. In Chicago, in 1896, James McDonough patented a similar process, and though he managed to make plates with three hundred lines to an inch, his factory could only produce three or four a day; after a huge investment of time and money the venture was abandoned.

Powrie and Warner thought they had solved these production problems. By the time they described their methods to Eastman, they had managed to inscribe six hundred lines per inch at a rate of three hundred and sixty plates a day by photographically printing the lines on a plate coated with a mixture of gelatin and potassium bichromate. This bichromate emulsion hardened when exposed to light, and after a number of complicated stainings and washings a series of fine red, green, and blue lines was left on the plate.

Eastman saw possibilities in this procedure. An option was taken on the Powrie-Warner process, which seemed even more workable when A. Fifield, a Kodak employee, suggested a better way to produce the line screen. Powrie and Warner had been using glass plates, but Fifield recommended that each of the thousands of thin sheets of celluloid be dyed with one of the three primary colors and then cemented together sequentially to form a large booklike block. Thin sheets could then be sliced off the edge of this slab of cemented leaves. Each of these new sheets, being composed of thousands of built-up sheets of alternating color, would make a perfect line screen. But after much work, the Powrie-Warner process, even with Fifield's improvement, proved impossible to manufacture in the quantity or quality that Eastman required.

Later, in 1904, Eastman became interested in a similar method then being worked on by the Lumière brothers in France. Taking up an idea first proposed in 1892 by McDonough, the Lumières dyed three batches of very small grains of potato starch (about a 15/1000 of an inch in diameter) red-orange, green, and violet-blue. The three separate grains were then mixed together, spread on a sticky plate, and the space between filled by sprinkling a very fine charcoal powder across the surface—the thousands of starch grain filters, in effect, replacing the lines. Eastman was interested in the starch grain screens, but he again discovered that the plates were too difficult to produce in quantity and decided against purchasing an option on the process. In 1907 the Lumières themselves began manufacturing the plates, which they called "autochromes," and at least in the hands of skilled photographers such as Edward Steichen, the autochrome became the most appealing color process of the first third of the twentieth century.

Clarke continued, as usual, to travel the Continent searching out the latest in color experimentation. Each discovery was followed by a few months of excitement, but in the end every process was abandoned as commercially unworkable. In Rochester, Eastman assigned Emerson Packard, a young chemist recently graduated from MIT, to work on the problem of color but, besides further proof of the enormous difficulties that stood in the way, not much came of the research.

In his 1869 book Les Couleurs en Photo-graphie, *the French inventor Ducos du Hauron described the subtractive method of making color photographs. Rather than adding beams of colored light together to create an image, du Hauron proposed sub-tracting the unnecessary colors from the full spectrum of white light. This du Hauron color photograph of Angoulême was taken in 1877. The Eastman Kodak Company's 1915 Kodachrome film used a subtractive process also.*

Eastman's tentative efforts to conduct in-house scientific research were on the right track. In many ways Clarke's work as a patent detective was not significantly different from the investigative efforts of the typical nineteenth-century photo supply house. He and Eastman were counting on the fact that someone outside the company would luck upon an adequate color process. But though at least some of Eastman's products had come through the door in the hands of free-lance inventors, the company's most significant products (the Kodak camera, transparent film, the Brownie) were Kodak inventions. At the time, however, there were only a few chemists on the Kodak payroll, and those few, working in small laboratories in the two-story Building No. 4 at Kodak Park, spent most of their time on production problems.

Late in 1911, during one of his European trips with Clarke, Eastman was given a tour of the Bayer Company, a large chemical manufacturing firm located in Elberfeld, Germany. Invited to lunch by Carl Duisberg, Bayer's head chemist, Eastman was asked about the Kodak research facilities. "We have seven hundred people in our organization," Duisberg is reported to have said. "How many have you got?" At the time Kodak employed less than ten trained scientists. After the meeting Eastman said privately to Clarke, "If Bayer can afford a research laboratory, we can."

Whether Eastman was convinced by wounded pride or by the fact that Kodak was indeed in dire need of a research facility, soon after the Bayer incident Clarke was asked to find a scientist capable of organizing and operating a large-scale photographic laboratory. Clarke suggested Dr. Charles Edward Kenneth Mees, an English chemist who had written widely on the photographic sciences and who was at that moment a joint managing director of Wratten and Wainwright, a small but well-known British firm that was one of the few photographic manufacturers to produce high-quality panchromatic plates.

The son of a Wesleyan minister, Mees had as a young boy been fascinated by the mystery of chemical reactions. At age ten, after watching a classroom teacher prepare chlorine, Mees asked if he could "handle the apparatus and make some." The teacher agreed, and as Mees recounted the story of that first experience with scientific experimentation, "By that time I [had] fallen in love, completely in love, with science." Though his father had looked forward to the boy training for the ministry, Mees set his mind on a career in science. At sixteen he enrolled at Saint Dunstan's College, a school that specialized in technical and engineering education. There Mees met Samuel E. Sheppard, a brilliant all-around student also interested in science.

In 1900 Mees and Sheppard left Saint Dunstan's for University College in London, where both enrolled in the chemistry department. The two had conducted a considerable number of practical experiments in makeshift home laboratories, and upon arriving in London they showed Professor Ramsay, head of the chemistry department, their notebooks. Ramsay looked over the work and told them, "You have done all the practical chemistry, all the laboratory work required for the final degree, so we can start you on research."

Mees began working on spectroscopy, the study of spectral wave lengths. Because Mees used photographs of the spectrum in this study, he inevitably found himself confronted with camera movement, plate sensitization, and the many problems associated with scientific photography. Mees also began using photographs to illustrate his notebook. He had borrowed a camera from a neighbor, a retired professional photographer who warned him that photography "will ruin your life. If you once start taking photographs, you will never do anything else." Mees assured the neighbor that his interests were of a more technical nature. A very technical nature as it turned out. "After a very little time," Mees remembers, "I began to wonder about the chemistry of photography. I wanted to know what happened to the plates when they were exposed to light and what happened during development and why the exposed part of the plates developed and the unexposed didn't." Mees put a few of these apparently simple questions to Ramsay and was "somewhat shocked" to discover that his professor knew "no more than I did." Ramsay suggested that Mees "try to find out some of these things," adding, "Wouldn't it be a nice subject for research?" Mees discussed the idea with Sheppard, and shortly thereafter the two equipped a laboratory and began a systematic study of the nature of photochemical reactions. As work proceeded, the two occasionally published the results of their research in *The Journal of the Royal Photographic Society*, and in 1903, on the basis of their photographic investigations, they were awarded undergraduate degrees.

After finishing their doctoral studies in 1906, Mees and Sheppard published their joint papers in a book entitled *Investigations on the Theory of the Photographic Process*. Mees once called this volume "the dullest book which had ever been written," but known simply as "Sheppard and Mees" it has become a classic in the field of photographic theory. Mees and Sheppard applied for postgraduate fellowships to continue their research, but there was only enough money in the university's fund for one scholarship, and since the two were equally qualified, it was suggested that they flip a coin to see who would win. Sheppard called heads. Heads it was, and Sheppard left for two years of study on the Continent.

Mees began looking for work in the photographic industry. Although F. C. L. Wratten, the founder of Wratten and Wainwright, thought the scruffy young scientist looked "like a golfer who had been out all night," he hired him. In fact, Mees was made a partner in the firm. Mees had practically no business experience, but Wratten insisted that he take part in both the research and the development of Wratten photographic products.

One of Mees's first assignments was to look into the chemical preparation and factory production of Wratten and Wainwright dye-sensitized panchromatic plates, which were sensitive to all zones of the visible spectrum. Mees decided that the existing two-step darkroom method of bathing the plates in dyes after they had been coated was too inefficient. He proposed that the emulsion be shredded, dye sensitized, and then flowed onto the plates. This method, though tricky, at least subtracted one step from the process. The Wratten and Wainwright panchromatic plates were still excessively sensitive to blue, so Mees further suggested that the company manufacture and market the yellow filter that was necessary to correct the color balance. Three types of these yellow filters were put into production, as was a green safelight filter, which at the time was the most efficient darkroom illumination available.

Mees's work with the absorption spectra of dyes led to one of the oddest misunderstandings of his career. A note in a January 1908 issue of *The British Journal of Photography* reported, "Any one possessed of the gift of 'reading between the lines' can be trusted to make startling discoveries, so we need not be so very surprised to find that Dr. Mees is unexpectedly credited with the production of a plate eminently suited to photograph spooks, and ghosts, or astral beings, as they are now styled in the most refined spiritualistic circles." In fact, Mees had been photographing spectra, lines of the spectrum, not spectral beings.

In 1909 Mees accepted a short-term consulting job with the American Bank Note Company, whose executives were worried that photography could be used to counterfeit currency. While in America, Mees wrote to George Eastman, whom he "regarded as the greatest man in the photographic world, "asking if he could visit Kodak Park. Eastman extended an invitation, and after the tour the two chatted for a half an hour. Mees remembered the conversation being about "American football, which was something," he said, "in which I had no interest whatever."

Though Mees was well acquainted with Kodak Limited, by then a British subsidiary of the American Eastman Kodak Company, he had no further contact with Eastman until January 1912, when he received a phone call from Clarke asking if Eastman could visit the Wratten and Wainwright factory in Croydon that same day. Mees was due to leave for Budapest to deliver a lecture on panchromatic plates. When Eastman arrived for the tour and suggested another meeting the following morning, Mees said he was sorry; could their talk be postponed until his return from Hungary? Eastman replied that he would have returned by then to America and told Mees "I think you had better come see me. I want to ask you if you will go to Rochester."

"What for, Sir?" asked Mees. "To organize a research laboratory for the Eastman Kodak Company and take charge of it," Eastman responded. Mees canceled his trip.

The offer seemed to Mees the perfect opportunity to reenter the field of pure research. "I was still anxious," he later wrote, "to return to the study of the theory of photography. The pressure of practical problems at Wratten and Wainwright had made scientific work difficult, and Mr. Eastman offered the very opportunity that I had always wanted. I was interested in the idea of industrial research, and I was enthusiastic about the possibility of an integrated study of the theory of the photographic process."

Only one problem remained: Wratten and Wainwright. Mees told Eastman that he "couldn't leave Mr. Wratten because he would not be able to carry on alone and therefore I could accept the offer only if he would buy Wratten and Wainwright." Eastman did so, paying one hundred thousand dollars for its capital stock, moving its operations to Rochester, and offering all current employees corresponding positions with Kodak Limited.

Though the thirty-year-old Mees felt that he was "too young" for such a job, Eastman dismissed the age issue with the comment, "That is a trouble that will get a little better each day." In April 1912 Mees went to Rochester to direct the design and construction of the new laboratory facility, which was to be erected on the site of the Kodak Park Building No. 3, an ivy-covered, one-story brick structure that had been built in 1891 as the original emulsion-making plant.

When completed, the new three-story building was divided into individual departments. Housed on the ground floor were facilities for the manufacture of Wratten and Wainwright plates and filters, as well as a research library. The chemistry and physics laboratories took up most of the second floor, and on the third there was a fully equipped photographic studio, a darkroom, a room with lead-lined walls for experimental X-ray work, and a small auditorium.

While the laboratory building was under construction, Mees began to assemble his staff. A number of those hired were American scientists: Perley Nutting, who had been in charge of the optics department of the National Bureau of Standards, was made head of the Research Laboratories' physics department. Loyd Jones, Nutting's assistant at the bureau, also came to Rochester, becoming head of the physics division after Nutting's departure. Another former government employee, Dr. Alonzo McDaniel, was placed in charge of the inorganic chemistry department.

So many of Mees's English colleagues were also hired that for a while much laboratory talk was conducted with clipped British accents, and around Rochester the arrival of all these scientists was known as "the English invasion." Samuel Sheppard was one of the first hired, as was John Crabtree, another expert in the chemistry of the photographic processes. John Capstaff, a former portrait photographer who had been employed at Wratten and Wainwright, was engaged to manage the manufacture of Wratten filters.

By January 1913 the new building was ready for occupancy and Mees's staff began work. The fact that the research laboratory was located inside the gates of the Kodak Park manufacturing facility sometimes created problems for Mees. His scientists, it seems, were unaccustomed to time clocks or indeed to any of sort of factory rules and regulations. A November 1913 memo to Mees from Kodak Park Manager James Haste read: "'The following men in your department have been reported to me as being at the dining hall before the whistle blows at noon; which is, of course, against the rules." Later that year Haste reported to Mees that "in looking over the Tardiness Report for the week ending May 6th I notice that the percentage of employees tardy in the Organic Research Laboratory is 37.5% and the Research Laboratory is 20.9%." Not good, especially in view of the fact that, as Haste added, "The total percentage for the whole plant is 6.9%."

When Mees had asked Eastman about specific assignments, the answer was simply, "Your mission is the future of photography." Mees responded that he thought it would be ten years before any profitable discovery would come out of the lab, a prediction that turned out to be uncannily accurate. In any case, work of both an experimental and applied nature was begun.

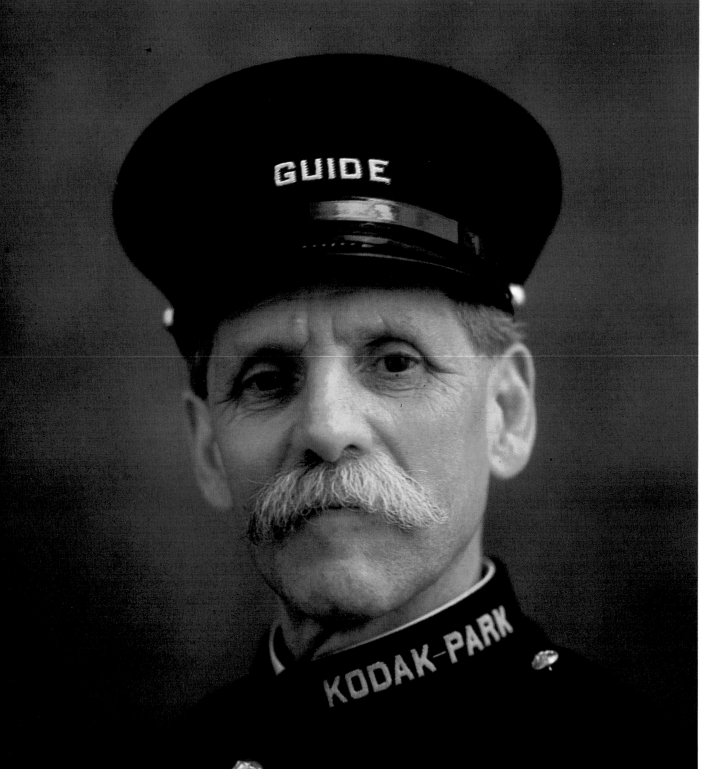

The organic chemistry laboratory undertook a study of the rate of decomposition of cellulose nitrate. Crabtree in the photographic chemistry department spent much of his time troubleshooting for problems such as tinting and toning of motion pictures, and Sheppard began what ultimately was to be very important work on the chemical nature of gelatin.

A few new products were developed in the lab during its first years. Shortly after arriving in Rochester, Mees collaborated with emulsion maker William Stuber and together they produced a fast, high contrast X-ray film emulsion. Mees also initiated a continuing collaboration with astronomers at Hale Observatory, periodically appearing, as astronomer William Miller remembers, with "pockets bulging with boxes of experimental plates especially prepared to meet the needs of staff members."

The most commercially adaptable product to come out of the pre-World War I research laboratory was a color product then known as "Kodachrome." John Capstaff, who had studied physics and engineering, had been tinkering with color photography before coming to Kodak. He continued his work in Rochester. By November 1914 Eastman was so satisfied with Capstaff's progress that an exhibition of thirty of his color portraits was mounted at the Memorial Gallery in Rochester. The following year similar displays were hung in London and at the Pacific Exposition in San Francisco.

Capstaff's Kodachrome film was a subtractive color transparency that made use of only two primary colors. Two negatives were exposed, one through a green filter and the other through a red. The negatives were developed and then bleached in a chemical bath, which both washed out the silver and hardened the remaining gelatin. The two negatives were then dyed in complementary colors: the green exposure being colored red-orange and the red exposure blue-

The two-color subtractive color process developed by Kodak scientist John Capstaff was commercially introduced in 1915 under the brand name Kodachrome. Two negatives were exposed through red and green filters respectively. When developed as gelatin reliefs, dyed in complementary colors, bound in register, and viewed as transparencies, the resulting Kodachrome film pictures were often capable of excellent color rendition.

(Opposite) The two-color Kodachrome process was especially suitable for portraiture. This study of a Kodak Park guide was taken in 1915 to exhibit the warm and relatively realistic skin tones produced by the mixture only of red and green light.

(Above) Two-color Kodachrome film was unable accurately to reproduce the colors of vegetation. Even still lifes, such as this handsome basket of fruit and vegetables, appeared thin and washed out, limiting commercial and noncommercial uses of the product.

green. The dyes soaked into the unhardened areas of the negative and thus produced a color positive. When the transparencies were attached face to face on a piece of glass and held up to the light, a color transparency was produced.

Kodachrome film worked well for portraiture. The combination of red and green produced acceptable skin tones. But since the two-color process lacked the blue sections of the spectrum, landscape rendition was poor. *The British Journal of Photography* commented that Kodachrome transparencies "have nothing of the pallid unsaturated appearance which has been characteristic of most color transparency processes. . . . In the past it has undoubtedly been difficult to make business in color transparencies, however good. . . . It remains to be seen whether the portrait color transparency will strengthen its position through the vehicle of Kodachrome."

Capstaff also adapted Kodachrome for use as movie film. In July 1916 a short film entitled *Concerning $1,000* was shot on the roof of the laboratory and in the garden of Eastman's house. Although the process had promise, the United States' entry into World War I interrupted work on both still and movie versions of Kodachrome film, neither of which met with commercial success.

In 1913, while pure and applied research was getting underway at the Kodak laboratories, Eastman was visited by Henry J. Gaisman, the inventor of the autostrop razor. Gaisman, who apparently had a predilection for things automatic, sketched out for Eastman his idea for an autographic (self-recording) piece of camera equipment. Earlier Gaisman had filed for a patent on the device, and while the examiner of patents agreed that it was entirely new, the application was refused on the grounds that there seemed to be no conceivable way the invention could be made to work.

Eastman disagreed. He immediately paid Gaisman ten thousand dollars for an option on the invention and then offered him a choice of receiving either a lifetime royalty on all cameras sold that incorporated his device or single lump-sum payment of half a million dollars, to be received after the camera was ready for the market. Gaisman apparently decided not to chance the wait and sold Eastman the invention outright for three hundred thousand dollars.

A camera that included the Gaisman invention was quickly developed, and in September 1914 the first "Autographic Kodak" was introduced. On the back of this new camera there was a small hinged door that popped open with the help of a spring. Inside the camera the usual double-thick paper on the back of Kodak celluloid film had been replaced by a new two-layer bipack, consisting of a thin sheet of red tissue and a piece of ordinary carbon paper. When the Autographic's door, which was located along the bottom edge of the film plane, was opened, the surrounding metal frame stamped softly down on the negative, impressing a half-inch wide rectangular border that ran the width of the film.

With the door open and the light shut off from the rest of the negative by the frame, the photographer wrote a short description of the picture on the back of the film. The pencil or stylus scratched the carbon paper, making it transparent. If the open door was held to the light for four or five seconds, light penetrating through the thin red paper traced a calligraphic photographic exposure along the lower edge of the negative.

In retrospect, the scrawl of handwriting at the bottom of the Autographic camera's pictures seems a little sloppy and disconcerting, which perhaps explains why, after twenty years of popularity, the autographic feature was finally dropped. By the mid-1930s the public no longer wanted, or indeed needed, a graphic aide-memoire scribbled on its prints. The picture's visual information was enough. At the time of its introduction, however, the aesthetic theory of popular photography was still in its nascent stages. Were snapshots simply visual records? The Autographic's on-film recording system seemed to imply that they were.

Clearly Eastman had the documentarian genre in mind when he bought Gaisman's idea. "This invention," he wrote Clarke, "has commercial advantages of a high order." Advertising copy for the Autographic camera argued that "any picture that is worth taking is worth a date or title. The places of interest you visit, the autographs of friends you photograph, interesting facts about the children, their age at the time the picture was made—all these things add to the value of the picture."

Certainly, for the most part, the public's appetite for photography was enthusiastically and naively empirical. Put simply, pictures were the mimetic proof that one had been somewhere at a certain time, and this accounts for the fact that the new class of amateur photographers recorded mainly people, places, and events. In any group of early snaps there are in equal proportion landscape shots, travel pictures, portraits, pictures of parties, houses, horses, and cars, photos of formal occasions, crowd shots taken at parks, beaches, picnics, and even attempts at photojournalism.

In 1897 the photographer Alfred Stieglitz had announced that "photography as a fad is well-nigh on its last legs, thanks principally to the bicycle craze." But Stieglitz was wrong. Perhaps the initial surprise at the ease of photography had diminished somewhat, but if measured by the number of camera sales, the public showed no indication of having grown bored with the sheer delight of picture taking.

Stieglitz was right, however, about one aspect of photography as it was popularly practiced. He had said that the public wants "no work and lots of fun," and there is every indication that this description was accurate. Though amateur photographers tried out almost every available genre, unlike most serious photography the vernacular modes were seldom epic, tragic, or even self-consciously lyrical. From the beginning snapshots were intended to record events worth remembering mainly for the fondness of their happy emotional messages. To a large extent, the unexpressed and unexamined snapshot aesthetic of the early twentieth century overflowed with bright sentiment. Very few snapshooters, it seems, grabbed a camera for the purpose of recording times of sadness, family disruption, or personal disaster. What was worth remembering was worth remembering; what was not was not photographed.

The prevailing sentiment of the first full years of the snapshot revolution was also conspicuously lacking in skepticism and uncertainty. Though cameras like the Autographic were very sophisticated machines, many snapshooters continued to enjoy them as they would a new toy. Hardly anyone seemed to question the epistemological status of the medium, and consequently most pre-World War I amateur photographs are entirely trusting.

The simple fact that most amateur film was sensitive only to bright daylight conspired to make snapshot content inevitably glowing, even luminous. Most pictures were taken outdoors, in parks, at the beach, in the backyards, in crowded city squares. At least in the seminal days of popular photography the average snapshooter seemed always to be elbowing around in a world busy with activity and movement. Even attempts at portraiture usually included all sorts of extraneous information. There is little doubt that this wide-frame shooting was at least in part encouraged by the camera's directions, which instructed the photographer to stand six or seven feet away from the subject. On the other hand, there is hardly any doubt that once the prints were brought home, the fields, streets, beaches, mountains, buildings off in the distance gave context to the photo's primary information.

During the first decade of the twentieth century an entirely new category of photographer had been created. Most nineteenth-century practitioners of the art had either been professionals (working commercial photographers such as Brady, Gardner, Nadar) or amateurs (Davison, Robinson, or Stieglitz himself). And of the two groups, the second was generally considered the more artistic. Thus Stieglitz's often bitter complaints about popular photography were both pioneering and a rearguard action. Stieglitz was working diligently to force the art world to

Experiments to adapt the two-color Kodachrome process were begun shortly after the introduction of the still technique in 1915. The first movie that was shot on Kodachrome film was a 600-foot film entitled Concerning $1,000, *written by Sylvia Newton, a Kodak employee, and starring, among others, Doris Mees (the daughter of laboratory director C. E. K. Mees), optical researcher C. W. Frederick, and various children of lab personnel.*

accept photography as a reputable artistic discipline. At the same time, he seems to have been worried that the influx of untrained and unserious snapshooters into the field would convince his critics that photography was nothing more than a mechanical, inexpressive medium able to be practiced by anyone buying a Kodak camera.

In 1909 Stieglitz, by then the acknowledged leader of an American art photography movement known as the "Photo-Secession," published in the magazine *Photographic Topics* a list of "Twelve Random Don'ts." Most of the warnings were of a loosely aesthetic nature ("Don't go through life with your eyes closed"), but two of the hints reminded popular photographers not to take themselves too seriously. First of all, Stieglitz said, "Don't believe you became an artist the instant you received a gift Kodak on Xmas morning"; and second, "Don't believe that the snapshot you have made is a 'genuine work of art' because some painter has asked you for a copy."

These proscriptions, which if heeded would have taken much of the delight away from photography, seem not to have been acknowledged by casual photographers. Definitions of artistry differ, or course. It is probable that snapshooters were often content with photographic records of the world, but it is also indisputable that no one, whatever the artistic pretensions, wants to take a bad photo. In fact, chances are that at some point, if only by accident, most camera users will take a very good picture.

In this way photography differs form the other arts. Almost any photographer, even conceivably a child with a Brownie, might manage to snap off a brilliantly composed, informative, even beautiful picture. That few could take these sorts of photos with the consistency of a gifted artist offered Stieglitz cold comfort.

In fact, despite Stieglitz's remark about painters, a significant number of both artists and writers were fascinated by the snapshot's indiscriminate and comprehensive visual memory. The French novelist Emile Zola, who had argued that "I only state facts," was an enthusiastic amateur photographer. While most of the art photography establishment in both Britain and the United States were fussing over focus and print manipulation, Zola had perceptively noticed that photographs stated facts with unchecked abandon. "You cannot say you have thoroughly seen anything," he wrote, "until you have got a photograph of it, revealing a lot of points which otherwise would be unnoticed, and which in most cases could not be distinguished."

Zola was not alone in his understanding of the brand new aesthetics of everyday photography. The painter Edgar Degas owned a Kodak camera and often took photos as compositional studies. Degas understood that the camera's lens framed scenes from new and unusual angles. A few steps to the left or right significantly changed the vantage point, and in the process altered the meaning of the picture. Degas, who in addition to his photographic studies also took what are called typical family snaps, seems to have instinctively understood that all those millions of untrained vernacular photographers were creating a new photographic aesthetic. Yet, as the critic Sarah Greenough has pointed out, it would be years before the photographic establishment "had the self-confidence to embrace these mundane incidents of modern life as worthy subjects or appreciate their lessons of pictorial structure."

The French painter Edouard Vuillard was an even more unabashedly casual snapshooter than Degas. His nephew remembers:

Vuillard owned a camera, a Kodak. It was an ordinary model, one of the bellows type. It was part of Vuillard's household. Its place was on the sideboard in the dining room. Sometimes, during a conversation, Vuillard would go to get it and resting it on some furniture or even the back of a chair, oblivious of its view finder, would point the lens in the direction of the image he wished to record: he would then give a brief warning, "Hold it please" and we could hear the clic...clac of the time exposure. The camera was then returned to its place, and Vuillard walked back to his seat.

Of course in any collection of snaps from this or other periods, there are an inordinate number of inexpertly composed, poorly focused, or even laughably inconsequential pictures. But these "mistakes" seemed unable to affect all those who had caught what one commentator called "the curious contagion of the camera." The Autographic Kodak answered the modern public's demands as well as any camera of the time. In its lifetime, there were almost twenty different models of the camera, ranging in price and size from the $23.00 No. 1A Autographic Kodak Junior camera to the $109.50 No. 3A Autographic Kodak Special camera, which was the first Kodak camera to be equipped with a coupled range finder, a mechanism that allowed the photographer to focus correctly by matching three horizontal lines in a small viewer placed on the front of the camera.

Indeed, in the twenty-five years since the introduction of the first Kodak camera, the sophistication of camera design had increased significantly. The lens of the first Kodak camera was simply two pieces of half-moon-shaped glass, only partially corrected for spherical aberrations and curvature of field. The next generation of Kodak lenses, though still fairly

The candor of early snapshots sometimes captured life at its most casual. In this 1908 photo taken of a roadside picnic, two women turn their heads as they hear the snapshooter's movement, while their friend George Eastman, apparently unaware of the photographer, continues to finish his lunch. This is an example of candid vernacular photography in its purest form—informal, unceremonious, and disarrayed.

unsophisticated, succeeded in correcting some of these faults. The Autographic camera, however, like many other models of the period, came equipped with an anastigmatic, or rapid rectilinear, lens. Before this new line of cameras, Kodak lenses had been unable to adequately remedy the astigmatic defect, which had the effect of blurring horizontal lines and sharpening vertical lines, or vice versa. As light was bent by the simple two-element meniscus lenses, it scattered. The new anastigmatic lens redirected the light by the clever compensatory design of the second glass element. The Rochester firm of Bausch & Lomb had supplied lenses for most early Kodak cameras, but in 1911 Christopher Graf, an optics specialist, was hired and in a year or so had designed the first Kodak anastigmatic lens.

Eight separate sizes of pictures were produced by the line of Kodak Autographic cameras. At the time most negatives were contact printed; the larger the film size the greater the size of the final print. Early Kodak roll films were described simply by camera name. In 1913, however, it was decided to give each size a three-digit number, beginning sequentially with number 101. The film produced for the Autographic camera differed from other films only in its backing. The smallest film size, A (for Autographic) 127 measured 1⅝ x 2½ inches, and the largest, A126, was 4¼ x 6½ inches.

There is no accurate figure of the number of cameras sold by the Eastman Kodak Company during the pre-World War I period, but certainly the number reached into the millions. In addition to the Autographic, the Eastman camera catalogs of this era list various sizes of box cameras, folding cameras, Brownie, folding Brownie, as well as the small vest-pocket Kodak camera, stereo cameras, and even several panoramic cameras. These last, which were equipped with a swiveling lens, took pictures up to 12 inches long and encompassed views up to 142 degrees wide.

Kodak also manufactured specialized types of cameras. In 1905 it had acquired the Folmer and Schwing Company, which had designed a sophisticated single-lens-reflex camera with a fabric focal plane shutter with a light-admitting slit that traveled quickly and evenly across the film plane. By 1915 the Folmer and Schwing Division of the Eastman Kodak Company was marketing about twenty kinds of these cameras, including a hand-held plate camera called the "Speed Graphic." During the formative days of pre-World War I photojournalism, Graflex cameras, and in particular the Speed Graphic, were the press photographer's camera of choice. By this time halftone reproduction of photographic images had become a common feature of many newspapers and magazines, and the majority of on-the-spot pictures of news events were taken with Graflex cameras.

The Folmer and Schwing Division also manufactured the Cirkut, a line of large-format panoramic cameras. The Cirkut took pictures as large as 16 inches high and encompassed views up to 360 degrees. A new portrait sheet film, intended for the professional market was also introduced in 1913, as was the "Kodopticon," a lantern slide projector. That same year Kodak also printed two important new publications: the first edition of *How to Make Good Pictures*, a 160-page fully illustrated instructional manual for amateur photographers, and the first issue of *Kodakery* a monthly magazine that published prizewinning pictures and offered advice on the latest Kodak products and processes.

Publications of this sort were regularly read by a new class of amateur photographers. These "serious amateurs" did not fully consider themselves artists; that category was reserved for those like Alfred Stieglitz or Edward Steichen who pursued photography as an avocation. At the same time, the readers of these magazines and manuals took the making of photographs much more seriously than the casual snapshooter. The serious amateur worked diligently to master photography's skills and was often the first to try out the newest technologies. In succeeding

From Stephan Lorant: *FDR; A Pictorial Biography* (Simon & Schuster)

Snapshooting was great fun, a game played even by the most prominent and prestigious families. In this early Roosevelt family Kodak snapshot, twenty-year-old Franklin Delano Roosevelt, his own camera in his hand, tries to dodge the attempt of another family member to catch him with the snap of a shutter lens.

Emile Zola once wrote that "You cannot say you have thoroughly seen anything until you have got a photograph of it." Zola had no doubt looked down from the spectacular superstructure of the Eiffel Tower many times, but this photograph, taken with a Kodak hand camera, revealed, as he wrote, "a lot of points which otherwise would be unnoticed, and which in most cases could not be distinguished."

The French painter Edouard Vuillard owned a Kodak camera that he used with an almost total disinterest in such finer points of photography as focus, movement, or light intensity. What Vuillard apparently cared most about, evidenced in this 1905 picture, was photographic composition, the play of light and shadow, and the fortuitous arrangement of people and objects as they were seen through the lens of a camera. Other French painters fascinated with the compositional aspects of the snapshot camera included Pierre Bonnard, Edgar Degas, and Camille Pissarro.

years this new breed of photographer would become one of the most active and important consumers of photographic supplies.

In the mid-1910s, however, much of the company's success was the result of the continuing growth of the snapshot market. The company had outgrown its present administrative facilities, and Eastman began planning a sixteen-story office building that would be erected on the site of the original State Street factory. However, in the midst of this expansion, the Goodwin celluloid dispute, which had been unresolved since the late 1880s, finally came before United States District Judge John Hazel. After Goodwin's death in 1900, the majority of stock in the Goodwin Film and Camera Company had been acquired by the Ansco company, a firm created by a merger of the Anthony and Scovill companies. As the controversy dragged on Eastman occasionally wished the whole Goodwin business could be settled once and for all. In fact, in 1900, Eastman had written to his attorney he had been "looking for somebody to sue us under

In 1901, when Jacques-Henri Lartigue was a six-year-old boy living in France, he was given his first camera. Other cameras, including a Kodak No. 2 Brownie, followed. Lartigue played with his cameras with the precocity and fervor of an inspired child. This picture, taken when Lartigue was approximately twelve years old, he later described as "an exciting duel in the dust." When Lartigue's youthful photographs were published almost fifty years later, the aesthetic genius of his unaffected eye was universally recognized.

The Autographic camera was designed to record both visual and written information. By opening a small metal door on the back of the camera and etching the negative with a stylus, a short aide-mémoire listing name, date, location could be inscribed at the bottom of each picture.

that patent." When later that year Anthony visited Eastman and threatened to do just that, Eastman told him "that if he would only sue us, there would be no hard feeling, it would be regarded as a friendly act." In 1902 Ansco finally brought suit against the Eastman Kodak Company for patent infringements. The chemical issues involved were so confusing that the first judge who heard the case commented simply that "the expert witnesses have given discrepant testimony on all essential matters."

However, on August 14, 1913, Judge Hazel ruled against Kodak and ordered the company to make restitution. Eastman was angered and disappointed but immediately wrote a check for five million dollars payable to the Ansco company. For the five million dollars Kodak was given a license to make use of the Goodwin patent. In the strictest legal sense Goodwin had been declared the inventor of flexible celluloid film.

The question of whether Hannibal Goodwin or George Eastman and Henry Reichenbach invented transparent celluloid film base has, despite Judge Hazel's ruling, never been adequately answered. Historians have found no reason to believe that Eastman and Reichenbach had ever heard of Goodwin before the filing of their patent application. The issue of production, however, is another matter entirely. As Eastman had argued before the court, his company had, at the very least, perfected the production of transparent film base. In other words, precise chemical formulas aside, the Eastman Kodak Company had developed, manufactured, and distributed the product and was thus responsible for its effect upon the world of photochemically reproduced images.

Celluloid film was the basis not only of the amateur snapshot film market but also of the fast-growing motion picture industry. By 1911, for instance, in addition to its regular snapshot film, Kodak was manufacturing over eighty million feet of motion-picture stock annually. No one, including Eastman, had anticipated or predicted the rapid growth of this portion of the photographic market.

The popular acceptance the movies had in fact proceeded at a speed similar to that of snapshot photography. By the mid-1890s, the Edison Kinetoscope viewer, which used fifty-foot rolls of Eastman film, had been installed in hundreds of small penny arcades around the country. The customer dropped a coin in the machine's slot and watched one of the minute-long films that had been shot in Edison's West Orange, New Jersey, studio. Other arcades had installed a competing system of viewing moving images known as the "Mutoscope." In 1895 W. K. L. Dickson had left Edison's company and with the backing of two entrepreneurs from Canastota, New York, devised this new system of watching moving pictures. The Mutoscope camera was, except for certain patent-evading details, much like Edison's. However, instead of the images being run past the eye on a continuous strip of film, the Mutoscope images were successively printed on a set of cards, which, when attached to a wheel and turned by a crank, allowed the images to flick past the viewers eyes like the pages of a child's flip book.

Despite competition, Edison was content with the Kinetoscope peep-box method of viewing motion pictures. He was afraid that the audience would become bored if these pictures were shown on a screen. But when others threatened to stage such shows, he relented. On April 23, 1896, the first Edison moving-picture projector, the Vitascope, was unveiled, and a crowd sat in the dark at Koster and Bial's Music Hall in New York City to watch a series of short films: a round of a prizefight, several pictures of dancers, and a documentary travelogue shot along the ocean front at Dover, England.

The audience was astonished (and sometimes frightened) by these moving pictures. *The New York Dramatic Mirror* reported that when the Dover seaside film was shown, "wave after wave came tumbling on the sand, and as they struck, broke into tiny floods, just like the real thing. Some of the people in the front rows seemed to be afraid that they were going to get wet and looked about to see where they could run to in case the waves came too close."

For the next few years these short movies were shown as fillers between vaudeville acts. In 1896 in Los Angeles Thomas Tally, who guessed that movies were at least as popular as the accompanying stage shows, opened what is generally considered to be the first establishment designed solely for the projection of motion pictures. Some of the customers entering Tally's arcade, never having been to an expensive stage show, thought the whole thing a hoax, so the proprietor cut a peephole in his lobby wall and gave nonbelievers proof of his claims.

Tally's experiment was such a success that during the next few years hundreds of small theaters, called "nickelodeons" because they charged a nickel a viewing, were opened around the country. To the Eastman Kodak Company this meant many more orders for both camera negatives and positive release stock. A side business that had begun in 1889 with a quanti-tatively insignificant order for twenty-five feet of Kodak film, now consumed miles of film.

The annual list of available Kodak products at the turn of the century was given various titles: The Kodakalogue *(1895);* The Witchery of Kodakery *(1900);* If You Want It, Take It—With A Kodak *(1901). By 1910, when over a million copies of the list were printed each year, it was known simply as* The Catalog.

For nearly fifty years the Graflex, with its fast focal-plane shutter and high-quality lens, was the press photographer's camera of choice. In this photo, taken by Jimmy Hare, one of the most active press photographers at the turn of the century, photojournalists covering a dynamite explosion at Communipaw, New Jersey, in 1911 climb over the piles of debris caused by the blast in search of the perfect on-the-spot dramatic photo.

In many ways, these projected "living motion pictures" were, at least in content and aesthetics, not significantly different than ordinary snapshots. Most of the makers of these films were not trained photographers. They simply drifted into moviemaking out of fascination with the process and a sense that this was a fairly easy way to earn a living. The most famous movie director of the period, Edwin S. Porter, had been initially hired by Edison in 1896 to work on machinery. A short time after starting work Porter was drafted to operate a camera. Having shown some skill in that aspect of filmmaking he was then put in charge of entire productions.

Though Porter apparently thought the fad for motion-picture photography would soon be over, throughout the 1890s and into the twentieth century he directed dozens of movies for Edison's company: newsreels, short comic sketches, travelogues, scenic views. In 1902 and 1903 Porter produced two films, *The Life of an American Fireman* and *The Great Train Robbery*, that would radically change the nature of the industry.

Both films were extended narratives. By creatively splicing together stock footage of a horse-drawn fire engine racing to a fire with studio-shot scenes of a woman and a child being rescued, Porter created a movie with twenty separate intercut shots. The movie-going public had never seen anything like this before. The 1903 *Great Train Robbery*, like *The Life of an American Fireman*, utilized jump cuts between scenes, was eight hundred feet long and lasted just under fifteen minutes. Despite warnings that its length would bore viewers, the public loved *The Great Train Robbery*, and it became so famous that nickelodeon owners often showed it as a teaser on opening day.

The audience for these films was far from sophisticated. Most nickelodeons were opened in the poorer sections of American cities, and, in fact, many of the movies' first customers were immigrants who spoke little English. But language did not matter. The movies, without the benefit of sound, spoke with the purely visual vocabulary of photography.

What the nickelodeon patron saw were images not significantly different than those seen in snapshots, that other new way of capturing the world on film. Film and camera lenses were slow, and consequently most motion pictures were shot either on open-air stages or out in the streets or countryside. *The Great Train Robbery*, for instance, was filmed on sunny days in the wilds of rural New Jersey. When the sun went behind the clouds, the movie cameraman, like the snapshooter, put down his camera.

The sensitivity of Eastman motion-picture film differed in no significant way from that used in the typical snapshot camera. In terms of light sensitivity, Kodak film was Kodak film. A few movie companies attempted to shoot indoors under banks of Cooper-Hewitt mercury vapor lamps, but the sun remained the most efficient source of light. This technical hindrance, however, seemed to coincide with the public's appetite for action-filled outdoor dramas. Cowboys, Indians, cops and robbers, chase sequences through parks and along beaches, even faked documentaries, such as Buffalo Bill's dramatic recreation of the Battle of Wounded Knee, were the standard features of this very energetic and trusting period of filmmaking.

In 1907, almost twenty years after their first contact, Eastman stopped by West Orange to meet Edison for the first time. Edison was, as always, concerned about competition. He asked whether it was true that his leading competitor, the French Pathé Company, was using seventy-five million miles of film a year. Eastman laughed and said not quite that much.
But the figure was close. In fact, millions of feet of transparent nitrocellulose film, both for motion pictures and snapshots, were being produced annually at Kodak Park. The next question, one that faced both Edison and Eastman, was how to encourage even further growth.

In 1915 Paul Strand, then a young photographer who believed that photography was capable of expressing "a range of almost infinite tonal values which lie beyond the skill of the human hand," walked the streets of New York with a Graflex camera using "straight photographic methods" to capture the people, buildings, and turmoil of the city. Taken on Wall Street, this photograph contains each of these three particulars in a single, masterfully composed shot.

Left:

Since the film stocks used in early motion-picture cameras were insensitive to all but the strongest light, most pre–World War I movies were shot on outdoor platforms. Not having to worry about sound, different silent movie scenes were often staged simultaneously on side-by-side sets, roofed only by muslin curtains draped above the actors and actresses to diffuse the harsh sunlight.

Above:

Edwin Porter's The Great Train Robbery, *produced in 1903 for the Edison Company, was one of the first fictional films to use intercutting of scenes to tell a complete story. Though only twelve minutes long, audiences were fascinated by the dramatic chase scenes and the inexorable drive toward the climatic shoot-out between bandits and posse. It was the single most popular and influential film of its time and prepared the way for the long narrative films that would turn movie making from a curiosity into a worldwide industry.*

Early in 1914 a large black touring car pulled up in front of the recently abandoned Kinemacolor studios in Hollywood, California. The complicated two-filter Kinemacolor process of making color motion pictures had been one of the many reviewed by George Eastman in his search for a commercially viable system of color photography. But though Kinemacolor had achieved some notable successes, a record of the coronation of England's King George V, for example, in the end, Eastman was proved correct. Few theaters would invest in the projection equipment required for these color movies, and by the end of 1913 the Kinemacolor company had gone out of business.

In the back seat of the car were Lillian and Dorothy Gish and Robert "Bobby" Harron, three of the most popular movie personalities of the time. The fourth occupant of the automobile was the director D. W. Griffith. Kinemacolor's buildings and back lots had been purchased by Harry Aitken's independent Mutual Film Corporation especially for Griffith's use. The director had chosen to move his stock company of actors, actresses, and technicians from New York City to Hollywood for a number of quite particular reasons. One, of course, was the weather. At the time, motion-picture camera stock was insufficiently sensitive to all but the strongest light, and since most scenes, interior or exterior, were filmed on outdoor stages, the sunny California climate allowed a longer and more reliable shooting season than the Long Island, Connecticut, or New Jersey locations usually favored by East Coast filmmakers.

But it wasn't just the California sun that drew Griffith to the West. It was the restrictive economic and artistic policies of an industry-wide regulatory organization called the Motion Picture Patents Company. Most of Griffith's career had been spent working for the Biograph film company, one of the constituent members of that organization. Griffith was Biograph's most successful director, but like all MPP companies, Biograph was interested in quick profits and was unwilling to spend more than the minimum necessary to produce motion pictures. Specifically, it forbade the making of long, expensive feature-length films and refused to allow the real names of its actors, actresses, and directors to appear on screen, fearing such publicity would encourage demands for higher salaries.

In the course of his seven-year movie career, Griffith had become convinced that both of these policies were ill-conceived. The future of the movie industry, he thought, depended precisely upon the exhibition of long narrative films featuring a cast of talented and recognizable movie actors and actresses. Oddly enough, Griffith had not always been so sure that motion pictures had any potential at all. Like many others in the early American cinema he had drifted from stage to movie acting in order to make a few quick dollars. In fact, Griffith at first had been reluctant to acknowledge that he had anything to do with these tawdry, lower-class film entertainments. He is reported to have remarked to his wife, the actress Linda Arvidson, "In a way it's very nice, but, you know, we can't go on forever and not tell our friends and relatives how we are earning our living."

Griffith's lack of faith in the importance of films did not last long. In 1907, after playing bit parts in several Biograph films, Griffith switched from acting to directing, and during the next six years the man who had worried that movies would ruin his career was responsible for over four hundred and fifty one-reel films. In these short movies, each about nine hundred feet in length and fifteen minutes in running time, Griffith had experimented with most of the filmic techniques now commonly associated with his name: close-ups, flashbacks, fade-ins and fade-outs, intercutting, crosscutting, camera placement, dramatic lighting, and rhythmic editing. As his interest in film language increased, so did his ambition to make longer, more complex movies. Griffith's employer, the Biograph company, let him make several two-reelers, but when the director was audacious enough to plan films twice that long they refused to put up the money.

Biograph was less interested in the future of filmmaking than in the accumulation of short-term profits. The Motion Picture Patents Company, popularly called "the Trust," had been

Lillian Gish has been described by a fan as "completely a being of lyrical loveliness." In this publicity photograph released at the time of the opening of D. W. Griffith's The Birth of a Nation, Gish appears not in her film role as the daughter of the radical reconstructionist Austin Stoneman, but instead as a screen personality. Though the Motion Picture Patents Company, a trust that included the Eastman Kodak Company, discouraged the creation of a star system, the demand for still pictures of Gish and other screen actors of the day confirmed the conviction of independent producers that the growth of the movie industry depended precisely upon the glamour and celebrity of its "movie stars."

formed in September 1909 by the leaders of the movie industry to control and protect their economic interests. At the time, films were relatively cheap to make; but they were even cheaper to copy. To discourage piraters, most movie companies printed a distinctive logo on each film frame. It was a simple matter, though, for duplicators to block out the trademark, reprint the film, and offer it as their own.

The suppression of film pirating was not the only rationale given for the creation of the Trust. Principally at issue was the use (or abuse) of Thomas Edison's motion-picture camera and projector. In the summer of 1907 Edison, who thought that patents on his movie camera and projector were being unfairly and illegally infringed upon, approached the Eastman Kodak Company with a plan to create a trade organization to consolidate his claims and to control patent evaders. Eastman agreed to cooperate, apparently convinced that Edison was indeed being cheated out of his fair share of the profits. Eastman was also concerned that the chaotic infighting between filmmakers would flood the market with increasingly cheap and shoddy products. "The chief advantage in my opinion," he said of Edison's proposition," was to be found in the regulation of prices, and the control of the renters, and the suppression of the dupers."

At the time Kodak was supplying most of the camera negative and motion-picture positive raw stock used worldwide for film production, and Eastman no doubt saw it to his advantage to have all of his film customers clustered together in one workable alliance. Kodak was also about to announce the creation of a new motion-picture film stock. Since early in the century, when the accidental ignition of the very flammable nitrocellulose stock had caused a number of terrible fires in theaters, Eastman had been investigating the possibility of a nonflammable, acetate-based "safety" film stock. The closely knit organization Edison envisioned would facilitate the introduction of "non-flam" film.

Thus, any order that could be brought to bear upon the film industry would be to the benefit of the Eastman Kodak Company. When he and Edison met, however, Eastman warned the inventor to be careful. "I told Mr. Edison," he said, "that I did not believe it would be a good thing for him to try to monopolize the whole cine business (producing, distributing, and exhibiting); that in order to give it its full development it needed several minds to originate the great variety of subjects required."

But complete control seems to be exactly what Edison had in mind. He had no way of dominating the movie business by means of the sale of raw film stock. That franchise belonged to Kodak and was the reason Eastman was consulted. Edison did, however, believe he owned sole rights to the most efficient and workable movie camera and projector then available. In fact, at least in terms of movie exhibition, Edison's patents were crucial. Though the invention of flexible roll film was certainly a major contribution to the development of moving pictures, if a machine to project these pictures had not been invented, moving pictures might have remained a small-time penny arcade amusement.

The poet and film reviewer Vachel Lindsay once called filmed photoplays, "An unbroken sheet of photography," a description as metaphorically exact as it is technologically tricky. It is true that a strip of motion-picture film is in essence nothing more than a sequentially exposed group of still photographic images. At least in that specialized sense, movie film is essentially no different than any other piece of film.

The difference is in the viewing of these pictures. Motion pictures create the illusion of movement; still photographs are static. To make the objects photographed on a strip of film appear to move, the connected images must pass before the human eye at a speed sufficient to create a physiological phenomenon known as "persistence of vision." This optical effect had been observed for thousands of years but was not studied in detail until the nineteenth century, when a number of scientists, among them Peter Mark Rôget, Joseph Plateau, and Michael

Faraday, performed experiments to study what Roget called this "striking" and "irresistible" illusion.

By the time Edison and others began using projected photographs to create the impression of action, it was known that if each of these linked pictures is held in front of the eye for a fraction of a second and the gaps between the transit of these images blocked by the action of a shutter, successively exposed photographs will seem to blend into each other. A string of these images, each flicked for a fraction of a second before the eye, would produce on the screen the illusion of movement. In purely mechanical terms, the most efficient device to effect this illusion, in other words, the best film projector, is that which most smoothly moves each film frame in and out of the eye's field of vision.

Ten years earlier, in 1896, when Edison had first shown moving pictures on a screen, his Vitascope projector had incorporated a clever feature called the "Latham loop," or the "American loop." Up to that time stress on the film as it was being jerked into place in front of the projection lens often caused the thin celluloid material to tear or break. A year earlier, in 1895, two brothers, Grey and Otway Latham, discovered that if the flexible film was bent into a small loop on either side of the film gate, tension could be reduced and the problem of breakage alleviated.

Later that year another inventor, Thomas Armat, developed a motion-picture projector that, in addition to the Latham loop, incorporated a shutter mechanism called the "maltese cross." This combination gear-and-sprocket device regularized the rate at which the shutter opened and closed, at least partially eliminating the flicker caused by the appearance of unevenly spaced images. Armat's projector worked so well that Edison bought it outright under what one film historian has called a "scandalous agreement." Edison marketed the product under his name; Armat's only credit for the design was a small metal plaque screwed onto the back of the projector.

It was the patents on both of these crucial mechanical inventions that Edison was seeking to enforce. In 1907, when he discovered an American film producer named William Selig had incorporated the maltese cross and American loop into his movie camera, Edison sued him and won. This legal victory gave Edison the exclusive American rights to any camera or projector that used the loop and cross combination. Unfortunately Edison had neglected to obtain patents overseas, and European moviemakers, including Charles Pathé and the Lumière brothers in France, seized upon this opportunity to include some of Edison's designs in their own cameras and projectors.

By the time Edison was seeking to control the film industry these French filmmakers were managing large and flourishing film companies. The Lumières had constructed a lightweight apparatus that was at once camera, projector, and printer, and during the late 1890s over a thousand short films were listed in their catalog. After 1900, however, the Lumières turned their attention from filmmaking to the production of photographic equipment and processes. Their place in the French film industry was taken by Charles Pathé, who, after building a motion-picture studio in Vincennes just outside Paris, had by 1908 become the world's largest movie producer, marketing twice as many movies in the United States as all the American film companies combined. Pathé, in fact, was Kodak's largest single purchaser of raw movie-film stock.

These European-made films, cameras, and projectors were being imported to the United States perfectly legally, and there was nothing, it seemed, Edison could do about it. The plan for a film industry organization that Edison presented to Eastman would of necessity have to be an international partnership that pooled all patents and inventions. Without the participation of all reputable international filmmakers, the arrangement would not work. As negotiations were proceeding, Charles Pathé visited Eastman in Rochester, and Eastman mentioned the Edison

idea. Initially Pathé seemed uninterested. However, when he discovered that Eastman had agreed to be part of the pool, Pathé, fearing that his supply of Kodak film stock would be cut off, agreed to join the Trust.

As news of Kodak's interest in the plan spread, Eastman received a call from Henry Marvin of the Biograph company. Biograph, which had begun business in the 1890s as the producers of the Mutoscope flip-card system of making motion pictures, had managed to evade Edison's patent restrictions by developing a sprocketless and loopless camera. Instead of using edge-perforated movie stock, the Biograph camera used pins to punch holes into the sides of the film as it moved through the camera. Eastman wrote of his conversation with Marvin:

He was very anxious to have assurances from me that we would not in any case cut them off, but I told him that all he needed was the assurance I gave him, viz: that we would not sign a contract until we had communicated with him and ascertained whether or not he was to have a license. Marvin stated that his camera, which had been declared not to infringe the Edison patent, makes negatives that are superior to those made by the Edison cameras and that he can print positives from such negatives on film perforated for the regular Edison exhibiting machine which registers more accurately than if made from sprocket-fed negatives.... I am inclined to think that he is entitled to consideration on the lines that he mentioned.

Just before the filming of D. W. Griffith's The Birth of a Nation *got underway, the Civil War photos of Mathew Brady's company were published in a four-volume edition entitled* Battles and Leaders of the Civil War. *Griffith's cameraman Billy Bitzer found a copy of the book in a local library. Since* The Birth of a Nation *was shot on Kodak's orthochromatic motion-picture stock, sensitive mainly to the blue and green zones of the visible spectrum, Griffith and Bitzer were able to pattern much of the film's look after Brady's wet-collodion photographic compositions with their near-orthochromatic overexposed skies and stark contrasts of men in arms.*

It clearly made little sense for Eastman to stop supplying any of his best customers. Biograph, Pathé, Edison, all competing film production units must agree to work together. In fact, he argued, any attempt to eliminate rivals would be counterproductive. As Eastman wrote to Strong, "I finally convinced them (the original licensees) that it was a fool thing to do — to try to bar out their competitors in any such way; that the result of it would be that they would bunch themselves together and make an opposition that would break up the whole scheme."

Finally, on January 1, 1909, the terms of the contract were written to the satisfaction of all parties, and the Motion Pictures Patents Company was formed. Nine manufacturers of movie films (Edison, Biograph, Vitagraph, Essanay, Selig, Lubin, Kalem, Star, and Pathé), one distributor (the American George Kleine) and one supplier of raw stock (Kodak) formed the Trust. The production companies promised not to sell or lease equipment to any firm outside the Trust, and Kodak pledged to sell raw stock only to patent company members. At first, the agreement called for a total ban on Kodak film sales to non-Trust members, but after hearing complaints from free-lance filmmakers such as the well-known travelogue photographer Burton Holmes, Eastman insisted on retaining the right to continue selling to small specialized filmmaking companies whose films did not compete with Trust products.

Kodak would add a one-half-cent surcharge to the price of the film sold to Trust filmmakers, and this money would be proportionately distributed as a royalty to members of the Trust. It seems clear, however, that even after negotiations had been completed Eastman still had doubts about the ultimate success of the Motion Picture Patents Company. Before signing the contract, he insisted that a clause be inserted that would allow Kodak to terminate the agreement with sixty days' notice.

Within months after the creation of the patents group Kodak's initial hold on the film market was challenged. In France, Charles Pathé announced that his firm would begin to manufacture its own sensitized stock. Pathé had not yet acquired the production facilities necessary to manufacture celluloid support, so it began regenerating Kodak stock. Exposed emulsion was scraped off out-of-date movies, the support recoated, and, almost worse to Eastman's mind, the film resold in Kodak boxes. Eastman argued that this was a "violation of our understanding." Pathé's project, however, was short-lived. The quality of the stock was so bad that after a few months Pathé decided to give up the regeneration process.

Soon afterward, Pathé found a source of virgin celluloid support and began producing and marketing small quantities of its own sensitized raw stock. At this point, Kodak, which had been selling Pathé about eighty million feet of raw stock a year, terminated all sales to the French company. The quality of the new Pathé film, however, did not match that of Eastman stock, and by the end of 1910, in spite of competition with Pathé, Kodak continued to dominate both the European and American markets.

It had been suggested to Eastman that he fight his film competitors by cutting prices, but he refused, explaining to Thatcher Clarke that "the best thing for us to do is to bring our products up to the very highest state of perfection and reduce our price when we have to. The trouble with the European administration the last eight or ten years has been that they consider price-cutting a panacea for all difficulties. My experience has been different from this. The money that we would lose by cutting prices between now and the time the concern gets going would keep us from starvation a good long time."

The "concern" in this case was Kodak's new acetate-based safety film, which, despite improvements, had for the most part been rejected by Trust members. The film produced acceptable images, but it broke very easily and the film cement used for splicing breaks was not effective on the acetate base. Added to these problems was the fact that the new stock cost one-half cent per foot more than nitrate film, a considerable amount of money to the cost-conscious producers of motion-picture entertainment. Eastman had hoped slowly to phase out the production of nitrocellulose stock, but so little acetate film was used that although Kodak continued to offer moviemakers both kinds of film, by 1911 hardly any nonflammable acetate stock was being manufactured.

In the meantime, the restrictive policies of the Motion Picture Patents Company had, as Eastman had warned, not discouraged competition, but rather the opposite. In 1910, in a further attempt to monopolize the motion-picture business, the Trust had created its own film distribution company, the General Film Company, which charged each of its ten thousand exhibitors a weekly license fee of two dollars. Since it was generally acknowledged that motion pictures shot on Kodak stock with Trust-protected cameras were far superior to any others available, most exhibitors, though outraged by the fee, had little choice but to go along with the agreement.

Only a few distributors, such as Carl Laemmle of the Independent Motion Picture Company and William Fox of the Great New York Film Rental Company, challenged this system. Laemmle, who after opening his first nickelodeon in 1906 had gone on to manage film exchanges in a number of American and Canadian cities, publicly attacked the exclusionary policies of the Trust. Laemmle placed advertisements in the trade papers featuring a leather-booted cartoon character named General Flimco. Flimco, like the Trust's General Film Company, stomped about in an effort to frighten and intimidate independent film producers and exhibitors. "I will rot in Hades," Laemmle's ad read, "before I will join the Trust, or anything that looks like a Trust."

In spite of the Trust's near monopoly on filmmaking, a few small outlaw film production companies continued to produce movies. These independent firms were sometimes called "blanket companies," after the blanket used to hide their illegal cameras. The Trust hired its own police force to search out and apprehend patent violators, and there are numerous stories of Trust detectives ("goons" to the independents) disrupting filming and breaking equipment.

As the director Allan Dwan, then working for the independent American Film Company recalled:

They always shot at the cameras. Their instructions were to destroy the cameras, since they were expensive and hard to get. Most companies only had one. So a lot of companies had to run for it and many went out of business on account of them. We'd always be working in the hills and they'd get up in back of a tree or up on a mound above you and wait for their time. Sometimes they'd wait until a fellow was cleaning the camera—we didn't have any studio for our headquarters—and take a shot at it, anything to destroy it. That was their job.

Despite the harassment, the independents refused to give up the fight. The exhibition of movies was simply too profitable a business for ambitious entrepreneurs to pass up. By 1908 ten thousand storefront nickelodeons had been opened and the public demand for a weekly supply of new fifteen-minute, one-reel movie shows was increasing. Laemmle, Fox, and other independent distributors, unwilling to pay the Trust's license fees, first turned to non-Trust filmmakers, such as Dwan's American Film Company, for movies and then began producing films themselves.

In the fall of 1910 Jules Brulatour, whose New York City photo-supply house sold raw film stock to the independents, visited Eastman. Brulatour was the American agent for Lumière, but—as he freely admitted to Eastman—the quality of both Lumière cameras and film was not close to that of equipment currently in use by members of the Trust. Independent cameraman and director Fred Balshofer once had Brulatour bring him a Lumière camera that was specifically designed not to infringe on Edison patents. It had no sprocket wheels, did not require perforated film, and was built to work without the patented Latham loop. After experimenting with the camera for several weeks, however, Balshofer simply could not make it work. Film twisted in the film gate, and when it was projected the uneven flicker of images made the movie all but impossible to watch.

Lumière raw stock was just as bad. As Brulatour said, the quality of the emulsion was unreliable and often it "would leave the support—there was no adhesiveness to it." To meet the independents' demand for adequate stock, Brulatour would sometimes buy Eastman film overseas and reimport it. Brulatour had first met Eastman early in 1910, when he and Lumière had toured the Kodak facilities in Rochester, and during the next few months he several times asked Eastman if a way could be found to supply the independents with Eastman stock. Eastman had said he was sorry but he was bound by the Motion Picture Patents Company contract.

But Brulatour kept asking, and finally at a meeting late in 1910 Eastman said: "Well, I would like to help you out Brulatour, personally. My relations with you have always been very cordial and if I can do anything for you I would be glad to do it."

Brulatour answered that if some arrangement could be worked out he would order eight hundred thousand feet of cine film per week. Eastman was surprised that the amount was so high. Aren't you exaggerating it? he asked. Absolutely not, Brulatour answered.

Eastman thought over the matter, and after meeting with MPP officials amended his contract to include the sale of film to the independents. At their next meeting, he said, "Well, Mr. Brulatour, we have decided and arranged to sell the independents film."

"I'm very glad of it," Brulatour replied, "for the independents, first, Mr. Eastman, and secondly for myself." Eastman answered that the company felt no obligation to deal only through Brulatour, but that he should "make us a proposition. We don't want to put anybody out of business. It has never been our purpose."

Shortly thereafter Brulatour became an Eastman agent and the independents for the first time were able to obtain Kodak stock legally. In many ways, Eastman's deal with the independents marked the beginning of the end of the Motion Picture Patents Company's domination of the film industry. Kodak continued to sell to Trust members, of course, but assuring the independents an unlimited supply of reliable stock had another, perhaps not surprising effect upon the nature of motion pictures. Trust officials had from the beginning argued on purely financial grounds that movies should be limited to one reel in length and the industry should avoid publicizing its actors and actresses.

The independents thought otherwise. Carl Laemmle, for one, believed that movie celebrities would draw more people to the theater and thus increase profits. In 1910 he offered Biograph actress Florence Lawrence a large raise in salary to join his Independent Motion Picture Company. Laemmle then planted a story in the press that Miss Lawrence, who until then was known only as "the Biograph girl," had been killed in a St. Louis streetcar accident. The next day, responding to his own lie, Laemmle denied the story and promised to bring both the actress and IMP's leading man, King Baggott, to St. Louis to prove that she was indeed still alive. Crowds lined up to see the pair of movie personalities, and the star system was born.

A few of the independents were also convinced that not only would movie audiences sit still for a film lasting more than one reel, but that they would be willing to pay higher prices to do so. In 1912 Adolph Zukor's famous Player's Company exhibited the three-and-a-half-hour filmed stage play *Queen Elizabeth*, which starred the aging Sarah Bernhardt. In the spring of 1913 the two-hour, nine-reel Italian epic *Quo Vadis?* was also imported. Both movies were unprecedented successes. *Quo Vadis?*, in particular, which was shown in legitimate theaters rather than nickelodeons, proved that, contrary to the Trust's policy, the full-length feature film was indeed very profitable.

Still, many of the Trust's companies refused to allow directors to film a movie longer than two reels. In 1913 D. W. Griffith, who had been responsible for much of the success of the

Biograph company, made his first four-reeler, a biblical epic entitled *Judith of Bethulia*, but Biograph officials were so upset by its length that Griffith was removed from behind the camera and assigned the less dangerous job of supervising producer. Griffith was incensed and a few months later left Biograph, accepting a job with an independent, Harry Aitken's Mutual Film Company. By early 1914 Griffith had taken his stock company of stars to Hollywood and was beginning work on what turned out to be the longest and most popular film of the era: *The Birth of a Nation.*

When Eastman's deal with Brulatour had made Kodak raw stock available to the independents, there were two types of cine film: camera negative, a slow, orthochromatic film, and motion-picture positive, an even slower film that had the high contrast necessary for projection. Though Cooper-Hewitt mercury vapor lamps were then being used occasionally for indoor shooting, directors and cameramen usually shot movies outside on sunlit platform stages.

Bright, direct sunlight caused problems for motion-picture cameramen similar to those encountered by amateur snapshooters. For example, in order to expose film adequately movie actors were often asked to stand facing directly into the sun, but harsh shadows would furrow their features. Griffith had partially solved this problem by hiring young, smooth-complexioned actors and actresses such as the Gish sisters, Mae Marsh, Blanche Sweet, and Bobby Harron.

The most ingenious solutions to the problems of light, however, were provided by Griffith's cameraman, G. W. "Billy" Bitzer. Since 1895, when he had begun shooting newsreels and travelogues for the Biograph company, Bitzer had been one of the cinema's leading film photographers. Bitzer's greatest successes, however, came after he was teamed with Griffith in 1908, and the two began experimenting with new lighting techniques.

Seeing Mary Pickford and her husband Owen Moore sitting on a bench one day, Bitzer realized that the reflection of light from white gravel at their feet had finely sculpted their features with soft light. Bitzer rigged up artificial reflectors to cause the same soft lighting effect on the set. Though at first some viewers, being accustomed to the even and hard illumination of direct sunlight, thought the frames were out of focus, this technique produced much more pleasing and glamourous images of movie actors.

In the 1909 film *Pippa Passes*, Griffith asked Bitzer to light a room so the viewer would be able to distinguish between various hours of the day. Bitzer inserted a sliding gate into the wall of the set, placed a mercury vapor light behind it, and, by gradually lowering the device, filled the room with the appropriate light. Later, Cecil B. DeMille's cinematographer Alvin Wyckoff would call this effect "Rembrandt lighting."

When Griffith and Bitzer began working on *The Birth of a Nation*, however, the sometimes flat effect produced by the orthochromatic stock often worked perfectly. Griffith's epic spectacle was a fictional recounting of the Civil War and Reconstruction periods. Coincidentally, many of Mathew Brady's wet-plate collodion Civil War photographs had been recently republished in a four-volume set entitled *Battles and Leaders of the Civil War*. Bitzer borrowed the volumes from a local library, and he and Griffith patterned the composition and lighting of most of the movie's battle scenes after Brady's photographs. In fact, some scenes in the finished movie so closely resembled these historical pictures that Griffith called them facsimiles.

Bitzer's camera was a hand-cranked Pathé model, which in 1914 was still illegal under the patent laws for an independent such as Bitzer to use. During each break in shooting the camera was immediately packed away, since any sign of the Pathé camera on Griffith's set would be evidence of a patent violation.

In its original version, *The Birth of a Nation* was composed of 1,544 individual shots, around fifteen times more than the imported *Quo Vadis?* The film had cost just over one hundred thousand dollars to make. When it first opened at the Liberty Theatre in New York City it ran

for forty-eight weeks and was the first movie popular enough to command a two-dollar admission price. Though Griffith's controversial interpretation of race relations following the Civil War was widely attacked, for its filmic accomplishments *The Birth of a Nation* was called "the greatest picture ever made."

By the time *The Birth of a Nation* was released in 1915 the power of the Motion Picture Patents Company had been considerably weakened. Kodak's 1911 decision to provide film to the independents had broken one of the Trust's main holds on the industry. By 1917, when the courts ordered it to "discontinue unlawful acts," the Trust had for all practical purposes ceased to exist.

On August 26, 1914, George Eastman wrote from London, "I reached here just a few days before war was declared, and as there was no use trying to do business, I turned around and came back home again." Conflict on the European continent would continue for almost three years before the American declaration of war on Germany in April 1917, but the disruption of Kodak's overseas business was almost immediate. Practically all Kodak Limited's export of photographic goods from England to the continent was interrupted. The French subsidiary, Kodak S.A.F., operated under wartime conditions, and the delivery of sensitizing dyes from Germany to the United States was almost completely halted.

Kodak Park was, for the most part, unaffected by the war. An organic chemistry laboratory was created to make up for the loss of the German dyes, and in all other parts of the plant production was increased to meet domestic needs. As the independent film producers grew in size and stature, orders for cine-film had increased proportionally. In fact, by the mid-teens the number of feet of raw movie stock manufactured at Kodak plants surpassed that of the production of amateur cartridge film. Even the demand for gelatin dry plates, which, despite advances in roll-film technology remained popular with some amateur and professional photographers, grew to such an extent that a new five-acre plant for their manufacture was built in Kodak Park.

Before the war, new photographic supplies had been regularly added to the Kodak line and old products updated. An experimental panchromatic movie stock, sensitive to all colors of the visible spectrum, was under development in 1913. The speed of Graflex camera film and amateur spool film was increased. In 1914 the Gregory Commercial Camera Company asked Kodak to manufacture a document-duplicating camera called the "Photostat." The number of cameras ordered was relatively small, but Eastman accepted the job and developed a high-contrast bromide printing paper to be used in this early photocopying process. And in 1915, A. J. Newton, a British colleague of Mees's, was brought to Rochester to organize the first Kodak photoengraving department. Newton's shop was set up to make the halftone plates for all Eastman publications. At Mees's suggestion it soon initiated experimental work on all aspects of the graphic arts.

The trademark *Kodak* had in so many ways come to stand for photography in all its modern forms, it seemed necessary to remind the general public in advertisements that "if it isn't an Eastman, it isn't a Kodak." When Kodak film survived Captain Robert Scott's ill-fated journey to the South Pole, the company was quick to publicize its contributions to the expedition. Theodore Roosevelt thought the Antarctic pictures "wonderful," and H. G. Ponting, Scott's official photographer, sent Eastman a few sample negatives taken on that trip and in an accompanying letter described in detail "what your films went through":

You must know that there was not sufficient room in our hut to store them. They had to be left outside, where they were subjected to temperatures that fell far below zero for many months together. They took over seven months on the voyage to the far South and, of course, passed through the tropics. They have, therefore, been subjected to extremes of heat and cold.

Opposite:
In 1913, after Commander Robert F. Scott's death at the South Pole, Herbert Ponting, the British expedition's official photographer, wrote a letter to George Eastman describing "what your films went through." This photograph of Scott's ship Terra Nova, *seen through the opening of an ice cave, was taken on a subfreezing Antarctic day. Ponting also recorded some of the expedition's exploits on movie film—an equally difficult task given the extreme conditions.*

I must further tell you, that as we kept our hut at a temperature of about 50 degrees Fahrenheit, there was often a difference of more than 100 degrees between the interior and exterior. This necessitated the very greatest care in the handling of photographic films and plates.

These films were bought in England in 1910. They arrived in the Antarctic in January, 1911. Some of them were taken to the South Pole, and were exposed on January 17, 1912. These exposed films were brought back by Captain Scott to the last camping place where my late chief and his two remaining comrades of the Polar party lost their lives in a terrible blizzard which raged for nine days.

These films lay beside their dead bodies for eight months before the search party, on account of the months of darkness, were able to reach the spot. They were then discovered and brought back to the winter quarters hut, where they were developed in January, 1913. The films have therefore passed through the tropics, through one Antarctic winter buried in the snow, and have lain through another winter in the temperature which must have fallen 80 degrees below zero, before development and after exposure; and they were two and one half years old. I have these negatives now and enclose a print from one of them. They must beyond all question be the most remarkable negatives in the world. Without them we should never have actually seen how Captain Scott and his companions looked when at the uttermost extremity of the earth nor what they found there, the tent of the Norwegian Amundsen, who reached this goal just a month earlier.

There was a drawback to all this success and acclaim. Kodak's commanding reach over the photographic marketplace had become so sweeping and extensive that in October 1911 the company was notified by the U.S. Attorney General's office that it was investigating possible Kodak violations of the 1890 Sherman Antitrust Act. The Sherman law and the 1914 supplemental Clayton Antitrust Act prohibited price discrimination tending to create a monopoly, interlocking directorates, and the acquisition of companies for the purpose of killing competition, all of which, the government charged, had been business policies of the Eastman Kodak Company.

Eastman, who during the Motion Pictures Patents Company disputes, had often argued against attempts to eliminate competition, thought this attack on the size of his company and its basic business practices ill-conceived. He refused, as he once wrote, to be intimidated by "newspaper attacks of the Ida Tarbell-Rockefeller type." He seems to have been genuinely distressed that the achievements of Kodak, both financial and artistic, were being devalued.

Eastman was certain that selling high-quality articles at a fair fixed price better served the public than debilitating price-cutting, product-cheapening wars between manufacturers of photographic supplies. He had never hidden his desire to create the largest photographic concern in the world. In Eastman's view, the ratio of size to service was easy to calculate: the larger the company, the greater the benefit for both consumer and businessman. In a long detailed letter to a business associate, Eastman frankly laid out his thinking on the issue; the letter, in effect, narrating a short commercial history of his own company:

I have stated that fixed prices have to do with distribution, and this is where the ethical claims of the manufacturer comes in. Why should a man, perhaps an inventor, who has an article which the public needs, be deprived of the best method of introducing it? It very often happens that the public does not know that it needs the article; it is not conscious of wanting it. As a rule the public has to be educated to its own needs. It does not see the merits in an article until it has been, so to speak, thrust down their throats and held there by some enthusiastic, imaginative person whose object is, of course to make money, but who knows he can only make it through giving the public something that he thinks the public ought to think it needs.

In order to make the article at a price where any one will buy it, he may have to invest a large sum of money in an installation for manufacturing it. If when it is ready for sale he is debarred

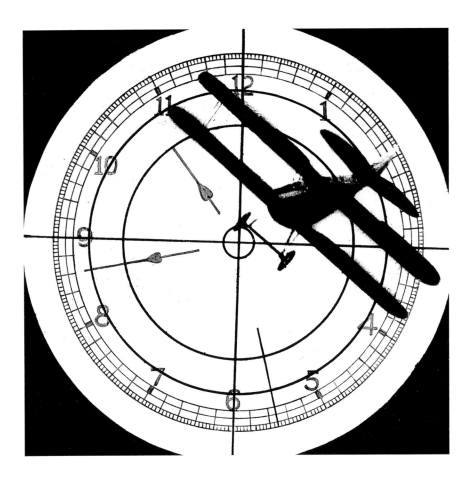

from employing the necessary agency for introducing it, he will be forced to offer it to a few large stores who are willing to take it, advertise it as a novelty, and drop it when its novelty is gone. Of course a man in the face of such a proposition will not engage in the enterprise.

Eastman was equally adamant about the ultimate effect upon the photographic marketplace of Kodak's acquisition of other photographic companies.

"It is perfectly true, as before stated," he wrote to one of his attackers, "that this company has absorbed a number of companies. Some of these companies have been purchased to avoid or settle patent litigation and as investments, but the most important ones have been purchased in pursuance of a definite line of policy which this company has now followed for many years. That is, to enable it to make a complete line of the very best photographic materials and apparatus...." Eastman continued:

As far as I know none of our competitiors who has made good goods has been unsuccessful in the last ten or twelve years, and none has been obliged to go out of business through the Eastman Kodak Company's methods of doing business. The enormous growth of the business caused by the broadening of the art by the inventions introduced by the Eastman Kodak Company has fed all of its competitors. Finally, the Eastman Kodak Company has for a number of years pursued the policy of reducing the prices of its products and also of adding valuable improvements to them without raising their prices.

Though he was sure his company had increased rather than decreased the aggregate market for photographic supplies of all sorts, Eastman understood the government's mood. "When the time comes," he wrote in response to an attack by Thomas Wallace of the Expo Camera Company, "we will comply with the law, notwithstanding our belief that such laws would deprive manufacturers of proprietary articles of a large part of their incentive for improving their goods and selling them on the merit system." "This letter," he concluded, "is intended for you personally, although I have not the slightest objection to your showing it to anyone, provided you show the whole of it."

None of Eastman's arguments convinced the attorney general's office, and on June 9, 1913, it filed suit against the Eastman Kodak Company. Two years later, on August 24, 1915, U.S. District Court Judge John Hazel rendered a verdict in the case. Kodak was found to have acquired a monopoly in the trade of photographic goods by signing exclusive contracts with the leading European paper manufacturers, by purchasing competing businesses, and by the imposition of fixed prices on its goods.

The decision was immediately appealed. However, as the long legal process of preparing documents and rearguing the case got underway, President Wilson declared war on Germany, and both parties to the lawsuit turned their attention to matters of the wartime economy. Eastman notified the Secretary of War and the Secretary of the Navy that Kodak would provide the government with any supplies it considered necessary for the war effort. Specifically, Eastman suggested that the company manufacture cellulose acetate, the chemical compound needed for the weatherproofing of airplane wings, and that it create and staff a photographic school to train men in the craft of aerial photography.

The acetate offer was almost immediately accepted. Photography, on the other hand, had never before been considered a critical part of warfare, and the government was slow to respond to Eastman's second proposal. While Kodak waited for an answer, Eastman asked Mees to come up with a workable plan for the uses of photography during wartime. In November 1917 the laboratory director wrote a long memorandum to Eastman in which he divided combat photography into two categories: tactical and documentary. "Documentary," he wrote, "consists in the taking of photographs both still and in motion as records of the progression or of the history of the struggle. Such recording work, while of great value and interest must, however, be entirely subordinated in importance to the tactical use of photography in the field."

Mees and William Folmer, the inventor of the Graflex camera, then went to Washington to offer their ideas and expertise to the government in person. The War Department again seemed uninterested, particularly in the aerial school proposal, and Eastman joked: "It may be that the government is afraid to accept any favors from one of the so-called trusts. Of course we are not paying any attention to such discrimination, but are trying to help out wherever we can."

Shortly after this visit, the government did ask that an aerial mapping camera and a film specifically designed for high-level photography be manufactured. By October 1917 Folmer had designed an automatic aerial camera nicknamed "Whistling Jim." In the initial years of the war the British Royal Flying Corps had taken numerous surveillance photographs, but their aerial cameras were bulky and difficult to operate. The airborne photographer had to lean precariously out of his cockpit seat to take pictures, a maneuver at once dangerous and, due to the awkward angle of the camera, not particularly effective. The automated Kodak aerial camera, loaded with fifty-foot rolls of film, was designed to solve these problems. Since the shutter rate and the speed of film advancing were controlled by a propeller-driven mechanism hanging in the plane's slipstream, the aerial photographer could man a machine gun while his camera automatically clicked off exposures. By the end of the war two hundred of the cameras had been ordered.

A few months earlier the federal government's food administrator Herbert Hoover had asked Kodak to "forgo all profit" on the raw cine-film stock needed by the Army Signal Corps, and Eastman agreed to the request. The newly formed photographic section of the corps was not particularly well organized. One motion-picture camera operator and one still photographer were assigned to each division, but many of the photographers were poorly trained, and those who made it to Europe before the end of the war seldom produced convincing or important footage. As one Signal Corps cinematographer remembered after the war:

We made up newsreels to send back home. We'd take a piece of film from here and a piece from there—they had no connection with each other whatsoever. . . . They were screaming for film, but there was nobody to make decisions as to what sort of film they wanted. So we gave them that film on venereal disease, Fit to Fight. *We used part of that one and mixed it with a second one and called it* Fit to Go Home.

Kodak was also asked by the National Association of the Motion Picture Association to assist in the distribution of morale-boosting Hollywood movies to army camps in France. The Committee on Public Information had been created in April 1917 to manage the propaganda side of the war effort, but there was such distrust between moviemakers and the CPI chairman, George Creel, that for a while the flow of Hollywood films to France was interrupted. It was only through the intercession of Jules Brulatour, chairman of the National Cinema Commission, that any sort of cooperation between the government and the major studios came about.

Because some of the scientists at the Kodak laboratories were British, interest in the European conflict at the lab began even before the U.S. entry into the war. Samuel Sheppard volunteered for service in the British armed forces but was declared "physically unfit," and Mees, who had taken up the study of Russian, suggested that he accompany a Canadian force to Siberia as an interpreter, a request that was also turned down.

Both continued their work. Mees oversaw Kodak's production of photochemicals, and Sheppard worked out a method of suspending pulverized coal in fuel oil for use in U.S. Navy ships. By the spring of 1918 Sheppard had developed a collodial mixture containing chemical "fixateurs" that stabilized the suspension of coal dust in the fuel oil, and the engines of a navy ship, the U.S.S. *Gem*, were for a time successfully run using this new type of fuel.

In the Kodak physics lab, Loyd Jones was asked to research improved methods of camouflaging ships at sea. During the summer of 1917, when the German submarine fleet was disrupting American marine shipping, the chairman of the Engineering Committee of the Submarine Defense Association wrote to Kodak asking that it collect data pertinent to the problem of high-seas visibility. At the time there was no purely scientific way of measuring the contrast between a ship and the featureless ocean behind it. Jones built a model ocean in his laboratory and floated small wooden ships in the tank in a variety of artificially created weather conditions. After measuring brightness, glare, and haze with a specially designed visibility meter, Jones suggested that ships be painted a grayish blue green. After the war ended the scientist published the results of his experiments, and work on camouflage was continued by the U.S. Navy.

In January 1918 the War Department finally decided that the formation of an aerial school in Rochester was appropriate. Before the war, photographs had been taken from balloons, kites, airplanes, and even by carrier pigeons. What Mees had called the "tactical" use of photography, however, was for the most part a new and undeveloped military science. In mid-March 1918 the first 250-member class arrived at the aerial school in Rochester and was housed in barracks constructed on the fourth floor of the new paper mill at Kodak Park. Schoolrooms were partitioned off in the same building, and students were fed at the park's cafeteria. When the aerial school was opened, its classes were divided into two disciplines: camera repair and basic photography. By the end of the war, 182 students had graduated from the repair school and more than 1,800, about a third of whom had no previous experience with photography, from the photographic section.

During World War I, it was common practice to take a set of two aerial photographs in quick succession so that the exposures nearly overlapped. When printed and viewed side by side, the

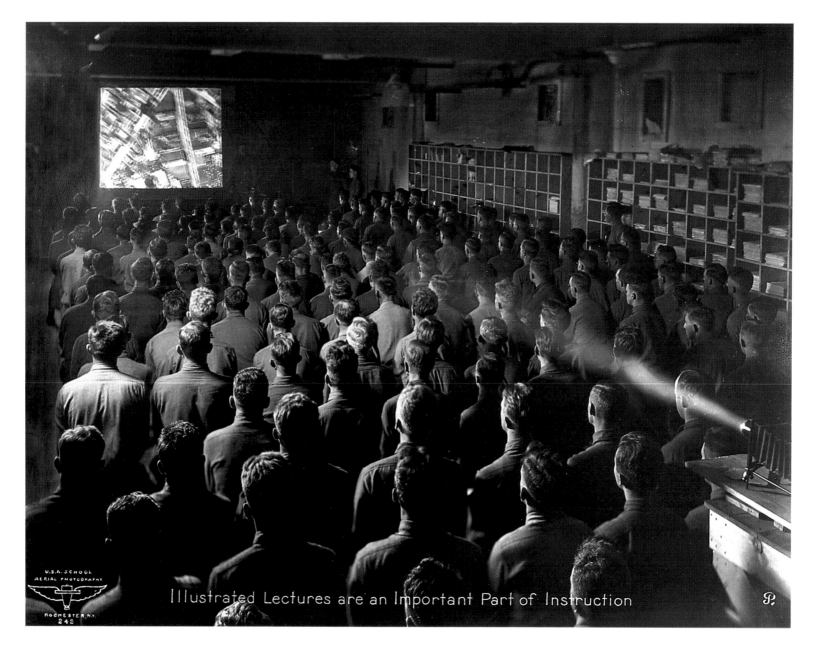

Illustrated Lectures are an Important Part of Instruction

In April 1918 a school was established in Rochester to train military personnel in all aspects of aerial photography: camera operation, film processing, interpretation of reconnaissance photographs. The 1,995 men who attended the school were based in a combination barracks-classroom in Kodak Park and were instructed by Kodak technicians and army advisers attached to the wartime school.

(Above) Students receiving instruction in the discipline of aerial photography interpretation.

(Opposite) A photo of the recreation room at the Kodak Park aerial photography school.

optical effect produced by these twin pictures resembles that of stereo photography. In fact, due to the ten-thousand-foot height from which these aerial photos were taken, the usual stereoscopic illusion of depth was greatly exaggerated; low hills looked like mountains and small depressions seemed to be deep valleys. This photographic phenomenon, called hyperstereoscopy, enabled the interpreters of aerial photographs to read each detail in the battle landscape as if it were writ large.

Students attending the aerial school practiced taking these double images during experimental flights over the countryside around Rochester and were instructed in the art of interpreting aerial information by military personnel attached to the school. Once trained in all aspects of aerial photography, exposure, development, and interpretation, students were sent overseas, where many of them joined the Photographic Section of the American Expeditionary Forces, then under the command of Edward Steichen.

When America entered the war Steichen was in New York City working with Alfred Stieglitz to promote photography as a reputable art form. About the issue of war, however, the two had radically different viewpoints. After hearing Stieglitz say that the sinking of the *Lusitania* "served them right," Steichen decided to "get into the war on the American side." Having always wanted to be a "photographic reporter," he volunteered for service in the Signal Corps

No Room for Worries
Y.M.C.A. - K.C. Hut

U.S.A. SCHOOL
AERIAL PHOTOGRAPHY

ROCHESTER.N.Y.
254

Photographs taken from airplanes flying high over the heavily trenched battlefields of World War I look to the untrained observer like little more than a series of abstract lines and shapes. However, when the aerial picture "has disclosed the information written on its surface," as Edward Steichen, whose Photographic Section of the American Expeditionary Forces was responsible for taking thousands of World War I reconnaissance photographs, including this view, once wrote, "it enters the category of 'instruments of war.'"

and was attached to its aerial reconnaissance unit. Steichen was quick to understand the importance of this new art as a "tactical weapon." As he later wrote: "The success with which aerial photographs can be exploited is measured by the natural and trained ability of those concerned with their study and interpretation. The aerial photograph is itself harmless and valueless. It enters into the category of 'instruments of war' when it has disclosed the information written on the surface of the print."

Late in the war, as equipment and know-how improved, military planners began to rely on this new sort of military information. Once an aerial reconnaissance plane landed, negatives were immediately developed and rushed by messenger to a nearby darkroom, where they were printed. Occasionally film was dropped from the reconnaissance plane by parachute to speed up the process, and army officers often were able to study enemy positions fifteen minutes after exposure. In the last five months of the war, as men from the aerial school began arriving in France, 1,300,000 photographs were taken by American airplanes, some shooting from as high as twenty thousand feet.

The documentary use of photography, as Mees had predicted, proved to be less crucial to the conduct of warfare. Signal Corps still photographers were issued Graflex plate cameras, either the 4 x 5-inch Speed Graphic or the 6½ x 8½-inch Cycle Graphic, but though these cameras were sophisticated machines, they were quite large. Together with filters and tripods, the still photographer's kit was a burden to carry around. In addition, military censors, unsure of what might be revealed, discouraged the distribution and publication of battle-front photographs. The still camera was usually present during most of the great military engagements of World War I, but few saw the grim and terrifying ordeal of trench warfare as captured on film.

The regulations of military censorship also covered amateur snapshooters. In 1910 Kodak had introduced a small folding camera called the "Vest Pocket Kodak." Shortly before the American entry into World War I, an autographic version of this camera was sold along with a small pigskin carrying pouch and was advertised as "The Soldier's Kodak Camera." Soldier-snapshooters were not allowed to take cameras to the front, and consequently most amateur photographs look like typical family snapshots—the difference being that the friends in the pictures are other doughboys and the places depicted are close to the battle lines of World War I.

Perhaps the most important use for snapshot photography at the time was, as Kodak advertised, "the pictures from home." Photos of babies born while their fathers were away, family gatherings, hometown celebrations, all of these were sent overseas to soldiers serving in France. The emotional security of a snapshot in the soldier's wallet was so strong that a little over twenty years later practically the same advertisement of a G.I. looking at a packet of pictures was published during the Second World War. Dress and destination were updated, but ideas and images remained almost identical.

By 1919, for the first time in history, photography had played an active role in the political, social, and military aspects of warfare. Despite the fact that the contributions of photography were sometimes slow to be understood, and its most powerful possibilities often sadly underdeveloped, no future war would be fought without its active participation.
In 1920 the newly elected president of the United States, Warren G. Harding, promised a return to "normalcy." For most that meant an end to the hardships of war and a beginning of that alternately leisurely and fast-paced decade known as the Roaring Twenties. For the Eastman Kodak Company "normalcy" was measured by the general public's tacit, almost offhanded acceptance of celluloid film as a daily part of their lives. In the little over thirty-five years since the invention of the Kodak camera and Kodak roll film, photography in most of its forms had evolved from a magical, somewhat privileged activity into a ubiquitous, everyday occurrence.

For instance, in 1920 alone at least five times as many snapshot cameras were sold as in 1914, the year the war in Europe began. Full-page halftone reproductions of up-to-date, informative, often sensational spot-news photographs accounted for much of the success for new tabloid newspapers such as the *The New York Daily News*. The twenties was also the decade when moving pictures first fully engaged the world's visual imagination. Each week luxurious, ornate picture palaces, decorated in Gothic, Renaissance, Empire, Moorish, or Egyptian styles, played

Though few genuine battle scenes were photographed during World War I, this panoramic shot taken with a Kodak camera of the burnt trees and muddy bomb craters that marked the no-man's-land separating enemy trenches is an effective representation of the conditions soldiers faced during that long, deadly war of attrition.

In the early 1920s nearly six thousand signs were erected by the Kodak advertising department on American highways to tip off motorists that there was a particularly interesting, scenic, or unusual "Picture Ahead."

new films portraying life only as it can be lived on the silver screen. For those reluctant to let the illusion end once they left the movie theater, there were fully illustrated movie magazines that printed behind-the-scenes stories about the stars. In 1910 a letter written to the Biograph film company was answered, "We regret to state that we are not issuing photographs of the artists comprising our stock company." Ten years later fan magazines distributed thousands of studio-produced photos of the most popular film personalities of the day.

The 1920s was also the era of the automobile. The private ownership of motor cars increased from slightly over six million in 1919 to about twenty-three million in 1929. Early in the decade Kodak found a way to associate the pleasures of motoring with the enjoyment of photography. Several teams of Kodak advertising men were sent out to drive along the country's most traveled highways and to choose particularly scenic areas. After the survey was completed six thousand small roadside signs were erected to tip off the traveler that there was a "Picture Ahead." When literal-minded readers complained that they looked in vain for a photograph hidden in the landscape, some of the signs were reworded to promise, "There's Always a Picture Ahead" — though the grammatical difference seems too small to justify the change.

Slightly more chic and stylized versions of full-color posters featuring the "Kodak Girl" were also introduced in the 1920s. In the beginning of the century Kodak Girls, with their long, blue-striped dresses and tidy hairdos, had been a little on the prim and dowdy side. One anonymous writer of the time described the charms of the turn-of-the-century Kodak Girl in couplets so breathless that it is not clear if the praise was serious or satirical:

> When I see her calm and bland   My eyes have snapped her face
> With her Kodak in her hand   In its witchery and grace
> Prepared to take a snapshot,   And have printed it, in color
>   sun or rain,   on my brain.

In any event, during the 1920s the Kodak Girl, who was known as "The Blue Girl" in England and "Dame Kodak" in France, was given clothing and hair styles more in tune with the times. If somewhat calmer in spirit than the typical twenties flapper, the new Kodak Girl was at least not as bland as her immediate predecessors.

Cameras also were fashioned to appeal specifically to the style-conscious women of the twenties. The well-known American industrial designer Walter Dorwin Teague was hired to create camera bodies with a classier and more elegant look. In 1928 Teague created the Series III "Vest Pocket Vanity Kodak," a metal and embossed leather camera that came in five colors: Bluebird, Cockatoo, Jenny Wren, Redbreast, and Sea Gull. Later that year Kodak introduced a Teague-designed camera outfit that included all the accessories necessary to maintain a cosmopolitan look while snapping pictures. Called the "Vanity Kodak ensemble," this chic camera kit contained a color-coordinated camera, lipstick holder, compact, mirror, and change purse.

During the 1920s Kodak first made substantial use of photographs in the newly introduced rotogravure pictorial sections of Sunday newspapers. Kodak full-page advertisements, which often ran on the back page of roto sections, were usually single portraits, actual-size reproductions of snapshots, or photos of the Kodak Girl taking pictures on an outing, at a party, or while motoring. Another type of advertising shot first introduced in 1923 was what is known

The Kodak Girl, described in a poem published in a 1901 Cornell University magazine as the "rose-crowned Lady Dainty of the Ads," had been introduced that year to promote Kodak products. By the twenties, the Kodak Girl, with her blue-striped dress, was depicted with her camera in hand, always ready to record the vibrant, leisurely life of the era on film. This illustration, published in the British magazine Punch *on June 16, 1924, is typical of the color advertising graphics of the time.*

Take a "Kodak" with you

The Cirkut camera, which was manufactured by the Folmer-Schwing Division of the Eastman Kodak Company until a court-ordered divestiture in 1926, could make panoramic pictures of up to 360 degrees. Eugene Goldbeck, a Texas free-lance commercial photographer, bought his first Cirkut in 1912 and for the next half century specialized in panoramic portraits of all sorts.

(Top) On the principle that the more people in a photo the more potential sales of prints, Goldbeck, unlike the photographer standing in the water in the center of this 1925 San Antonio, Texas, baptism, set up his Cirkut camera to capture as much of the crowd as possible. According to Goldbeck, even his competitor bought a picture that day.

as the "corner curl." To make sure customers would remember to tell their local photofinishers to use Velox developing paper, a print was shown with one corner turned up revealing the Velox brand name printed on the back of the paper. Of all advertising techniques employed by Kodak, the corner curl is perhaps the longest lived, still appearing in many contemporary print and film advertisements. (For many years it was used together with the word *Kodak* as the company's logo.)

The era of "normalcy" also marked an end of sorts to the United States government's antitrust suit against the Eastman Kodak Company. In 1915, when U.S. District Court Judge Hazel ruled against Kodak, Eastman wrote to a friend: "Twenty-five years from now, this phase will be looked on with the same derision as our 'free silver' experiment. By that time damn foolishness will no doubt be directed into some other activity."

Though World War I had interrupted the appellate court litigation following this decision, the final 1921 court decree was not as free of the trust-busting impulse as Eastman might have wished. Judge Hazel declared that Kodak must sell its interest in six of the photographic companies it had acquired: the Premo and Graflex camera firms, the Artura paper company, and three dry-plate manufacturers, Seed, Stanley, and Standard. With these disposed of, the company was directed to refrain from purchasing any other photographic concerns. In addition,

the company was ordered to eliminate the exclusive sale of Kodak products at fixed prices by dealers.

While Kodak was stripped of a few of its manufacturing lines, the 1921 consent decree could have been more damaging. The company was allowed to retain its most profitable businesses: Kodak brand cameras and film. The court chipped away some of Kodak's assets, but it left practically undisturbed the company's dominance over the still and motion-picture film markets.

In most ways, both sorts of film had changed very little since the turn of the century. Kodak film was, as the company advertised, Kodak film. Despite differences in negative size, all Kodak orthochromatic snapshot films were uniformly manufactured. The same was true of raw movie stock. After the failure of moviemakers to accept nonflammable acetate film, Kodak had continued, with two major exceptions, to coat its standard emulsion on a nitrocellulose base. In 1924, after a number of disastrous hospital storage-room fires, Kodak introduced acetate-based X-ray film, and within a year or so the manufacture of X-ray stock on a nitrate base was discontinued.

The second product sold only on acetate stock was 16mm home-movie film. By and large, professional movie stock remained a nitrate-based film. If the correct care was taken by professional movie projectionists, nitrate-based film was acceptably safe. For home use,

(Above) Climbing to the roof of the Grand Palais with his Cirkut camera one day in 1927, Goldbeck was able to take a panoramic view of "Paris: The World's Wonder City," stretching from the Eiffel Tower at the far right of the photo to the Grand Palais at the extreme left.

MOVING PICTURES

On the morning of November 12, 1928, the S.S. Vestris, *its cargo shifting in heavy seas, listed to one side and was about to sink. After the order was given to abandon ship, Fred Hansen, a* Vestris *crewman, brought his $8.50 folding Kodak camera on deck and began taking pictures. Upon returning to New York on one of the rescue ships that had arrived to pick up survivors, Hansen was sought out by the picture editor of the* New York Daily News, *and the following day the amateur photojournalist's dramatic shots of the disaster were published.*

however, Eastman absolutely refused to supply anything other than nonflammable "safety" film. In 1912 Edison had written to Eastman asking about the availability of film for use in a household kinetoscope machine he was interested in putting on the market. Eastman answered: "Concerning the cellulose acetate film which we are furnishing you for your Home Kinetoscope, we beg to say that we believe the article to be a perfectly safe one for use in such an apparatus or we would not consent to supply it. In our opinion the furnishing of cellulose nitrate for such a purpose would be wholly indefensible and reprehensible."

As the virtual inventor of popular photography, Eastman was always interested in the potential of the amateur movie market, but he had been shown no safe and workable system of home viewing. In 1914 F. W. Barnes, the manager of the Hawk-Eye Works, had designed an experimental home-movie camera that could be converted into a projector by replacing the back of the camera with a projection lamp house. The camera worked well enough. The film, as usual was the major problem. The Barnes camera used the dangerous 35mm nitrate stock, and, even if that had been acceptable, the cost of processing was prohibitively high. Like all motion-picture projection positives, it was necessary first to develop the camera negative and then print it as a positive on another length of stock. The cost of this two-step process, it was thought, would limit the numbers of those interested in making and projecting home movies.

At the Kodak laboratories John Capstaff decided that this price problem could be partially alleviated if the original camera negative was developed into a projector positive by the reversal process. The reversal method had been described and occasionally used as early as 1862. After a piece of exposed film is conventionally developed into a negative, the unfixed film is bleached in a bath of acid bichromate or acid permanganate. The acid changes the silver into a soluble salt, leaving a positive image of silver halide, which is then washed away. The unexposed silver halide remaining is exposed to full light and developed to form a new silver image. This positive can be projected in the same way as professional movie film.

The obvious advantage of the reversal method over the negative-positive process was that it saved film. Its major disadvantage was of a purely technological nature. If the film was perfectly exposed, enough silver halide crystals would be left unexposed in the emulsion to produce an acceptable positive. However, if the film was overexposed, too few silver halide crystals would be left and the positive would be light and lack contrast. Alternatively, if the film was underexposed, too many grains would be left and the positive would be too dense and dark. Since this film was designed for use by the average amateur it was necessary to relieve the home-movie maker of the responsibility of taking precisely exposed pictures.

As Mees observed, a way had to be found so that "you press the button and we do the rest." Capstaff's solution to this problem was to control or "time" the second exposure. In other words, the reversal of an overexposed negative required careful underexposure to form a positive. In the same way it was necessary to overexpose an underexposed piece of film. Clearly this was a painstaking and delicate task, and when World War I interrupted Capstaff's work no commercially viable method of timing the reexposure had been discovered.

The reversal process had another, perhaps surprising advantage over the usual two-step printing procedure, and this further contributed to the importance of Capstaff's postwar work on the problems of amateur cinematography. Quite early on Capstaff had noticed that reversal pictures were considerably less grainy than those printed by the usual negative-positive procedure. After puzzling over the phenomenon for a while, Capstaff realized that it could be explained by an examination of the grain size in the original negative. Since the largest grains of silver halide in the emulsion are the most sensitive to light, a good deal of the changed silver in the negative will have originally been quite sizable crystals. In the reversal process, these are bleached and washed out. The crystals left for reexposure will thus have been the smallest and consequently will, when projected, produce a much less grainy picture.

After arriving in Athens, Greece, on vacation with Isadora Duncan in 1921, Edward Steichen, who had left his own camera behind, borrowed a Kodak camera from the headwaiter at his hotel, climbed the hill to the Parthenon, and asked the dancer to pose between two columns of the temple's portal. "The idea," Steichen has written, was to capture "her most beautiful gesture, the slow raising of her arms until they seemed to encompass the whole sky."

Believing some of the few remaining technical problems associated with reversal processing about to be solved, Capstaff asked designers in the Hawk-Eye camera factory to build a portable home-movie camera. In the summer of 1920 the first experimental model of the Cine-Kodak camera was delivered, and Capstaff and his associates began developmental work on a marketable home-movie system. Their first requirement was that the film be acetate-based rather than nitrate-based. Eastman was so insistent that only safety film be used that even after acetate-based Cine-Kodak film was introduced a special burn check was instituted to make it impossible for nitrate stock to be processed.

The second guideline laid down for film design was related to the first. It was discovered that to retain picture quality, the image could be no smaller than one-sixth the usual 1 x ¾-inch dimensions of professional motion-picture film. This worked out to 10mm, which after the addition of the 3mm on each side of the picture needed for sprocket holes, produced a 16mm size. The 16mm format thus had two advantages: adequate exposures could be obtained, and it was unlikely that 35mm nitrate film could be slit in half and slipped into a home camera or projector.

The first Cine-Kodak camera was hand cranked, which created a few unsuspected problems. When Kodak sales personnel heard that work on the new home-movie outfit was close to completion a few asked to take the camera home over the weekend to try it out. Since the Cine-Kodak camera was designed so that one turn of the crank would expose eight frames, a double turn was necessary to match the standard sixteen-frames-per-second running speed. Capstaff's assistant Harris Tuttle instructed each of the sales people to "practice cranking the camera and make sure you are turning the crank two turns per second before loading the camera."

One of the first to borrow the camera was a Kodak sales official. After the film was returned for processing the following Monday morning, Capstaff and Tuttle discovered that the negative was so badly overexposed that there was hardly enough silver left for adequate reversal processing. When the film was projected it became obvious what had happened. Suspecting Capstaff was trying to impress the sales department with the amount of film that would be sold if the fast-cranking instructions had been followed, the official had cut the cranking speed in half. When film is run through the camera at less than the usual sixteen-frames-per-second projection speed exactly the opposite effect is produced on the screen. Exposing the film at half speed, for instance, and projecting it at the normal rate, will double the number of images seen, thus doubling the rate of movement in the film. By cranking the camera once rather than twice per second the Kodak salesman had unintentionally produced a movie in which people comically chased each other around in Keystone Cops fashion.

By 1921 Capstaff had enough confidence in the camera, film, and reversal development that several test films were shot to show Eastman the result of his work. A few of the reels were assemblages of the sort of events the average family might want to film: picnics, parades, parties. Another 16mm movie, called *Some Chemical Reactions* was taken of work in the research laboratory. The most impressive, at least to Eastman and Kodak officials, was a home movie entitled *A Child's Birthday Party*, the documentary account of a party given for Charles Gleason, the ten-year-old son of the organist who played at Eastman's receptions. Charles's mother, who was both director and cameraman recalled: "They wanted someone who knew absolutely nothing about movies so they could be sure that anyone at all could load the camera. I was terrified." The actors and actresses playing themselves in this early example of cinema vérité seemed to have few such apprehensions. As Mrs. Gleason described the plot of the film:

It opened with a nurse spreading a tablecloth on the grass and putting on dishes of goodies, jams and marshmallows. Charles and a little friend promptly began feeding each other marshmallows and jam. It was wonderful. The children threw mud at each other and fought magnificently. The

The 16mm Cine-Kodak home-movie camera, introduced in 1923, was the moving-picture equivalent of the snapshot camera. Children's parties, vacations, even home-town parades were recorded for home viewing.

neighborhood dogs and cats joined in the fun. After they were well messed up the nurse took them off for a washing. The shaggy dog and cat tromped all over the tablecloth licking the other children's faces. Someone shooed away the animals and the nurse set the tablecloth again and brought on a cake. There was a scrap among the children and one washed the face of a little girl with a piece of cake. It was a wonderful film. I don't think I ever saw a better one.

The acting, directing, camerawork, and production quality of *A Child's Birthday Party* apparently convinced Eastman that a system for the making and showing of home movies could be successfully marketed. In many ways this idea of amateur cinematography was a direct descendant of the original notion of snapshot photography. The camera was lightweight and easy to operate. All the photographer needed to do was point and press the button. Once a strip of film was exposed, it was sent back to Kodak, where, by the reversal method of film processing, the company did the rest.

When the Cine-Kodak movie camera and the Kodascope projector were introduced in June 1923 the processing was done on twin-reel racks that were rotated in tanks of processing solution. The reexposure time necessary to reverse each strip of negative film to projection positive was hand controlled by the machine operator. Though this system worked well enough, in a few years it was replaced by a continuous-processing machine that ran the film through six-foot vertical glass tubes. As the film progressed through the tubes, the machine operator could visually judge the amount of reexposure necessary. Eventually even this stage in the processing was eliminated by the invention of a photoelectric cell that tested the density of each negative and automatically adjusted the amount of reexposure necessary.

At first the making of home movies was a relatively expensive hobby. A fifty-foot roll of film, enough for a two-minute home movie, cost $3.50. The price of the entire amateur outfit, including camera, projector, tripod, and screen, was $335. For the average consumer, who could for instance, buy a complete Vanity Kodak ensemble for $15, this was a prohibitive price.

Other uses were found for the 16mm movie system. In 1921 Harris Tuttle shot what are apparently the first 16mm medical films on record: accounts of a child suffering from a disorder called Oppenheim's disease, a surgical operation, and the delivery of a baby by caesarean section. In 1922 Sigurd Bo, a Rochester brick manufacturer, asked Tuttle to make an industrial film to record a new method of making fireproof bricks and cement blocks. Later that year, researchers undertaking a time study of workers at Kodak Park wondered if a slow-motion film could be made to ascertain why one worker was able to perform 25 percent more work than another. Tuttle designed a hand crank that allowed the camera to make sixty-four exposures per second. When this film was projected at forty-eight frames per second, the movements of the workers were slow enough that the time-study experts could measure each worker's motions in detail.

The possibility of using 16mm films in the classroom was also studied in the early 1920s. In 1926 a two-year experimental teaching film program was conducted with the cooperation of two professors, Ben Wood of Columbia University and Frank Freeman of the University of Chicago. Ten thousand students in twelve cities were shown films on a range of academic subjects. The results of the investigation proved that films could be used effectively in the classroom, and in 1928 a Kodak subsidiary, Eastman Teaching Films, was incorporated. By the end of the year close to one hundred classroom movies had been produced. In fact, the quality of 16mm film proved to be so good that in the late 1920s Hollywood 35mm films were reprinted onto the smaller stock and, like today's videocassettes, either rented or sold.

On the whole, however, the Cine-Kodak remained a home-movie camera, the motion-picture equivalent of a snapshot camera. Osa Johnson, the wife of documentary and adventure filmmaker Martin Johnson, described George Eastman carrying a 16mm Cine-Kodak camera "everywhere he went" while accompanying the Johnsons on a 1926 photo-safari to Africa.

With a Cine-Kodak home-movie camera, a mother celebrating her child's birthday could become a motion-picture director. The back lawn was her set, the children her feature players, and the usual disordered scenario of children eating and playing party games her plot.

*George Eastman's friends, the filmmakers
Martin and Osa Johnson, specialized in the
documentation of the landscape and wildlife of Africa. Eastman, who backed many
of their expeditions, joined the Johnsons
on a month-long safari in 1926, often photographing animals and events with the recently introduced Cine-Kodak 16mm
movie camera. This scene is from the Johnsons'* 1935 documentary* Baboona.

Eastman and Johnson had first met in 1923, when Johnson had asked Eastman to invest in an earlier expedition. Eastman listened to the proposal and answered:"I have seen some of your interesting pictures, Mr. Johnson, and I have no doubt that as you go along your work will be of increasing importance, but unfortunately I have made it an inviolable rule never to invest in private enterprise. Good morning—and thank you for coming to see me."

Johnson did not give up. Halfway to New York City he got off his train and boarded another back to Rochester. Again Eastman agreed to see him. "I was so anxious to make it clear that you couldn't lose by investing in a motion picture to be made of the animals at Lake Paradise that I guess the whole thing had the sound of a money proposition," Johnson explained.

"Am I to understand," Eastman replied with a smile, "that you're not promising me a super-colossal return on my investment? I must say I like your frankness, Mr. Johnson. I'll invest ten thousand dollars in your idea, and you may use my name freely in securing more."

Three years later Eastman joined the Johnsons and the naturalist and filmmaker Carl Akeley in Africa. During the 1920s, documentary films, especially those that recorded travels to strange and exotic locales, were almost as popular with moviegoers as fictional Hollywood films. Akeley, who had invented and patented a lightweight movie camera, was a trained naturalist, and through his efforts many natural history museums were encouraged to collect and distribute filmed records of wildlife and other such natural phenomena.

One day while on the photographic shoot, Eastman and the Johnsons came upon a rhinocerous grazing in a field. As Osa Johnson told the story: "We had no way of knowing what Mr. Eastman would do under the circumstances and were completely unprepared when he started toward the animal, taking pictures with his little camera as he went."

"Suddenly," Johnson continued, "the big beast decided to resent Mr. Eastman, snorted, lowered his head, and charged. Never have I seen a greater exhibition of coolness than Mr. Eastman now displayed. Instead of turning and running, which anyone else would have done, he stood quietly, still facing the animal, and when, snorting and ferocious, it was within perhaps fifteen feet of him, he simply sidestepped it, like a toreador, and actually touched its side as it passed. All of which Martin caught with his own camera."

During the twenties the most prolific users of motion-picture stock remained the makers and exhibitors of professionally produced feature films. The transformation of the movie business from an arcade amusement into a major national industry was already underway when the Motion Pictures Patents Company was dissolved in 1919. The struggling independent movie producers to whom Kodak began supplying raw stock in 1911 had set up production and distribution conglomerates and were dominating the industry to an extent undreamed of by the members of the Trust. In Hollywood, where many of the independents had gone to escape the Trust's detectives, film companies such as Paramount, United Artists, and Metro-Goldwyn-Mayer had established studios and an organized system of making movies, and each week millions lined up at neighborhood theaters to see the newest Pickford, Chaplin, Fairbanks, Swanson, or Valentino photoplays.

For the Eastman Kodak Company the number of feature-length films being shot on Hollywood sets and the breadth of their distribution translated into millions of feet of raw stock. The negative cost alone of D. W. Griffith's 1916 epic movie *Intolerance* is reported to have been close to four hundred thousand dollars. In its original rough-cut version *Intolerance* was two hundred thousand feet long and ran for eight hours. But even at thirteen thousand five hundred feet, its final length, release prints of the movie required hundreds of thousand of feet of stock.

Increases in the quantity of film manufactured were matched by substantial changes in the quality and variety of motion-picture stock. By 1929, as the age of the silent movie was about to end, Kodak manufactured dozens of kinds of professional motion-picture raw stock. In 1916

there had only been two: an orthochromatic camera film, which could only be used in daylight
or under ultraviolet-rich arc lamps, and a slow-speed positive film.

To capture acceptably lifelike images on orthochromatic stock was one of the movie
cameraman's foremost worries. Since the ortho film emulsion was sensitive only to the blue and
green ends of the visible spectrum, red objects, causing no change in the silver salts, registered
black on the screen. This red blindness caused two problems. The contrast between areas of
exposed blue green light and areas of unexposed red light was exaggerated, a photographic
effect early cinematographers called "soot and whitewash." Even more problematic was the fact
that the predominantly red flesh tone of the faces of actors and actresses often appeared very
dark. Odd-colored makeup was often applied to compensate for the film's insensitivity to red,
and actors and actresses working on silent-film sets sometimes resembled pale, expressionless
ghosts.

When composing scenes, most motion-picture cameramen used a small filter called a "C-49,"
which transmitted only blue light, to which orthochromatic film was sensitive. A panchromatic
film stock had been available to moviemakers on an experimental basis since the mid-teens, but
this new film made no major improvement upon film photography until 1922, when Kodak's
cine-negative panchromatic film was introduced. The dramatic difference between the two
emulsions is perhaps most apparent in the photographic qualities of two of the most well-
known documentary films of the twenties.

In 1920 the explorer Robert Flaherty decided to make a full-length movie that told the story
of the daily life of a Hudson Bay Eskimo and his family. It was not his first try at Arctic

filmmaking. A few years earlier Flaherty had been hired by Sir William Mackenzie to explore the Nastapoka Islands in Hudson Bay. Shortly before the expedition departed, MacKenzie suggested that Flaherty take along one of those "new-fangled" motion-picture cameras. The explorer knew next to nothing about photography, but he bought a movie camera and spent three weeks in Rochester learning the basics of motion-picture filmmaking from Kodak technicians. When he returned to the Arctic later that year, Flaherty shot twenty-five thousand feet of film, which upon his return he edited into a six-thousand-foot exhibition print.

Unfortunately, while further editing the film in a Toronto cutting room, Flaherty lit a cigarette. A spark was dropped on the highly flammable nitrate stock and thirty-five thousand feet of the original negative was destroyed. When in June 1920 the filmmaker returned to the North to shoot another film he was more careful. Negative stock was stored well away from the small stove that heated his hut, and when it was necessary to protect it from the thirty-degrees-below-zero temperatures of the Arctic, Flaherty warmed the film inside his coat.

Despite all these difficulties, the filmmaker's orthochromatic stock was in all other ways well suited to the task of filming in the harsh, almost entirely depthless landscape of Hudson Bay. The high-contrast ortho stock enabled Flaherty to separate visually the snow and hoarfrost background of the Arctic from the darker tones of the film's main characters, Nanook and his Eskimo family. At the same time, the fundamentally monochromatic fabric of life in the Arctic,

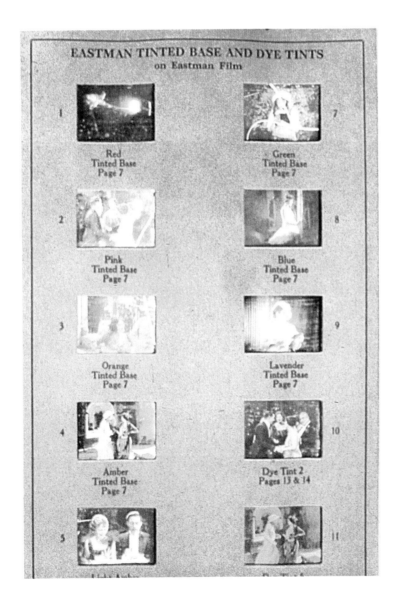

During the early 1920s Kodak's positive release film was available in a variety of colors. Most silent filmmakers used one or another of these colored supports to enhance dramatic moods. Red stock, for instance, was employed in fire scenes to foster fear and excitement, while light amber might enhance the tenderness of a filmed love scene.

Documentary filmmaker Robert Flaherty's first two major movies, the 1922 Nanook of the North, the story of Eskimo life in the Arctic, and the 1926 Moana, a record of Samoan society, were photographed with entirely different film stocks. Nanook was shot on blue-green–sensitive orthochromatic film, which accentuated the harsh, practically colorless landscape of Hudson Bay. When the filmmaker began to photograph in the South Seas, the introduction of panchromatic film had extended the range of movie film to include the red part of the spectrum, thus allowing Flaherty to capture the warm, multihued modeling of light so typical of the tropical climate of Samoa.

what one reviewer called the "regional atmosphere of grim infinitude," seemed to flow seamlessly across the screen.

Nanook of the North was released in 1922 to such critical and commercial success that producer Jesse Laksy commissioned the making of another documentary film. Though Laksy told Flaherty to "bring me back another *Nanook of the North*," the subject matter of the new film, life among the Polynesian people on the South Seas island of Samoa, could not have been more different. The wooded hills and valleys of Samoa were lush, dense with detail, and often brilliantly hued. Flaherty began shooting his film with the standard ortho stock, but when the first reels of footage were printed the images were disappointingly flat.

Luckily the filmmaker had brought along a few cans of the newly introduced Kodak panchromatic stock, and as an experiment he loaded his camera with a roll of the color-sensitive film. Flaherty's wife, Frances, wrote that when this film was screened, "the figures jumped right out of the screen. They had a roundness and modelling and looked alive and, because of the color correction, retained their full beauty of texture." Flaherty had already shot forty thousand feet of film, but he decided to abandon all the ortho footage and reshoot the entire movie.

Flaherty cabled Kodak from Samoa asking for more panchromatic stock, which the company sent, with the warning that the film had not as yet been tested for use in a full-length film. Despite Kodak's caution, Flaherty committed himself to the new film, painstakingly processing it in the total darkness of an island cave. Though the finished film, which was titled *Moana*, the Polynesian word for "sea," was less dramatic than *Nanook* and did poorly at the box office, the beauty of its photography proved crucial to the acceptance of panchromatic film. Within a few years, almost all Hollywood filmmakers and cinematographers acknowledged the ability of pan film to capture accurately shades of color and to reproduce finely the flesh tones of the human face. By late 1928, when Kodak introduced Type II and III cine-negative pan films, hardly any movies were still being shot with orthochromatic stock, and in 1930 its production was discontinued.

During the first decade or so of motion-picture exhibition, the public was so taken with the simple fact that things appeared to move about realistically on the screen that they usually forgave the sometimes poor print quality of the films. By the mid-teens this wide-eyed fascination began to give way to an increasingly demanding visual sophistication. For instance, a 1915 *New York Dramatic Mirror* review of Charlie Chaplin's *The Tramp* praised the structure, characterizations, and tempo of the film with a vocabulary borrowed from theatrical criticism. At the end of his review, the critic added somewhat tentatively, "The photography at times might have been a little clearer, and there were instances where working a little closer to the camera would have brought the comedy of his [Chaplin's] expressions out better."

Both of these comments were, of course, early attempts to work out a critical language adequate to this new genre. Despite film titling and musical accompaniment, silent movies are in essence visual experiences. Even when deprived of words, the superior silent-film actor or actress was able to communicate a remarkable range of emotions. The best still photography had always been able to capture the character of the human face. Motion-picture photography at its finest photographed thoughts. At the same time, it was also quite clear that all the great stars of that day (and of this) possessed a sometimes unaccountably becoming and seductive quality particularly alluring when viewed through a camera lens and captured on film. In a word, they were photogenic.

Gloria Swanson, for instance, was said to have a "camera-proof" face. Despite Swanson's long jaw and slightly bug-eyed look, during the twenties she was the screen symbol of cosmopolitan elegance and refined charm. A similarly inexplicable photographic magnetism turned a former gardener, dishwasher, and taxi dancer named Rodolpho di Valentina into

By the end of the age of the silent film, continuing improvements in camera, duplicating, and print film stocks encouraged actor/directors such as Buster Keaton and Charlie Chaplin to create subtle pictorial effects. Chaplin's peril in this scene from the 1931 film City Lights (above right) is accentuated by the looming play of light. Keaton, on the other hand, faithfully cranking his machine in the Chinatown episode of The Cameraman (above), is depicted as a small hapless figure in a world of uncontrolled kinetic mayhem. Both are films, not staged plays, primarily visual art, emulsion magic.

Rudolph Valentino, one of the silent era's most singularly successful male actors. Though *The New York Times*'s March 1921 review of Valentino's breakthrough movie, *The Four Horsemen of the Apocalypse*, devoted only one line to the star, its description of the entire movie's "kinetic photography" at least hinted at the compelling seductiveness of the film. "His pictures, for example," the reviewer wrote of the film's director, Rex Ingram, "are smooth and soft, and yet as distinct as the sharpest photography could make them; they are effectively lighted; and their dramatic, as well as purely pictorial, value has been as moving and still objects."

311-189

A 93-182

A good deal of the photographic quality of these films, was without doubt the work of the first generation of great motion-picture cinematographers: Billy Bitzer, Karl Freund, Charles Rosher, Karl Struss, William Daniel, and Alvin Wyckoff. As expertly photographed as many of these films were, however, the pictorial quality of release positives still remained a problem. As *The New York Times* reported in a 1921 profile of a motion-picture laboratory, "Most people, and especially those who have had to wait until Monday for the Kodak prints which the corner drugstore promised them on Saturday, know that when the cameraman turns the crank of his machine in the studio he exposes negative films from which positive prints have to be made before any pictures can be seen in a theater, but there are few who have any more than a vague

Left:

First appearing on the screen in early Mack Sennett-slapstick comedies, Gloria Swanson was by the miracle of motion-picture photography transformed into one of Hollywood's most celebrated and regal stars. The movie industry, which before the war had been held in the grip of the Motion Picture Patents Company, became by the mid-1920s a national phenomenon. What had begun for Kodak as a small side business now consumed as much film as any of the other sectors of the photographic community and produced glamorous images, which, as the film historian George Pratt has written, transfixed movie audiences sitting "spellbound in the darkness."

Above:

The first Academy Award for cinematography was presented in 1928 to two veteran cameramen, Charles Rosher and Karl Struss, for their work on Sunrise, a lyrical film directed by F. W. Murnau. Perhaps the least well-known of the world's influential photographers, silent film cinematographers such as Rosher, Struss, Karl Freund, and William Daniels in many ways equaled the famous directors of the period in the authority and magnetism of their work. As Kodak continued its close cooperation with Hollywood through the twenties and thirties, cinematographers waited, as one cameraman has written, "like a bunch of sheep. When Eastman sent out a new batch [of stock]—'This is going to do so and so'—well, all the cameramen wanted to try it and see it."

In 1926 Kodak scientist John Capstaff was sent to Hollywood to make test shots (above and right) using the two-color Kodachrome film movie process he had first developed in 1916. Twentieth Century-Fox was interested in the color process, which it named "Nature Color," and a few films including the 1930 London Revue *were made in two-color Kodachrome, but for what appear to have been budgetary reasons use of the process was abandoned.*

idea of how the thousands of feet of positive film can be obtained from the milky-white negative that comes out of the camera."

During the first two decades of professional filmmaking all of these positives were made by printing the original camera negative on fine-grain stock. So many release prints were churned out each week that original negatives often simply wore out. Consequently, in prewar American cinema, most films were shot with two cameras set up side by side. The first was operated by the chief cinematographer, and its negative was used for printing domestically distributed films. To save the expense of shipping reel after reel of exhibition prints overseas, the assistant cameraman shot a complete second negative.

When the demand for increased number of release prints rose in the early twenties, duplicate negatives were sometimes made from projection positives. This reprinting process noticeably diminished the quality of the new negative. The prints made from this second generation duplicate negative were much grainier and lacked the tonal scale of the original. In 1928 this problem was alleviated when Kodak introduced the first 35mm motion-picture duplicating film. What millions of movie viewers saw on the screen at their local movie house now more closely represented the photographic print quality of the films as they had originally left the movie lab.

As the technological sophistication of film stocks increased, so in turn did the demand of the audiences for lusher and more realistic movies. Lavish productions such as *Why Change Your Wife?*, Cecil B. DeMille's titillating domestic drama, and *Ben Hur*, the director's equally extravagant biblical epic, outdid in pure spectacle anything as yet seen on the screen. Each week people attending these movies sat, as the film historian George Pratt has said, spellbound in darkness. The movie audience could drift off into imagined worlds while at the same time allowing themselves to be convinced that these films contained messages and meanings applicable in the real world outside the darkened theater hall. What these films most noticeably lacked to marry the illusion of picture shows to the verisimilitude of off-screen life was color.

Many motion-picture color processes had been introduced, Kinemacolor, Dufaycolor, Gaumontcolor, for instance, but in the end none of the complicated camera and film procedures was commercially successful. As early as the late nineteenth century individual movie frames had been hand colored, but even with the development of the 1905 Pathé five-stage stenciling process, this method of producing colored films had proved too laborious. A much simpler — though obviously less accurate — way to make color was to dye the entire strip of celluloid. Only one color at a time was viewed on the screen, but tinted stocks were adopted as the best of all alternatives by many silent filmmakers.

Robert Sherwood's 1924 review of the Douglas Fairbanks film, *The Thief of Baghdad*, for example, describes the movie as having "a marvelous fairy-tale quality — a romantic sweep which lifts the audience and vaporizes it into pink, fluffy clouds." It is possible that Sherwood's metaphorical pink clouds actually looked that color on the screen. In 1921 Kodak had begun manufacturing its cine-positive tinted stock in nine colors: lavender, red, green, blue, pink, light amber, yellow, orange, and dark amber. To turn white clouds pink, the noon sky blue, or burning fire red, the filmmaker simply printed that scene on the appropriately colored stock.

For a while in the mid-twenties Kodak seriously considered introducing the Capstaff two-color Kodachrome film as an alternative to the cine-positive colored supports. Capstaff was sent to Hollywood to take test shots of stars. The Fox Film Corporation was sufficiently impressed that it built a processing laboratory and made at least one movie in a version of Kodachrome film called "Nature Color." The Fox project was short-lived, however; after 1930 the attempt to make films in Nature Color was abandoned.

Perhaps the most successful color-film process of the twenties was the two-color cemented-positive system devised by the Technicolor film company. Two thin films specially manufactured for Technicolor by Kodak were exposed in a camera equipped with a beam splitter. This optical device divided the red and green zones of the spectrum and directed each of the beams to separate negatives. These color records were developed to produce positive gelatin-relief images. Using the subtractive method, the films were dyed cyan and magenta, the colors complementary to the original red and green records, and cemented back to back.

In 1923 at the beginning of a thirty-year collaboration with Technicolor, Kodak manufactured its first technicolor film stock, called "Kalmus Positive," after Herbert Kalmus, the founder of Technicolor. Though not widely used during the twenties, individual color scenes were shot in such movies as DeMille's *The Ten Commandments* and Douglas Fairbanks's *The Black Pirate*.

The arrival of the first optical methods of recording sound on film in the late 1920s signaled the end of the era of the silent motion picture. In the early 1920s, while on a trip to Paris, George Eastman had been filmed delivering a "little speech" by the French moviemaker Leon Gaumont. Gaumont's "Chronophone" film system linked a record player to a movie projector to produce synchronized sound. Eastman hated the idea, calling it "fakery." But phony or not, sound motion pictures would soon almost entirely replace the photographically subtle and aesthetically satisfying silent movie.

In 1930 the flamboyant producer-director Howard Hughes made a movie called *Hell's Angels*. The film, which is otherwise notable for its introduction of Jean Harlow to movie audiences, was also in many ways emblematic of all the technological changes taking place in the motion-picture industry. *Hell's Angels* was originally intended to be a silent film, but before its release Hughes decided to take advantage of the new sound technology and reshot the movie. Most of the movie was shot on black-and-white panchromatic stock. Here and there in the film, such as during a night flight episode, Sonochrome, a tinted stock specially prepared so that its dyes would not interfere with the sound track, was used for special effect. There were even a few scenes filmed in a two-color subtractive process.

In 1930 a "talkie" photographed on pan stock with occasional tinted and color sequences was about as technologically advanced a film possible. That cinemagraphic state of affairs would soon change. In less than ten years color could be captured on a single strip of 16mm film. In less than five years, cine-negative panchromatic film would be replaced by Kodak's Supersensitive negative panchromatic film. And two years after the release of *Hell's Angels*, the first full-length, three-color Technicolor film was exhibited.

All of these film stocks, as well as their still equivalents, would, as the Eastman Kodak Company entered its fifth decade, be developed by the Kodak Research Laboratories. In the future, the growth and progress of photography would be directed by the theoretical and developmental works of trained scientists. In a very real sense photography would become a science as well as an art.

In the mid-1920s scenes shot in the Technicolor two-color cemented positive system appeared in a few of the most popular films of the time. Printed on specially produced Kodak dye-imbibition stock, color segments, such as this scene from the 1925 Phantom of the Opera *(above)*, occasionally spotlighted certain episodes in predominantly black-and-white films. Since most of a film's scenes, such as this frame from the 1923 Ten Commandments *(left)*, were monochromatic, the shift to color added emphasis to the select episodes of the film's story.

In 1923 Karl Brown, Billy Bitzer's assistant on many D. W. Griffith movies, filmed director James Cruze's The Covered Wagon, *a monumental western epic, which, according to one critic, "combined qualities of Mathew Brady and Frederic Remington." Westerns were also in some sense travel pictures, photographic tours through the exotic and unfamiliar valleys and mountains of the Far West that in the nineteenth century had been the stock-intrade of photographers such as William Henry Jackson. Late in the 1920s, after the transfer of some Hollywood movies onto 16mm stock,* The Covered Wagon *was one of the most popular films rented from the Kodascope Library.*

One night in the late spring of 1926, as the ship carrying him toward Martin and Osa Johnson's base camp approached Port Sudan on the Red Sea, George Eastman had a dream. It was the sort of dream, at once technological, commercial, and artistic, that could have come only to a man of Eastman's vision and experience. In his sleep Eastman envisioned a new system of color movie photography. Upon waking, he wrote a long detailed letter to Frank Lovejoy, vice-president and general manager of Kodak, in which he outlined the entire process: the scientific principles behind the new color technique, the factory methods needed for its production, and even the advertising campaign that would precede its introduction.

Actually, the technology was not new. The additive lenticular technique of producing color photographs Eastman described had been patented by the French inventor R. Berthon in 1908. The Berthon process is in some ways similar to the screen-line technique of making color transparencies. One important difference between the two is that instead of etching a series of alternating red, green, and blue lines on a glass plate, Berthon covered the camera's lens with a three-banded color filter. Each of the filter's bands allowed only one color of light to enter the lens at that point. That particular color was then refracted by the lens and directed to the film plane.

The second major difference between the lenticular method and most screen-line techniques was that Berthon had designed a unique sort of film. Lenticular film is manufactured by running the stock through steel rollers that corrugate the surface of the film with rows of tiny convex embossments so small they are only visible with a microscope. These minute corrugations (about 550 per inch) are shaped like—and in fact perform—the same function as miniature lenses.

Imagine, for instance, scattered light rays reflecting from a bright apple. As these rays strike the lens, the red filter band only allows the red rays to enter the camera. As this light is directed by the lens to its appropriate place on the film plane, it is bent or refracted by the tiny embossments. Each lenticular lens on the film records the light once again in bands. The original separation of light by the camera filter is thereby reproduced on the film, the band of red light appearing on the film as a small exposed line. The green and blue sections of the spectrum are similarly recorded.

Lenticular movie film is processed by the reversal method. When shown through a projector with filters matching those originally covering the camera lens, the lenticles redirect each band of light through the appropriate filter. On the motion-picture screen, these colors appear as very small lines of color, which when seen from far enough away meld together to produce a color image.

C.E.K. Mees, the Kodak lab director, agreed that the process was sound and Kodak purchased the right to the lenticular additive process from its current owners, the Société Keller-Dorian-Berthon, the ever-busy John Capstaff was assigned to study its commercial feasibility. The major problems of the system were technological. The embossing of the film was tricky. It was also necessary to design workable color filters. And, like all additive methods of projecting color, the filtering and refiltering of light called for by the Berthon process significantly reduced the intensity of projected light. Since lenticular film was also nearly impossible to reprint, it was not likely that these sort of color films would ever be commercially exhibited in large theaters. As a home-movie system, however, it had potential. When shown on a small screen separated by a few feet from the projector, the image quality was not only acceptable, but very good.

On July 28, 1928, two years after Eastman had written Lovejoy, the Kodacolor home-movie system was introduced at a well-advertised party held on the grounds of Eastman's home. Invited to the event were a few of the most celebrated industrial, political, and educational leaders of the day: Thomas Edison, General John J. Pershing, and Adolph Ochs, among others. All were given an opportunity to try out the movie camera: Pershing photographing Eastman,

Eastman taking film of Edison, and so forth. Toward the end of the day, the Kodacolor stock was taken to the Kodak plant, where it was developed and edited. That evening, as the party ended, color film of the afternoon's events was shown in the music room of the house.

As usual, testimonials were solicited from the famous guests. Edison, always interested in mechanics, commented: "It is a very simple process, a simple solution of what was thought to be a complex problem. Years ago I worked on color problems myself and made a complete failure of it." Fairfield Osborn, president of the American Museum of Natural History, considered its use in "bringing nature in colors into the school." Owen Young, chairman of the board of directors of General Electric, was impressed by the "organized research" that had developed Kodacolor film. And Pershing commented, succinctly, "Amazing; wonderful."

The most perceptive and, indeed, most prescient comments about the new color film came from Major General James G. Harboard, president of the Radio Corporation of America. Harboard was interested in the long-range commercial, military, and social effects of the invention:

This is the greatest development in photography since the moving picture itself. It comes at a fortunate time, in view of the present development of sound movies. We have just had action and

On July 28, 1928, home-movie Kodacolor film, which combined bands of lenses embossed in the film with a three-color camera filter to produce color movies, was formally announced at a party held on the grounds of George Eastman's Rochester home. In attendance were some of the most celebrated figures of the day, including, not surprisingly, Thomas Edison, whose work on movie-camera technology was customarily linked with that of George Eastman, the man most responsible for the development of moving-picture film stock.

Kodak's international photography competitions during the late twenties and early thirties drew millions of entries. The winner for best foreign photograph in the 1931 $100,000 contest was Luis García Gurbindo's photo of the running of the bulls in Pamplona, Spain (above). In 1929 Frank Kunishige of Sacramento, California, was awarded a prize for his 3-A Kodak Special shot (opposite). These photographers were serious amateurs, a venturesome and resourceful sector of the nonprofessional photographic community intent upon technical expertise and high-quality images.

sound together. It may have a good deal of influence upon the development of television. If we have television with color photography, it will make as much difference over ordinary television as the difference between color photography and ordinary black-and-white pictures. This should be its greatest affiliation with radio. It also might have considerable military importance, as it should make possible much more accurate pictures in colors than in mere black and white—especially in airplane pictures, and in showing up camouflaged objects.

In 1928, of course, none of these advanced technologies were available. Moving pictures viewed on television, whether in black and white or color, had as yet not challenged those seen on the motion-picture screen. Aerial photos in color were highly unusual. Motion pictures that combined sound and color were a relative rarity. And, certainly, the replacement of black-and-white snapshots by full color photographic prints was as many years away.

In fact, of all the new media Harboard mentioned, only radio played an active role in Kodak's present business. In 1928 Kodak sponsored a half-hour radio show, the chief purpose of which was to remind listeners of the pleasures of weekend photography. The program, which despite its length was called "The Kodak Hour," had as its usual guest speaker the radio personality Angelo Patri. Between presentations of recorded music, Patri slipped in celebrations of snapshot photography, and other members of the cast, "The Front Porch Gang," as they were called, described photography's uses in family situations.

In 1930 this first show was followed by two others: "The Kodak Mid-Week Hour," which aired on Thursday evenings, and "The Kodak Weekend Hour," which ran on Friday nights. Two of the segments of the midweek show, Edgar Guest's reading of a poem and a narrative description of a famous family's snapshot album, were again intended to extol the emotional satisfactions of home photography. An article in *The Kodak Salesman*, an in-house magazine published to keep the company's salesmen abreast of products and promotions, articulated this idea clearly, if often with more than a touch of overstatement:

Analysts of advertising know that Kodak advertising copy rests on the deeply embedded emotional structure that underlay human behavior in primordial days, as now. Whether his medium is The Saturday Evening Post *or* The Tanktown Local, *the fellow who writes a Kodak ad has an advantage. In offering a device with which people can record kin, possessions and pastimes, he deals with joys, yearnings and vanities that for centuries have been the instinct of the race.*

Accordingly, many of the most popular Kodak cameras of the twenties and thirties were designed to appeal to the extended family. Brownie cameras came in six bright, attractive colors. The Boy Scout Kodak and the Camp Fire Girls' Kodak cameras were each manufactured with scout logos imprinted on the body of the camera. A Gift Kodak camera was offered complete with a cedarwood presentation box. A snazzy Walter Dorwin Teague–designed box camera with a geometric art deco pattern on its face was called the Beau Brownie. And in the middle of the decade the popular molded-plastic Baby Brownie was introduced. Like the pioneering 1900 Brownie camera, the Baby Brownie cost only one dollar.

During the early 1930s the spool size of a few Kodak films was reduced. This decrease in bulk made possible the manufacture of a number of small lightweight cameras, such as the Six-20 series. In addition, advances in photographic emulsions contributed to a reduction in the size of a negative needed to produce acceptable pictures. These increases in film sensitivity had an equally important effect upon that other genre of popular photography: amateur cinematography.

The film used for 16mm home movies, especially for Kodacolor films, remained expensive. In 1928 a Kodak executive suggested that a double set of exposures could be made on a single strip of film if pairs of half-width frames were first run forward, exposing one side, and then again backward through the camera, exposing the other. In 1932 an 8mm camera and projector was manufactured that made use of this trick. By then, emulsions were sensitive enough that once both sets of small frames were exposed, the film could be developed by reversal. After processing, the strip was slit down the center and two of its ends cemented together. By reducing the need for film by half, the 8mm camera significantly expanded the use of snapshot cinematography.

In 1930, to commemorate the fiftieth anniversary of Eastman's entry into the photographic supply business, a gold-colored Anniversary Kodak camera was designed. The camera was to be given free of charge to any boy or girl who celebrated a twelfth birthday that year. Over half a million were produced by the May 1, 1930, giveaway date, and within two or three days the entire shipment was gone.

In 1930 Eastman turned seventy-six. Fifteen years earlier he had written to a friend: "Between you and me, this is the most varied and interesting business in the world. It embraces, at one time or another, almost every problem that comes up in science, art and industry." As the busy postwar years passed, though, some of Eastman's oldest and closest friends and partners had died: Henry Strong in 1919, Thacher Clarke in 1921. In 1931 Edison, with whom Eastman's name had inevitably become linked, would also die.

There had also been a changing of the guard in the commercial world of European photography. In 1927 Eastman and his longtime customer and sometime competitor Charles Pathé decided to merge their respective manufacturing companies in France. Pathé continued to produce and market movies, but the cine, still, X-ray production, and distribution facilities of both companies were combined, and a new firm called the Société Kodak-Pathé was formed. In 1929 Pathé, who had been made managing director of the combined company, left the business entirely and retired to the Riviera.

For many years Eastman had been a very wealthy man, but as he had said in a rare interview, published in *Hearst International* magazine in 1923, "If a man has wealth, he has to make a choice, because there is the money heaping up. He can keep it together in a bunch and then leave it for others to administer after he is dead. Or, he can get it into action and have fun, while he is still alive. I prefer getting it into action and adapting it to human needs, and making the plan work."

Making money work was exactly what he had quietly been doing since at least 1912, when, under the pseudonym "Mr. Smith," Eastman had contributed a million and a half dollars' worth of Kodak stock to the Massachusetts Institute of Technology. For a few years, there was wide speculation about the real identity of Mr. Smith, particularly in the small community of those rich enough to donate such a sizable gift. Two New York philanthropists suspected each other of being the donor, and the wife of one millionaire privately told friends that her husband was indeed *the* Mr. Smith. After years of this sort of talk, Eastman tired of the issue and gave Dr. Richard Maclaurin, the president of MIT, permission to make his name public, adding, "I have saved myself annoyance somewhat at your expense heretofore, and it will no doubt be a relief to you to get the matter off your mind."

Eastman had, in fact, given away so much Kodak stock that in 1923, after rumors had circulated around the company that the gifts signaled his retirement, a letter was sent to all employees listing his donations. Writing that his "major interest in life is to guard the continued success of the Kodak Company and the welfare of its people," he went on to explain that by contributing to educational institutions he had insured that a great deal of Kodak stock would remain undisturbed after his death. The accounting of donations listed seven large gifts:

MIT	*$4,500,000*
University of Rochester	
School of Music	*$3,000,000*
College of Arts and Science	*$2,500,000*
Medical School	*$1,500,000*
College for Women	*$1,500,000*
Hampton Institute	*$1,000,000*
Tuskegee Institute	*$1,000,000*

Parents! Children! *This Camera* FREE
to any child born in the year 1918!
(Any Child whose 12ᵗʰ Birthday falls in 1930)

Go to a Kodak Dealer and accept one…complete
with Roll of Kodak Film FREE! *Pay nothing, buy nothing*

A Gift of 500,000 Cameras
to the Children of America
In Commemoration of the 50ᵗʰ Anniversary of Kodak

On May 1, 1930, to commemorate the fiftieth anniversary of the Eastman Kodak Company, specially designed Brownie cameras were given free of charge to any child who celebrated his or her twelfth birthday that year. Five hundred thousand cameras were manufactured, and within two or three days all were gone from dealers' shelves.

THE SCIENCE OF
PHOTOGRAPHY

Period cameras can be as instructive as any historical artifact. The Six-20 Brownie held in this advertisement, with its circle K logo and vertical enamel and stainless-steel strips, was manufactured, as the inscription above the lens states, in the United Kingdom by Kodak Limited. This information in the photograph, along with the fact that the camera was marketed from 1934 to 1941, enables social historians to identify and make a few deductions about the period. The style advertised, open, sunny, and confident, is perhaps typical of that in vogue in 1930s Britain.

Eastman had also invested millions in the building and staffing of dental clinics. The first of these facilities opened in Rochester in 1917, and in 1919 alone over forty-eight thousand parents and children had been treated, forty-two thousand of whom had only been able to afford the five-cent-per-visit minimum fee. Eastman was so pleased with the success of the venture that other dental dispensaries were planned, the largest of which, the London Clinic, was opened in April 1929.

At the same time, Eastman's interest in the welfare of children, educational institutions, and other charities was matched by his concern about the continued prosperity of those employed by the Eastman Kodak Company. The bonus given to all workers in 1899 was, in 1912, formally instituted as the wage-dividend plan. As Eastman explained, this unusual profit-sharing plan was meant to insure that "employees engaged in an industry that is paying extraordinary dividends to its share holders are entitled to some recognition outside their fixed wage."

At the time, 10 percent per annum was the normal dividend expected on shares. As Eastman saw it, if dividends went above this percentage the employees should benefit. It was decided that each year the employees' wage dividend should equal 35 percent of any stock dividend over this 10 percent. These payments would be based on the salary earned by each worker during the previous five years of employment. To illustrate how this worked, Eastman's statement explained that the previous year "the extra dividends to holders of common stock have amounted to 30 percent. Thirty-five percent of 30 percent equals 10½ percent, which divided by five equals 2.1 percent of each of the five years' wages." On July 1, 1912, the first year that the plan went into effect, a total of $282,249.39 was divided among the 5,179 worldwide employees of the Eastman Kodak Company.

For many years Eastman had also been interested in music and musical education. Concerts regularly were given in the ballroom of the house he had built on East Avenue a couple of miles away from his Rochester State Street offices. Music, he thought, would provide the leisure most

During their mid-1930s crime spree, two unlikely outlaws, Clyde Barrow and Bonnie Parker, posed along a roadside for a few snapshots. Some of these cheeky pictures, all bluff and jaunty brigandry, wound up in the possession of photography collectors and were used by director Arthur Penn when stylizing the gestures of the actors Warren Beatty and Faye Dunaway in the 1967 film Bonnie and Clyde.

needed to escape, at least momentarily, the "drudgery" and "sheer work, unpleasant, but inescapable" necessitated by "the irksome and wearing nature of industrial employment."

"Do not imagine that I am a reformer—far from that," Eastman said of the relaxation provided by music. "It is simply," he continued, that "I am interested in music personally, and I am led thereby, merely to want to share my pleasure with others." In addition to sponsoring the creation of the Rochester Symphony Orchestra, Eastman was also the principal backer of the University of Rochester's Eastman School of Music. Of the music school, Eastman wrote to a friend, "It has given me more fun in my old age than anything I have ever tackled. When you come to think of it, it's a joke that one who is totally devoid of musical ability is trying to steer one of the largest musical enterprises ever proposed."

Throughout all these projects Eastman remained intimately involved in what he called "the general policy and development of the future" of his company. He no longer burdened himself with specific business or manufacturing problems. In 1923 he had turned over the day-to-day management to two longtime employees, William Stuber and Frank Lovejoy, and joked that he was thinking of taking two six-month vacations a year.

In most ways, Eastman was of that rare breed of public men who devote their lives to singular achievement in a specific area of public life. He had never married. His closest friends were either old business associates or Rochester neighbors who had known him since childhood. To these people he was a warm and generous friend. Osa Johnson once wrote that though she always addressed him as Mr. Eastman, he was extremely "kind, sensitive, resourceful and versatile." While in camp on the African plains, cooking was his favorite hobby. Once when Eastman was baking a bitter-plum pie, Johnson slipped and called him Pop. Eastman grinned and teased her into explaining that she had meant Top...Old Top.

When Eastman left camp at the conclusion of his 1926 African trip, Johnson saw him off at the train station. "Back to the world of fraud and front," Eastman joked. "At any rate, wherever I happen to be, it's going to be nice to think of you two—your fine work together—your fine lives together."

To most people, Eastman remained the man who by creating the Eastman Kodak Company had radically altered the course of photography. On the occasion of his seventy-fifth birthday, an editorial in *The New York Times* reviewed Eastman's achievement:

If everyone who has got pleasure from a snapshot or a movie film were to express gratitude to the man who initially made it possible, George Eastman would be the most bethanked man in the world on the seventy-fifth anniversary of his birth. The films that his factories produce each year would, it is estimated, reach ten times around the globe, and there is not a corner of the earth which has not been exposed to them, or to which they have not carried fleeting or treasured images. There would be special supplementary thanks, what the Scotch call a "bethankit" that after his three score and ten he has found a way of filling even the shadow world with colors such as objects have in God's world of nature.

But as congratulations and awards mounted up, Eastman's energy waned. "I shall probably go down to the office oftener," he said early in 1931, "but I do not expect to do any work there again." Arteriosclerosis and the minor ailments of old age slowed him down even more. A vacation trip to his hunting camp in North Carolina was planned for the summer of 1932, but during the late winter of 1931 and 1932 Eastman seldom left his house.

On March 14 a group of old company friends arrived to witness a codicil to his will assigning most of his remaining money to the University of Rochester. Eastman seemed in a good mood, joking that each of the witnesses would receive a twenty-dollar gold piece. He then went upstairs.

Eastman's longtime secretary Alice Whitney Hutchison stayed behind to collect a few papers. As she was about to return to the office, she heard the sound of a gunshot. Eastman had ended his life. The note left read, "My work is done. Why wait?"

When George Eastman entered the field of photographic research, experimentation was a craft. Fifty years later it was a science. The "Edison shotgun method," as one Kodak researcher called the old trial-and-error method of research, had been for the most part replaced by a meticulous and measured study of the scientific laws governing the behavior of light-sensitive chemicals.

The older methodology had no doubt achieved remarkable results. In the 1880s, for instance, Eastman chemist Henry Reichenbach, by virtue of instinct, education, and experience, had come up with a formula for the preparation of transparent celluloid stock. It worked, though Reichenbach would have been hard-pressed to explain why. And even Eastman himself, mixing compounds over his mother's kitchen sink, had created the best dry-plate emulsion of the era. But those days were over.

George Eastman's vacations from work generally took the form of long camping trips. Though internationally renowned as a businessman and an inventor, Eastman was to his friends a relaxed and gracious companion, his most memorable contribution to the success of these expeditions being his generally acknowledged skill as camp cook.

In 1922, to commemorate the tenth anniversary of the founding of the Kodak Research Laboratories, scientists working with John Capstaff on the development of amateur cinematography made a short satirical film called *Out of the Fog*. The movie, which recounted in very broad strokes the story of the so-called 1912 invasion of Rochester by British scientists, was intended as a surprise anniversary present for the laboratory's director and founder, C. E. K. Mees. In fact, Harris Tuttle, who was principal director, cinematographer, and processor of the film, came very close to being fired after Mees noticed him rushing to hide the unedited stock each time the director entered the room.

Most of the lab's accomplishments to date were caricatured in the film. Loyd Jones, for instance, who had worked on camouflage techniques during World War I, dressed in a sailor suit and was filmed taking visibility readings of a toy warship floating in a dishpan. But it was Mees who was the movie's principal protagonist. Camera equipment was taken to a beach on Lake Ontario just a few miles north of the city to shoot a sequence spoofing Mees's first landing upon the shores of America. As the rowboat bearing a Mees lookalike came into view, out of the fog, the future laboratory director could be seen standing erect in the bow of the boat. On the shore his fellow scientists held signs welcoming him to "Darkest America."

In detail, disposition, and, clearly, in sense of play, this home movie accurately summed up the working life of the first industrial laboratory created especially for the scientific study of the photographic process. In 1912, when the lab was established, the idea of industrial research was relatively new. Earlier in the century, Charles Steinmetz had convinced General Electric that it was in the interest of the company to create and staff a laboratory to study "commercial applications of new principles," and within a few years other companies, including Western Electric, Du Pont, Goodrich, Parke-Davis, E.R. Squibb, and Kodak had followed suit.

Shortly after arriving in Rochester, Mees had gone to General Electric headquarters in Schenectady, New York, to ask advice of Willis Whitney, the director of the G. E. laboratory. But besides cautioning Mees to "leave the men to run the laboratory and just see that nobody interferes with them," Whitney had few concrete suggestions about how industrial laboratories ought to be formally organized. Most of the work at the G.E. lab was proceeding pretty much on an ad hoc basis. Whitney told Mees that he had asked some of his scientists to read technical journals and had also tried to set up a weekly colloquium to discuss new research, but he had only been partially successful in institutionalizing these discussions. It seemed to Mees that formalizing the free flow of ideas between scientists was crucial to the intellectual life of a laboratory. One of the first decisions he made as director was to schedule a weekly multidisciplinary roundtable discussion at which all could hear about work being conducted in labs down the hall from their own. At first these meetings were not difficult to run. When the Kodak research laboratory opened in 1913, it employed only about twenty scientists, and it was relatively easy to call the entire staff together for one of these brainstorming sessions. But as the number of research personnel grew from forty in the lab's third year of operation to eighty-eight in its seventh, and as the lab's budget rose from about fifty-thousand dollars in 1913 to almost three hundred and fifty thousand in 1920, Mees saw the need for a more organized system.

Mees's 1913 scratch-pad diagram outlining the division of responsibilities had split the laboratories into three departments: physics, chemistry, and practical photography. In time, this initial assignment of responsibilities evolved into a centrifugal configuration of assignments intended to draw the work of each department toward a central goal. Mees called this sort of structure "convergent." Arrayed around the edges of this wheel-like organizational chart were the three original departments, each now further subdivided. The chemistry department, for instance, included colloid, physical, organic, and photochemical divisions. Lines from each of these departments led inward to photographic theory, the experimental basis of research, and then to the hub of the innermost circle: practical photography.

Mees imagined the entire laboratory arrayed not as an army but as an orchestra. "It is not the duty of the laboratory head to command his scientific staff," he said. "It is his duty to lead it." When he and Eastman had first discussed his job, Mees was pleased to be allowed to report directly to the head of the company. Information filtered through a series of other corporate officials, Mees argued, would not arrive at the president's office in its original form — if it arrived at all. The inevitable checking and cross-checking of ideas as they wound their way through the chain of command would stifle the genuine creativity that was at the core of scientific research. As Mees said in a speech to the National Research Council:

The real problem in directing research is what research shall you do and when shall you stop doing it. The decision is usually in the hands of some very important body. Now, in my opinion, the best person to decide what research work shall be done is the man who is doing the research, and the next best person is the head of the department, who knows all about the subject and the work; and after that you leave the field of the best people and start on an increasingly worse group, the first of these being the research director, who is probably wrong more than half the time; and then a committee, which is wrong most of the time; and, finally, a committee of vice-presidents of the company, which is wrong all the time.

From his own experience Mees knew that productive research was most often a slow, cumulative process, but he also recognized that sometimes "the wilder the scheme, the better it works." "People don't make discoveries; they stumble on them," he added. Once, in the early days of the laboratory, even Eastman, whose instincts about the necessity of unfettered thinking Mees had always trusted, wondered about the day-to-day effectiveness of the lab. Eastman began reading aloud from a sheet of paper listing experimental projects that had led nowhere and asked Mees to justify the failures. Mees told Eastman that he was looking at the wrong list.

In 1922, as a surprise gift to Kodak Research Laboratories director C.E.K. Mees, a satirical film entitled Out of the Fog, *which chronicled the early days of the lab, was produced using the newly developed 16mm Cine-Kodak home-movie system developed by Kodak scientist John Capstaff. Mees had envisioned the laboratory facility as a modern version of the research institute described by the English Renaissance philosopher Francis Bacon as a "House of Solomon," manned, in Mees's words, by "a great company of fellows . . . in the pursuit of knowledge." Here a research scientist appearing in the film, which concluded with Mees ceremoniously accepting the keys to the laboratory, takes on-the-set stills with a Kodak folding camera.*

We make many mistakes, the director told the president, and we know why they're no good. Maybe, Eastman responded, a discussion of present failures will prevent a repetition of future failures. No, Mees replied, we won't make the same mistakes; we'll make new ones, and these will lead to our successes. The profits on these successes, he concluded, will in the end more than outweigh the cost of all our failures.

For anything important to come of their work, industrial scientists must on all accounts be left free to follow the paths of pure research. At the same time, as Mees argued in detail in his now classic 1920 book *The Organization of Industrial Scientific Research*, the mission of an institution such as the Kodak Research Laboratories is "to supply the technical information on which an industry is operated." In 1912 Mees had told Eastman it would take the lab about ten years to come up with its first profitable product. Though no one in the lab felt pressured to make a delivery on that date, in 1922 a demonstration of Capstaff's home-movie system was shown to Eastman just as this ten-year period was about to end.

Discoveries of a more theoretical nature took slightly longer; but during the second and third decades of the lab's existence these too followed. Mees had begun his photographic career as a university research scientist. One of the in-house jokes of the movie *Out of the Fog* was that when the Mees character was handed the keys to the research lab he was carrying a battered suitcase labeled "H&D curves." Computed by two scientists working in England in the 1880s, Ferdinand Hurter and V. C. Driffield, the Hurter and Driffield curves were the first significant, and in some ways most important, practical representation of the relation between exposure and image density.

In the late nineteenth century, when Hurter and Driffield had become interested in the science of photography, there was no acceptable way to measure quantitatively the sensitivity of photographic emulsions. Photographers judged the amount of exposure necessary for any particular picture by experience. In order to compare the sensitivity of two brands of plates they simply guessed; one emulsion seemed to need a little less exposure time or a little less light intensity than another. Hurter and Driffield thought that a scientific law must be found to quantify accurately each of these factors.

The two scientists decided to calculate the amount of silver built up after the development of a photographic negative as a function of its exposure to light. Since it was difficult to measure the very small silver differences between one negative and another, they projected light through the negative and gauged silver buildup in terms of relative opacity; the more silver, the more opaque and vice versa. The amount of exposure they calculated as the product of time (the length of exposure) and intensity (the strength of the light). With these variables in hand, Hurter and Driffield conducted a number of experiments in which they discovered that density of a negative increases arithmetically as its exposure to light increases geometrically. In other words, each increase of one unit of density is caused by a logarithmic increase in exposure.

After plotting these changes in density and exposure on a graph, Hurter and Driffield discovered that an odd curve was formed. At low levels of exposure very little density was created. This section of the curve they called its "toe." At a certain point on the exposure scale, however, density increased dramatically and efficiently. This straight uniform line was the graph's slope. Hurter and Driffield also discovered that at some point, in spite of the increase in exposure, the rate of density increase began to drop off. This section of the graph was described as its "shoulder."

The two scientists named this S-shaped graph the "characteristic curve." For each emulsion then, a certain measurable amount of exposure caused the most visible changes in the light-sensitive material. Below this measure of exposure increase the negative was underexposed and above that level it was overexposed.

Clearly, the most important section of the curve was the straight slope. It was on this line that the contrast between densities was most important. In fact, the steeper the slope the greater the contrast. An emulsion that produced large differences in density with small increases in exposure was described as a high-contrast emulsion. Conversely, if the emulsion reacted slowly it was judged as being of the low-contrast type. In theory, by using this diagram a photographer could take a perfectly exposed negative by either adjusting the intensity of light by means of aperture changes or varying the time of exposure with shifts in shutter speed.

When Hurter and Driffield published the results of this research in the *Journal of the Society of Chemical Industry* in 1890, they announced, "The production of a perfect picture by means of photography is an art; the production of a technically perfect negative is a science." Unfortunately the difference between the "perfect negative" and a "perfect picture" was not easily measured.

In the early 1920s, as theoretical research into such issues resumed after the First World War, Loyd Jones of the Kodak laboratories began to study the relationship between negative quality and tone reproduction. It was immediately clear to Jones that there was no simple one-to-one correspondence between the density of a negative, what he called its "objective" value, and the "subjective" or pictorial value of a photographic print. A scientific method must be found, Jones thought, to compare the objective and subjective. After showing prints to a number of observers and asking them to rate each picture, Jones plotted this information on a graph containing the characteristic curve of the negative and concluded that for most viewers perfect contrast is only vitally important in the middle-tone regions. Above and below those areas a perfectly exposed negative had little effect on the subjective appreciation of print quality.

As these and similar studies continued, other scientists at the laboratory were examining in detail each constituent part of a piece of photographic film: the cellulose support, the silver halide, and the gelatin in which that photosensitive chemical was suspended. The first of these, the transparent cellulose support, had been under continual study since it was first introduced in 1889. After the prewar commercial failure of nonflammable cellulose acetate professional movie stock, members of the organic chemistry division of the laboratory were assigned to study the reactions that took place when cellulose was combined with acetic anhydride. Cellulose-acetate film used large quantities of acetic acid and acetone, both of which were produced from the distillation of wood. In 1920 Kodak purchased a methanol factory in Kingsport, Tennessee, hoping to reduce the price of acetate film. Though the production of an adequate and inexpensive acetate-based film for still and motion-picture film proved elusive, as a result of this early work, Tennessee Eastman began manufacturing a number of related acetate-based chemicals and fibers in addition to photographic celluloid.

Research into gelatin silver-halide emulsions contributed even more significantly to the understanding of the photographic process. It had long been known that there were "good" and "bad" gelatins. In the winter of 1882 George Eastman's batch of "bad" gelatin had come close to ruining the company. At the time, photographic researchers knew that something in the gelatin could sensitize or, as it had in Eastman's case, desensitize the silver halide. But they did not know what caused the change in sensitivity.

In the early twenties, a group of scientists headed by Samuel Sheppard began testing various gelatins. Sheppard, who had been Mees's closest associate since their school days at Saint Dunstan's, was a brilliant but sometimes demanding man to work with. One day, when the owner of a bar and grill across the street from Sheppard's office turned his radio up full blast, Sheppard went over and politely asked the man to lower the volume. The bar owner refused. Sheppard solved the problem with the skill and ingenuity of a working scientist. He went back to the laboratory and rigged up a static generator that jammed the radio's incoming signal.

Overleaf:
As early as 1935, when U.S. Army captains Orvil A. Anderson and Albert A. Stevens took aerial shots from a balloon hovering thirteen miles above South Dakota, the Kodak Research Laboratories cooperated with those interested in high-altitude aerial photography. The Anderson-Stevens photo from the balloon of the earth's horizon (top left) was in 1935 the highest vertical photograph ever made and encompassed the largest area ever seen through a single lens. The aerial photo (center left), taken on the same day, shows approximately 105 square miles of south-central South Dakota. The geometrically shaped cultivated fields at the left contrast dramatically with the grasslands and the erosion lines branching off the White River in the lower part of the photo.

In August 1938 Bradford Washburn, at the invitation of Kodak scientist Walter Clark, took this photo (bottom left) of the Sheridan Glacier near Cordova, Alaska, from a height of 3,000 feet, using the newly developed high-resolution Kodak SS Pan Aero film. Several years later, in June 1942, Washburn used haze-cutting Kodak infrared film to record from 15,000 feet Alaska's Mt. McKinley during a storm.

Similar persistence and creativity were applied to the study of gelatin. Since photographic gelatin is made from clippings of calf hide, it inevitably contains organic impurities, many of which are clearly the result of the cow's diet. Separating and identifying each of these impurities was a tedious task. However, in November 1923, after long hours of laboratory work, Sheppard wrote to Mees: "We have the animal, apparently to a certainty, genus and species, but in a sense it is like having a bear by the tail. The solution of the mystery is remarkable ... we have, pour ainsi dire, discovered the philosopher's stone of emulsions."

The question, Sheppard continued, was whether this discovery should be published, patented, or kept secret. When Mees had accepted the position of research director he had convinced Eastman that results in the field of pure research should be published for the benefit of the entire scientific community. Eastman agreed, with the added proviso that such publications not hurt the business of the company. The gelatin discovery clearly fell into this gray area. "I feel sure," Sheppard's letter continued, "that if we hide it under a bushel, that said bushel will be removed by others before long. Because there is a certain ripening of events, and, like fruit, if one does not pluck them at their time, another will, or they will fall of themselves."

After consultation with Eastman, Mees decided that the results of the research on photographic gelatin were so significant that a patent should be obtained. Two years later, after more study, an application was submitted describing the discovery. Sheppard and his assistant J. H. Hudson had extracted an organic sulfur-bearing substance from "good" gelatin that caused an immediate increase in the light sensitivity of the silver halide. This compound was identified as an allyl mustard oil, which reacted with the surface of the silver halide particles to form "small, mostly ultra-microscopic nuclei, such as silver sulfide." The bear that Shepard had by the tail was, in fact, not the calf itself, but what it liked to eat. Recounting this important and startling discovery, Mees told a lecture audience, "Twenty years ago we found out that if cows didn't like mustard there wouldn't be any movies at all."

The discovery of the existence of small sensitizing bits of silver sulfide led Sheppard to speculate further about the relationship between the light-sensitive properties of silver-halide images and the mysterious and as yet unexplained formation of invisible latent images in a silver-halide emulsion. In 1917 M. B. Hodgson, an employee of the Kodak laboratories, had watched silver develop on a microscope slide. It seemed clear to Hodgson that the change from silver halide to pure silver had started from spots on the surface of each crystal.

Sheppard surmised that these spots could possibly be places where the silver sulfide from the gelatin had attached itself to the surface of the crystals. This formulation was called the "concentration speck theory." The sulfide concentration specks thus act as catalytic centers from which the reduced silver grows like strands during development.

Two British physicists, R. W. Gurney and N. F. Mott, using the laws of subatomic quantum mechanics, added to the concentration speck theory by speculating that these centers collected electrons knocked from bromine atoms contained in the silver bromide compound. After much research at the Kodak labs, T. H. James further argued that these developmental centers were in a sense self-propagating, that they were autocatalytic, the deformed silver ions at the sensitivity centers serving as links between the reducing agents of the developer and the speck.

While these subatomic studies of latent-image development were underway, other Kodak scientists were working on optical methods of sensitizing the silver halide. In 1873 the German chemist H. W. Vogel had discovered that certain organic dyes would extend the range of the emulsion to include the green and yellow zones of the visible spectrum. This made possible the so-called orthochromatic film stock. (Actually orthochromatic, which means "proper colors," does not accurately describe these emulsions. They are relatively insensitive to red and therefore not entirely color corrected.)

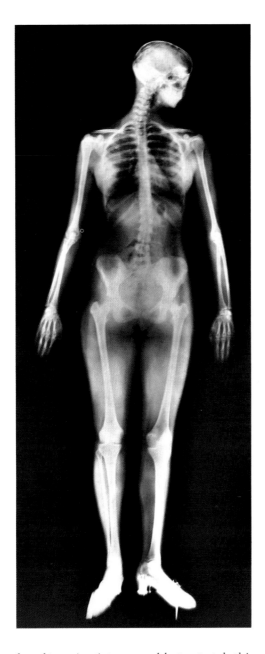

"Beauty's Bones" was the caption under the world's first X-ray snapshot of the entire human body, published in a 1934 edition of Kodak's Applied Photography. *Kodak had manufactured X-ray supplies since 1896, some as small and compact as the cardboard-lined packets designed for dental work. This radiographic photo was taken on a 72x32-inch sheet of specially prepared X-ray film.*

Overleaf:
In 1934 the two Leos, Leopold Mannes and Leopold Godowsky, fearing that their three-year contract with Kodak would expire before they had finished their work, showed Kodak Research Laboratories director C.E.K. Mees a two-color film stock processed by the controlled diffusion of developing chemicals. The quality of the color reproduced seemed to Kodak satisfactory enough for plans to be made for its commercial introduction. But the preparations were suspended later in the year when the two researchers developed a much superior three-color version of the process.

After Vogel's breakthrough, other scientists were able to stretch this sensitivity as far as the red zones, and by the turn of the century there were a number of panchromatic emulsions that were sensitive to the entire visible spectrum. All of these dyes were complex organic compounds, and though Kodak was able as early as 1913 to produce an experimental panchromatic movie film, it had not at the time begun fundamental research into dye sensitization.

In 1928 two British chemists, Frances Hamer and Olaf Bloch, had published a series of papers describing the very efficient sensitizing capabilities of fifteen cyanine dyes. Mees immediately assigned Leslie Brooker, a young organic chemist, to begin experimenting with these and other sensitizing dyes. In 1930 Hamer also joined the company to continue experimental studies in the field. As work progressed, Mees, who followed this research closely, discovered that combinations of certain of Brooker's dyes sensitized the emulsion far beyond the sum of their individual properties. In other words, they supersensitized the emulsions. This super emulsion was first put to practical use in the 1931 preparation of Wratten hypersensitive plates for press photographers. A year later they made possible the first supersensitive panchromatic motion-picture film.

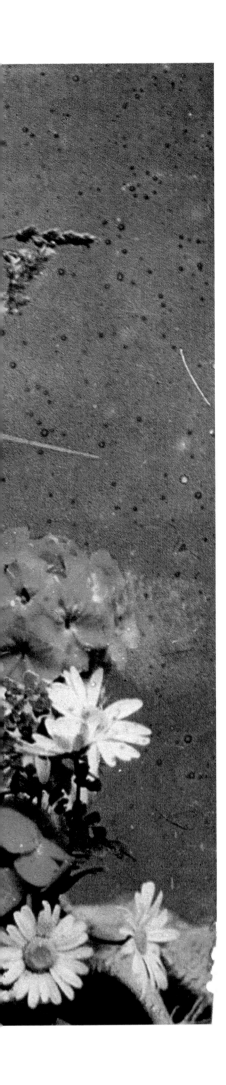

A different sort of sensitization research was hurriedly begun shortly after Agfa, a German film company, announced that it had found a way to use gold to double the emulsion's exposure speed. A number of Kodak chemists, including A.D. Nietz, had been assigned to experiment with various sensitizing chemicals. Work proceeded at a seven-day-a-week pace, but little progress was made until Nietz, who was afflicted with multiple sclerosis, casually happened to toss some of his medicine into a small batch of emulsion. When the emulsion was tested it was found that the sodium thiocynate, an ingredient in Nietz's medicine, had significantly increased its speed. Further experiments by John Leermakers with sulfur, gold, and thiocynate produced a highly sensitive emulsion, and Kodak was once again back in competition with Agfa.

By 1928 the budget of the Rochester laboratory totaled over one million dollars a year, and at the British factory in Harrow another research facility was established in a former public house named "The Good Will to All." When it was initially established, the British lab, which was organized by Mees's friend Walter Clark, worked on factory problems such as the analysis of current films and papers, but within a few years it too began important theoretical work.

In 1920, eight years after he first came to Rochester, Mees had written Eastman a letter outlining his thoughts about the future of photography. "I am aware," Mees wrote, "of the danger of such an attempt and of the fact that a large proportion of these prognostications will probably prove incorrect. Nevertheless, I thought that it would interest you to have such a summary." Among the most important items on Mees's list were motion-picture photography, X-ray work, and industrial and commercial photography.

Mees predicted a doubling of the use of motion-picture film, especially for use in schools and colleges, an expansion of the use of photography for industrial measurement and record keeping, the application of X rays to study metals, the growth of aerial photography as a surveying tool, the replacement of photographic plates by film in the photoengraving process, and the use of simple "high-grade" cameras by amateur photographers. Teaching films never became as ubiquitous as Mees might have wished, and often many of these advances were slow in coming, but in most ways Mees was remarkably clairvoyant.

In two very important instances, however, Mees was wrong. In 1920 Mees had guessed that "it does not appear that any great development is possible in the direction of an increased sensitiveness in negative-making materials." By the end of the decade, research into the nature of gelatin, latent-image formation, and dye sensitization had indeed significantly increased the speed of photographic negatives.

Mees's other error was one of omission. He had mentioned that color-separation techniques would be developed for both movie and still photography, and indeed much work was accomplished in this field. What Mees could not have predicted at the time was the coming of a new color process, one in which without filters or separate negatives three colors could be captured on a single piece of film.

The ideal research community, as Mees saw it, would be a convivial band of high-minded, exceptionally well-educated, hard-working gamblers. Time after time he had seen the longueurs of an individual's lab work yield sudden and unsuspected results. Mees had also watched cooperation between researchers quicken the commerce of ideas. In short, he understood the importance of brains, conjecture, and risk in the scientific workplace.

As a young man, Mees had been fascinated by the life and works of the sixteenth-century scientist and statesman Francis Bacon. He was well aware of Bacon's somewhat scandalous reputation. As Lord Chancellor of England, Bacon had been tried by Queen Elizabeth's court, found guilty of "peculation," and sent to the Tower. Whatever Bacon's personal failings, Mees wrote, there is little doubt that this difficult man must be counted as "one of the greatest intellects that ever lived."

Two of Bacon's ideas seemed to Mees especially useful to those engaged in industrial research. The first was the absolute primacy of observation and experimentation, the crucial importance of approaching all problems by means of the scientific method. The second of Bacon's contributions to the research community, what Mees called his "noble dream," was the notion that scientific discoveries inevitably increase the aggregate wealth of mankind.

Clearly Bacon's philosophy was preindustrial and precapitalist. Improvements in methods of production and the profit motive probably never entered his mind. But, according to Mees, what Bacon could not forecast he at least prefigured. "Perhaps," Mees wrote, "as we did more science and learned more about it, we could improve methods of production. If you could improve methods of production, you could increase wealth. What Bacon thought of, in fact, was applied industrial science."

Research in these Meesian-Baconian terms was a gamble, a wager between science and society over the ultimate worth of risky and time-consuming experimentation. This bet, Mees contended, was fairly safe to take:

In ordinary gambling, the odds are weighted against you, and if you win half the time and lose the other half, you will come out a loser in the end because the odds are weighted against you. In research, they are very much in your favor provided that the research is carried out by competent people; that is, by the average skilled man available for research work. The odds depend, of course, on the men. What is required is the ability to recognize a discovery when it is seen. People don't make discoveries; they stumble on them, but they may recognize them.

Sometimes in the course of the research, Kodak scientists stumbled upon unexpected facts and theories, sometimes they simply tripped over each other. By the late twenties, the three-story research facility built in 1913 was overcrowded. Even after the stock-market crash of 1929, when staff levels were slightly reduced, it was still apparent that too many scientists working on too many projects were sharing too small a space. Since a good deal of emulsion work required complete darkness, sets of heavy drapes were hung in the doorways and corridors separating laboratories. Laboratory protocol required a warning shout on entering or exiting these light locks. Occasionally a lab worker, intent upon the problem at hand, forgot to announce himself or herself. One scientist, after being knocked flat in a doorway, looked up indignantly and snapped, "I was thinking."

The construction of a new and larger laboratory building in 1931 solved some of these traffic problems. It did not, however, alter the lab's long-standing tradition of creative stumbling. Scientists were allowed, even encouraged, to go their own ways. Conditions were not exactly chaotic, but nor was lab time strictly budgeted to the single task at hand. Sometimes "things happen," Mees said, "without any sign of efficiency or plan." And not all of these "things" related directly to photography. Kenneth Hickman's discovery of an efficient and simple method of concentrating vitamin A, for example, lay at the end of a research route so circuitous that even Mees was surprised by the results.

Hickman had joined the staff of the Kodak Research Laboratories in 1925. His first assignment was to come up with a way to recover the valuable silver inevitably left in photographic fixing baths. Gathering up the precious metal by electrolysis seemed to be the smartest solution to the problem. In fact, it turned out that the electroplating techniques he devised worked so well that Hickman was sent to Hollywood to teach his methods to technicians at Metro-Goldwyn-Mayer. In his spare time, the scientist was also helping out in Capstaff's amateur movie laboratory.

"The early 16mm film cameras were great fun," Hickman once said. "And we in the lab were encouraged to expose film for the plant to practice processing. The pictures, however, were rather dreadful, photographically speaking, with smudged, blurry highlights. This, it seemed to me, was halation caused by light reflected from the back of the film. I smeared the reverse side of half a roll of film with red ink, let it dry, and put it in the camera. The pictures on the smeared half were notably better than the unsmeared."

Hickman had with one leap of scientific logic invented the notion of a film antihalation layer. There were, however, practical problems with the inked backing. In warm weather the antihalation layer became so tacky that a roll of film could not be unwound. Hickman suggested the chemicals used in the antihalation be thoroughly dried in a vacuum oven. At the time, though, little theoretical research had been undertaken in the area of high-vacuum distillation. Hickman experimented with various technologies, and within a few years he had designed highly efficient vacuum pumps.

While out taking a walk during his lunch hour, it suddenly struck Hickman that there might be other, nonphotographic applications for his work on high-vacuum technologies. Noticing bottles of cod-liver oil lined up in a drugstore window, he wondered whether "the dread of daily spoonfuls of the foul-tasting curative" might be alleviated if "whatever it was that cured you could be concentrated by distillation and put into a pill." The curative turned out to be vitamin A, and by 1938 Hickman's work with high-vacuum molecular stills resulted in the formation of Distillation Products, Incorporated, a Kodak subsidiary engaged in the manufacture of vitamin A pills.

The single most significant product developed in the Kodak laboratories was the result of an equally serendipitous set of circumstances. Sometime in 1921 or 1922 George Eastman received a letter from Frank Damrosch, the brother of the musician and conductor Walter Damrosch. Would Eastman be interested in meeting two young musicians, Leopold Mannes and Leopold Godowsky, who in their spare time were experimenting with color photography? Eastman, who

Mannes and Godowsky alternated between careers in music and science. As schoolboys they had collaborated on hundreds of color photography experiments, none of which were completely successful until after their 1930 decision to join the staff of the Kodak Research Laboratories. Sometimes whistling classical music to time darkroom operations, "Man and God," as one Kodak staffer called them, succeeded in 1934 in developing full-color Kodachrome film.

Right:

The brilliance of color photographs in the late 1930s was in part a function of patterned lines and specks of color. Older color processes, such as Dufaycolor, Autochrome, Finlay Color, and Agfacolor, had line screens that were either clotted or criss-crossed with color particles. By comparison, the Kodachrome dye image, even when enlarged, seemed smooth and grainless.

Below:

During the four years Leopold Mannes and Leopold Godowsky spent developing Kodachrome film at the Kodak Research Laboratories, innumerable test strips of film were exposed and processed. These pieces of film, next to which the two handwrote their notes, are among the last experimental strips developed before the commercial introduction of the new color film.

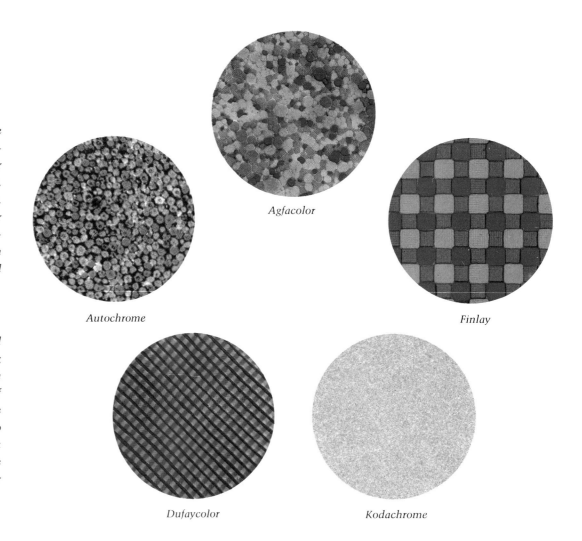

Agfacolor

Autochrome

Finlay

Dufaycolor

Kodachrome

Left:
The Vivex color process, introduced in Britain in 1931, was advertised as "the first in any country to be solely used for a competent and prompt service in the making of prints from sets of colour-separation negatives." Vivex's bold, fetching colors were sometimes used, as in this 1939 advertisement for canned goods, to catch the consumer's eye. After the beginning of World War II, the process was discontinued.

Below:
Brilliance of hue and greater light transmission were two of Kodachrome film's advantages over other color processes, as this 1942 comparison between examples of Kodachrome cut-sheet film (left) and Dufaycolor pack film (right) shows.

over the years had been shown dozens of color technologies, agreed to the request. He was impressed with their work—not enthusiastic enough, however, to make any sort of commitment to Mannes and Godowsky.

In 1922 one of these names resurfaced when Mees received a letter from a colleague, Robert Wood, the chairman of the Experimental Physics Department of Johns Hopkins University:

This is to introduce to you my friend Leopold Mannes, who has worked on a system of color photography which appears to have some novel features which I think will interest you and your company. It occurred to me that you might offer him the facilities of your laboratory for a few days, for I feel sure that he can produce better results under better working conditions. . . . He uses no color screens and can print colored positives from his color negative. The process is quite simple, and the results which I have seen look promising.

Mannes and Godowsky had been close friends since attending high school together at the Riverdale Country School in New York City. Both had come from families well known in the New York musical world. Godowsky's father, Leopold Godowsky, Sr., was a respected concert pianist and composer. Mannes was the son of violinist David Mannes and pianist Clara Damrosch Mannes. One of his uncles was the conductor Walter Damrosch and another was Frank Damrosch, the Eastman friend who had first brought their names to Kodak's attention in the early 1920s.

In 1917 Mannes and Godowsky went to a Manhattan theater to see a film entitled *Our Navy*. The movie had been made by a four-color additive process. There is no record of their response to the subject matter of the film. What interested them most was the color rendition, which both agreed was terrible. Mannes and Godowsky were still in high school at the time, but after a little library research into the principles of additive color, they rigged up a color camera and began experimenting with various filter and lens combinations. Setting up shop in their school physics lab, they managed to correct somewhat the parallax problem caused by the use of multiple lenses—a remarkable achievement, considering that they were untrained schoolboys.

They then left for college, Mannes going to Harvard, where he majored in music and minored in physics, and Godowsky attending the University of California, taking courses in chemistry and physics while playing violin in the Los Angeles Philharmonic Orchestra. Though at first this mixture of disciplines seems surprising, it is actually neither odd nor unusual. The musical arts, for instance, demand a combination of patience and inspiration analogous to the mixture of tenacity and creativity required by the scientific method. In the same way, musical measures share with the permutations of science a direct intellectual bloodline. Each is in its own way a sequential, incremental, and indeed mathematical discipline. In time, these twin talents would serve Mannes and Godowsky well.

In their college years they continued their experiments with additive color during holidays and summer vacations. At one point they thought an acceptable additive color system was at hand. Reducing the number of colors used to two (as, for instance, Capstaff had done during the development of the early Kodachrome), Mannes and Godowsky constructed a double-lens camera that exposed side-by-side images on a single strip of film. Since the parents of both part-time inventors were well-known figures in the New York theater world, they managed to convince S. L. Rothafel, the impresario of "Roxy" movie-house fame, to let them try out their invention in one of his establishments. The color rendition of their two-color film was apparently quite good, but when the projectionist complained about the difficulty of adjusting the lenses necessitated by this new system, Mannes and Godowsky, though unhappy, agreed.

After graduating from college, they returned to New York City, where they took up double careers, working full time as professional musicians and part-time as photographic researchers.

Shortly after Kodachrome film was introduced, astronomical photographers began
using the new stock to take color pictures
of various outer space phenomena. This
1939 Eastman wash-off relief print of the
rings of Saturn (left) was made from a
Kodachrome negative. Other astronomical photo studies, such as this late 1930s
Kodak Research Laboratories infrared
view of a solar corona (above), allowed scientists to make new discoveries about the
physical makeup of the galaxy.

By then, they had decided, as Godowsky said, "to switch from multiple lenses to multiple layered film — in other words, from the optical approach to the chemical approach."

This was a considerable, and it turned out, crucial change in working methods, especially in view of the current state of color film. During the twenties most color processes, whether motion picture or still, depended in one way or another on optical devices. Lumière's Autochrome process, Louis Dufay's Dufaycolor, and Clare Finlay's Finlay Color were all additive color transparencies taken and viewed through screen-line filters. Though difficult to make and reproduce, these types of pictures were undoubtedly the most accurate and pleasing version of color stills on the market.

For the most part, the production of movies in color also employed optical principles. The Eastman Kodak Company's Kodacolor home-movie system was basically a screen-line technique, using film and camera filters to make and project color records. Professional movie color was slightly more sophisticated. By 1932 the Technicolor Corporation had begun making high-quality three-color films. Their camera, however, which used a beam splitter to expose three separate negatives, was a large, bulky device, difficult even for professionals to operate. Professionals were also required to develop and print Technicolor film. The three strips were processed by developing each negative into a gelatin-relief image on a specially prepared Eastman Kodak matrix stock, dying all three with complementary subtractive colors, and then carefully printing them in register on a clear gelatin stock. Films in Technicolor were bright and extremely engaging, but there was no way the technology could be brought down to the level of the average photographer.

Clearly the most efficient method of producing color on film should resemble that used to make ordinary black-and-white pictures. In fact, such a process had been patented in 1912 by the German inventor Rudolph Fischer. Fischer proposed that three emulsion layers, each sensitive to one of the primaries, be coated in succession upon a photographic support. Incorporated into each of these layers were chemical substances called "color couplers" that would react with developing fluids to liberate subtractive dyes in each emulsion layer.

In this process, now called chromogenic development, no screens, special filters, or complicated series of lenses are necessary. Color is produced purely by chemical development. The exposed silver halides, are as usual, changed to silver in proportion to the amount of exposure. Simultaneously dyes are created in each layer. When the silver is bleached away, a three-layer color image, composed only of dyes, remains. In theory, this idea was fine; in practice, Fischer was unable to discover a way to stop the dye-forming color couplers and sensitizing dyes from wandering between layers.

When their friend Robert Wood wrote to Mees in 1922, Mannes and Godowsky had already begun to experiment with dye couplers. Their experiments, however, were hampered by a lack of supplies and by inadequate facilities. Since no multiple-emulsion film or plates were available on the commercial market, Mannes and Godowsky had to make their own. Working in the bathrooms and kitchens of their parents' apartments, they carefully scraped the emulsions off single-emulsion plates, added the color couplers, and recoated the plates. Mees, who had often supplied other researchers with special emulsions, offered to help out. After a meeting at the Chemist's Club in New York City, at which he was shown examples of their work, Mees agreed to send Mannes and Godowsky color-sensitive multiple-layer emulsions prepared to their specifications.

Mees's proposition simplified their emulsion work, but it did not solve the problems of money or laboratory space. Fortunately a secretary working at the Wall Street offices of the investment firm of Kuhn, Loeb and Company, who had met Mannes earlier that year, mentioned their work to her employers. Shortly thereafter, Lewis Strauss, a young Kuhn, Loeb representative, knocked on the door of Mannes's apartment and explained that his company might be interested in investing in color research.

Strauss asked if he could see some examples of their work. Mannes and Godowsky explained the process, made several exposures, and set to work in the kitchen developing the color pictures. It happened to be very cold that day, which slowed the action of the developing fluids. After the usual thirty-minute development period the images were still unformed. The two inventors, worried that their increasingly bored benefactor might leave, sat Strauss in a living-room chair and entertained him with a selection of Beethoven sonatas. Between movements, Mannes and Godowsky laid down their instruments and rushed to the kitchen to check the plates. When they were ready, the pictures (and perhaps the music) impressed the banker. After reporting back to his employers, Strauss returned with the offer of a twenty-thousand-dollar loan.

By 1924, with the assistance of Kuhn, Loeb's money and Mees's plates, Mannes and Godowsky were able to patent a two-color process utilizing a double-coated plate. The most significant suggestion included in the patent application was an explanation of what is known as controlled diffusion. By carefully gauging the amount of time necessary for the developing fluid to create an image on the top layer, Mannes and Godowsky were able to leave the second layer unchanged. In other words, the developing fluid was kept from wandering from one layer to the next. Controlled diffusion was, however, so complicated a processing technique that it was not considered commercially practical.

In the meantime, Mannes and Godowsky pursued their musical careers. Mannes was awarded a Guggenheim fellowship, and Godowsky traveled the concert circuit as his pianist father's violin accompanist. In their spare time they continued to work on multilayered systems of color photography. By 1927, with controlled diffusion in mind, they began exploring a new method of producing color. They decided that rather than including color couplers in each emulsion layer it would be more efficient to put them in the developing fluid. This ingenious idea eliminated the old problem of wandering color couplers. Each coupler would be introduced by controlled diffusion and thus each layer would be cleanly dyed. The chief problem with this method was that the sensitizing dyes necessary to produce color records in each layer also tended to wander.

In 1929, with money running out, Mannes and Godowsky once again met with Mees at the Chemist's Club. Mees, who had followed and encouraged the work of the two part-time chemists, knew that in the Rochester laboratory Leslie Brooker had succeeded in creating dyes that were both nonwandering and highly effective as sensitizers. Mees realized that if Brooker's dyes were made available to Mannes and Godowsky the two might be able to solve the remaining problems associated with their controlled diffusion process. He made them an offer: Kodak would pay Mannes and Godowsky thirty thousand dollars up front to pay off the Kuhn, Loeb loan. Each would also be given seven thousand five hundred dollars a year in salary as well as royalties on any patents taken out by Mannes and Godowsky before the association with Kodak.

In November 1930 the offer was accepted. Six months later, after initially working in a laboratory set up in a Broadway hotel room, Mannes and Godowsky moved to Rochester. Not surprisingly, they found the city to their liking. The laboratories were better equipped and the technical assistance they received from Kodak scientists was crucial to the ultimate success of their process.

Rochester was also, not coincidentally, the home of the Eastman School of Music, and a short time after their arrival Mannes and Godowsky were regularly performing with groups of local musicians. Music also played a major role in their laboratory work. Since it was necessary for all experimental work on these color-sensitive emulsions to be undertaken in complete darkness, development time was counted off by whistling bars of classical music.

"We had to be absolutely exact," Godowsky once said, "about intervals of as little as a second and a half, and we had to measure these intervals in total darkness. Stopwatches were no

Though the widespread use of color film by amateur photographers was many years away, shortly after it was introduced Kodachrome film was tested by a variety of photographers. Two advertising photos (top right and lower left) from the 1930s prefigured its use as a popular portrait film, both for close-up shots and for more interpretive pictures that evoked mood and ambience by means of color. The 1940 Kodachrome sheet-film study of calypso dancers (center) by Harold Edgerton is one of the earliest color photos taken with electronic flash, a technique that was developed in the late 1920s and early 1930s but that did not become available to all amateur photographers until the 1970s.

good—we couldn't use one with a radiant dial, because of the effect it would have on our sensitive materials; and, anyway, we found watches were less accurate than whistling the final movement of Brahms's C Minor Symphony at the regular speed of two beats to the second. But how could you go into all that with a scientist who'd never so much as heard of the C Minor Symphony?"

The three-year period specified in their contract with Kodak was due to finish at the end of 1933. Since an adequate color process had not as yet come to fruition, both inventors thought, as Godowsky once said, that they "were in line for the axe." "It was obvious," Godowsky added, "that our only chance of survival was to invent something in a hurry—something that the company could put into production and make money on. And that something was Kodachrome film."

Early in 1934, their jobs temporarily saved by Mees's offer of a one-year contract extension, Mannes and Godowsky showed the director a two-color home-movie process. Mees was enthusiastic and immediately recommended to management that plans be made to market the product. Manufacturing and marketing difficulties slowed the film's introduction, and in 1935, just as Kodak was about to introduce the two-color film, the two inventors succeeded in perfecting a much superior three-color version.

On April 15, 1935, the new product, borrowing the name "Kodachrome" from the earlier Capstaff color process, was formally announced. Kodachrome was first offered as a 16mm

Most photojournalists waiting for the arrival of the German dirigible Hindenburg *carried large-format Speed Graphic cameras loaded with black-and-white film. New York Sunday Mirror photojournalist George Sheedy was an exception. His 35mm camera was loaded with what the paper described as "Kodachrome natural color film." After being knocked down by the blast of the explosion when the Hindenburg crashed, Sheedy managed to expose his roll of film, which was flown to Rochester for development and then back to New York, where, on May 23, 1937, a selection of the pictures appeared in a double-page spread of the* Sunday Mirror's *magazine section, becoming the first news photographs ever published in color.*

home-movie film. Like the American stripping film included in the 1888 Kodak camera, it was necessary to return Kodachrome film to the factory for processing.

Kodachrome color transparency film consisted of five layers attached to a celluloid support. In descending order, from top to bottom, these were: a blue-sensitive layer containing a yellow dye to trap all blue light, a strip of clear gelatin, a blue-green-sensitive layer, another strip of clear gelatin, and finally a blue- and red-sensitive layer. Three color records were thus produced on a single piece of film: blue in the top, green in the middle, and red on the bottom. Each of the layers was one to three micrometers thick — much thinner than the width of a human hair. It was necessary to coat each of these layers in complete darkness with less than a 2-percent deviation in thickness.

The processing of the film was even more meticulous. Twenty-eight separate steps were involved. First the entire film was conventionally developed, bleached, and reexposed to light. Dye creation and silver destruction in each layer was then accomplished by allowing the developing fluid to replace successively the silver images in each layer with its appropriate subtractive dye: cyan in the bottom red layer, magenta in the middle green layer, and yellow in the top blue layer.

In 1912 George Eastman had guessed that color photography might have "quite a vogue." The history of Kodachrome during the few short years after its initial introduction certainly bore out that prediction. In the first years after its invention, three new motion-picture versions of Kodachrome were brought out: a 16mm sound-recording stock, one that could be used by artificial light, and an 8mm home-movie type. In September 1936 two Kodachrome cartridge films were made available to still photographers, one for 35mm cameras and another for Kodak Bantam Special cameras.

All of these films produced transparencies. At first, Kodak returned the processed film to photographers in uncut strips. But by 1938 each transparency was individually mounted in a 2 x 2-inch cardboard "Readymount." That same year the Kodaslide color transparency projector was also introduced. Both of these products are now considered responsible for the growth of interest in 35mm photography — particularly among amateur photographers.

The acceptance of Kodachrome film by commercial photographers was more immediate. In 1937 *The Milwaukee Journal* was one of the first newspapers to publish full-color Kodachrome photos in its rotogravure section. *The National Geographic*, which had previously published Autochrome and Finlay Color photos, printed its first Kodachrome images in an April 1938 article titled "Austria Kodachromes from a Candid Camera."

In 1939, one hundred years after the invention of photography, a world's fair was opened in New York City. Since the early 1880s Kodak had mounted exhibitions in dozens of such expositions. For the first time, however, the company constructed its own building. Displays of all sorts of Kodak products, amateur and professional, were put together. But it was a 187-by-22-foot series of projected transparencies hanging in the Hall of Color that was to the general public the single most impressive example of photography in the show.

Shortly after the initial announcement of 16mm Kodachrome film, Mees had written: "With the coming of this new process amateur movies will be in color. There is no longer any need for us to pretend that the world is in monochrome, and to represent the glorious world in which we live by a gray ghost on the screen." Yet it would take years before color prints approaching this quality could be held in the hand. A number of years would also pass before moviemakers and artistic photographers were given the opportunity to take full advantage of tripack color films. And black-and-white photographs would never be completely superseded by those in color. But the revolutionary nature of the Kodachrome process had changed the nature of twentieth-century photography almost as radically as roll film had transformed the nineteenth-century world of glass-plate picture taking.

By the time the Hall of Color opened, Mannes and Godowsky had left Kodak. Mannes returned to New York, where he was appointed assistant director of the Mannes School of Music, which his father had founded. Godowsky moved to Westport, Connecticut, continuing photographic research in a small laboratory he called "Kodak Park Westport." Both men were retained as consultants and occasionally returned to help with the laboratories' continuing research into the understanding and improvement of color technology.

A Kodak executive had once joked that only "man and God" could have created Kodachrome film, which was in more than one sense absolutely true. Mannes and Godowsky understood the implications of that statement in terms slightly less metaphysical. It was the process, the intellectual and technological creativity, that in the end accounted for the invention of Kodachrome film. Mannes understood the implications, and in a speech delivered at George Eastman's house in May 1952, by then remodeled to house a photographic museum, he explained:

Looking back on the years during which Kodachrome was evolving gives one a strange perspective on what an invention really is. I think if I were asked to define it, I would say that invention is primarily the art of getting out of trouble. There is very seldom such a thing strictly speaking, as an invention.

Rather, it is almost always a conglomerate of ideas, each one "thought up" to avoid some difficulty. One starts working on a so-called invention with some sort of definite goal in mind. Often as not, even the goal may undergo a significant change during the long period of work in achieving it.

Mees would have agreed completely. And so would have George Eastman.

Preceding pages:
Though snapshot camera production halt-
ed almost completely during World War II,
in the years leading up to the war the 1941
Target Brownie Six-20 camera, the 1936
Kodak Bantam Special camera, and the
1938 Kodak 35 camera (left to right) were
often used by casual, advanced, and seri-
ous amateur photographers of the time.
During the war the U.S. Navy adapted the
Kodak 35 camera (fourth from left) to be
attached to submarine periscopes. The
1938 Super Kodak Six-20 camera (right),
with its fully automatic exposure control
system, was the most advanced snapshot
camera of the era.

Opposite:
"The great pictures," a 1938 double-spread
advertisement in Life *magazine asserted,*
"are made on Kodak film." One of the
great pictures used to illustrate this claim
was Life *photographer Margaret Bourke-*
White's tightly composed, geometrically
balanced study of New York City's George
Washington Bridge. In 1932 Kodak had
also provided Bourke-White with twenty
thousand feet of movie stock for a docu-
mentary film about life in Russia.

All of a sudden, just as it was about to celebrate its one-hundredth anniversary, photography came of age. Until the 1930s photography had been an adolescent medium, adventuresome, exciting, a little ungainly, sometimes lacking in direction. It had not defined itself with any confidence. Was it primarily a folk art, a poor man's painting? Did it only document? Was it simply a chemical and mechanical craft? A science? Could photography challenge the other plastic arts in privilege and stature?

That the shaping of these questions coincided with an era of social and political unrest may, indeed, simply be coincidental. It seems reasonable to suppose that worldwide economic depression and the dark days preceding World War II should have prompted the medium to respond with a corresponding frugality. In a certain sense, however, austerity measures missed photography. In all its forms, amateur and professional, artistic and documentary, still and moving, the medium flourished.

The 1931 Eastman Kodak Company's $100,000 international amateur competition, staged just two years after the Wall Street stock-market crash, drew three million entries. After a downturn in attendance from 1931 to 1933, motion pictures were more popular than ever. It has been estimated that during the thirties sixty million to seventy-five million people went to the movies each week. In 1936 *Life* magazine, the first American mass-market periodical devoted chiefly to the reproduction of photographs, appeared on the newsstands. The magazine's prospectus was replete with a single transitive verb: *to see.*

To see life; to see the world; to witness great events; to watch the faces of the poor and the gestures of the proud; to see strange things—machines, armies, multitudes, shadows in the jungle and on the moon; to see man's work—his painting, towers and discoveries; to see things thousands of miles away, things hidden behind walls and within rooms, things dangerous to come to; the women that men love and many children; to see and take pleasure in seeing; to see and be amazed; to see and be instructed.

Life is now known as the seed ground of American photojournalism, the virtual inventor of the multiple-page photographic essay and the first American publication to give privilege to visual information. But as the excited listing of its intentions suggests, *Life* was more than just a news magazine. All of photography's other important genres and modes were represented. In a single issue there were pictures of babies, capricious pets, movie stars (also capricious), bizarre accidents, landscapes, consumer goods, and in fact just about any person or thing that might possibly be the subject of a good picture.

During the thirties the political uses of the medium were recognized by the United States government. The Farm Security Administration, charged with the management of the agricultural crisis, created a photographic section. Roy Stryker, the head of the section, hired forty-four photographers and dispatched them to various parts of the country to collect visual data. Pictures were needed to confirm social conditions, and Stryker knew what sorts of empirical proof he wanted. Sometimes he asked for "good slum pictures"; occasionally for images full of American abundance ("pour the maple syrup over it," he once wrote). Most of all he wanted lots of pictures. By the end of Stryker's tenure at the FSA and its successor, the Office of War Information, a little over ninety thousand negatives had been exposed.

The idea that photography could be classified as an art form was given formal recognition in 1937, when Beaumont Newhall, a young curator at The Museum of Modern Art in New York, organized a retrospective exhibition entitled *Photography 1839–1937*. It was the museum's first major photography show. Before this retrospective, the history of photography as an art form existed as little more than a batch of unsorted images. Newhall gave it historical shape, organizing, categorizing, and structuring the museum's photographic collection. In its review of

The Historical Section of the Farm Security Administration was created in 1935 to
document the Depression with photographs. The majority of the nearly one hundred thousand photos in the FSA archives,
such as Walker Evans's 1935 study of a
Reedsville, West Virginia, gas station
(right), were made in the sharp, high-contrast Dickensian language of black-and-
white film. Late in its tenure, however, the
FSA supplied a few of its photographers
with Kodachrome film. Color photos, such
as Russell Lee's 1940 shot of a rural family
meeting at the Pie Town (New Mexico)
Fair (below), sometimes depicted hard
times in an equally discerning, though
brighter and more spacious light.

Opposite:

One of the first to gauge the commercial
possibilities of 35mm Kodachrome film,
Ivan Dmitri took a variety of color pictures
in the late 1930s that were reproduced in
magazines such as the Saturday Evening
Post, Vogue, and House and Garden. This
Dmitri color shot of an airplane flying over
Manhattan was featured on the cover of a
1939 issue of American Leica magazine. It
was one of the first color photographs to be
printed on a magazine cover.

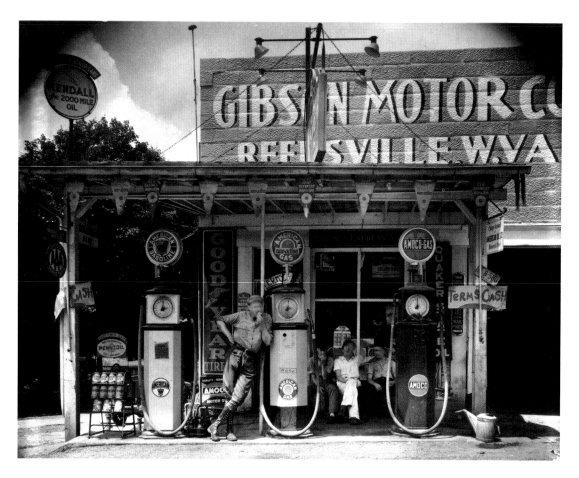

the show, *The New York Herald Tribune* congratulated photography on the breadth and depth of its imaginative reach:

One sees the camera as the technically triumphant instrument of exact depiction, as a sensitive medium of artistic record, as a device creating new imaginative worlds out of its own limitations and possibilities, going on to exploit its deliberate distortions of light and form for their own sake until finally even the camera itself disappears, leaving the abstract "shadowgraphs" of Man Ray and others.

Simultaneously, one sees it reaching out to report the whole of experience, developing motion, penetrating to the structure of the atom and of the giant star cluster. One sees it spreading in another sense, first to books, then to current magazines and newspapers and advertisements and its own pictorial theaters, until it makes the daily world of modern man a pictorial world to a degree beyond anything in human experience.

To the Eastman Kodak Company, the success of photography in the 1930s was the payoff following years of chemical and mechanical research. Kodak had been known mostly for its consumer goods. The snapshot revolution of the late nineteenth century and the snapshot craze of the early twentieth century had, by the twenties and thirties, inextricably intertwined photography into the fabric of modern life. Home cameras, for instance, remained one of the mainstays of the company's income. Each year since the introduction of the Kodak camera in 1888, half a dozen new or updated snapshot cameras had been added to the Kodak line. For the most part, these were designed to be used by untrained snapshooters.

A major portion of Kodak advertising copy was directed specifically at this market. "Snapshots you'll want tomorrow," one tag line reminded people, "you must make today." In 1934 Edward Steichen was commissioned to take a series of photographs to illustrate ads of this type. Steichen, who by this time was working chiefly as a fashion photographer for *Vogue* and *Vanity Fair* magazines, was interested in making these pictures as "realistic" as possible. As this particular campaign was based on the idea of people looking for the first time at a new set of snaps, Steichen chose what he called "everyday people" to take part in the sessions. While the photographer set up his compositions, the amateur models were given "nondescript" pictures to look at. Just before making the exposures Steichen substituted "lively snapshots" of people who might appeal to those models. As the models spontaneously responded to the new snaps, the photographer clicked off a picture.

The fact that the spontaneity in these pictures was skillfully contrived hardly makes a difference. In the first place, few would disagree with the notion that snapshots are often terrifically engaging. (Even the hoariest aesthetician smiles at his own family snaps.) Secondly, all amateur snapshooters know that to be in the right place at the right time is one of the requisites of good picture taking. Steichen made it his business to be so situated, but with perseverance and luck the average picture taker could emulate the professional's skill. The picture selected as the grand prizewinner in the 1931 $100,000 amateur competition was a snap of a girl on a British beach silhouetted against the setting sun. It was the kind of photo that could be, and was, taken by a part-timer with a well-made camera, good film, and a quick eye.

During the thirties a similar advertising campaign argued that "the great pictures are made on Kodak film." The phrase "great pictures" had a double meaning. In its most literal sense it referred to the work of great photographers. Accordingly these full-page spreads featured high-quality photos by well-known professionals such as Arnold Genthe and Margaret Bourke-White. At the same time, the advertising slogan implied that at least a portion of the credit should be granted to the common denominator shared by these photographers: Kodak film.

By the mid-thirties, after the 1931 introduction of Kodak's Verichrome film, very good photos were much easier to take. The marketing of Verichrome was the first significant change in Kodak amateur roll film since the marketing of noncurling stock in 1903. A product of laboratory research into the supersensitizing properties of dye combinations, Verichrome, as its name suggests, was a fairly truthful black-and-white film, generally sensitive to most of the visible spectrum.

Verichrome was also a very forgiving film. Its emulsion had a wide latitude. Latitude is usually defined as the range of exposures over which a satisfactory photograph can be obtained. Clearly, if the amount of exposure necessary to produce acceptable contrast is expanded, the photographer's task is simplified. In other words, the wider and larger the film's exposure range, its latitude, the more forgiving it is of mistakes in speed or aperture adjustment.

Verichrome film's wide latitude was a boon to the amateur who picked up his Brownie box camera, pointed it, and clicked off a shot. Some of the errors the untrained snapshooter might make (too much light, too little light) were offset by the film's fairly broad tolerance. After the introduction of Verichrome film the typical snap was more responsive to the visible spectrum and more charitable to amateurs who knew next to nothing about the craft of photography.

There were various sizes of Verichrome roll film, which the user could select from by film number. Prior to 1913 Kodak films had been identified by camera. For instance, the 1½ X 2-inch film designed to fit the Pocket Kodak camera was called "Pocket Kodak film." However, as new cameras were marketed that used the same size of film as an older camera, it was decided to number the films sequentially in the order in which they had been introduced. The 120-size Verichrome film, for instance, which measured 2¼ x 3¼ inches, had been first manufactured for the No. 2 Brownie camera in 1900.

After 1916, there had been only two additions to this list: 616 and 620 films, which, though wound on thinner spools, were identical to 116 (introduced in 1899) and 120 in size. In 1934, however, a new and ultimately very significant film size was first marketed: 135. At the time all Kodak films were contact printed; that is, negative and print positive sizes matched exactly, and though the relatively small proportions of 35mm film were alright for projection purposes, they were considered too tiny to be of much use for making prints.

Since at least 1912 cameras had been constructed to make use of short tag ends of 35mm film discarded by moviemakers. At first, most of these cameras were advertised as a low-cost way to produce lantern slides. The film was cheap—a fifty-foot roll contained eight hundred frames—and when projected the quality of the pictures was very good.

In the early twenties the German designer Oskar Barnack was one of the first to build a camera specifically designed to take advantage of the small film. Barnack's camera, which was called the Leica (after its manufacturer, Ernest Leitz), was intended to produce negatives from which prints could be enlarged. The Leica was a very small camera with a very short focal length and an extremely good lens. Both these features jacked up the supply of exposure, allowing quick, concentrated bursts of light to strike the film. Since the intensity of light was so strong, less exposure time was required by the Leica. Unlike most large-format cameras, which were unable to take interior pictures without the assistance of explosive flash powder, the 35mm Leica often could operate effectively by the illumination available inside a normally lit room.

Though many serious photographers still preferred the easily printable negatives produced by larger cameras, the merits of the "miniature" 35mm were immediately recognized by a few of the most important photojournalists of the time. After experimenting with the new small camera in the 1920s, the German news photographer Erich Salomon discovered in many instances acceptable photos could be made in locations heretofore unexplored by the camera. Slipping into a League of Nations conference room, with the small camera inconspicuously held

SMALL CAMERAS
DOCUMENT THE WORLD

*Anton Bruehl, who is sometimes consid-
ered "one of the first masters of advertising
color photography," took this color shot of
dancers in a nightclub in 1943. The expressive blend of dramatic movement and vivid hues evident in this photograph was,
after the introduction of Kodachrome film,
increasingly used to arrest the reader flip-
ping through the advertising sections of
mass-market magazines.*

Opposite:

*The Eastman wash-off relief process, in-
troduced in 1935, was an imbibition color
dye-printing technique whereby relief positives were made from separation negatives, dyed the appropriate subtractive
colors, and then squeegeed one at a time
onto a fixed-out sheet of photographic paper. This brightly colored Chevrolet advertisement was produced in the late 1930s
using the process.*

DELUXE CHEVROLET CO

MATCHLESS PERFORMANCE
CHEVROLET RADIO

YOUR TICKET of
TO THE
WORLDS
FINEST
RADIO
PERFORMANCES

CHEVROLET 6 TUBE RADIO

GENUINE
PERMANENT
ANTI-FREEZE

in his hand, Salomon was able to make exposures without attracting the attention of the assembled diplomats. A British photo editor nicknamed these new sort of pictures "candid photographs," and by the mid-thirties a few photojournalists, such as Alfred Eisenstadt, André Kertész, and Henri Cartier-Bresson, were also carrying 35mm cameras on assignment.

In spite of these successes, Kodak, and in particular its lab director, C. E. K. Mees, still considered the minisized 35mm negatives too small and grainy to be satisfactorily enlarged. Its possibilities as a consumer product were too limited. On the other hand, the German camera industry was so well known for the quality of its workmanship that in 1930 Kodak entered into negotiations with August Nagel, one of the best-known German camera craftsmen. In 1928, after working for and managing a number of camera manufacturers, Nagel had founded his own firm: Dr. August Nagel—Factory for Precision Mechanical Work. During the next few years the small plant produced well-respected, top-of-the-line cameras such as the Recomar, Pupille, and Volenda.

A Kodak retail and wholesale subsidiary had been opened in Germany at the beginning of the century, but in 1927, as the demand for film in this part of Europe rose, Kodak acquired Glanzfilm AG in Berlin-Koepenick and built a modern film factory. According to the German photographic magazine *Die Deutsche Fotoindustrie*, when Kodak representatives asked Nagel to consider selling his factory, Nagel "decided to increase the efficiency of his plant through close cooperation with the most important photographic enterprise in the world." Thus in 1931, a new Kodak subsidiary, Kodak AG, which included administrative and sales offices, the Glanzfilm factory, and the Nagel camera works, was formed.

The first cameras off the line at the Nagel works after its merger with Kodak were a roll-film version of the Nagel Vollenda, an improved lightweight Brownie 620, and two small cameras, the Vollenda Junior 620 and the Junior 620. Considering their relatively high cost, many of these cameras sold quite well, but Nagel and Kodak had in mind a slightly different and more popular type of precision instrument: a high-quality, but relatively inexpensive 35mm camera. At the time the main problem with 35mm miniatures, besides the negative size, was their expense. As a 1934 article in the *Kodak Trade News* explained:

While miniature photography on motion-picture film has attracted a large number of amateurs, it has not done so to the extent that it deserves. Miniature cameras that have appeared on the market until now are all of the most expensive precision type, with all sorts of sophisticated technical features. The latter makes them first-class photographic instruments, but they also make miniature photography, which is basically inexpensive, very costly. This is why miniature photography became the domain of a class of wealthy amateur and professional photographers. The less affluent amateur cannot participate, because precision instruments of this type are beyond his means.

Nagel set out to reduce the cost of the miniature camera, and in 1934 the first Kodak AG precision 35, the Retina, was announced. Though one German photo magazine named the Retina "the new Kodak People's Camera" and remarked on its reasonable price, one of the first models available in the United States cost $54. True, the price of the Retina was considerably less than the two-hundred- to four-hundred-dollar price tag of a Leica, but in 1934 a No. 2 Brownie cost only $2.50, a Jiffy Kodak Six-20 $6.75, and a Vest Pocket Kodak Special $25.

In the two years before the first Retina was replaced by a slightly improved version, a little over sixty thousand of the cameras were sold. Though this figure does not match the hundreds of thousands of snapshot cameras bought each year, it is also not an inconsiderable number. In fact, most of these precision-built 35mm cameras did not wind up in the hands either of working professionals or of everyday snapshooters. Retina cameras were purchased by a relatively new class of photographers now generally known as "serious amateurs."

During the first fifty years after the introduction of the home camera, the majority of sales were made to those who took out their cameras only at important events: parties, vacations, ceremonies. These pictures were usually taken as visual keepsakes. The snapshooter did not particularly care about how the camera worked; it was only important that it did the job. To the serious amateurs photography was a hobby, a hobby they pursued with a single-mindedness sometimes exceeding that of professional photographers. Some simply liked to operate the equipment; others were bent on pursuing more aesthetic goals. To many, of course, the allure of photography was its unique combination of art and technology. Not surprisingly, the serious amateur was often the first to try out a new technology. Professionals were accustomed to their old equipment, as were snapshooters. The serious amateurs, having the hearts of technicians, were open to anything new.

In spite of the Retina's success, many Kodak officials remained unconvinced that miniature cameras would ever become very popular. The 35mm was still too expensive for the mass market, and enlargements of the pictures it produced were not up to the quality of the average contact print. In 1933, however, two new very fast 35mm films, Kodak Supersensitive pan film and Kodak Panatomic film, were developed in the laboratory. Charles Case, a former managing director of Kodak Limited, argued that if one of the double row of sprocket holes were eliminated from these films, a 28 x 40mm negative, 25-percent larger than the original stock, could be produced. This increase in negative size almost entirely eliminated enlargement problems.

The new film was given the number 828, and a new line of cameras, the Bantam, was designed to make use of it. Bantam cameras were the snapshooter's equivalent of the 35mm miniature. The first two marketed were sold for $5.75 and $9.75 — lens quality (f/11 and f/6.3, respectively) accounting for the slight difference in price.

Kodak had been involved in the study and manufacture of lenses since at least 1913, when the first anastigmatic lens, designed to prevent light rays from registering as two short lines in different focal planes, was designed specifically to fit Kodak cameras. A year later C. W. Frederick, the first full-time optical specialist, was hired. It was his mathematical computations that enabled Kodak to develop quickly the ten-inch f/4.5 and twenty-inch f/6 lenses needed for World War I aerial cameras. To manufacture efficient lenses of this size that corrected the distortion problems associated with high-altitude photography was, at the time, a rather remarkable feat.

In the days before electronic computational machines, the creation of new lenses was a tedious, time-consuming business. Lens design, which involves the tracing of the angle of refraction of rays of light as they travel from one medium to another, is a precise mathematical science. These angles must be accurately predicted and measured so that all rays come together at a precise point on the film plane. Aberrant rays, which cause a variety of distortions, must be redirected.

The light-gathering capabilities of a lens are described as a function of the capability of the glass unit or units to correct distortion. This is further measured by the aperture size, an "f" number obtained by dividing its focal length by the diameter of the lens. The smaller this "f" number, the faster, or more efficient, the lens. The aperture of the lens first used by Daguerre was approximately f/15. By the 1920s lenses as fast as f/2 were available. In fact, a lens manufactured specifically for the 1923 Cine-Kodak home-movie camera was measured at f/1.9.

In addition to its mathematical indices of refraction, lens designers also had to consider the optical properties of various glasses. Through the 1920s it was generally acknowledged that the best lens material available contained barium oxide. This sort of glass was manufactured only in Germany, France, and England. When the export of this glass was interrupted during World War I, studies were begun to discover whether other equally efficient glass compounds could be domestically produced. During the 1930s Frederick Higgins, an MIT-trained optical mathematician, with the help of a group of Kodak Research Laboratories' chemists headed by Samuel Sheppard, began investigating so-called rare-earth oxides. These studies, which continued throughout the thirties, culminated in 1941 with the manufacture of a rare-earth lens for use in high-altitude aerial photography.

Kodak lens manufacturing had, since the early teens, been the responsibility of the Hawk-Eye Works, a factory located across the Genesee River from Kodak's State Street offices. Initially this building had housed the Blair Camera Company. By the late 1930s the entire operation was turning out a list of fairly specialized photographic products, including lenses and precision camera parts.

One of Hawk-Eye's less well-known, but nonetheless financially significant, products had very little to do with photography. Shortly after the stock-market crash of 1929, Hawk-Eye Works managers began looking for further ways to utilize their optical manufacturing capabilities. Other companies had been making small glass "cat's-eye" reflectors. These glass buttons, called somewhat pretentiously "auto-collinating catadioptric units," were attached to the backs of bicycles or wagons or to roadside signs to alert approaching motorists. Since the Hawk-Eye Works was engaged in the manufacture of glass anyway, a machine was designed to snip ends off tubes of glass. These snippets were then curved and back-coated with aluminum. Well into the 1940s, when plastics began to replace glass in such products, over five million cat's-eyes were manufactured each year.

The principal responsibility of the Hawk-Eye Works remained the manufacture of Kodak camera lenses. Miniature cameras, in particular, due to their short focal length and small negative size, required very sophisticated lenses. In 1936, a year after the introduction of the first low-priced Bantam camera, manufactured mainly for the amateur market, the Kodak Bantam Special was announced. This camera, which came equipped with an unusually fast f/2 lens, cost $110. Clearly it was not a piece of equipment that the snapshooter might casually pick up.

The 1938 Kodak Super Six-20 was an even more intricate, expensive and, for its time, advanced camera. The $225 Super Six-20, designed by Joseph Mihalyi and styled by Walter Dorwin Teague, was the first camera to incorporate a fully automatic exposure system. This folding camera, called the "clam shell" because of the peculiarly acute curve of its body, used a photoelectric cell to read the amount of existing light and to adjust the aperture accordingly. The camera was not very reliable (Kodak technicians called it the "boomerang" since it regularly shot back for repairs), but it was ahead of its time.

The most striking fact about the mechanical sophistication of all these cameras is the date of their introduction. The 1930s was the era of worldwide depression, a retrograde time, when it would seem a consumer-driven business such as Kodak would cut back its production of expensive items. A glance down the list of two dozen or so cameras that first came on the market from 1932 to 1938 seems to suggest otherwise. It is true that inexpensive cameras remained available to the average snapshooter. In 1934 the Baby Brownie cost only one dollar. The Bantam, at $5.75, was quite a bit more expensive, but it too was priced low enough to appeal to the general public. However, many of the other cameras introduced during this era were top-shelf, high-ticket pieces of equipment. In other words, the prevailing trend in Kodak camera design was toward increasing sophistication and expense.

The growth of the serious amateur market certainly contributed to this drift. Amateurs who considered photography a hobby were generally those with enough cash to purchase the precision equipment required to make good pictures. While most snapshooters were content to press the button and let the photofinisher do the rest, photography enthusiasts insisted on doing it all themselves. In 1914 George Eastman had expected the Kodak developing tank to

The most affecting and pleasing color cinematography of the 1930s and 1940s was produced by the Technicolor three-strip imbibition process. Using camera and print stock specially prepared by Kodak, movies such as the wide-canvas, handsomely costumed Civil War epic Gone with the Wind *were shot in appropriately "Glorious Technicolor."*

Opposite:

Movie film is projected frame after frame, twenty-four photos per second, and though the illusion of movement is produced by persistence of vision, moviegoers often seem to leave the theater with a single immutable image etched in their imaginations. As silent film actress Louise Brooks has written of the soft-focus glamour image of stars such as Greta Garbo, seen here in the 1936 Camille, *"No matter how many times I've seen her in films, that's how I always see her. She is a still picture—unchangeable."*

Left and below:

Greg Toland was perhaps the most creative cinematographer of the 1930s and 1940s. His "acknowledged brilliance," as American Cinematographer *magazine argued in 1942, placed him "in the most nearly ideal position any Director of Photography has enjoyed since the halcyon days when D. W. Griffith and Billy Bitzer were between them creating the basic technique of the screen." Two of Toland's most innovative films were the dramatically lighted dust-bowl story* The Grapes of Wrath *and* Citizen Kane, *in which extreme depth of field created an effect that, as the cinematographer wrote, made the audience "feel it was looking at reality, rather than merely at a movie." Both movies took advantage of improvements in camera and lens design as well as the increases in the light sensitivity of Kodak camera stocks such as the 1935 Super-X and the 1938 Super-XX.*

The shift from a "realistic" world rendered in black and white to the imagined, "theatrical" realms of color was used to great effect in the 1939 Technicolor film The Wizard of Oz, *in which a conjured land is brought alive with brilliant hues, and in* The Adventures of Robin Hood, *in which the bright greens of Sherwood Forest and the vivid reds of royal heraldry evoke the pageantry of medieval England.*

become as popular as the snapshot camera. Yet most amateurs couldn't be bothered with film processing and continued to take their negative film to photofinishers. Photography enthusiasts, on the other hand, were proud of their technological brand of self-reliance. They not only wanted to develop their own film, they insisted upon doing so. They studied the photographic lingo, and at meetings of miniature camera clubs they argued about competing products with a vocabulary up to then only used by professionals and laboratory researchers. During this era fine-grain developers were created to complement the fast 35mm film, and many serious amateurs turned into self-described "darkroom bugs."

In fact, they loved the art and science of photography with a passion usually unmatched by the typical working professional. One such buff, Kalton Lahue, wrote a history of the Kodak Retina camera, fondly remembering that precision instrument:

In addition to its substantial features at a reasonable price, the Retina had two other factors working mightily in its favor. One was the aura of quality—that indefinable attribute that man recognizes as the ultimate he can produce. When picked up in hand, the Retina was a perfect fit—it belonged—and the silky smoothness with which it responded to man's adjustments was natural. It looked, felt and behaved like a champion and the black leather finish (trimmed with a combination of black enamel and nickeled finish on the exposed metal parts) served to accentuate the feeling of confidence one felt when holding a Retina in hand—despite the fact that such a finish was less expensive to furnish at the time than one of chrome.

But the looks of a champion are worthless unless it truly performs like a thoroughbred and herein rested the Retina's second success factor—it excelled at its appointed task.

In 1937 about twelve and a half thousand photographs were submitted weekly to *Life* magazine. Five thousand of these pictures came from photographic syndicates. Two thousand five hundred were the work of *Life* staff photographers, correspondents, and researchers. The remaining five thousand were contributed by amateur photographers.

In a single issue of *Life*, then, the pictures of well-known photographers such as Edward Steichen or Alfred Eisenstadt were printed alongside the work of photographers whose names would be unrecognized and whose reputations might rest on a single submission. Some of these photos (both professional and amateur) were taken with 35mm miniatures; others with larger format cameras. A few were simply snapshots. All, however, proved that photography, even in times of economic and political crisis, had become seamlessly interwoven into the fabric of the contemporary world.

Photography's next task was to authenticate its stature, to prove its message universal, unforgettable, and utilitarian.

If the most memorable photographs taken during the years immediately preceding the Second World War were tacked on a wall, few would be in color. In retrospect that fact seems altogether understandable. Politically and socially, the thirties are generally considered a tenebrous era, the deep shadows of which were only occasionally interrupted by sudden, luminous highlights. The particular beauties of black-and-white photography, its command of contrast, its graphic directness, its fine manipulations of light, qualify it as the perfect documentarian complement to the era.

This is not to suggest that color photography was entirely absent from the photographic landscape of the thirties. By 1939 Kodachrome was available in a number of formats: 16mm film (with sound), 35mm cartridge roll films, cut-sheet films for larger format cameras. But all Kodachrome images were in one way or another viewed as transparencies; color prints would not come along until the early forties. And though the graphic reproduction of color slides in mass-market magazines was slightly quicker to arrive, it too was a rarity in the thirties. No doubt the technology was in place. Since Kodachrome dye images contained no metallic silver, they could be enlarged at will. As a *National Geographic* photo editor, Louis Marden, said, "The minute we saw this stuff projected, we knew the millennium was here for magazine color reproduction." But even into the early forties the preponderance of photographs printed in picture magazines such as *Life* and *Look* continued to be in black and white.

During the thirties color photography had also been made available to the motion-picture industry. Early in the decade Technicolor had abandoned its two-color cemented positive technique for the much more pleasing and vivid three-color imbibition process. But making movies in Technicolor was expensive, and this limited the number of color films produced each year. In fact, prior to 1939, when *Gone with the Wind* and *Wuthering Heights* won Academy Awards for color and black and white, respectively, there had been only a single cinematography category. Until this time, color was, in most peoples' minds, an extra, a special attraction.

In 1939 the photographic business of the Eastman Kodak Company was divided into three practically equal parts: amateur, professional-commercial, and 35mm motion picture. The amateur market was further subdivided into still and cine categories. In 1935, when Kodachrome 16mm film was introduced, Mees bet Frank Lovejoy, the current president of Kodak, that within five years black-and-white home movies would be replaced by color films. Kodachrome was so clearly a superior product that Mees won the wager in less than three years.

Mees did not chance the guess that a similar shift would take place in the amateur still market. Certainly, with the increasing popularity of the 35mm miniature camera and the 1936 introduction of Kodachrome film in that format, the number of color photographs taken each year had increased dramatically. But as yet, the overwhelming majority of amateurs continued to take black-and-white pictures. Cameras that used film in formats other than 35mm were still considerably less expensive, and, most important, black-and-white photos could be viewed as prints.

Most professional and commercial photographers also stuck with black and white. Indeed, many had become masters of the medium, mechanical, chemical, and artistic virtuosos. Instinct and a good eye, as always, separated great photographers from the merely competent, but for all, the scientific study of the structure and behavior of the silver image had eliminated a good deal of the guesswork involved in picture making. Simply put, most of the working photographers of the era understood in remarkable detail how photochemical images were captured, developed, and printed.

Even art photographers, who had usually insisted that sensibility separated them from more mundane users of the medium, became attentive technocrats. Edward Weston, for instance, was one of the founders of a small group of photographers called "f/64." Weston was a "straight," in some sense "realistic," photographer. Using fast film and very small apertures (thus the name f/64) Weston took straightforward photos of things: people, plants, landscapes, architecture. "The camera," he wrote, "should be used for a recording of life, for rendering the very substance and quintessence of the thing itself, whether it be polished steel or palpitating flesh." But like all other members of the f/64 group, Weston was also a perfectionist when it came to the making of photographs. "Unless," he once wrote, "I pull a technically fine print from a technically fine negative, the emotional or the intellectual value of the photograph is for me almost negated."

Straight photographers of the Weston type also were insistent that their pictures encompass a very extensive depth of field. Photographic law dictates that the wider the lens opening the less light is accurately focused on the film plane. To compensate for the lack of sharpness, the distance between lens and film (the focal length) is adjusted. When a photographer focuses on a single object, however, only a certain area in front of and behind this point remains sharp. By limiting the amount of light entering the lens (stopping down the aperture), the photographer can reverse this process and increase the area in acceptable focus. The larger the area in focus, the greater the depth of field.

Camera mechanisms could not alone create the sharpness and depth favored by the f/64 straight photographers. The film had to be capable of registering this detail. When less light enters a stopped-down lens aperture, the amount of exposure decreases. Larger, more sensitive grains of silver halide in the emulsion could compensate for this loss, but this would lead to larger clumps of developed silver and unacceptably grainy prints.

The solution to this grain-sharpness problem was to increase the light sensitivity of the emulsion without increasing the grain size. By the late 1930s, scientists in the Kodak laboratories had succeeded in extending this range by combined research into the areas of dye sensitization and supersensitization, gelatin and emulsion making, and developing fluids. Improvements in each of these factors allowed photographers to make full use of the highly sensitive panchromatic films marketed during this era.

The seemingly autonomous efforts of aesthetics and science, one concerned with image and emotion, the other with density and contrast, crossed paths in the work of Ansel Adams, another of the original members of the f/64 group. Adams's zone system of photography was in a certain sense a shrewd synthesis of pure research and original artistry. Adams, who had met Weston in the late 1920s, would have completely agreed with that photographer's technoartistic credo. "The real test," Weston wrote, "of not only technical proficiency, but intelligent conception, is not in the use of some indifferent negative as a basis to work from, but in the ability to see one's finished print on the ground glass in all its desired qualities and values before exposure."

This approach was the basis of Adams's zone system. To make great photographs, Adams argued, the photographer must take into account four variables: the sensitivity of the film, the brightness or luminescence of the scene, the amount of exposure, and the method of

Opposite:

In the early 1940s Kodak cooperated with the Technicolor Corporation in the development of a single monopack stock from which three separation negatives were produced to print the release film. This technique was first utilized on location shots for the 1943 film Lassie Come Home.

Left:

The large and bulky Technicolor three-strip camera was particularly well suited to the in-house productions of cartoon features such as Walt Disney's 1932 Flowers and Trees, *the first three-color film shot in Technicolor.*

In 1941 color prints from Kodachrome transparencies were first introduced. Produced in two sizes (2¼ x 3 inches and 5 x 7½ inches), these Minicolor prints were among the most highly saturated color prints of the day. Prints made from 8 x 10-inch Kodachrome professional sheet-film transparencies, called Kotavachrome prints, were produced in sizes ranging from 8 x 10 inches to 30 x 40 inches.

development. First the photographer must previsualize his picture by measuring luminescence on a ten-zone scale; the darkest tones being at one end, the lightest at the other. He then can decide subjectively where on this scale the most artistically significant tones of the scene should fall. With this information, the photographer is able to manipulate contrast through the amount of exposure and development. The result, if the photographer has accurately controlled each variable, will be a print that is perfectly expressive of the photographer's understanding of the scene.

The Adams zone method was intended primarily to produce images that had, as he once wrote, "aesthetic/expressive intentions." In other words, finely articulated, beautiful photographs. Other 1930s photographers, the documentarians, were not so sure that production of beauty was the only business of the photographer, particularly in view of the pressing social conditions of the Depression years. Some of these documentarians, such as *Life* magazine's Margaret Bourke-White, were professional photojournalists. Others, such as Berenice Abbott, worked independently.

The best-known group of documentarians, however, had been hired by Roy Stryker for the Farm Security Administration's efforts to provide documentary evidence of the Depression. The government was looking, as Arthur Rothstein, the first photographer hired by the FSA, wrote, "to justify the New Deal legislation designed to alleviate" these conditions. The gray area between documentary truth and political propaganda seemed less important to Stryker than the camera's ability to spur the country into action. By the late thirties, when Stryker transferred his efforts from the Farm Security Administration to the Office of War Information, political circumstances in Europe increased his sense of urgency. "I know your damn photographer's soul writhes," he wrote to FSA photographer Jack Delano, "but to hell with it. Do you think I give a damn about a photographer's soul with Hitler at our doorstep? You are nothing but camera fodder to me."

Whatever the political and ideological purposes of the photos taken during Stryker's years at FSA/OWI, at the time these photographs had an almost immediate impact upon the way Americans viewed social conditions. FSA/OWI pictures were published in newspapers, in magazines (*Life* and *Look* for instance), and in book form (such as Sherwood Anderson's paean to small-town America, *Home Town*). Ansel Adams had said to Stryker, "What you've got are not photographers. They're a bunch of sociologists with cameras." That these camera-carrying sociologists could often bend the truth, as recent discussions of FSA working methods has proved, was, to those who saw the pictures, fundamentally unimportant. There in dense, believable black and white was the way things were. The camera did not lie.

In many ways, despite the apparent distance between the f/64 group, with their insistence upon purely aesthetic expressiveness, and the documentarians, with their taste for social truth, the two groups had exploited the medium of black-and-white photography with a skill and sophistication unmatched by earlier photographers. Each had wrung from silver halide chemistry a view of the world expressed mainly in the contrast between highlights and shadows.

The visual language of motion pictures was also primarily expressed in a black-and-white vocabulary. By the late 1920s orthochromatic stock had given way to cine-panchromatic film. However, contrary to the prevailing trends in still photography, which called for sharpness and increased depth of field, most cinematographers during the 1930s continued to favor a softer, more diffused look. Even as the new panchromatic stocks became more sensitive to the light, the style remained the same. Partly a matter of economics (the less lighting needed the cheaper the production cost), the soft style was mostly an artistic choice. One cinematographer of the time put it simply: "Sharp photography is not artistic photography."

Sharp photography was also not considered capable of creating the glamorous images that drew moviegoers week after week into the darkened theaters. The twin attractions of allure and illusion were, during the thirties, mainstays of what has been called the Hollywood dream factory. On the silver screen, movie stars, whether they were playing gangsters, G-men, or the privileged denizens of high society, had to look larger and more beautiful than life. The quality of the individual's photographic image, its ability to charm, entice, and enthrall was what counted above all. Indeed, as the screen actress Louise Brooks once wrote, it was often a single image that remained etched in the memory:

When you think of it, what people remember of those stars is not from films, but one essential photograph: Dietrich—heavy-lidded, sucked-in cheeks/Keaton—sad little boy/Crawford—staring self-admiration/Gable—smiling, darling. And when I think of Garbo I do not see her moving in any particular film. I see her staring mysteriously into the camera. No matter how many times I've seen her in films, that is how I always see her. She is a still picture—unchangeable.

Most motion-picture studios at the time had a distinctive style. Warner Brothers' films, for example were usually brightly lit; MGM movies, starker and more contrasty. As the Eastman Kodak Company introduced films with increased sensitivity, each of these studios simply adapted the improvements to complement its particular look. Though the new stocks were in fact capable of rendering increasingly greater detail, cinematographers underutilized the films. Movies were not meant to be realistic. Cinematographers were light modelers, and their subjects were the stars of the day. Actors and actresses, not their environment, were the focus of the audiences' attention. As one cinematographer of the time wrote after the introduction of Plus-X camera stock:

The film itself now does half the work of separating the different planes of your picture. People stand out more clearly from their backgrounds. Even separating the planes in close shots—the little matter of keeping a coat lapel from blending into the background of a garment—of giving an illusion of depth to the faces and figures—is easier with the new film.

The most significant exception to this approach was the work of cinematographer Greg Toland. During the late 1930s Toland had experimented with stark, dramatic lighting in such films as the 1939 *Wuthering Heights* and John Ford's 1940 *The Grapes of Wrath*. The images in this last movie, an adaptation from John Steinbeck's novel about migrant workers, seem to have been influenced by the sort of documentary still photographs then being widely circulated by the Farm Security Administration.

Toland's most revolutionary adaptation of these deep and sharp still techniques came in 1940, when he was hired by Orson Welles to direct the photography of *Citizen Kane*. When the two first met to lay out the cinematographic plan of the movie, Welles told Toland to let "the Hollywood conventions of movie-making go hang if need be," a suggestion Toland was more than glad to follow.

The custom that Toland was most eager to let go hang was the soft, single-plane glamour photography preferred by most studios. In 1938 Kodak had introduced Super-XX motion-picture camera film. The stock was four times faster than its immediate predecessor, Super-X, without any noticeable increase in grain. Around the same time a fine-grain duplicating stock had also been marketed. These stocks, together with improvements in motion-picture camera and lens design, set the stage for Toland and Welles's creation of what in movie terminology is called "deep-focus photography."

Much like the f/64 group, Toland stopped down the aperture of his camera to sizes, as he wrote, "infinitely smaller than anything that had been used for conventional interior cinematography." By carefully coordinating film, camera, and lighting, Toland was able to keep

Though the majority of photographs taken during World War II were in black and white, this Office of War Information picture of an A-20 bomber and its crew, shot by Alfred Palmer in 1942, was exposed on the then relatively new Kodachrome color stock.

in focus a depth of field extending from eighteen inches to infinity. In scene after scene, people and objects in the foreground share visual importance with those in the background. Like Weston, Toland saw deep focus as a way to portray life accurately and realistically. "Both Welles and I," Toland wrote, "felt that if it was possible the picture should be brought to the screen in such a way that the audience would feel it was looking at reality, rather than merely a movie."

As startling, powerful, and groundbreaking a movie as *Citizen Kane* turned out to be, the realism of deep-focus black-and-white photography was not the only issue at hand. If Mees had been correct that after the introduction of Kodachrome film the "glorious" world no longer need be viewed in monochrome, then the illusion of reality could best be accomplished by taking pictures, still or motion, in color.

Late in administrator Roy Stryker's tenure at FSA/OWI, a few photographers had been provided with Kodachrome color transparency film. Though only a little over a thousand of the near ninety thousand exposures taken by Stryker's photographers were made on color stock, the difference in mood, tone, and perhaps verisimilitude is at once apparent. In spite of the clear signs of poverty, the appearance of blue skies, bright orange billboards, and even the scrubby grass and mauve dirt make these few color documentary photographs somehow more spirited and vibrant than similar scenes shot in black and white. Which version of reality is the more reliable is a question that probably cannot be answered.

In one way or another, all photography creates its own truth. The year before work on *Citizen Kane* began, production of another film had ended. That movie was *Gone with the Wind*, and its cinematographical legacy is probably no less important than that of Welles's later black-and-white film. Unlike the filming of *Citizen Kane*, there was considerable on-the-set controversy about cinematographical issues. Part way through the filming, Lee Garmes, the original cameraman, was fired by producer David O. Selznick. The cinematographer had been using a new type of Technicolor stock with, as he later explained, "soft tones, softer quality...but David had been accustomed to working with picture-postcard colors." Indeed Garmes had very closely described exactly the type of color Selznick wanted, color that would make the audience "gasp" at its beauty.

As it turned out, the color tones of the movie were often not as hard and sharply rendered as Selznick might have wished. *Gone with the Wind*, like Griffith's *Birth of a Nation*, is a historical melodrama, a cinematic rendering of the Civil War era swarming with detail and lush with emotion. "Picture-postcard" colors, as Selznick rightly imagined, encouraged viewers to focus on each character and incident as if it were a single discrete part of the sweeping historical pageant that passed before them. In that limited sense, color separated and sharpened photographic planes no less effectively than Toland's deep-focus techniques. But the rhetoric of color, and particularly the luxurious tones of the Technicolor three-strip imbibition dye process, also soothed and excited the viewer. The elegant clothing of the main characters, the brightly colored flags and uniforms of the soldiers, even the glow of Atlanta burning against the night sky, all conspired to produce an illusion that had little to do with verisimilitude.

Gone with the Wind was in most ways a respite from reality. It expressed emotions that if photographed in black and white would have reminded moviegoers of the stark contrasts dividing the world outside the darkened theater.

Three weeks after the bombing of Pearl Harbor on December 7, 1941, the United States Navy released the first photographs of the destruction. Allowing the public to glimpse visual proof of the disaster, ships on fire, the partially sunken U.S.S. *Arizona*, Americans courageously battling against an enemy that struck suddenly and without warning, was not simply an act of goodwill on the part of the navy. By the time the pictures were nationally published in newspapers and magazines, the United States was at war with Japan, and documentary photography had been requisitioned as part of the war effort. Seeing was no longer simply a matter of believing; it had, with a not-so-subtle shift of emphasis, become the surest way to spread the sense of urgency, alarm, and patriotism necessary to fight a good war. Pictures, in short, were great pieces of propaganda.

During the First World War the government had been slow to understand the uses of the medium. It had been particularly laggard in its dealings with the Eastman Kodak Company. The antitrust battles between Kodak and the government no doubt affected the War Department's point of view, as did its inexperience with the tactical and documentary uses of photography. Twenty years later, as the likelihood of another world war was fast becoming a certainty, the government was much less reluctant to request—even require—corporate contributions.

The shift in the political climate does not completely explain this dramatic turnabout. By the late 1930s and early 1940s the Eastman Kodak Company had also changed. Its research and development facilities, its manufacturing expertise, and the broad scope of its nonphotographic chemical research had in all ways expanded the company's ability to contribute. Even before the United States's declaration of war, Kodak had signed letters of intent with the government offering to manufacture photo-related products such as height-finders and aiming circles, artillery telescopes and aerial cameras.

As the United States shifted from a peacetime to a wartime economy the country's industrial capabilities were retooled to accommodate the demand for military goods and hardware. Since the First World War, Kodak had acquired manufacturing expertise in areas other than the production of photographic supplies. Tennessee Eastman, for example, the company's chemical subsidiary, had expanded its research into cellulose-acetate film to include other acetate-based materials. One of the first jobs Tennessee Eastman was assigned by the government was to step up production of synthetic yarns and fibers to replace the natural fibers such as silk and wool then in short supply. The National Research Defense Council also asked Tennessee Eastman to

As part of its contribution to the war effort, Kodak manufactured a variety of range-finding telescopes, such as this height-finder used by a U.S. Marine Corps long-range antiaircraft battery on Rendova Island in the South Pacific.

manufacture a highly explosive acidic-based substance called RDX (Hexamethylene Tetramine Nitrate). By the end of the war almost a billion pounds of this explosive, which was used in torpedoes, depth charges, and other sorts of bombs, came out of the Holston Ordnance Works, a Tennessee Eastman factory erected just a few miles away from the subsidiary's Kingsport factory.

In Rochester other nonphotographic war work included the building of pontoons in Kodak metal shops, the manufacture of metal components for various underwater apparatus, and the design of VT (variable-time) fuses. VT fuses were small, six-inch-long detonators operated by radio control. As a bomb fell toward the ground, waves from the five-tube radio contained in the VT fuses were transmitted toward the earth. When the bombshell reached about seventy feet above ground level, the radio signals triggered a detonating switch, exploding the warhead just above the target.

Kodak's most secret and scientifically sophisticated work for the government began early in 1943 when Mees met with Leslie R. Groves, an army brigadier general who explained that he wanted Kodak to take part in the secret development of a new weapon: an atomic bomb. Mees wondered why a company like Kodak had been approached, to which Groves's assistant, Colonel Kenneth Nichols, is reported to have responded, "Do you know any better qualified?" Mees agreed that few laboratories had so successfully combined pure and applied research, and soon after Kodak chemists, physicists, engineers, and administrators were shipped either to

The Kodak 35 camera, first introduced in 1938, was adopted by the U.S. Navy during World War II as the standard submarine camera. When equipped with a periscope attachment, the camera recorded events above the sea, such as the sinking of torpedoed enemy ships.

SMALL CAMERAS
DOCUMENT THE WORLD

Most of the work produced by Edward Stei-chen's Naval Aviation Photographic Unit was taken on black-and-white film. Occasionally, however, such as in this shot of a sea battle and in the documentary film The Fighting Lady, *Kodachrome film was used effectively to depict the smoky yellow glow of gunfire during battles fought on the open seas.*

physicist E. O. Lawrence's research facility in Berkeley, California, or to Oak Ridge, Tennessee, where a uranium-separating plant was then under construction. Both locations were so secret that they were referred to by Kodak scientists as "Shangri-la" and "Dogpatch," respectively.

Most of Kodak's work on the project was conducted at Dogpatch, the uranium-enriching facility at Oak Ridge. "The problems at Oak Ridge were massive," according to Wesley Hanson, who before the war had specialized in color research, "and we learned to solve them as we went along. It was not so much a research project as a chemical plant operation, and it was a completely new experience for me." The administrative and engineering problems aside, in 1944 the first shipment of U-235 was sent from Oak Ridge to the project's testing grounds at Los Alamos, New Mexico.

All these perhaps surprising war-related projects were accompanied by a slow but eventually almost complete cessation of Kodak's consumer film business. In 1942 the War Production Board ruled that Kodak should cut production of its amateur film to 50 percent of the previous year's level and reduce its professional, commercial, and movie film output to 76 percent of the 1941 rate. The following year absolutely no amateur cameras were produced.

Film for amateur use, in fact, became so scarce that the caption under a *Collier's* magazine cartoon of a woman showing friends her latest snapshots read: "When we get film we try to make each picture count. This is one of our backyard, our four children and their families, a neighbor boy home on furlough, my sister and her husband, and a corner of our bed of

gladioli." Photographic supplies unrelated to the war effort were so strictly rationed that one Kodak advertising manager imagined his job being to convince people not to buy "what we haven't got to sell anyway."

The war also interrupted nonessential laboratory research. A little over five years earlier the invention of Kodachrome seemed to be the harbinger of a photographic revolution. Photographs in color, many predicted, would soon replace black-and-white representations of the world. As it turned out, about twenty years would pass before that forecast was realized. In 1941, however, the move toward color was brought one step closer with the introduction of two types of color prints: Minicolor (in two sizes, 2¼ x 3 inches and 5 x 7½ inches) and Kotavachrome (sheet films ranging in sizes from 8 x 10 inches to 30 x 40 inches). Both of these types of pictures were printed from Kodachrome transparencies on three-emulsion-layer color-sensitive white paper and made use of the Kodachrome controlled-diffusion process.

In 1942, in response to the German Agfa company's 1935 development of a negative-positive color film, Kodak introduced Kodacolor print film. Unlike the Kodachrome color-transparency process, both the Agfa and the Kodak films contained color couplers in the emulsion itself. These "incorporated" couplers were immoblized in each of the three emulsion layers by long chains of carbon atoms called "fatty tails." Since Agfa had patented its formulas, Kodak chemists came up with a version of the carbon compounds that was "protected" by shorter, less water-soluble chains. The film, however, still had problems with light absorption, dye stability,

SMALL CAMERAS
DOCUMENT THE WORLD

During World War II most of Kodak's film production was requisitioned for use in the war effort. Photographs that documented overseas battles were a major part of this mission. Published in Life *magazine in 1945, W. Eugene Smith's shot of a marine demolition team blasting a bunker on Iwo Jima's Hill 382 was seen by those back home as a powerful reminder of the on-going war's destructive potential.*

and excessive graininess. The prints were also expensive (seventy-five cents for the smaller Minicolor size, three dollars fifty cents for the larger ones), and as the war took more and more of the company's time, further research on consumer color was for all practical purposes halted.

The "protected coupler" concept was instrumental, however, in the creation of a film adaptable for aerial photography. Since the First World War, Kodak, at the urging of George W. Goddard, a young Signal Corps photographer, had been experimenting with the production of high resolution, fine-grain films for use in high-altitude reconnaissance work. Goddard had asked Mees in 1924 to make what he called a "negapositive," a reversal film that would eliminate the time-consuming task of printing each negative. The Capstaff reversal process, which had been designed to produce inexpensive home-movie film, was adapted to meet Goddard's requirements.

Night photography also seemed to Goddard something that should be of interest to Kodak. On November 20, 1925, the photographer had constructed an eighty-pound flash bomb, loaded it and his aerial cameras in a small army plane, and flown over the roof of Kodak's Rochester offices, where Mees and his associates were waiting with the equipment necessary to measure the luminescence of the blast. At about 11:00 P.M. that night Goddard dropped his bomb.

As C.E.K. Mees had predicted before World War I, aerial photography remained the medium's most important tactical contribution to the conducting of warfare. This black-and-white aerial shot documenting an invasion landing was taken in 1945.

The photo (above), taken from the air by Charles Kerlee, a member of Edward Steichen's Naval Aviation Photographic Unit, is of a Curtiss SB2C Helldiver coming back to the U.S.S. Hornet *after a bombing mission in the South China Sea.*

The microfilming of letters reduced the bulk of mail to about one-fiftieth of its normal weight. Kodak's V-Mail microfilm system, first created during the 1940 German siege of Great Britain, was responsible by the end of the war for the easy transport of nearly a half billion letters.

A—You read a letter in your boy's own writing, like that above (actual size).   letters—in the form of photographic film. C—On this one roll of 16-mm.
B—The three small boxes in the photograph contain over 5000 of these   film—shown in slightly reduced size—1700 letters have been photographed.

Kodak created, U.S. Government adopts "V···-MAIL"...
for communication with our men on distant fronts

YOUR BOY writes you a letter on a sheet of paper — regular letter size. This is photographed on Kodak microfilm — is reduced in size to about a quarter of a square inch ... Now it has only 1/100 of the weight of normal mail.

With thousands of other letters — 85,000 letters weighing 2000 pounds weigh only 20 when reduced to microfilm — it is swiftly flown from his distant outpost to America.

Here, again through photography, the letter addressed to you is "blown up" to readable size — folded, sealed in an envelope, and forwarded to you. It is as clear as the original writing. It really is the writing of your boy because it's a photographic print.

And your letters to him, which you write on special forms, go by the same space-saving, time-saving V···- Mail.

Kodak developed and perfected the process ... Pan American Airways and British Overseas Airways, the two great pioneers in transoceanic air transport, blazed the air trails ... and the three companies, as Airgraphs, Ltd., offered the service to the American and British governments.

IN APRIL, 1941, under the trademark "Airgraph," England first employed the system to solve the problem of getting mail to and from the forces in the Near East. The Airgraph System was gradually expanded until it knits

the British Empire together with about a million letters a week — personal and official.

And now the men serving overseas in the American armed forces also have the benefits of this form of speedy correspondence.

Airgraph, or V···- Mail as it is called here, is an adaptation of Kodak's Recordak System which has revolutionized the record-keeping methods of thousands of banks and business houses. Many records of the U.S. Census, Social Security, and Army Selective Service are on microfilm — error-proof, tamper-proof, lasting photographic copies of the original bulky records ... Eastman Kodak Company, Rochester, N. Y.

SERVING HUMAN PROGRESS THROUGH PHOTOGRAPHY

Late in the war about a thousand subminiature cameras were secretly manufactured for the OSS for use by agents in occupied Europe. Called the "Eastman M.B." (for "matchbox"), the camera was built to be disguised, if necessary, in a standard matchbox.

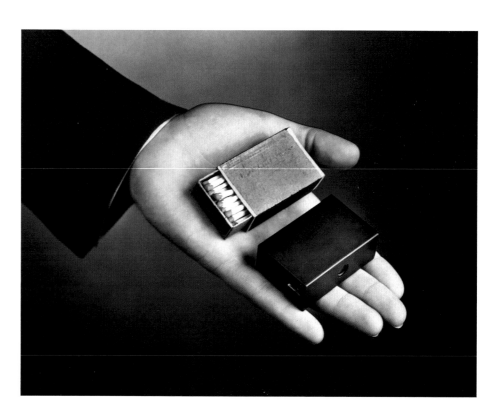

*Hollywood director George Stevens, then
attached to the U.S. Army, was present in
April 1945 when Russian and American
troops met at the Elbe River in Torgau,
Germany. This rare 16mm Kodachrome
color film frame, taken by Stevens's unit,
documents that meeting.*

Unfortunately neither he nor Mees had thought to inform anyone else in the community of the experiment, and as Goddard drove into the city from the airport, the streets were full of people, many of whom were speculating that an explosion at Rochester's central heating plant had caused the intense illumination of the night sky.

After the invention of Kodachrome transparency film, Goddard once again traveled to Rochester, this time to question Mees about the possible uses of the new Kodachrome color film in aerial work. Color photographs, Goddard explained, would provide the readers of reconnaissance pictures with new levels of information. Objects on the ground that heretofore had blended monochromatically into one another would, when viewed in color, be seen "as the eye perceived" them.

Kodachrome did indeed produce more "realistic" color images, but two problems with the film had to be overcome before high-altitude pictures could be useful. The first was the continuing problem of atmospheric haze. Kodachrome worked well when exposed at reasonable distances from its subject, but when photographs were taken from thousands of feet up, sharpness and resolution were lost. Leopold Mannes and Leopold Godowsky, who had returned to the Kodak laboratories as consultants just before the war, and Walter Clark, the former head of Kodak's research laboratory at Harrow, spent months taking test shots from a B-18 airplane, and by 1939 they were able to develop a fairly fast, aerocolor-balanced Kodachrome stock.

The second problem was the time and care necessary to develop the film. By 1938 a technique known as selective reexposure had reduced the number of steps in the procedure from twenty-eight to eighteen, but, even at that, the training and equipment required made processing in the field all but impossible. Research into a film that employed "protective couplers" contained in each emulsion layer had by this time begun, and by the middle of the war an effective Kodak Aerocolor film was invented. Because these films were, like Koda-chrome, viewed as positive transparencies, many of the most unsatisfactory aspects of Kodacolor print film, a product using a similar color coupler technology, were adequately averted.

Movie stock, like other sorts of film, was solicited to help win the war. Shortly after the beginning of the war President Roosevelt established the Bureau of Motion Picture Affairs to encourage Hollywood filmmakers to produce morale-boosting movies such as the 1943 musical revue This Is the Army, *which starred, among others, Ronald Reagan.*

Mees had predicted in 1918 that photography's most significant contribution to the waging of war would be its ability to provide tactical information. It has been estimated that close to 90 percent of the intelligence data gathered during the Second World War came from aerial photographs. Eight million square miles of the earth's surface were photographed in both color and black and white. Flash-bombs of upwards of a billion candlepower were dropped when photographing at night over enemy territory. Aerial pictures were sometimes taken from a height of six miles. What had begun in the early days of the First World War as an experiment now was a military necessity. As Army Air Force Commander H. H. Arnold explained in a 1944 article entitled "How We Fight with Photographs," "A camera mounted on a P-38 often has proved to be of more value than a P-38 with guns."

As prescient as Mees was in 1918 about the tactical and strategical uses of photography, he seriously underrated the future of documentary photography in wartime. One of Kodak's earliest military assignments was in the form of a request from the United States Navy to plan and organize a photo center in Washington, D.C. This facility, Kodak was informed, would house studios and processing laboratories for both motion-picture and still photography, editing rooms, camera repair shops, and even "hot and cold rooms" in which to test supplies being forwarded to tropical or arctic regions.

The work of the Naval Photo Center was very close in spirit and intention to that of the photographic group of the Farm Security Administration. Though its mandate was much wider and its work conducted on a much grander scale, the center was envisioned as a clearinghouse of politically useful visual information. Some of the pictures taken by navy photographers that

passed through the facility were sent directly to military planners. Many of the photographs, particularly those showing gallant American GIs in action around the world, were approved by military censors for publication in the mass media. All had a single overriding purpose: to help win the war.

One of the most famous photographers to make use of the center was Edward Steichen, who at the age of sixty-two somehow managed to convince the navy to commission him as a lieutenant commander in the photographic unit of its Training Literature Division. Traveling the Pacific under Steichen's direction, most of the photographers in this unit preferred smaller, faster 35mm cameras over the bulky Speed Graphic, which was the standard service issue. Film was not a problem. Rationing regulations had assured military photographers a continuing supply of both black-and-white Kodak panchromatic stock and Kodachrome film. Eight-by-ten-inch sheets of Kodachrome were, in fact, so plentiful that occasionally photographers in Steichen's unit secreted the color stock out of navy headquarters and traded it on the open market for 35mm cameras.

As World War II wound on, battle films became increasingly grim and realistic. By the time the war was over, scenes of American soldiers suffering, as in the 1949 Sands of Iwo Jima, were much more common than they had been in the early confidence-building days of war.

The 1945 Japanese surrender aboard the U.S.S. Missouri,
which ended World War II, was documented in
this 8 x 10-inch Kodachrome film print.

That color was so dispensable seems in hindsight an anomaly. Kodachrome color transparency film was available to most World War II photographers, but its use was the exception rather than the rule. Very late in the war, when victory seemed assured, *Life* magazine photographer George Silk exposed a few rolls of color film while covering the war in Italy. The caption accompanying Silk's pictures suggested that an increased use of color might indeed have contributed an unprecedented sense of realism to the photographic documentation of war:

These pictures also show that ordinary black-and-white photographs have not done full descriptive justice to the war in Italy. They have omitted the soft browns and grays of the ruined Italian towns, the bright shocking redness of freshly spilled blood, the incongruously gay colors of spring in the midst of battle.

There are at least two purely technological reasons why color seldom showed up on the pages of mass-market magazines. In the first place, processing remained tricky, and secondly, most of the World War II photographers were accustomed to black and white. They knew how to manipulate the film, and some, such as Carl Mydans, the *Life* photojournalist, personally developed their own photographs in the field. The single emulsion layer of black-and-white film was also a tougher, more stable stock. It could survive varied climates and film cans could be shipped without fear of damage. All sorts of ad hoc procedures were possible when working with the sturdy black-and-white stock. Photographers in the Pacific theater, for instance, were told that when transporting film the correct ratio of film to dehumidifier was one pound of rice or tea leaves per two hundred feet of motion-picture or still film.

It is also likely that color images were thought too lurid and sensational. Throughout most of the war, photographs from the front were distributed to boost morale. Not until September 1943, when *Life* magazine published George Stock's photos of the aftermath of battle on Buna Beach in New Guinea did people back home see for the first time pictures of dead American soldiers. And even then the editors of *Life* felt it necessary to justify the publication of such alarming and depressing photographs:

Why print this picture, anyway, of three American boys dead upon an alien shore? Is it to hurt people? To be morbid?
These are not the reasons.
The reason is that words are never enough.

In that light, it can only be imagined how early in the war magazines would have responded to photos such as Silk's that also displayed "the bright shocking redness of freshly spilled blood." It would take twenty years for the press and the public to be ready to see the carnage of war in full color, but then, during the Vietnam War, the attitude of both toward the good fight would have changed considerably.

It should not be imagined, though, that the black-and-white images produced during World War II lacked expressive power. In intimacy, insight, and compositional power nothing like these pictures had ever emerged from any previous theater of war. But like the politically motivated FSA/OWI documentary photographs that preceded them, these pictures were unabashedly rhetorical. Just before the D-day invasion of France, Allied commander Dwight Eisenhower had written in a memorandum to his staff, "Fundamentally, public opinion wins wars." There were few vehicles that carried the weight of public opinion more efficiently than photography. Field photographers knew this implicitly, or at least articulated it in their own terms. As George Silk once said about the apparently disinterested eye of documentary photography, "There is no such thing as being unbiased. You'd have to be a neuter to be unbiased, and if you were unbiased then nothing would be worth reading that you wrote or took."

Of all photography's genres none was more forthright about its partiality toward the Allied cause than the motion-picture industry. When film rationing figures had been released early in the war, Kodak was required to reduce the amount of stock sent to Hollywood by only one quarter. And, in fact, even a good deal of that stock was used specifically for Hollywood-produced training films. In 1942 the Office of War Information had formed the Bureau of Motion Picture Affairs to administrate the movie world's contributions to the war effort. In Hollywood, military groups such as the Air Force Motion Picture Unit were set up to make use of the motion-picture industry's expertise. Ronald Reagan, for instance, then a member of an air force training crew, was the off-screen narrator of a secret movie made early in the war to prepare pilots for possible bombing runs over Japan. Skillfully put together out of existing footage, the film simulates a long-range bombing sortie over the Japanese islands. As the pilot imagines himself watching landmarks appear on the screen and prepares to select his target, Reagan's carefully scripted descriptions of tactical procedure talk him in.

Many of Hollywood's most famous actors and directors were attached to one or another of these military movie groups. Gene Kelly and Tyrone Power, for example, were assigned to the Naval Photo Center in Washington, and John Huston, Frank Capra, John Ford, and William Wyler worked either directly for the War Department or were assigned to another service branch. Capra was one of the most prolific of these Hollywood wartime directors. Called to Washington by none other than General George Marshall, Capra was given his orders by the chief of staff:

To win this war we must win the battle for men's minds. [General] Osborn and I think films are the answer, and that you are the answer to such films. Now, Capra, I want to nail down with you a plan to make a series of documented, factual-information films—the first in history—that will explain to our boys in the army why we are fighting, and the principles for which we are fighting.

"I'll make you the best damned documentary films ever made," Capra answered. The seven-part "Why We Fight" series was used when indoctrinating new recruits, exhibited in commercial movie theaters, and, with dialogue translated into either French, Spanish, Portuguese, or Chinese, shown at Allied bases all over the world.

Hollywood proper also contributed to the war effort, making a series of combat films designed to show Allied soldiers in their best light and the enemy at its worst. These early movies, with uplifting titles such as *Salute to Courage*, *To the Shores of Tripoli*, and *The Devil with Hilter*, were by the middle of the war gradually replaced by slightly more realistic films such as *Bataan* and *Guadalcanal Diary*. Though still blatantly propagandistic they at least succeeded, as film critic James Agee wrote, in depicting the average GI as less than a superhero, as a typical, though idealistic American: "naive, coarse, primitive, honest, accomplished and true."

Motion-picture films played another, perhaps even more novel, role in the life of the average GI. In the late 1930s Kodak executive Charles Case, who had been chiefly responsible for the use of miniature film in the Bantam camera, was asked by H. H. Balfour, a member of parliament in Britain, if the microfilming of letters might decrease the bulk and weight of the mail then being sent overseas by air. In fact, Kodak had been in the microfilm business since 1927, when a subsidiary called the Recordak Corporation had been formed. Making use of the recently introduced 16mm Cine-Kodak, a machine was designed to synchronize the one-per-second filming of canceled checks. The Recordak microfilm system was so successful that by the end of the decade department stores, insurance companies, newspapers, libraries, and even the national census bureau had begun recording and storing data in this miniature format. In 1933 New York district attorneys had used a microfilm reader to prove in court that handwriting on different canceled checks matched, and in 1938 a federal court for the first time accepted microfilm as evidence.

The Recordak system, however, required that documents be displayed on a microfilm reader, and this ruled out its use by soldiers at the front. By 1940, with air traffic reduced to a minimum by the German siege of England, interest in the microfilming of mail was renewed. The British government again asked Case to study the idea. A small corporation called Airgraphs was formed, with Kodak, Imperial Airways, and Pan-American Airways as partners. Case had found that with current high-contrast emulsions the 16mm negatives used for microfilming could easily be enlarged into 4 x 5-inch prints. Photocopying machines were specially designed to accommodate letter-sized documents, as were processors and printers, and in August 1941 Queen Elizabeth sent the first Airgraph letter, a message to the commander of British forces in the Mid-East. The Airgraph system worked so well (it reduced bulk to one-fiftieth of the normal amount and cost to one-fifth) that after the American entry into the war, the company was renamed simply "V Mail." From then until the end of the war, nearly half a billion microfilmed letters were sent to and received by soldiers all over the world.

During the war, Kodak's large-scale operations on the European continent practically shut down. In Germany the factory of Kodak AG, like its American parent company, was put to work producing war supplies. (Coincidentally, AG also manufactured time fuses.) Late in 1943, when Allied bombing raids over Germany intensified, the film plant at Koepenick was so seriously damaged that film production was transferred to a factory in Prague. With the partitioning of Germany after the war, the Koepenick plant, located ten miles inside the Russian sector, was taken over by East German authorities. Offers were made to Kodak to reactivate the plant, but they were declined.

Throughout most of the war years the Kodak-Pathé facilities at Severan and Vincennes likewise produced war material for the German occupying forces. On the day of the liberation of Vincennes, German SS troops still held French resistance fighters as prisoners in the city's ancient castle, which they threatened to blow up, captives and all. Mlle José M. Boichard, a Kodak-Pathé engineer, volunteered to negotiate with the German soldiers. After some discussion with the commander of the fort, an Austrian officer not attached to the SS, it was agreed that the prisoners would be released before the castle was destroyed. As the castle gate opened the prisoners ran out. The assembled Kodak-Pathé employees then waited for the explosion. But Mlle Boichard had apparently been so persuasive that, unbeknownst to the SS soldiers, the Austrian commander had cut the detonating wires.

In 1945 the Kodak annual report listed in detail the range of products produced by the company during the war. In addition to dozens of nonphotographic products, such as gunsights, ordnance supplies, and pontoons, Kodak had manufactured film "at an annual rate of more than five times the yearly average of all snapshot film used by amateurs in the United States in the immediate prewar years." The report also stated that "the annual rate of deliveries of sensitized photographic paper to the armed forces and for war-related purposes, based on the first half of 1945, was more than six times the average prewar consumption in the United States used for snapshot prints."

Once the war was over and people were ready to resume normal lives, deprivation, so throughly a part of the wartime economy, was replaced by a desire for well-being and a demand for all the good things that had been missed. Pictures were one of these things.

"Photo Fans Must Wait: Film Supplies for Civilians Won't Come Till Late 1945," read a small headline in the August 16, 1945, edition of *The New York Daily News. The Washington Post*, running the same Eastman Kodak Company press release, slanted the news a little differently: "Plenty of Film Late This Year." The same day's issue of *The Boston Advertiser* spun the story in another direction: "Film? Not in Picture: No Ample Supplies for Civilians Until Late This Year, Eastman Says."

Whether photo materials were still scarce or about to be bountiful was a fine and, in a certain sense, felicitous distinction. During the four years between the attack on Pearl Harbor in 1941 and the end of the war in 1945, the civilian use of photographic goods, like that of other consumer products, had been strictly rationed. Most of Kodak's industrial output was directed toward the hard business of making war. Leisure, relaxation, and enjoyment were, if not frowned upon, at least not activities essential to the winning of a war. After the end of the war, when soldiers returned home and the usual traffic between consumer and economy was renewed, people enthusiastically shopped for all the merchandise missing the last few years from the shelves of their favorite stores.

A 1946 *Collier's* magazine cartoon depicted a five- or six-year-old boy posing, a little awkwardly considering his age, for a customary baby-on-the-blanket photograph. "Because we couldn't get film when you were three months old, that's why," the parents explain to the squirming, impatient child — a fact that, if the estimated number of amateur photos taken during the war is correct, was without exaggeration.

By 1941 1.1 million snapshots were taken annually, a little over twice the number taken six years earlier in 1935. Then came the war years, when, according to economic analysts, so few snaps were made that the figures were not worth recording. During the first full year after the resumption of civilian supplies, the count jumped to 1.5 million and in less than ten years increased to just over 2 billion. In 1954, of the estimated 53 million families in the United States, 38 million owned cameras, a market that Kodak forecasters predicted would substantially increase when picture-taking teenagers, who at the time consumed about one quarter of the black-and-white still film sold, reached adulthood.

Despite the 1935 invention of Kodachrome film, the 1942 introduction of Kodacolor prints, and the 1946 announcement of Ektachrome color stock, sales of black-and-white film continued throughout this period to dominate the market. As late as 1953, 16 percent of amateur stills were made on color stock, certainly a considerable increase over the 2 percent taken in 1941, but an almost insignificant increment given the revolutionary change in photography brought about by the introduction of the Kodachrome film technology.

Before color photography's market share could change, it was necessary to sort out some of its major problems, not the least of which was Kodak's often confusing use and reuse of brand names. In September 1945 this issue was resolved when Mees wrote a memo to the staff of the Kodak Research Laboratories explaining that in the future "the prefix 'Koda —' is to be used for materials processed by the company and 'Ekta —' for those processed by the user. The suffix '— chrome' is to be used for reversal materials and '— color' for non-reversal materials." (Kodachrome film by this definition was a company-processed reversal product, a transparency; Kodacolor a company-processed negative-positive print film; Ektachrome a user-processed reversal film; Ektacolor a user-processed print stock. Kodak no longer adheres to these distinctions in using its trademarks.)

Given the interrelation of each of these color processes there was in the Kodak laboratories an inevitable cross-fertilization of research ideas. One chemist experimenting with a particular technology often came up with a hunch that might help a fellow scientist working down the hall on a completely different problem. Wesley Hanson, for instance, had been engaged early in the war in an investigation of the possible adaptability of Kodachrome slide film for use in

professional motion pictures. He was having little luck. To generate the thousands of release prints needed by Hollywood, it was necessary to make an intermediate, a duplicate negative of the Kodachrome positive. "In other words," as Hanson later wrote, he was "making copies from copies. The quality was just terrible, and it had been a major problem for seven or eight years."

Hanson decided that if a simple negative-positive process, like that of black-and-white photography, could be worked out, multiple prints could be manufactured from original or duplicate negatives. The Kodacolor film process, in which the color couplers were incorporated in the emulsion rather than the developer, was such a technology, but its color rendition was poor. Hanson explained:

In the theory of subtractive color process, each image color absorbs only one of the three primary colors, or one-third of the spectrum. Thus the cyan dye supposedly absorbs only red, the magenta only green and the yellow only blue.

Alas, it doesn't work that way. The yellow dye does its job quite nicely, but no magenta and cyan dyes are available to take out only the light of the corresponding complementary colors,

green and red, respectively. This leads to color degradation problems with blue and green reproduction and brightness problems with yellow and red, when prints are made from the negatives.

A way had to be found to mask or block the undesirable absorptions. Hanson continued:

Lying in bed one night in February of 1943, I thought if you had the coupler itself colored and you destroyed that color when you made the dye, then you had an automatic mask right there.

I got up the next morning and wrote down the idea, then I went to the labs and told [Kodak chemist] Paul Vittum. He said, "I think we've got something on the shelf that might do it.... Let's try one."

So that same day we ran an experiment and, sure enough, it was colored and it was a coupler and it worked. We were off.... It took many more inventions to make the whole thing work. But the idea had been proven.

By using a yellow-colored magenta coupler and a salmon-colored cyan coupler, blue light was kept from degrading the intensity of red and green layers of the negative. The result of this

"Dear Mr. Weston," George Waters of the Kodak advertising department wrote to photographer Edward Weston in August 1946, "I am wondering if you would like to make an 8 x 10 Kodachrome print for us of Point Lobos." Weston answered that he "didn't know color," but he had such a love for the landscape around Point Lobos that he would "hate to see it murdered in color by an 'outsider.'" This study by Weston of a shell (opposite), taken in 1947, is one of the series of Kodachrome film transparencies resulting from Waters's initial offer. Ansel Adams's late 1940s Kodachrome film photograph of California's Yosemite Valley (above) was also used by Kodak for advertising purposes.

masking is a brick orange negative. As Hanson explained in a 1977 speech:

Thus, in printing, only the cyan peak is printed, resulting in saturated yellow and magenta images that produce clean, bright reds, because the unwanted green and blue absorptions of the cyan dye are cancelled out. The colored coupler has a red orange cast to it. The color is destroyed where the image is formed, but where there is no image, the colored coupler remains. Because the absorption is the same over all the picture area, the whole process negative (masked with the colored coupler) looks red orange.

Hanson's idea for masking negative film with colored couplers made possible the 1949 introduction of an Ektacolor negative-positive sheet film for professional photographers. But in spite of the improvements in Kodacolor and a substantial increase in full-color advertisements by Kodak, the snapshooting public continued to take black-and-white pictures. In 1950, the year after an improved Kodacolor film came on the market, the percentage of color pictures taken by amateurs rose only a single point, and three years later, though the aggregate number of color prints produced rose from 31 million to 74 million and that of color transparencies went from 86 million to 179 million, both color processes combined still commanded only 13 percent of the market.

In the late 1940s Kodak's mass-market advertising was separated into eight distinct groupings: picture taking with Verichrome film, picture taking in color, popular cameras, fine cameras, accessories, home movies, teenagers, and "photo fans." The first two categories reflected the conflicting claims of the two technologies. The casual snapshooter would have preferred full-color pictures. But quality, which Kodacolor film lacked, counted, as did price — color was more expensive. And there was also ease. In 1948, rephrasing the original Kodak camera slogan, it was advertised that with the black-and-white Verichrome film, "You press the button, it does the rest." For those savoring the almost unprecedented good life of the postwar period, anything that saved labor, whether it be a washer, dryer, freezer, or, indeed, fault-free film, was accepted as another of the miracles of modern life.

On the other hand, the two types of cameras advertised, popular and fine, indicated a widening split between the serious amateur and the unsophisticated amateur sectors of the photographic public. During the first ten years after the war, Kodak introduced about a dozen new Brownie camera models. Since the introduction of the one-dollar Brownie in 1900, this camera model had been the workhorse of the amateur market. By 1950 the Brownie Hawk-Eye camera, equipped with a newly popular flashbulb attachment, cost only $6.95 and was used by both adults and children to take millions of simple, no-fuss photographs.

At the same time, Kodak continued to manufacture and produce 35mm cameras for those with a more serious interest in photographic technology. These were, as one camera historian has written, "the golden years of the American 35mm." Neither the German nor the Japanese photographic industries had fully recovered from the war; it was the age in fact when the phrase "Made in Japan" had a less than approbatory connotation. This state of affairs would not last long. By the late 1950s the Japanese were producing high-quality, low-priced 35mm cameras, and Kodak would respond in 1963 by introducing the Instamatic camera, but that radical change in marketing strategy was still ten years away. Despite competition from domestic camera manufacturers, such as the Argus and Bosley firms, Kodak marketed over two dozen 35mm models during the decade immediately following the war. These cameras ranged in price from the $34.75 Pony 135 to the $70.60 Kodak 35 to the $168.50 Retina IIa camera. For the time, of course, these were fairly pricey cameras, but since they were 35mm models, they could be used to take high-quality Kodachrome slides. In fact, throughout this period the number of color transparencies taken each year (and projected in sometimes tedious home slide shows) was more than double the number of color prints annually produced.

Opposite:
During the postwar years group portraiture, always one of the mainstays of popular photography, was promoted even to the youth market. In this 1949 Kodak advertising shot by Ralph Bartholomew, Jr., cheerful, athletic teenagers pose for a friend holding an inexpensive Kodak box camera.

POSTWAR PROSPERITY

In the 1950s some of the most colorful photographs made in the snapshot genre were taken on 8mm Kodachrome home-movie film. Continued improvements in camera design and film emulsions made the motion-picture recording of family events, as in these 1957 frames of a child and her dog, an increasingly popular variation on the snapshot family album.

The other medium in which high-caliber color was available to the amateur was that of home movies. Within five years after the introduction of Kodachrome 16mm and 8mm film, over 50 percent of home movies were shot in color, and by the early 1950s that proportion of color had risen to nearly 100 percent. Amateur movie making was a relatively expensive proposition. Movie cameras ranged from fifty to three hundred dollars in price, and a projector and screen could double that amount. But the color rendition of the Kodachrome film process was so good that in the amateur market black-and-white home movies almost entirely disappeared.

Since 16mm and 8mm Kodachrome film used a color-reversal process that produced a single print it was fine for low-volume home exhibitions. Professional movie producers, however, needed thousands of release prints, and it was while attempting to work out a solution to this problem that Hanson had begun pursuing the idea of colored couplers. In the meantime, another group of Kodak researchers, directed by color expert Ralph Evans, continued to look for ways to solve the Kodachrome release-print problem. Initially they decided that if a low-contrast second-generation "internegative" could be developed in conjunction with a higher-contrast print film then the complicated controlled-diffusion Kodachrome film process could be eliminated during the post-production stage.

At the time, the majority of color films were still made by the Technicolor three-strip dye-transfer process. Though the Technicolor Corporation held patents on this technique, Kodak had since the early twenties manufactured all the film required by Technicolor: the camera-separation negative stock, the matrices required for printing each of the three colors, and the final print stock. In addition Kodak scientists had worked on dye formulas and during the forties helped Technicolor develop an incorporated coupler film.

So close was the relationship between the two companies that in 1947 the United States government filed an antitrust suit charging that Kodak and Technicolor had attempted to control the business of color cinematography through a series of licensing agreements. Within months Kodak signed a consent decree in which it agreed to provide to other film companies with many of its color patents; some at no charge and others for a fair royalty. Initially, Technicolor's experience and expertise was of such a high level that even after the release of

© The Walt Disney Company

The Walt Disney Company and other makers of documentary films often used small portable 16mm cameras and 16mm Kodachrome film to record wildlife in its natural habitat, as in this scene from the 1953 film The Living Desert.

In 1954 Daan Zwick and George Higgins of the Kodak Research Laboratories worked for a few months in the special-effects department of Twentieth Century-Fox learning how Kodak films were used in Hollywood. When the scientists were about to return to Rochester, Marilyn Monroe autographed pinups for them. Zwick's (above) read, "Dear Daan, remember me in your emulsions," and Higgins's was inscribed, "All I am I owe to Kodak and you."

these patents few were able to compete. And in any case, Hollywood producers were still looking ahead to a cheaper color technology that was less time-consuming to expose and process than the complex Technicolor system. As was Kodak.

In 1948 the first step toward a new professional color movie stock was taken when Nick Groet, one of the few Kodak scientists without a college degree, suggested that the results of color-negative experiments he had made while working on a professional sheet film be applied to the movie-stock problem. Groet urged those working in the Kodachrome film lab to coat 35mm stock with the emulsions used for the sheet film, expose it in a motion-picture camera, and then print it on the high-contrast incorporated coupler print film previously developed by the Evans group. As Daan Zwick, who worked in this lab, remembered, Groet guessed that the result would "knock our eyes out, and he was right."

The color reproduction of the new film was excellent. However, one problem remained: the images were excessively grainy and unsharp. Working together, however, Hanson and Groet invented the concept of "coupler starvation." In order to decrease the grain size they double-coated each layer: the upper one containing large, fast grains and the lower one small, slower grains. The top layer, which reacted quickly to light, was dye-starved (it produced smaller than usual amounts of color), while the slower bottom layer was given enough couplers to compensate for the difference. Together the two layers produced more than adequate color rendition without the usual large dye-image grain sizes.

The print film produced to complement this 35mm motion-picture negative stock was also the result of an ingenious idea. Kodak scientists had discovered that the eye is most sensitive to detail in the magenta image, less so in the cyan, and least able to discern detail in the yellow. They therefore rearranged the conventional ordering of emulsion layers. The magenta, being the most important was on the top, the cyan in the middle, and the yellow on the bottom. Microscopic measurements of the film certified that the film was several times sharper than any previously developed.

When a strip of this film was projected, however, something appeared to be wrong with this very reasonable scientific logic. As Hanson remembered:

The stuff was absolutely unsharp. Everyone was yelling "focus, focus" but the film wouldn't focus. This was backwards from what we expected. We had been completely led astray by the resolving power measurements. The picture was completely fuzzy and looked terrible. We had to find out what was the matter.

When the film was reexamined researchers found that there were two answers to this problem. The first was that the high magnification required of motion-picture film skewed the microscopic measurements. Second, it was discovered that light from the bottom layer, which contained the largest and slowest-developing crystals, was bouncing back up and double-exposing the top layers. After long hours of work and the input of George Higgins of the Kodak Physics Department, Groet decided to include soluble magenta and cyan dyes in the film to "mop up" the green and red light before it had a chance to bounce back to the upper layers.

By early 1950 both the color negative motion-picture camera film and the color positive print film were ready. The production of these films, however, remained an obstacle, particularly the manufacture of the multilayer print film. So many coating steps were required that it was thought that the film might be prohibitively expensive. In 1954 Theodore Russell, who was then working in Kodak's Emulsion Research Division on an experimental mixed-grain Kodachrome emulsion, decided that if a hopper could be devised with different slits for different emulsions then multiple layers could be simultaneously spread on the film base. After a few mechanical adjustments were made it was found that this machine (called "Joe Hopper" after the biblical Joseph's coat of many colors) not only worked well but that as a bonus each layer could be made thinner and thus more concentrated.

In 1950, before the days of Joe Hopper, the first batches of Eastman color-negative film and Eastman color-print film were produced at Kodak Park. During the next couple of years the new film was used sparingly; most notably in *Royal Journey*, a 1951 documentary movie account of Princess Elizabeth's tour of Canada and Warner Brothers' 1953 fictional film *The Lion and the Horse*, both of which were shot and printed on the new stock.

As the 1950s began, Hollywood producers, always anxious to attract larger audiences while at the same time cutting costs, became increasingly attracted to color cinematography. To meet this demand companies such as Du Pont, Ansco, Cinecolor, and others tested a diverse variety of color technologies: three-color, reversal, even two-color techniques. At the Kodak laboratories John Capstaff worked out a way of stripping three separation negatives from a single film support and continued to work on a lenticular color film similar to the Kodacolor film first introduced in 1928.

No one doubted the demand for this new photographic technology. As Hanson, who had

In 1949 Kodak reintroduced a hand-coloring process invented in 1940 by Jack Crawford's Flexichrome Company. By this method, a black-and-white relief positive was made from a single panchromatic negative, dyes were applied directly on the film with a brush, and the resulting color picture printed on a separate support. Since specific colors were chosen, sometimes arbitrarily, by the individual colorist, Flexichrome photographs, such as this picture of cookies made in 1950 by an unidentified artist, were often more interpretive than "realistic."

been intimately involved with developments in color since the early 1940s said:

We were entering technology unlimited. The whole motion picture industry was just dying to get better color film—all we had to do was to learn how to make it so they could use it. The same was true for the whole field of amateur photography. We just had to come up with the technology. We never had to worry about whether anyone would buy it. We knew they would.

Early in 1950 Kodak sales personnel began to take serious notice of a new visual medium: television. Radio had been used intermittently to describe and sell Kodak products, but for the most part the company continued, as it had done since the late nineteenth century, to concentrate its advertising efforts in the pictorial print media. Images were Kodak's stock-in-trade. In 1902 George Eastman had noticed that a new Kodak catalog was about to be published without a picture on its cover and ordered it redesigned. "Photography is our business," he told the salesman responsible. "Use it."

Though television was not by the strictest standards photographic, it was so popular and its rapid growth so remarkable that it could not be ignored. With the help of J. Walter Thompson

Company, which for many years had been Kodak's chief advertising agency, the sales staff compiled a list of shows with which Kodak might want to be affiliated: a Dave Garroway program, an Alfred Hitchcock mystery series, "From Sea to Shining Sea" (a series of regional documentary vignettes), "Now See This" (portraits of "people as people"), "Eye Cue" (a variety show based on viewer participation), and a "light but warm serial of family life."

Though some of these programs eventually appeared on television with other sponsors, Kodak opted for a family story entitled "Norby." Starring David Wayne, "Norby" was the continuing account of the usually whimsical trials, travails, and tribulations of a small-town bank clerk. The show, which one Kodak writer called "not quite a classic," was rather long in development and did not appear until 1955. After the airing of a few episodes it was canceled.

The following year Kodak was offered the sponsorship of two other comedies: "Father Knows Best" and "Ozzie and Harriet." The latter was chosen, and for the first time the company entered the world of large-scale televised advertising. "Ozzie and Harriet" was a family program, and much like the 1920s radio program "Front Porch Gang" it was an ideal vehicle for the forwarding of Kodak's most important consumer product: snapshot-album photography. In

The Kodak dye-transfer process, developed by Louis Condax and Robert Speck, was introduced in 1946 to replace the 1935 Eastman wash-off relief process. Three separation relief positives are each dyed one of the appropriate complementary colors and successively squeegeed onto a sheet of photographic paper. Very subtle shades of color can be reproduced, as in this dye-transfer print of dinnerware by Louis Condax.

One Sunday morning in 1954 Walter and Virginia Schau were heading toward California's Lake Shasta for a day of fishing when a tractor trailer just ahead of them lost its steering and crashed into the guard-rail of the Pit River Bridge, its cab left dangling forty feet above the water. As her husband and another motorist struggled to save the driver, Mrs. Schau clicked off the two exposures left in her Brownie camera. The photos won that year's Pulitzer Prize for on-the-spot news photography.

1957, when partial sponsorship of the top-ranked variety program "The Ed Sullivan Show" became available, Kodak again agreed to participate.

Kodak television commercials hardly differed, at least in content, from the company's usual print ads. The occasions of family photography were celebrated, as were the latest and most reliable Kodak products. In that sense, despite the new medium, not much had changed since the days when George Eastman had made a short list of applications for the Kodak camera, the company's first promotional booklet. Though the clothing, equipment, and itineraries might have changed, "Travellers and Tourists, Bicyclists and Boating men, Parents, Sportsmen and Camping Parties and Lovers of Fine Animals," continued, as Eastman had predicted, to record everyday life with snapshot cameras.

Television did not, of course, spring full grown from a technological void. Even Kodak had been, since the mid-thirties, involved with the science and engineering problems of the new medium. Though the company was mainly involved in the production of supplies for conventional photography, many correctly surmised that this new electronic-imaging system would also make use of film. Certainly one of the principal virtues of television was that it was able to transmit pictures pretty much "as they happened." In other words, it had an intrinsic theatricality and spontaneity. Like radio, it could be presented live. But as one Kodak manager of the time said about the possibility of a full line-up of simultaneously staged and broadcast programs, "They just couldn't have it live...there ain't that much ham in America."

Thus, even in the late 1930s, when television was still a curiosity, Kodak began working with the Bell Laboratories on methods of transmitting photographically filmed images over the electronic airwaves. The initial problem faced by technicians was the ratio of film (running-speed frames per second) to the cycle frequency of television. In the late 1920s, when optical sound recording on film (recording sound via light waves) was in its formative stages, Loyd Jones and Otto Sandvik of the Kodak Research Laboratories had studied the flicker characteristics of film speed and discovered that if the standard sixteen frames per second were raised to twenty-four per second, the quality of optical sound would be increased. By the early 1930s the twenty-four-frame figure had become the industry standard. Since the frequency cycle of television transmission was equivalent to thirty frames per second, it was necessary to discover a method of synchronizing the two ratios.

Work on this problem continued at the RCA, Bell, and Kodak laboratories, and a number of projectors, such as the Kodak model 250 television projector, were constructed to synchronize the ratios. Television producers also faced a similar problem with the re-recording of live programs for syndication. In 1949, after years of research conducted jointly with the Allan B. Du Mont Laboratories and the National Broadcasting Company, Kodak introduced the Eastman television recording camera, a 16mm camera that was used for continuous recording of an image on a television screen.

The small, sometimes fuzzy images seen on the tiny screens of the earliest televisions were valued less for their pictorial quality than for the simple fact that people could be entertained by moving pictures in the comfort of their homes. Actually, it is not clear whether anyone even thought of the medium as being in direct competition with most sorts of photography. Television, as the word implies, is the electronic transmission and reproduction of an object over a distance. Photography, on the other hand, is chemical writing with light. The graphic difference between the two — the first flickering bits of energy, the second a series of continuous tones — was perhaps not as obvious then as now.

Electronically reproduced pictures had little effect upon the spread of photochemical images in mass-market magazines. The popularity of *Life*, for instance, or *Look*, *National Geographic*, or any of the other principally pictorial publications of the time was unaffected by the arrival of television. In 1952 there were television sets in only about 35 percent of the homes in America, and even for those who had TV the range of programs that could be seen was fairly limited. Variety shows and dramatic presentations were the most popular programs then available. Televised news was in its infancy: fifteen minutes each evening of world events reported in the style of radio announcing. Two years earlier war had broken out in Korea, and television might have been expected to have been quick to cover the war. But television technology was still in its formative stages, and for the most part the Korean conflict was a living-room war only to the extent that images from the front appeared in newspapers and magazines.

Many of the photographers sent to Korea were veterans of the previous war, as indeed were most of those who bought and perused the publications. Perhaps a writer in *U.S. Camera* was on the right track when he wrote that "John Q. Public [likes] to see close-ups of war in the comfort of his home...likes to sit back in his chair and have things done for him without having to expend more than a minimum of energy." Maybe "Mr. Public" was not quite as casual about these images as the writer suggests, but there is no doubt that the demand for pictures was high. The results of a 1951 survey showed that pictures illustrating "National Defense" and "Foreign War" were by a fairly large margin the most sought-after by magazine buyers.

The public's appetite for war pictures was shadowed by a demand for the kinds of images we now associate with television: "Accidents and Disasters," "Crime," "Sports," "Beauty Queens," "Glamour Girls," and "Children and Babies." These mixed genres, rife with excitement and loaded with everyday emotions, were representative of the high place photography had assumed in the corporate life of the culture. The collection and dissemination of information by visual means had become an accepted fact of life — pictures told stories, pushed products,

By careful control of the dyes used in the Kodak dye-transfer process, as in these Louis Condax landscapes printed from the same set of relief positives but in entirely different hues, color could be rendered re-alistically, as in the autumn print (right), or manipulated to change the season, as in the depiction of spring (opposite).

amused mothers and fathers, warned of the dangers of war, linked people together. In the days before the growth of television, they were the universal and shared language.

The Eastman Kodak Company was more than happy with this mass broadcast of photographic images. The graphic reproduction of any kind of picture was a boon for photography. The more the culture came to depend upon photographs for visual information, the wider the spread of photography in general. Kodak had been involved in the graphic arts since the hiring of A. J. Newton, a British printer, in 1914. Mees, in particular, had throughout his tenure as head of research at Kodak been interested in this area of photographic technology. Though he once "congratulated" the audience at a graphic arts convention "for being the only industry that had survived for a hundred years with no technological changes," the charge, as Mees no doubt knew, was not entirely fair.

It is perhaps true that the graphic arts industry was slow to take advantage of new technologies. At least until the mid-1930s most photoengravers continued to print from high-

contrast wet-collodion plates, a technique successfully accomplished only by the most expert. In 1920, when writing to Eastman about the future of photography in general, Mees had maintained that "the future of the [graphics] industry depends on whether, by the use of such radical changes as film instead of wet plates, and an automatic camera, the present difficult photographic process can be accomplished by one which can be operated by the same semi-skilled labor as the rest of the photoengraving process."

The first of these changes came in 1934, when Kodak introduced its line of Kodalith graphic arts products: transparent stripping films and high-contrast developers. Improvements in these graphic arts products, such as special restrainers to increase developing time, were followed in the 1940s by the introduction of Kodak contact screens. These graded-density screens, containing the dot structures necessary for halftone printing, were designed to be placed in contact with the negative film being reproduced and to provide the printer with much more highly resolved tone reproduction.

The photographic portrait, whether of an individual or of a family, as in this classic 1930s Bachrach studio picture of the Joseph P. Kennedy clan, was during the postwar years one of the brightest prospects in the field of professional photography. Portraits had since the daguerreotype days been one of the medium's most popular genres (Bachrach, in fact, has been in business since 1869). During the 1950s ornately framed enlargements and "living walls" of family pictures were promoted by Kodak as an appropriately stylish method of home decoration.

Kodak had also, for obvious reasons, been very interested in improved methods of color printing. Kodachrome slides were eagerly greeted by magazine photo editors, but the reproduction of color still often involved a skilled retouching of negatives, positives, or printing plates. In the late 1930s two Kodak scientists, Alexander Murray and R.S. Morse, invented an electronic machine that optically scanned a color transparency and made the separation negatives necessary for the preparation of printing plates. The scanner was then sold to Printing Developments, Inc., a subsidiary of Time, Inc., and after further improvement was used to print the color sections of the Time-Life family of magazines.

Even with these improvements in graphic arts techniques, however, most magazines used color sparingly. Only large-scale advertisers could afford regularly to use the new technology. Though many photographers thought that color had seldom surpassed the painted color postcard stage, bright, exuberant color turned out to be the perfect medium for the promotion of products during the fifties. Early in the decade the production of high-quality color-negative prints was still a few years off, but for advertising work, an older and in some ways subtler color-printing technology was available.

In 1935 Kodak had introduced a method of making color prints called the "Eastman wash-off relief" process. Three separation negatives were made from an original color photograph by rephotographing it through color filters. From each of these, gelatin-relief positives were produced, which when dyed the appropriate complementary colors could be printed in register upon a specially prepared sheet of gelatin-coated paper. Dye-drying times were quite long, however, and the process did not fully take hold until 1946 when the Kodak dye-transfer process was introduced. The improved chemistry of this procedure was the work of Louis Condax and Robert Speck, two New York City photographers and color printers whom Mees had asked to join the Kodak laboratories in 1940. Since the intensities and colors of the dyes used in this process could be skillfully controlled, the color, mood, and message of these images was able to be manipulated almost at will. Condax, in particular, was known as one of the masters of this medium.

Each of these improvements in the graphic reproduction of photographs contributed to the continued dominance, indeed the prominence, of photography in the pictorial life of the postwar era. Nothing exemplifies this trend better than the interest in large-size photographic portraiture. After improvements in Ektacolor film and Ektacolor paper in the mid-fifties, commercial photographers were able to make high-quality prints suitable for framing from color negatives. Decorating magazines encouraged their readers to hang such pictures in "home galleries." In 1956 Kodak mounted an exhibition of portraits in a Manhattan apartment to demonstrate just how elegantly appointed a room could become when adorned with handsomely framed photographs.

Studio Light, a Kodak publication aimed specifically at the commercial trade, suggested that photographers promote the idea that a "living wall" of pictures was for most young families the favored way to create that always desired "homey" effect. Besides, as the magazine informed professional photographers, payment plans could now be arranged:

Nobody will argue with the statement that credit selling and credit buying have become as American as apple pie and baseball. And the "black eye" once associated with credit selling no longer exists. Even the dignified New York Stock Exchange sponsors a time payment plan for the purchase of securities, and nearly half of all luxury automobiles are paid for on time! In fact, there is an honest incredulity in the remark one friend will make to another, "You mean you paid cash?"

One credit arrangement that seemed especially appealing to professional portrait photographers was the "baby plan," whereby pictures could be scheduled to match each memorable stage of a child's growth. In the pre-World War II years about two and a half million babies were born per year in America. By 1947 that figure had almost doubled. Hundreds of snapshots were being taken of each of these five million children, and each year millions of the popular 3½ x 5-inch sized studio portraits were processed and sent to grandparents, aunts, uncles, or just about anyone who might conceivably have an interest in how much a child had changed in the past twelve months.

Thus when Kodak was approached in 1950 by the owners of New York City's Grand Central Terminal with a plan to decorate the east balcony of the station with a huge rear-projection photograph, there was some doubt about the technical problem involved, but much less about the subject matter. The first of these 18 x 60-foot "Colorama" panels was made from three exposures produced by New York photographer Valentino Sarra. In the middle section (the largest), a mother was seen photographing her two children. In each end panel were close-ups of the boy and girl. In succeeding years new Colorama displays were produced and hung,

In 1953 The Robe, *a biblical epic shot in the newly introduced Eastman color negative film and projected in the wide-screen CinemaScope format, was the third-largest revenue-grossing film ever made, coming in just behind the 1915* Birth of a Nation *and the 1939* Gone with the Wind. *Though the wide-screen format would undergo changes during the next few decades, within that same time period Eastman color films would entirely replace the older Technicolor dye-imbibition process.*

mostly images created by Kodak staff photographers, though now and then a guest photographer such as Ansel Adams was hired.

The fifties, at least in terms of economic growth, was the golden age of amateur and professional photography. In 1938 the Eastman Kodak Company employed about 39,000 people worldwide. By the mid-fifties that figure rose to just over 73,000. Net earnings also increased dramatically during the fifties from 50 million dollars in 1953 to almost 100 million dollars in 1957. During the five years after the end of World War II nearly 150 million dollars was invested in plant modernization, much of that money spent to expand and update the facilities at Kodak Park. And in 1951, 15 million dollars was spent by the Kodak Research Laboratories alone. In fact, by the middle of the decade Kodak was operating four separate photographic research laboratories: Kodak Park in Rochester, which employed just over 700 people; Kodak Limited in Harrow, England, with a staff of 230; Société Kodak-Pathé in Vincennes, France, with 180 persons; and a small Kodak Australasia lab in Abbotford, Victoria, with about 70 scientists. Among the four locations close to 400,000 square feet of space had been allocated to research.

As public reliance upon and enjoyment of photography surged along, dozens of new products were developed and introduced: in 1951 an inexpensive Brownie 8mm movie camera and Ektalux flasholders; in 1952 a new infrared aerial photographic film for night photography and the Recordak Bantam microfilmer; in 1953 the Brownie Holiday camera and special Hawk-Eye lenses for TV work; in 1954 Kodak Ektachrome film for miniature cameras and Ektacolor film in roll-film sizes.

In nonphotographic areas, Kodak organized a company called Texas Eastman to manufacture gas- and oil-derived chemicals. In 1952 Kodak's Tennessee Eastman subsidiary, which had been set up in 1930 to provide cellulose acetate for filmmaking, began manufacturing a synthetic yarn that was given the brand name "Chromspun." And Distillation Products Industries, founded in 1938, was now manufacturing and marketing vitamin E in a variety of forms. Each of these companies also maintained laboratories with a combined staff of about 450 people.

Besides its work on acetate fibers, Tennessee Eastman, in collaboration with production specialists at Kodak Park, had succeeded in finally producing a workable acetate film. Kodak's long search for a commercial non–nitrate-based film support, which had been initiated before the turn of the century, resulted in the 1948 introduction of a cellulose triacetate "safety"

The first full-length film shot and printed on Eastman color stock was Royal Journey, *a documentary account of Princess Elizabeth's tour of Canada produced by the Canadian National Film Board in 1951.*

Along with photographic supplies, the Eastman Kodak Company produces a number of diversified products, many in the related field of organic chemistry. One of those products, Chromspun, a synthetic fiber manufactured by the Eastman Kodak Company subsidiary Tennessee Eastman, was advertised in this studio shot taken in 1952 by commercial photographer Edward Fitzgerald.

motion-picture film, for which the following year it won an Academy Award. Shortly thereafter, however, Du Pont began marketing a polyester-based film support that, as one scientist working on the project said, "convinced everyone concerned that this could well become the photographic film base of the future." In 1955, after much research into the nature of poly-ethylene terephthalate (PET) support, Kodak signed a licensing and manufacturing agreement with Du Pont, and by 1960 many commercial film products were coated on this Estar base.

The 1949 award for safety film was followed by another Oscar a year later presented for the development of Eastman color negative and Eastman color print films. Hollywood had reason to be grateful. Unlike the market for still photographs, which was in most ways unaffected by the arrival of television, the movie industry had after the war suffered a serious decline. In 1946 Americans spent 20 percent of the money they had budgeted for entertainment on movies. By 1950 the percentage had dropped to 12. Whether this decrease was a function of life-style (family activities taking precedence over movie going) or the result of increased television viewing is still an issue of debate among scholars of the period. In any case, fewer people attended films each week and the major studios were anxious to find some way to regain their audience share.

The size of its film screens, especially when compared to the small 12- or 14-inch televisions then available, was one of Hollywood's most obvious advantages over its competitor. Accordingly, many of the most popular films of the fifties were either filmed on wide-gauge 60mm or 70mm stock or optically squeezed onto 35mm film by anamorphic lenses and then blown up on the screen by reprojecting the images through compensating lenses. Twentieth Century-Fox's 1953 *The Robe*, shot by means of the anamorphic Cinemascope process, was not only the most popular movie of the year but at the time the third most lucrative film ever made, coming in just behind the 1915 *The Birth of a Nation* and the 1939 *Gone with the Wind*.

Filmmakers also tried to draw customers to the theater by making three-dimensional stereoscopic movies. Three-D movies made use of pretty much the same principal as still stereoscopic techniques popular in the late nineteenth century. In the 1920s a few "anaglyph" 3-D color films had been made by simultaneously exposing separate films through red and green filters for left- and right-eye views. When these were printed and viewed through a pair of glasses with one green and one red lens the illusion of depth was created. Paramount Pictures made a few short films in anaglyph 3-D, which it called "Plastigrams," but the color was not very good, and, besides, the effort to look through the glasses gave many people headaches. In the 1950s this method was replaced by one in which the two images were exposed through polarizing lenses and viewed through equivalent glasses. After the movie was shot, the two images were projected in register, and the lenses, by allowing each eye to see light vibrating only on a single, polarized plane, created the illusion of depth. There was some initial interest in these films but they also caused headaches, and, anyway, the public soon tired of the trick. (In 1954 Kodak introduced a stereo still camera—none had been manufactured since 1925—but interest in this sort of photography also quickly waned.)

Of all the new film processes color was the most lasting and commercially successful. After the dissolution of the Kodak-Technicolor licensing agreements, the major studios were, as Hanson said, "just dying to get better color film." Not only a better film, but a cheaper film. At first it was necessary to make separation negatives from the camera film, and that was time-consuming and expensive. The 1956 introduction of Eastman color intermediate film, which could be used as a master positive to generate the duplicate negatives needed for thousands of release prints, at least partially solved that problem, and by the mid-fifties over half of the films made in Hollywood were in color.

As a result of the United States government's suit against Kodak and Technicolor, a number of independent film-processing labs were established. Some, such as Warnercolor and

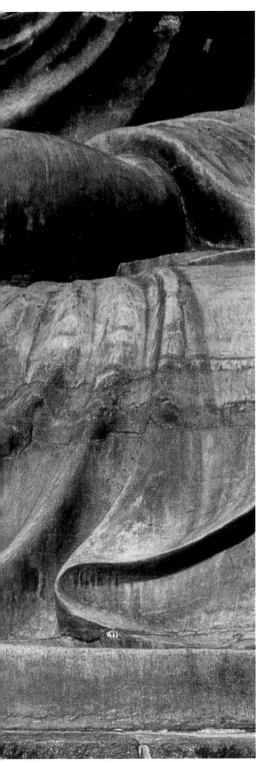

When Nicholas Muray, best known for his work in the field of advertising photography, went on vacation he took along a 35mm camera and rolls of Kodachrome film. Like all travelers, Muray recorded exotic sights, landscapes and seascapes, and the unfamiliar people he encountered. Unlike most of those who carry cameras on their trips, Muray was a professional photographer, and the pictures in his travel album are perfectly and expertly exposed.

Kodak has traditionally believed that anything good for photography is good for the Eastman Kodak Company. Consequently when Kodak was asked in 1959 by photographer Ivan Dmitri to sponsor an annual exhibition entitled Photography in the Fine Arts *at The Metropolitan Museum of Art, it agreed to do so, with the proviso that* its contributions be anonymous. The resulting exhibitions, which concluded with a large show at the 1964–1965 World's Fair, were both popular and controversial. Viewers thought the exhibitions wide ranging and provocative. Museum photography curators such as Edward Steichen considered Dmitri a self-knighted Sir Galahad of photography. But at the very least, the photographs exhibited, such as Henri Cartier-Bresson's Madrid 1933 Playground in Spain *and Andreas Feininger's* 1951 Web of Yellow Garden Spider, *reasserted the deservedly high standing of photography in the world of the visual arts.*

Metrocolor, were closely linked to specific studios and shared their names; others, Movielab, Deluxe, and even Technicolor, were independent entrepreneurs. By the mid-fifties, however, all specialized in the processing of Eastman color film.

Oddly enough, as Hollywood filmmakers began to market their films to television, this figure began to reverse itself. Since most television broadcasts were in black and white, the studios, seeking to save costs, dropped the production of these films. By the late fifties only about a quarter of each year's movies were filmed in color.

In 1955, after the filing of the second major government suit against the company during the postwar period, Kodak signed what is now known as "the consent decree." The U.S. attorney

Marc Riboud's Weird Hills: Lush Rice Paddies and Bitter Labor, *shown in the final* Photography in the Fine Arts *exhibit in 1965.*

Above right:
Ernest Haas's Venice: Gondola in Blue Fog, *which was exhibited in the first* Photography in the Fine Arts *show.*

general had claimed that Kodak's practice of including the cost of processing in the price of Kodachrome film restrained trade in the photofinishing industry. It is not clear whether this was indeed the company's motive. By the fifties the chemicals and equipment needed for processing the "Ekta-" brands of color film were widely available. In addition, Kodachrome film processing, even after reductions in the number of steps required, remained a complicated and time-consuming process, probably beyond the capabilities of most trained independent processors. In any case, Kodak agreed to sell the film as is and to release the formulas necessary to process Kodachrome film.

At the same time, and even more significantly, the company also agreed to provide photofinishers with all the information and materials needed to process Kodacolor print film. During the discussions before the settlement of the suit Mees had argued that Ektachrome, which, like Kodacolor and Eastman color films, contained color couplers directly in the emulsion, and which consequently was much easier to process, would become the most popular color process. Mees also thought that many amateur photographers would use the simplified Ektachrome film developing kits now to print their high-quality transparencies. He was wrong. As Eastman's 1888 complete system had proved, most amateur consumers wanted to see their pictures in the form of hand-held reflection prints and had no particular desire to process the photos themselves.

The Kodak idea from its inception had been based on the freedom from work provided by a division of labor. As the first promotional booklet had promised amateurs:

The Kodak Camera renders possible the Kodak System, whereby the mere mechanical act of taking a picture, which anyone can perform, is divorced from all the chemical manipulations of preparing and finishing pictures, which only experts can perform.

In other words, you press the button, we do the rest.

Initially, of course, the Kodak snapshot camera was returned to the factory, where it was opened and the film processed. After the introduction of daylight-loading film, however, when

A portrait of Georgia O'Keeffe by Yousuf Karsh, exhibited in the fourth Photography in the Fine Arts.

film could safely be removed from the camera, anyone with the materials and know-how could develop film and make prints. Solio paper, on which photos could be printed by exposure to sunlight, and Velox paper, printable by gas or electric light, further expanded the possibilities of non-Kodak photoprocessing. In other words, the way was opened for the creation of an independent photofinishing industry. Which is exactly what happened.

In 1910, for instance, Glen Dye, a former portrait photographer, invented his first printing machine and founded a company called PACO (Photographic Alliances Corporation). George Eastman, who apparently saw the growth of the mass-market photofinishing industry as a blessing to the buyers of his film, had only one complaint. Would Dye, he asked, include a "K" in his company's name? By the 1920s, now operating as PAKO, Dye built his first mechanized printing machine, the PAKO printmaker, which automatically conveyed each print through developing, fixing, and washing baths.

Through the 1920s all prints were developed by contact with an original negative, and even after mechanization, each cut-sheet paper print was handled by the processor one at a time. As such, the consumer photofinishing industry had not attained the technological expertise of those who developed and printed motion-picture stock. John Crabtree, who had joined the Kodak Research Laboratories in 1913, specialized in the rack-and-drum methods used by motion-picture processors and together with Glen Matthews wrote a book entitled *Motion Picture Laboratory Practice*, which for some years was the motion-picture processors' bible. But the continuous-processing techniques did not completely pass over into the world of consumer photofinishing until the 1930s, when Kodak, among others, introduced contact printers with semiautomatic exposure control. In England, a World War I veteran and former filmmaker named Captain Will Barker built one of the first "dip-and-dunk" film processors. About the same time Kodak introduced the Kodak Velox Autometric, which employed a selenium photo-cell to control the amount of light needed to make a print.

Late in the 1930s, with the increasing popularity of the miniature cameras, efforts were made to produce the projection printers necessary to enlarge the small 35mm negatives. In 1937 Kodak first manufactured its Velox rapid projection printer to "open new avenues for increased photofinishing business by making fixed magnification enlargements from miniature negatives on Velox rapid paper." Surprisingly, this machine still made use of single cut sheets of paper. Not until the late 1940s, when Kodak introduced its Continuous Paper Processor and PAKO announced its Pakoline machine, were prints made on long rolls of paper. The Kodak machine turned out 2,400 prints per hour, a huge advance compared with the one-at-a-time contact-printing methods.

By the 1950s a flourishing photofinishing industry had sprung up to meet the continuing and increasing demand for photographic prints — for black-and-white prints, that is. The printing of color was a wholly different matter. Both Kodak and the German company Agfa, Kodak's major competitor in the field of color photography, still considered the processing of color too difficult for independent photofinishers. In Agfa's case specialized companies were trained to develop and print the film, while Kodak continued to require the return of Kodachrome and Kodacolor films to its Rochester plant.

After the signing of the 1955 consent decree, Kodak stepped up work on an inexpensive and uncomplicated color printer able to be used by independent photofinishers. The result of this research was the Type IV C color printer, which, together with improvements in color print paper, enabled many small companies to add color printing to their already large business of black-and-white photoprocessing. As Hanson has said of the post–consent decree period, "This was a major change in the whole color-film processing industry. The huge worldwide photofinishing industry that we know today grew up on Kodacolor film. It just took off."

Though the quality of prints produced for the consumer market by these commercial labs was quite good, it was not even close to being good enough for a certain sector of the photographic world. "Fine work for exhibition," critic Peter Stackpole wrote in his review of the 1959 Metropolitan Museum of Art's show *Photography in the Fine Arts*, "can't be put through a hopper." Few serious photographers or lovers of fine photography took Stackpole's dictum as anything but the absolute gospel truth. Since the earliest days of the medium most creative photographers had either printed their own pictures or carefully supervised their production. One of the lessons of the Ansel Adams zone system of print previsualization was that strict control of all aspects of the photochemical process was an absolute necessity if high-quality aesthetic work was the photographer's goal.

Kodak had, at least since its 1897 exhibition of art photography, encouraged work in all photographic genres. Though the company had been popularly known as the creator and principal supplier of the consumer mass-market, its business had never been dominated by this

In 1950 Kodak was invited to install a continuing series of 18 x 60-foot color transparencies on the east balcony of New York City's Grand Central Terminal. Many of these huge photographic murals depicted amateur photographers taking pictures in particularly photogenic situations or locales. Though Ansel Adams called these Kodak displays "aesthetically inconsequential but technically remarkable," he regularly contributed to the project. As a rule the millions who passed through the station were uniformly struck by the magnitude and capacious sweep of these brilliantly lighted examples of color photography. The Colorama display at the top of the page is by Adams, that at the bottom by Ralph Amdursky.

single neighborhood of the photographic community. In 1950, for example, the sale of amateur goods amounted to about 26 percent of Kodak's business, professional and commercial equipment for 27 percent, and professional motion pictures for 9 percent. (The remaining 38 percent came from sales of cellulose and other chemical products.) In other words, it was far from accurate to consider the snapshooter Kodak's only or most important customer.

Kodak had always cultivated all these clients. Particularly the high-profile (and high-end) professional market. Eastman and many of those who succeeded him as managers of the Eastman Kodak Company were convinced that anything good for great photographers was good for all photography. In the forties, for instance, George Waters of the Kodak advertising department had asked Edward Weston, Ansel Adams, Charles Sheeler, and Paul Strand to experiment with Kodachrome film. Kodak offered to purchase those transparencies it thought suitable for advertising purposes, which it did, titling ads displaying Weston's Kodachrome photographs as "Edward Weston's first serious work in color."

Kodak's relationship with most art photographers had been equally amicable, and when Ivan Dmitri approached the company in 1958 with a plan to mount an annual exhibition of great photographs it was decided that the funding of such a show would be in the interests both of

photography in general and Kodak in particular. It was also decided, perhaps with recent antitrust suits in mind, that while Kodak would underwrite the project, no mention would be made of the company's involvement. Thus when the first of the Dmitri-organized *Photography in the Fine Arts* exhibition opened in 1959 it was formally announced as a joint undertaking of *Saturday Review* magazine and The Metropolitan Museum of Art.

Dmitri, whose real name was Levan West, had begun his artistic career as an etcher. After the invention of Kodachrome film he became interested in the commercial possibilities of the new medium and, after acquiring the nom de plume Ivan Dmitri, was one of the first to have

Since 1935 KINSA competitions, the annual Kodak International Newspaper Snapshot Awards, have been sponsored by the Eastman Kodak Company and many daily newspapers in the United States, Canada, and Mexico. Amateur photographer John Milhaupt's black-and-white multiple exposure of a lunar eclipse was a prizewinner in the 1946 KINSA competition.

color work printed in mass-market magazines. Dmitri's skills as a promoter of color photography apparently did not desert him when organizing the "Photography in the Fine Arts" program. The prospectus for the nonprofit organization listed its ambitious, though seemingly reasonable, goals succinctly:

The goal of Photography in the Fine Arts will be reached when leading museums and art centers, here and abroad, maintain departments of photography with their own curators and budgets for purchasing superlative photographs for permanent collections; and when commercial galleries find it worthwhile to buy and sell photographic prints on a basis parallel with other art forms.

Lake with Weeds *is the title of this 1956 KINSA contest winner by Horst Ebersberg.*

One of the most spectacular and singular travel pictures of the 1950s was made on May 23, 1953, when Sir Edmund Hillary took this Kodachrome film photograph of his Sherpa climbing partner Tenzing Norgay soon after they achieved their goal of being the first men to reach the summit of Mt. Everest.

To fully legitimize the venture, Dmitri asked for the cooperation of James Rorimer, then director of The Metropolitan Museum of Art, who told him, "Get together an exhibition of photographs and if in the estimation of a group of museum directors it is worthy of being hung in museums, I will hang it in The Metropolitan." This Dmitri did, approaching everyone from the Pulitzer Prize committee to advertising agencies to "authorities in the field of photography." After assembling 438 photographs (197 in color, 241 in black-and-white), Dmitri assembled a jury panel consisting of among others Rorimer; Edward Steichen, director of the Department of Photography at The Museum of Modern Art; Dorothy Seiberling, art editor of *Life* magazine; Beaumont Newhall, director of the George Eastman House; Alexander Liberman, art director of *Vogue*; Alfred Frankfurter, editor of *Art News*; Joyce Hall, president of Hallmark cards; Stanley Marcus, the department-store owner and art collector; and Frank Baker, senior art director of McCann-Erickson advertising agency. When this distinguished and varied panel had finished its work, approximately one hundred and forty photographs were chosen, and late in 1959 an exhibition was mounted. Then the firestorm hit.

In February 1960 Steichen wrote to Dmitri:

After the manner in which I expressed myself at the January, 1959, meeting in your studio, and in view of all that has followed, it should not surprise you to learn that I have no interest whatsoever in being connected with the continuation of your "Photography in the Fine Arts" project. My principal reason for this is that in my estimation the whole undertaking is the most damaging thing that has ever happened to the art of photography.

Steichen went on to argue that a significant number of museums did indeed have photography departments and that "your pretense that this venture would initiate the collecting of photographs by art museums, and persuade them to consider photography as an art, may, on the whole, have been due to ignorance." "You may," Steichen continued, "have been oblivious of these facts, and consequently failed to recognize the fallacy of your position as the Sir Galahad of photography, but, being a New Yorker, you must surely know that The Museum of Modern Art has exhibited, collected and purchased photographs almost from the time of its inception."

In fact, Steichen's description of Dmitri as Sir Galahad was beside the point. The chief complaints about the show as articulated by Peter Stackpole in the September 1959 issue of *U.S. Camera* were that the jury was unsuitable, that many of the photographs came from commercial, and thus not artistic, sources and that the quality of some prints was dubious. In sum, Dmitri had asked the wrong people to judge the wrong photographs and had neglected to warn them that print quality counted above all.

The issue that hovered most menacingly over all of these complaints was the old and unresolved conflict between low and high art. PFA jurors had had the effrontery to display the work of amateur photographers next to that of well-known and highly praised art photographers. This simple fact, Nina Howell Starr wrote in her review of the show, "scandalizes serious photographers." Creativity, she argued, belongs in the province of the truly creative; sensibility counts, as does seriousness. "One comes away from the exhibition," Starr complained, "hungry, hungry for print quality, hungry for aesthetic experience, hungry for expansion of sensibility, and hungry for communication that is part of the creativity offered by all works of art."

But to others, such as The Metropolitan Museum's Associate Curator of Prints Carl Weinhardt, who served on a second PFA jury, it seemed "clear that photographers need desperately to be judged at least occasionally by people who are willing and able to look at their work as pictures—or 'art' if you will—and not just as photographs. Endless judging of photographs by photographers who use their own home-grown criteria, and never measure against a longer esthetic yardstick, can create a dangerously inbred situation."

By 1964 even Beaumont Newhall had had enough of this yardstick stretching. In reply to an invitation to join that year's PFA jury, Newhall wrote to Dmitri that in 1962 he, photographer Ansel Adams, and Ralph Steiner had suggested that the work of thirty-eight photographers be included in that year's show:

To my embarrassment and surprise, the jury rejected the work of more than half of the photographers who responded to our urging—including some of the most established photographers of today, such as Aaron Siskind and Richard Avedon.

All of the jurors were old friends, respected museum colleagues, highly skilled in the connoisseurship of painting. But is it fair to photographers to ask museum directors who have little knowledge or understanding of photography to sit in judgement of their work? I would not feel qualified to judge abstract-expressionistic painting; an exhibition of paintings chosen by photographers or photographic critics would perhaps be an interesting show, and possibly a popular one, but hardly of significance in the field of painting.

Just how the Kodak advertising department took this criticism is not clear, though certainly the anonymity of the company's financial contributions kept it out of the argument, and the fact that amateur work was included would not have been particularly alarming. When PFA went out of existence after a large exhibit at the 1964–1965 World's Fair, the issues raised by the show were unresolved: did amateurs belong in the same hall with acknowledged artists? Or was it true, as Morris Gordon wrote, that "Ivan Dmitri had painfully wounded the egos of the writing clan?"

Whatever the answer to these questions, by the end of the immediate postwar period photography, in all its forms, was more popular than ever. Art photographers were beginning to claim their rightful place in museums. Commerical photography, much of it in color, was engaging the attention of marketers. Things could be sold if the picture was good enough. The movies were using the graphic boldness of film technology to draw audiences away from their TV screens. Even the snapshooter was getting some recognition.

Before the war, Kodak, in cooperation with ninety U.S. newspapers, had organized a competition for amateur photographers called the Newspaper National Snapshot Awards. Wartime shortages had suspended the contest, but after it was resumed in 1947, the number of publications involved and the number of entries continued to rise. The questions raised by PFA critics were in no way answered by the quality of the pictures winning snapshot awards. Some were on par with professional work, others well below that level. Many amateur winners were, in fact, clearly imitators of one or another art photographer. Not until the next decade would this resemblance be reversed: art photographers attempting to mimic vernacular snapshooters. But then the art and business of photography, which had bloomed in the genial fifties, would be forced to engage the fractious, discontented world of the sixties and seventies.

The worldwide serious amateur sector of the photographic community grew steadily during the postwar period as greater numbers of nonprofessionals took up the hobby of 35mm photography. Marc Riboud's 1958 photo of a crowded Japanese picture-taking outing, though perhaps not representative of most serious amateur photographers' excursions, nonetheless is illustrative of the accelerating growth and sophistication of this segment of the photographic market during the 1950s and 1960s.

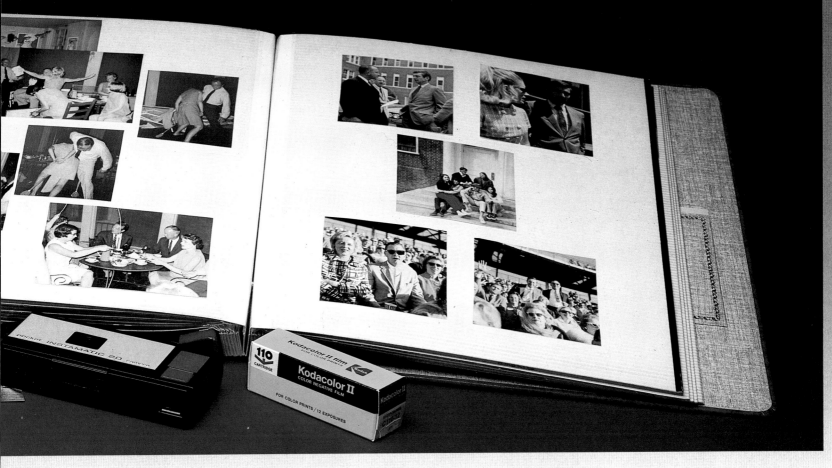

Preceding pages:
*Though Kodak continued to manufacture
sophisticated 35mm cameras such as the
1954 Retina IIIc camera (left) through the
late 1950s, it was the 1963 Instamatic
camera (center), a cartridge-loaded camera that used 35mm-wide Kodachrome
and Kodacolor film, which was the most
ubiquitous Kodak camera of the 1960s.
In 1972 Kodak introduced its Pocket
Instamatic camera (right), designed to use
effectively 16mm film of relatively fast
speed and wide latitude. The Kodak Car-
ousel tray was used for easy viewing of
slides.*

On August 15, 1960, Dr. Charles Edward Kenneth Mees died in Honolulu, Hawaii, where he had spent the five years since his retirement studying marine invertebrates, delivering occasional lectures, and talking to anyone who shared his interests in science, industry, and the affairs of the mind. Mees had been an Eastman Kodak Company employee for forty-four years when he left Rochester. He had been hired by George Eastman in 1912 to chart "the future of photography" and had gone on single-handedly to organize what became the world's largest and most productive laboratory devoted to research in the field of photography. By 1947 so many new and significant Kodak products had come out of Mees's laboratories that *The Saturday Evening Post* profiled the "Doctor of the Darkroom":

The middle initials of Dr. Charles E. K. Mees, a British resident of Rochester, New York, do not stand for Eastman Kodak, as is sometimes seriously assumed. The mistake, though, is understandable. Mees, Kodak, and the science of photography are inseparable, frequently indistinguishable, and impressively interdependent. Doctor Mees is related to every thumb that snaps a shutter, to every overexposed shot of Aunt Bella at the seashore, to pictures of an atom fissioning and plates of stars invisible to the eye. For thirty-five years Mees has directed research for the Big K of Rochester, world's largest photographic firm. He has taken science by the hand and led it, often brusquely and belligerently, to such epochal advances as panchromatic film, amateur movies and color pictures.

Though the *Post* writer perhaps overstated his case somewhat, there is no doubt that Mees, with his great technical expertise and equally impressive management skills, had influenced Kodak policy as no one had done since George Eastman. No single man, of course, had been primarily responsible for Kodak's phenomenal success. When Eastman died, the company was already being managed by his successor, William Stuber. And in the years before Mees's death Frank Lovejoy, Thomas Hargrave, Perley Wilcox, and Albert Chapman had been presidents of the Eastman Kodak Company.

By 1960, the "Big K," as the *Post* called it, had net earnings of more than 100 million dollars per year, employed 75,000 people worldwide, and had slightly over 100,000 shareholders. Kodak had also in its first seventy-five years diversified its operation. It was no longer just a supplier of photographic goods. Up to 30 percent of its business was in the field of cellulose derivatives, distillation products, and other industrial chemicals. In the public mind, however, few of these products contributed to Kodak's repute.

To most, the Eastman Kodak Company was a manufacturer and merchandiser of photographic supplies, the world's largest and most powerful. Only the United States Treasury used more silver per year than Kodak. It marketed more cameras per year than any other company in the world, and so much film came off Kodak coating alleys that the sprocket perforations punched out each day weighed more than a ton. In less than a century, Kodak's "Familiar Yellow Box" came close to being an icon, and one of the world's most recognized symbols.

In the years since George Eastman had begun hand coating dry plates in a downtown rented loft, the upstate New York city of Rochester had become the industrial and research capital of the world of photography. Photographers came to Rochester seeking advice (Ansel Adams, among others, thought its weather awful), as did all those in the business of buying or selling products associated with photographic goods. In 1947 this unlikely, medium-sized American city also became home to an international center for the exhibition and study of photography. After Eastman's death his home had been occupied by Alan Valentine, the president of the University of Rochester. When Valentine left the university in the mid-1940s, the house, according to provisions in Eastman's will, was converted into a photography museum. The obvious choice to head the museum was Mees, who in 1947 was elected Eastman House's first president.

Photography had been Mees's passion since his days at University College—though not his only one. Throughout his career he had been a tireless lecturer and writer, and while his eight books and more than one hundred and fifty papers and pamphlets had been mostly about photography, Mees had found time to speak to accountants on cost control, to West Point cadets on military strategy, and to archaeologists on the culture of the Nile Valley. The last of these topics, Egyptology, was a particular Mees favorite. "Even the Roman Empire," Mees, the dedicated researcher once wrote, "presents too fleeting a base for fundamental principles."

In 1951, while on a lecture tour, Mees discovered that the large artery in his left leg was blocked. He immediately sought medical help, but doctors discovered that the damage was so great that the limb's amputation was necessary. After being fitted with an artificial leg, Mees wrote: "The thing is purely mechanical. After all, I don't do my work with my feet; I do it with my head. I told the doctors that the only amputation that would really bother me would be one at the neck." Reports of Mees's legendary capability for endless talk seem to bear this out. Mees would sometimes play golf with friends, who remember him as one of the few on the course who could continue speaking and speculating even through his own backswing.

After Mees's death two permanent legacies were established to memorialize a lifetime's work in photography. At Eastman House, a Mees gallery was set aside to trace the history of the science and technology of photography. Though an Eastman House curator is reported to have groused, "Did Rembrandt save his brushes?" the Eastman House technology archive continues to be one of the most popular and instructive of the museum's exhibits.

The second memorial dedicated in the laboratory director's name was the Mees Observatory at the University of Rochester. Mees had been long fascinated by astronomy and in particular the uses of photography in astronomical studies. In the early days of the lab he had slipped specially prepared photographic plates to friends working at observatories. In fact, Mees had been directly responsible for many of the photographic efforts made by the Eastman Kodak Company in the fields of pure and applied scientific research: radiography, infrared photography, celestial mapping, microphotography, and spectrographic analysis.

Scientific photography, unlike all the other routine pictorial uses of the medium, is customarily concerned with precise measurements. Sometimes, as in photomicrography, it enlarges objects so small as to be invisible to the human eye. At other times, film is capable of recording light so distant from earth that it is visible only through huge telescopic lenses. Some types of scientific photography, infrared, for instance, can capture wavelengths of light unobservable by the human eye, while others, such as X-ray film and nuclear tracking plates register the existence of what Wilhelm Roentgen had called a "new kind of light."

Within a year after Roentgen's discovery of X rays in 1895, Kodak entered the market to supply film for both medical technicians and for those few photographers who, taking commercial advantage of this curious type of picture taking, had opened "Roentgen studios" that advertised "X-ray sittings." Kodak even introduced an X-ray printing material, but the speed and density of the paper were unable to produce adequate pictures, and the product was discontinued. Most X-ray studies at the time were recorded on glass plates. However, when World War I interrupted the supply of glass from the European continent, film seemed the obvious choice of materials to meet the military demand for this relatively new diagnostic device. In 1918, just after America entered the war, Kodak introduced Eastman Dupli-Tized X-ray film. This new film was light in weight and reliable, and since it was coated with a high-speed emulsion on both sides of the support, it had the added advantage of allowing technicians to reduce the amount of exposure.

Like many other Kodak products, X-ray films were continually improved in the succeeding decades. By the early 1960s the film was so fast that the dosages of dangerous radiation were reduced to a fraction of what they had been in Roentgen's day. The time necessary to develop

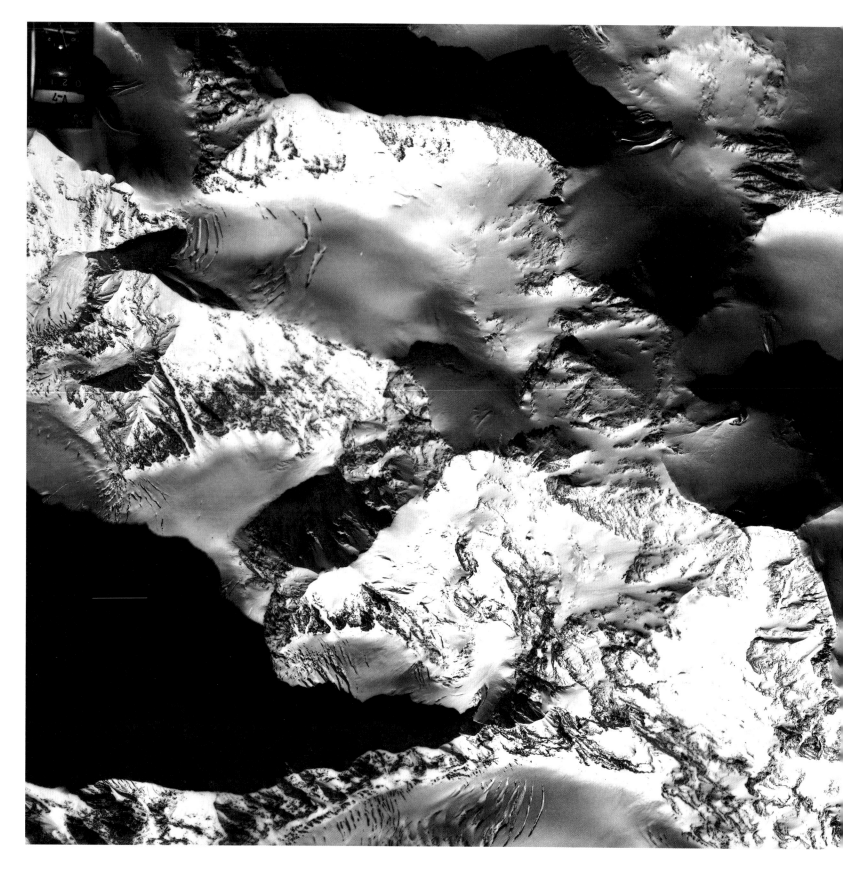

During the late 1950s, Kodak manufactured an ultrathin space-saving aerial film stock to be used in the cameras of the United States government's very secret high-altitude reconnaissance airplanes, the U-2s. Photographs using this film were taken during Francis Gary Powers's ill-fated 1960 U-2 flight over Russia and were used by President John F. Kennedy to reveal the building of nuclear missile bases in Cuba. This photograph was taken directly above Alaska's Mt. McKinley from a U-2 at an altitude of sixty thousand feet on September 6, 1960.

the film was also reduced when the Kodak RP (Rapid Processing) X-Omat processor was introduced in 1965. An earlier model had reduced the turnaround time from an hour to six minutes, but with this new machine radiographs were available for study ninety seconds after exposure.

Similar products were manufactured for the use of X-ray examination in dentists' offices and for what industrial users called "nondestructive testing." Compared to its medical applications the commercial use of X-ray film seems fairly pedestrian and commonplace. Welds in large structures are checked for faults. The smallest parts of machines can be recorded in minute detail. Roentgen's "new kind of light" has also been employed on hundreds of special occasions, such as the 1964 study of Michelangelo's *Pièta*, undertaken shortly before it was shipped to the United States to be exhibited at the 1964–1965 New York World's Fair.

Film has also been used to detect other sorts of radiation. In 1949 it was discovered that a batch of Kodak X-ray film had mysteriously become fogged. Julian Webb, a Kodak scientist who had worked at Oak Ridge during the war, suspected that the radiation released by above-ground testing of nuclear bombs might be responsible. After much research Webb discovered that radioactive materials rising above the Alamogordo, New Mexico, test site had traveled a thousand miles northeast and settled in the Wabash River basin. There they were washed into the river by the rain. Not coincidentally, the fogged X-ray film had been packed in strawboard, manufactured in Vincennes, Indiana, with Wabash River water. Webb's detective work revealed that radioactive particles had traveled by a circuitous route, from Alamogordo, New Mexico, to Vincennes, Indiana, and finally to Rochester, New York, where, invisible to the human eye, particles in the strawboard packing had fogged the film.

Kodak officials viewed this scenario, Webb has recalled, "with a certain amount of skepticism." But Webb persisted, asking Al Ballard, another veteran of Oak Ridge, to conduct further experiments. After collecting a container of freshly fallen snow, Ballard measured its radioactivity. It was much higher than was expected. The issue was raised once again with management. It was entirely possible, company managers were told, "that one could easily visualize a scenario in which most things entering Kodak Park would be contaminated with radioactivity and that the coating alleys, i.e., Kodak, would be shut down."

It was time, apparently, to take the problem seriously. A ten-foot-square stainless-steel tray was positioned on the roof of Building No. 59 in Kodak Park. When it rained or snowed samples were collected. According to Carl Zuehlke, who had worked with Ballard on the original tests, "Frequently we would go for several weeks finding results which were only slightly above background, [but] when a new bomb test was carried out in Nevada, and later in Russia, almost invariably we would find a sharp increase in radioactive fallout a few days later." Kokak continued to monitor the radioactivity levels on a daily basis through the 1950s.

About the same time Kodak was approached by the United States government to test the nuclear debris collected by air force planes flying through radioactive clouds created by Russian bomb tests. "The hope was," Zuehlke remembered, "that the nature of the nuclear process used by the Russians could be inferred by a chemical characterization of the fission products. The difficulty was that perhaps 99 percent or more of the debris collected probably better represented a Kansas cornfield or other ambient dirt."

Henry Yutzy, then head of Kodak's Emulsion Research Division, came up with a solution to the problem. Yutzy mixed a sample of the dirt with a photographic emulsion that contained no hardener and spread the mixture on a glass plate. The radioactive particles exposed the silver halide. The emulsion was then hardened. When the dirt and unexposed emulsion were washed away, black, radioactively exposed spots were left. These were then scraped off and quantitatively measured.

"We never learned—or at least I never learned—whether this procedure was successful," Zuehlke noted. "The samples were brought to us, from somewhere, by a courier carrying them in a briefcase handcuffed to his arm. He returned a week later with his attached briefcase to pick up the concentrate. We presume that the effort enjoyed some success, since the entire operation was repeated a number of times."

By the early sixties Kodak was involved in other areas of government-related work, some of it secret and classified, some that would in time become very well known. Aerial photography had, since the First World War, been one of Mees's many enthusiasms. After the war Kodak continued, at the instigation of George Goddard and the Army Air Force, to study the problems encountered by high-altitude photographers. In fact, in 1935 Captain Albert Stevens had taken an experimental Kodak infrared film aloft in a balloon and made the first photograph that clearly showed the curvature of the earth.

Infrared film records rays of energy that are longer than light waves and invisible to the human eye. Since these rays are not absorbed or reflected to the same extent as visible light, the world as it is recorded on infrared film is very different than that captured by ordinary film. Police photographers, for instance, use infrared to examine powder burns caused by close-range gunshots. Since chlorophyll contained in plants strongly reflects infrared radiation, ecologists use the film to see changes in the health of vegetation. During World War II, infrared film's ability to examine chlorophyll allowed surveillance photographers to tell the difference between artificially colored camouflage cloth and natural foliage.

The most significant postwar uses of aerial film occurred in the late 1950s after President Dwight Eisenhower proposed an "open skies" policy, whereby both Russian and American aerial reconnaissance pilots would be given the right to photograph freely each others' military sites. Though Eisenhower had joked in a 1955 meeting with Soviet Premier Nikita Khrushchev that during the last war the Russians would have given "a great many rubles to have had good photography of the enemy's positions," the "open skies" plan was rejected.

In the meantime, the Central Intelligence Agency had been building and outfitting a high-altitude spy plane dubbed the "U-2." Various aeronautic and photography companies were approached to work on the project, including Kodak, which in secrecy designed a very thin film that could be loaded on the plane in large quantities. Though U-2 flights over Russia were responsible for tens of thousands of photographs, the fate of one particular flight, that taken by Francis Gary Powers on May 1, 1960, will, of course, always be associated with the project. After Powers's photo-reconnaissance plane was shot down that Sunday morning, the world was able for the first time to see the sort of high-altitude pictures now possible.

Similar flights continued in other parts of the world, however, and in October 1962 another U-2 aircraft took pictures over Cuba that would have an even more dramatic effect upon world affairs. Again using specially manufactured thin Kodak film, U-2 aerial cameras took pictures of what appeared to be the construction of a Russian nuclear base on the western end of the Cuban island. When President John F. Kennedy first saw enlarged sections of the long rolls of aerial film, he thought that the missile launchers looked "like little footballs on a football field." The "little footballs" were considered photographic proof. On October 22, Kennedy went on television and, pointing to one of the aerial photographs, said that they were "unmistakable evidence" that Russian bases were being erected in Cuba.

In 1918 Mees had correctly predicted that the "tactical" use of aerial photography would be its greatest contribution to warfare, but even he might have been surprised when men carrying cameras were propelled into earth-circling orbits by rockets. It is not that Mees had neglected the photography of outer space, it's just that most of his work had been devoted to looking outward rather than inward. Since 1912, when the astronomer George Ellery Hale questioned Kodak about the possibility of photographing through the telescope at California's Mt. Wilson, Mees and others in the lab had mixed small quantities of the special emulsion needed for long astro exposures.

Since the task of astronomical film and plates is to record light many times less intense than that seen on earth, the exposure times required of their emulsions are so long that after a certain period what is known as reciprocity failure takes effect. For most photographers, who open the shutter of their camera for a fraction of a second, reciprocity failure presents no problem. Astronomical exposures, however, can last up to an hour. By the late 1940s Kodak had begun preparing small quantities of special astro emulsions marked by the letter "A." These films and plates had a fairly short shelf life and were sold as special orders. (Even today, spectroscopic products are "nonreturnable.") The same was true for color-sensitive astronomical plates. The new dye-sensitized emulsion with improved sensitization in the red and infrared range allowed scientists to study star systems never before recorded. Beginning in the early 1950s three space-mapping programs were undertaken with the help of Kodak spectroscopic plates: the Northern Sky Survey of 1952, the Southern Sky Survey of 1973, and the New Northern Sky Survey in 1987. Each of these projects enabled scientists to gather information about the position of previously discovered stars and to identify objects in outer space.

In an odd turnabout, the one planet that scientists had been unable to photograph was the earth. Billions of photographs, of course, had been taken on the earth. It was also possible to attach a camera to a microscope and record earthly life too minute to be seen with the naked eye. Surprisingly, prior to 1971, when Kodak introduced a special photomicrographic film, these sorts of pictures were taken with a high-definition Ektachrome stock initially designed for aerial photography. With the new photomicrographic films, biologists were able to take pictures of objects magnified many thousands of times and to study close-up photographs of objects as small as the taste buds of a guppy and as intricate as the patterns on the wing of a butterfly. But though high-altitude pictures such as Stevens's infrared photos succeeded in capturing the curve of the earth on film, no pictures of the entire planet seemed possible.

This suddenly and dramatically changed in the 1960s. As early as 1959 an Atlas missile carrying an automatic camera had been sent into space, but though the photos taken on this flight clearly showed sections of the earth from a height of seven hundred miles, it was not until manned missions began in 1962 that the planet was seen in all its spectacular beauty. Through the late 1950s Kodak had been involved in the production of ultrathin Estar-base film used on the first experimental space flights. But it was John Glenn's historic first manned orbital flight that transformed the act of photographing in space. As Glenn wrote of a photo taken on Kodak film on February 20, 1962:

Since this was the first U.S. manned orbital flight, this was the first landmass picture taken following launch approximately 23 minutes earlier. On this flight I used a 35mm hand-held camera. Probably the most significant thing about the photograph is that it pointed out to all of us the value pictures from space would have for mapping, weather analysis, etc., in work that has since been refined to a high degree with other equipment on other flights and other projects.

On subsequent flights, both manned and unmanned, Kodak products were used for a variety of scientific and engineering purposes. Sixty-two cameras loaded with Kodak films allowed scientists to monitor the performance of the rocket that thrust *Mariner IV* into space on its trip to Mars, and Kodak instrumentation-recording papers were used to record the progress of *Gemini V*. Not all the pictures made on these expeditions were technical. Some were taken by astronauts purely for the pleasure of recording the radiant colors and magnificent abstract patterns of earth. Scott Carpenter, the pilot of *Aurora VII*, wrote of the sun setting:

The beauty of this panorama is overwhelming. The brilliance of the colors and the sequence in which they appear defy description, and I was anxious to record it photographically so others would understand. Even at the time, however, I was consoled by the thought that, in contrast to the ever-changing aspect of sunrises and sunsets as seen from the surface of the Earth, those viewed from space were destined to be forever the same.

Mees had once written that "the destroyer of stability is knowledge," though he clearly meant the knowledge gained by scientific and industrial research. Carpenter's photos would have no doubt seemed to him discerning in a specifically aesthetic manner. Eastman had told Mees that his job was "the future of photography," but neither could have seen this far over the horizon.

In 1951, shortly after the amputation of his leg, Mees gave the major address at the American Chemical Society's diamond jubilee dinner. Mees spoke about chemistry, biology, and astronomy in terms of the responsibilities "which the chemist must accept for the application of science to the future." At the end of that speech he restated his belief that "the advance of science is the hope of mankind." But, he added, "Man cannot live by bread alone; the function of science is not merely to add to our ease of living. Nourishment, shelter, health, and leisure are not ends in themselves. We need a minimum of all of them, but many of those who have raised the human spirit and have made man but a little lower than the angels have lacked the material comforts of life. More precious than these—vital in the true sense of the word—is freedom. In this sense we must all stand united—academic and industrial scientists alike—all who have worn the toga and taken the vows of science."

In the decades following that speech the science of photography would take part in this struggle as never before. The world would be flooded with pictures, not all of them as temperate and gratifying as Mees might have liked.

Abraham Zapruder, a dress manufacturer who had recently moved to Dallas, agreed with his secretary. "How many times," she asked him the morning of November 22, 1963, "will you have a chance to have a crack at color movies of the president?" Zapruder rushed home and picked up his Bell & Howell camera, loaded it with 8mm Kodachrome color film and was back in Dealy Plaza in downtown Dallas shortly after twelve o'clock. Finding a spot partway between

The blue-striped dress was gone, as was the box camera held at waist level by most of the Kodak Girls who since the turn of the century had appeared in Kodak camera advertisements. But the small cartridge-loaded Instamatic camera raised to the eye of this 1963 version of the Kodak Girl was perhaps the most efficient, foolproof, and popular camera ever marketed by the Eastman Kodak Company—over 70 million of the cameras sold worldwide.

Abraham Zapruder, a Dallas, Texas, dress manufacturer, was a skilled amateur photographer, and when on November 22, 1963, the chance arose to photograph the motorcade of President John F. Kennedy as it passed through Dallas's Dealy Plaza, Zapruder loaded his home-movie camera with Kodachrome film and awaited the president's arrival. When Kennedy's car appeared in his viewfinder, Zapruder pressed the camera's button and for the following 8.3 seconds exposed the most momentous and horrifying 152 frames of home-movie film ever taken. Optically enhanced image by Robert Groden.

the Texas Book Depository and a highway overpass, Zapruder attached his zoom lens and waited for the arrival of the presidential motorcade.

At approximately twelve-thirty the Lincoln carrying President John F. Kennedy, Texas Governor John Connally, and their wives turned into the plaza. Zapruder raised his camera. A freeway sign blocked his view of the car. A second later, as the motorcade came into view, Zapruder squinted through the viewfinder and pressed the button on his camera. The president raised his hand to wave at the crowd, but the look on his face was strange, Zapruder thought. It seemed to be saying something like, "Oh, they've got me."

For the next incredible 8.3 seconds the amateur photographer continued to follow the car with his camera, exposing 152 frames of the most historically significant home-movie stock ever taken. When it was discovered that Zapruder's film was the only photographic evidence of Kennedy's assassination, it was acquired by *Life* magazine, which the following week printed selected strips of the color movie. In the days after the killing, law-enforcement investigators analyzed each frame of the film in an attempt to ascertain how many bullets had been fired, their trajectory, and the intervals between shots.

Zapruder was not the only person in Dealy Plaza that day with a camera. As soon as he heard the rifle retort, Captain Cecil Stoughton, Kennedy's official photographer, immediately reached for his telephoto lens. But Stoughton was too far behind the action to get a picture. Bob Jackson, a *Dallas Times Herald* photographer, looked up and saw a gun barrel being withdrawn from the window of a building across the street. But there was not time to take a photo. (Jackson would be much quicker with the camera three days later when Kennedy's accused assassin was himself assassinated.) In addition, perhaps dozens of others in the crowd that day were carrying snapshot cameras, though it is not known exactly how many took photos or how many were too stunned by what they saw to take pictures.

What is clear is that the world had become thoroughly seasoned to the culture of cameras. Though by the mid-1960s electronically transmitted images were beginning to replace picture magazines as the primary carrier of visual information, many of the most enduring memories of the weekend following the assassination remain those captured by photochemical means. Bob Jackson's dramatic picture of the Sunday, November 25, shooting of Lee Harvey Oswald now seems etched in the historical record, as does Stoughton's photograph of Lyndon Johnson taking the oath of office in the crowded cabin of *Air Force One*. In a certain way, cameras seemed aesthetically and intellectually to satisfy the appetite for information. As *The New York Times*'s television critic John Corry wrote of the power of still photographs: "Television couldn't match anything like that; its technology worked against it. Images on television move too fast to be digested."

Across the entire spectrum of society the demand for photochemical images was never greater. In all divisions of the photographic market (professional, artistic, amateur, serious amateur) picture taking continued its postwar boom. More cameras were purchased, more images exposed, and more photos processed than at any time in the history of the medium.

The single most remarkable indicator of photography's continued accelerating growth shows up in the amateur wing of the picture-taking community. In the late 1950s Kodak camera designers had been attempting to develop a machine that would outdo even the original Kodak camera and the first Brownie in reliability and ease of operation. Since before the war the 35mm format had become increasingly popular, especially for the taking of color photographs, but Kodak's Japanese competitors were beginning to secure a large share of this camera market. What was lacking was an inexpensive 35mm snapshot camera, what Mees had called an "Aunt Molly camera," that would equip the amateur with equivalent capabilities.

Like George Eastman's original Kodak camera, this new piece of equipment would have to be part of a complete system. Thus in the late 1950s Kodak engineers initiated a secret design plan known as "Project 13." When work on it was wrapped up in 1961, the new camera crafted by this group was called the "Instamatic," and as one historian has written, "It was probably the best-judged market coup in commercial photographic history."

The integrated design of the Instamatic cameras was a marvel of industrial engineering. The plastic bodies could be mass produced, as could the high-quality acrylic lenses. The cameras had a short focal length and small aperture (43mm, f/11 lens), which meant that they were capable of taking quite sharp photographs. The usual double row of sprocket holes per frame were replaced by a single perforation per frame, which allowed the negative size to be increased to 28 x 28mm. Since the frame was square, the cameras could be held either vertically or horizontally with no change in picture ratio. And, with only one sprocket hole per frame, a fresh, unexposed negative could be brought into the film plane with a single press of the advance lever.

After its introduction in 1954, high-speed Kodak Tri-X film was often used by photojournalists to cover current news and sporting events and even the active lifestyle of the period. This contact sheet of Tri-X film was taken indoors in existing light by Dan Weiner while documenting a typical day in the life of James Conkling, president of CBS Records. According to the caption printed under the Weiner photographs, which were selected for the March 1957 issue of Fortune *magazine, each episode of the executive's life was functional, fast-paced, and separated into millimoment slices: "James Conkling lives like a TV program, on a split-second schedule. While he brushes his teeth, his wife shows him a breakfast menu, which may include chocolate pudding. By nine o'clock he is on the train for Manhattan...."*

KODAK SAFETY FILM   TRI X FILM

The code name of Project 13 was "easy load," and it was that feature which most fully insured the commercial success of the Instamatic cameras. The apparently simple act of handling film in a camera had always been one of the major difficulties encountered by unpracticed amateur photographers. At any stage in the threading, rewinding, and unloading process, film could be accidentally exposed. The 1963 "Kodapak" film cartridge almost entirely eliminated this problem. The Instamatic was designed to accept a small plastic container of 126-size film that could be easily snapped into the camera. When the number appearing in a small window on the back of the plastic carton indicated that all the film had been used, the entire cartridge could be disengaged and taken to a processor. The snapshooter need never touch the actual film.

The 126-size film cartridges came loaded with one of three types of film: black and white, color print, and color transparency film. By 1958, however, Kodacolor print film had been introduced in the 35mm size, and it was this stock, albeit specially perforated for this camera, that beyond doubt was the most popular with Instamatic camera users. Kodacolor was a wide-latitude film, which when used in this camera produced adequate color prints with an absolute minimum of effort. In other words, the Instamatic was what is known as a "film burner," a camera that inspired photographers to snap away relentlessly. Perhaps not since the 1888 introduction of the initial Kodak camera had the slogan "You press the button, we do the rest" been as seductive. The sales of 126 film were so strong that at first photofinishers had difficulty catching up. However, many soon realized that lengths of the 35mm film could be joined together and put through the type of continuous developing then being used to develop motion-picture stock. The mass printing of pictures from Kodacolor film was even further simplified by the 1968 introduction of RC (resin coated) paper, which dried about three times faster than the usual baryta-coated print stock.

The Instamatic camera/film cartridge system worked so flawlessly that dozens of other camera companies were licensed to manufacture cameras that accepted the units, but in the end it was the Instamatic camera that dominated the amateur market in the decade following its introduction. Over seventy million of these cameras were sold during the 1960s, practically replacing the old revered box camera. (Early Instamatic camera models were quite cheap, under twenty dollars, a price even further reduced when some dealers gave customers a rebate if they turned in their old Brownie.) In 1972 the trend toward small reliable cameras was further advanced when Kodak introduced the Pocket Instamatic camera. The 110-size film produced for this subminiature camera was manufactured from 16mm-wide stock and had a remarkably small 13 x 17mm negative size.

Both these cameras were equipped with flash capabilities. The flashbulb had been invented in Germany in 1929, and at first it was used much like old "open flash" exploding powder. The camera's shutter was opened, the bulb illuminated, and the shutter closed. By the late thirties, however, photojournalists began to rig up shutter-synchronized flash units. The image of the cigar-chewing press photographer reaching into his pocket for a bulb to insert in the flash gun of his Speed Graphic camera became a movie cliché. By 1940, when Kodak had introduced the Six-20 Flash Brownie, its first synchronized flash camera, amateurs also were able to take pictures by the artificial light of a bulb. By the mid-1950s, when the Brownie Starflash became the first Kodak camera with a built-in flash holder, flash had become standard on many amateur cameras.

The first Instamatic camera was equipped with an electrical "hot shoe" that accepted a flash holder, but in time even this system was improved. In 1965 Sylvania Electric Products introduced a four-shot pivoting "flashcube" that could be attached to the camera. This feature allowed the amateur photographer to take four photos without stopping to change bulbs.

Opposite:
By the 1950s improved techniques in ultra-high-speed photography enabled photographers to stop action in slices of time as small as 1/10,000 of a second. Harold Edgerton, the MIT scientist responsible for the development of the electronic flash, took this 1975 shot on High-Speed Ektachrome film of a fan blade whirring at 3,600 RPM through the flame of a Bunsen burner as part of an experiment in visually studying changes in the density of air.

Wherever an especially interesting, significant, or inspiring vista is to be found, there are sure to be snapshooters around, all intent on capturing what they see on film. By the mid-1960s, when Thomas Consilvio took this photograph for his book Snapshooters, *the memories retained by most amateur photographers were warmed by the hues of color film, an aesthetic tool that a Kodak advertising campaign had described as capturing "all the wonders of awakening life."*

In 1974, when the Kodak Tele-Instamatic 608 camera was introduced, a pop-up "Flipflash" bulb was first marketed.

The Tele-Instamatic camera, as its name implies, had two lenses, one for normal shooting and a telephoto to photograph objects at a distance. A few late models of the Instamatic, such as the Tele-Instamatic 708 camera, also had a built-in exposure-control device that automatically corrected for light intensity. The Kodak Ektralite camera, first marketed in 1978, was even more sophisticated. This camera not only included electronic flash, which had been invented by Harold Edgerton of MIT in the 1930s and had been marketed by Kodak in 1940 as the Kodatron electronic flash unit, but it also automatically read coded notches on the film and adjusted itself to the appropriate film speed.

Each of these models was what is known as a "point-and-shoot camera." All the casual photographer needed to do was snap a cartridge in the camera, target the subject through the viewfinder, press, slide, or push a lever, and get ready for another picture. When all the exposures had been used, the cartridge was removed from the camera, taken to the photofinisher, and within a few days the prints were ready. In 1890, with a developing and printing schedule of about six thousand negatives a day, Eastman had written that "our orders are usually fulfilled within the limit of time given in our advertisements—ten days." By 1974 the Eastman Kodak Company's computer-controlled color printer allowed photofinishers using this processor to develop and print six thousand negatives in one hour.

That neat ratio does not begin to gauge how popular an activity it had become to take pictures. A little more than 5,000 of the 1888 No. 1 Kodak cameras were manufactured before the camera was discontinued in 1889. In the fifteen years of the 1901 No.1 Brownie camera's life about 500,000 were built. During the 1960s and 1970s, 70 million Instamatic cameras were sold. Even more significant, it was estimated that while the average snapshooter exposed four rolls of film a year, Instamatic camera owners used eight.

There is no way, of course, accurately to count the number of snapshots taken since the introduction of the first Kodak camera in 1888. Trillions likely. There are, though, a number of ways to indicate the influence of these pictures upon the way the world saw and remembered. Snapshots are a unique vernacular form of artistic endeavor. They can, and have, been made by very young children and very old adults. To take such pictures requires no special skill. The snapshot's appearance on the stage of pictorial art around the turn of the century ushered in a new breed of image maker, and though the fascination with picture taking was first called a fad, the craze never let up. Once amateurs discovered that they could easily make images, they did so with an abandon that cheerfully ignored the birthright and entitlement of artistic privilege. Anyone could photograph anything he or she wished, and that simple fact broadened the base of artistic entitlements. "Call it, for want of a better phrase," the American historian John Kouwenhoven has said of the invention of popular photography, "the democratization of vision."

Amateur photographers using the first Kodak cameras were instructed to stand with their backs to the sun, letting the light fall brightly on the subject facing them. Often, depending upon the angle of the sun, this maneuver added an extra figure to the photo, that of the shadow outline of the picture taker. In this 1966 shot, Lee Friedlander, one of a loosely defined group of photographers interested in the aesthetic of the snapshot, quotes a line from the history of amateur photography, letting a featureless, perhaps ominous, shadow create a double portrait of unusual power.

Of all the on-the-spot news photos taken during the dramatic 1960s, Eddie Adams's picture of the February 1968 street execution of a suspected Vietcong infiltrator by a South Vietnamese officer remains one of the most memorable and iconic of the age. Fast, reliable film, such as Kodak Tri-X film, and the quick reflexes of photojournalists collaborated during this decade to produce an album of similar telling photographs. As one commentator wrote of photos such as Adams's, "It was the still picture that fixed the image, that called forth the editorials, that will stick in memories."

The prevailing spirit of this opening of vision was from the beginning impressionable, curious, and often unaffected. Most vernacular photographers simply glanced through the viewfinder and clicked away, and in the process they included much more of the world than they had intended. Only later, when their prints were returned, did they notice all those things that the relentless eye of the camera had captured. And as Kouwenhoven has argued, "The cumulative effect of one hundred and thirty years of man's participation in the process of running amuck with cameras was the discovery that there was an amazing amount of significance, historical or otherwise, in a great many things no one had seen until snapshots began forcing people to see them."

Many of these unnoticed things were not much more than diary entries in the social and political history of particular eras: the style of clothes once in vogue, for instance, or a political banner that just happened to be included in an otherwise average portrait. Some of the things that slipped into these pictures turned out to be significant in unforeseen ways. In 1981 a snapshooter in St. Peter's Square in Rome accidentally captured a handgun being raised as Pope John Paul II rode past the crowd. Another amateur photographer's picture of the crowd immediately following the shooting included a man running away with what appeared to be a gun in his hand. Both photos were used by police as clues in their attempt to discover the identity of the man or men who had attempted to assassinate the Pope.

The bulk of the billions of snaps taken since the invention of the amateur camera are not so celebrated. They record unexceptional events, significant solely to the few who participated. They are family pictures in the strictest sense; only those in the immediate household of family, club, or work respond to their emotional appeal. Looking through a family album after his mother's death, the French critic Barthes came upon a snapshot of his mother at age five. "I

studied the little girl's face," Barthes wrote about this photo, "and at last rediscovered my mother."

Snapshots like that of Barthes's mother were usually not what professional photographers or curators called "good pictures." Print quality could vary. The untrained snapshooter often exposed film badly, and since the pictures were mass processed mistakes were often not corrected in the development and printing stages. Often vernacular photographers did not frame their pictures with an artistic eye. Most were interested simply in the objects captured, not the abstract and pleasing relationship of shapes. And even then, this sort of photographer sometimes blundered badly, slicing off body parts, tilting the frame precariously, snapping at precisely the worst time.

By the mid-1960s, however, some professional "artistic" photographers were discovering that these apparently "bad" pictures were capable of yielding unusual and meaningful insights. "I am a passionate lover of the snapshot," Lisette Model wrote, "because of all photographic images it comes closest to the truth. The snapshot is a specific spiritual moment. It cannot be willed or desired to be achieved. It simply happens to certain people and not to others. Some people may never take a snapshot in their lives, though they take many pictures."

Though the precise requirements of this "snapshot aesthetic" are still a matter of dispute among photographic historians, it is clear that during the 1960s and 1970s photographers such as Garry Winogrand, Lee Friedlander, Wendy Snyder McNeil, and Emmet Gowin in one way or

Well into the 1960s, color photography was considered ill-suited to the coverage of war. In photojournalist Eddie Adams's words, color pictures were too "lush," too "nice." One of those who did take color shots was Life *magazine photographer Larry Burrows, who favored Ektachrome film stock because, as his son said of photographs such as this picture of a helicopter hovering over a jungle outpost, "It produced the greens and the browns which were the hallmark colors of Vietnam."*

another found some inspiration in vernacular photography. Winogrand, who is one of the iconic figures of this unaffiliated group, was uncomfortable with the phrase, but as John Szarkowski has written, even he understood the emotional and artistic referent that underlay the term:

> The term "snapshot aesthetic" was coined to give a name to the open-ended character of this imagery, so different from the familiar ideal of good pictorial design, with its taut assemblage of interlocking shapes. Winogrand thought the label idiotic and pointed out correctly that the prototypical snapshot was—at least in intention—rigidly conceptual, even totemic. At a deeper level, however, there was perhaps some justice to the term, for the snapshooter and Winogrand agreed that the subject was everything. The difference between them was that the snapshooter thought he knew what the subject was in advance, but for Winogrand, photography was the process of discovering it.

This insistence upon discovery and, in fact, photographic verification was shared by the most influential group of photographers working during these decades: the photojournalists. Though television was throughout the turbulent two decades from 1960 to 1980 beginning to become the world's everyday lingua franca, press photography had never before played such a critical role in the dissemination of political and social information. In previous times of discord photographers had seen conflict from a distance (the World War I photographers), documented with compassion (the FSA photographers), or recorded as best they could the valor, fortitude, and fright of soldiers (the World War II photographers). But during the sixties photojournalists acted as political advocates, going as close as they could to any event without worrying about the consequences—either to themselves or society.

By 1955, after the introduction of Kodak's Tri-X black-and-white 35mm film, the majority of photojournalists had exchanged their 4 x 5 Speed Graphics for smaller, more portable 35mm cameras. Before the introduction of Tri-X film most press photographers had used either Kodak Super-XX roll film or Kodak panchro press B 4 x 5 sheet film. Both these films were fairly fast. With flash they could acceptably capture most scenes and events. The Tri-X emulsion, however, was four times as sensitive to light as the earlier films.

The immediate consequence of this new film, which can be seen in *Life* magazine stories of that year, was that with the combination of miniature camera and fast Tri-X film, press photographers were able to work in available light. This meant that in many situations the photojournalist was able to raise his camera quickly and snap acceptably sharp pictures on the spur of the moment. When covering the Vietnam War, for instance, almost all photographers used Tri-X film, and lots of it. David Douglas Duncan is reported to have carried at least sixty rolls when he went into the field, and Larry Burrows would routinely put the film in his socks, where, he once said, "it's handy to get at."

One of the most famous photographs of the era, Eddie Adams's shot of the street execution of a prisoner by a South Vietnamese general, is as emblematic as any of the universal, almost casual use of this fast film. In February 1968 Adams went out on what seemed to be a typical assignment:

> As we walked back to the car, we saw that the South Vietnamese had just grabbed this guy....
> We saw them walking down the street. And so like any newsman, we followed up on the story;
> we continued photographing [the prisoner] in case somebody were to take a swing at him or he
> fell or whatever. So we just followed them down to the corner where they stopped for a minute,
> and...some guy walked over—we didn't know who he was—and...pulled a pistol out. As soon
> as he went for his pistol I raised the camera thinking he was going to threaten him. I took a
> picture. That was the instant he shot him. I had no idea it was going to happen. He put the pistol

back in his pocket and walked over to [us] and said "He killed many of my men and many of your people." And he walked away.

The effortlessly fluid reflex gesture of raising a camera to one's eye is perhaps the most incontrovertible proof of the existence of the universal camera culture George Eastman had envisioned. Whether it was Abraham Zapruder looking at a president through the lens of a home-movie camera or one of the 70 million Instamatic camera owners taking pictures at a picnic or a photojournalist covering wars both domestic and foreign or an art photographer attempting, as Lee Friedlander once said, to capture "all that the camera can consume in breadth and bit and light," millions of photographers now automatically lifted their cameras whenever they saw something worth recording. In fact, Garry Winogrand became so addicted to the possibilities inherent in this gesture that after his death in 1984 it was discovered that he had left close to a third of a million exposures unedited and in some cases unseen.

As wide ranging in style and content as were photographs in each of these genres, none were as riveting as the snaps taken by that group of part-time photographers who worked full time for the National Aeronautics and Space Administration. Cameras had been on board all manned and unmanned space vehicles since John Glenn's 1962 orbital flight. In 1965 one of these cameras, loaded with specially manufactured Kodak Ektachrome film, was even carried outside the spacecraft and pictures were taken from a vantage point one hundred miles above the earth. If not always solemn, the exercise was at least one that all amateur picture takers could understand. When Edward White stepped out of the *Gemini IV* module with a 35mm camera attached to his hand-held maneuvering unit, fellow astronaut James McDivitt looked out the window and began snapping his own record of this historic first space walk. As an international audience listened in to their conversation, the two dueling snapshooters joked with Houston Mission Control officer Gus Grissom about their work:

"Is he taking pictures?" Grissom asked McDivitt.
"Of the ocean, this is my only guess," McDivitt answered.
"Take some pictures." Grissom commanded.
"Get out in front where I can see you," McDivitt told White.
"Okay."
"Where are you?"
"Right in front now."
"Hey, Ed, smile."
"I'm looking right down your gun barrel, huh? All right."

Four years later, in 1969, a similar scene was enacted when two other astronauts, Buzz Aldrin and Neil Armstrong, took what are perhaps the most well-known travel shots ever exposed. Three years earlier the unmanned *Lunar Orbiter II* had been sent to photograph the moon to determine possible landing sites. For this mission Kodak had manufactured a dual lens camera that it loaded with film capable of being processed on board the ship. The Bimat processor designed for the *Lunar Orbiter* missions developed film by squeegeeing together and pulling apart two webs of wet developing chemicals. Once the film had gone through the Bimat processor, images were electronically scanned and the resulting signal sent to earth, where it was recorded by a Kodak-supplied readout device.

On November 28, 1966, the Kodak camera, film, and processing system was responsible for what was called "the photograph of the century," a close-up of the sixty-mile-wide, two-mile-deep moon crater Copernicus. "On first seeing this oblique view of the crater Copernicus," NASA administrator Oran Nicks wrote, "I was awed by the sudden realization that this

The Eastman Kodak Company's relationship with the National Aeronautics and
Space Administration began as early as
1959 when an unmanned Atlas missile
carrying an automatic camera loaded with
Kodak film took high-altitude photographs of the curvature of the earth.

By 1962, when John Glenn made the first
U.S. manned orbital flight, specially produced ultrathin Ektachrome film was used
to record the astronaut's reactions during
lift-off. As he flew over the earth, Glenn
himself took pictures with a hand-held
35mm camera.

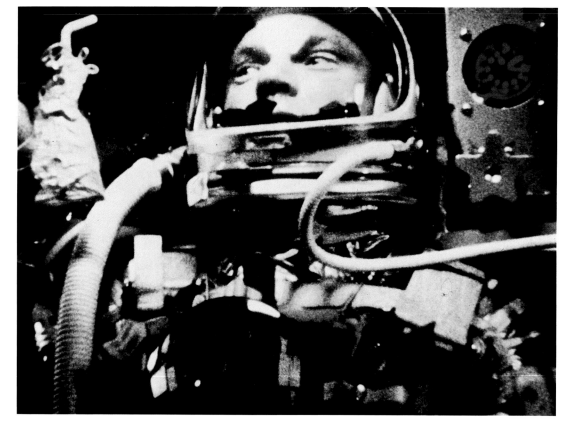

In 1965 James McDivitt held his camera to
the window of the Gemini V space module
and snapped shots on Ektachrome film of
his fellow crew member Edward White
during his historic first walk in space.

Opposite:

The most famous travel snapshot ever
made was taken by Neil Armstrong in July
1969 when he asked fellow astronaut Edwin "Buzz" Aldrin to pose for a picture on
the moon. Kodak, as with all the previous
manned flights, provided film for the Apollo XI mission. For this flight Kodak also
manufactured a specially designed "walk-
ing-stick" stereo camera used to take photos of three-inch–square sections of the
moon's surface.

prominent lunar feature I have often viewed by telescope is a landscape of real mountains and valleys, obviously fashioned by tremendous forces of nature."

Three years later men carrying cameras were able to take close-up pictures of the moon's surface. For the 1969 *Apollo XI* moon mission, Kodak manufactured a 35mm stereo camera mounted on the bottom of what looked like a walking stick. To obtain highly resolved color photos of three-inch-square sections of the moon, the astronaut pushed the stick against the soil and pulled the camera's trigger. These stereo photos were the first to allow scientists to study in detail a portion of undisturbed lunar surface. (Aldrin and Armstrong may have also set a distance record for "lost" travelers' cameras when they intentionally left the stereo unit on the moon.)

As crucial to the success of the mission as these scientific photos were, it was the snaps Aldrin and Armstrong took of each other that remain the most universally appealing. Using 70mm Kodak Ektachrome film, the two moon photographers took dozens of shots that are in most ways typical of the travel genre: each posing for the other in front of their lunar vehicle, next to the flag they had just planted, or against the backdrop of the spectacular lunar landscape—pretty typical stuff, though clearly not exactly what Eastman had in mind when he recommended that "travellers and tourists" could use his products to "obtain a picturesque diary of their travels."

By the early 1970s the Eastman Kodak Company had become fondly, if not irreverently, known to photographers as the "Great Yellow Father." Since the 1880s Kodak had advertised its products with a variety of slogans—"You press the button, we do the rest," "You press the button, it does the rest," "Capture your memories on Kodak film"—but it had been the familiar yellow film box that had been its longest standing and most effective method of product identification. Early in the century a few shipments had gone out packaged in blue boxes, but dealers complained that the change confused their customers, and from then on the color yellow connoted Kodak film.

Dozens of competitors had challenged Kodak's dominance of the film market, particularly during the postwar period, when film boxes of different colors had begun regularly appearing on the shelves of photo dealers. The American 3-M Company, for instance, marketed its film in white and blue containers. But green and gray, the signature colors of the Japanese Fuji Company and the German Agfa Company, respectively, were the hues that most frequently contested with Kodak yellow for a film buyer's attention. During World War II, the research and sales operations of both of these companies, like those of photographic concerns all over the world, were interrupted by the affairs of war. By 1948, however, Fuji was again marketing a color film, and a year later Agfa resumed production of its prewar color products.

In spite of this renewed competition, the Great Yellow Father continued to steer the general course of the photographic market. In a certain sense, it also standardized the film industry, particularly in the important area of color film processing. After the great surge in sales of color stock following the introduction of the Instamatic cameras in 1963, the number of independent photofinishers able to process color rose accordingly. Few took advantage of the 1955 release of the controlled-diffusion formulas necessary to develop Kodachrome stock, the procedure was just too complicated, and the processing of that film remained almost entirely within the Kodak preserve.

But the processing of Kodak's two incorporated coupler film stocks, Ektachrome and Kodacolor, were well within the capabilities of all processors. The problem for independent photofinishers was the lack of industry-wide conformity. No single processor could afford to change chemicals each time a different brand of film was handed in. Since Kodak was the single largest vendor of film, most adopted Kodak's twin processing systems: C-41 for color

Between 1939 and 1967 two Academy Awards for cinematography had been given annually, one for black-and-white photography and the other for color. After 1967, with almost all films shot on Eastman color film, only a single prize was given. Color was no longer simply an added attraction, as it often was in the fifties. It was now used with a sophistication previously reserved for black-and-white cinematography. Three of the movies that won Academy Awards in the late 1970s were particularly notable for their subtle uses of color photography: Nestor Almendros's 1978 Days of Heaven, for its references to American artists such as Andrew Wyeth and Edward Hopper; Vilmos Zsigmond's 1977 Close Encounters of the Third Kind, for what American Cinematographer magazine called a blending of "an aura of fairy-tale wonder with here-and-now realism;" and John Alcott's 1975 Barry Lyndon for its low-lighting effects and its use of color to imitate old master painting.

The Czech photographer Josef Sudek used a Kodak Panoram camera, out of production since the early twentieth century, to photograph the streets, canals, and landscapes around Prague. Pictures taken in this photographic format and others earned Sudek the title "the poet of Prague."

negative films and E-6 for Ektachrome reversal stock. The majority of film manufacturers followed suit. By the late 1970s, Fuji, Agfa, 3-M, and others were manufacturing film that could be processed in either C-41, E-6, or a close equivalent.

While processing was becoming standardized, the film itself was undergoing major changes. Photographic scientists had long recognized that improvements in emulsions were regulated by what they called "the emulsion research triangle." This schematic drawing has three sides, each corresponding to one of the features of emulsion: speed, granularity, and sharpness. Each of these properties are interdependent, though not always happily. To raise the speed of a film, for example, it is often necessary to enlarge the silver-halide grain. This increase in size inevitably makes the film more grainy and thus less sharp. To increase sharpness, on the other hand, grain size is reduced; but then speed is also reduced.

Of the three sides of the emulsion triangle, speed has come to be employed as the most common measure of film sensitivity. By the 1950s there were a variety of ways to measure speed, all in one way or another calculated from characteristic curves of the sort formulated by Hurter and Driffield in the late nineteenth century. By the 1960s, however, Kodak and other manufacturers were describing the speed of their products by means of an arithmetic pattern devised by the American National Standards Institute. In this system a doubling of each number signifies twice as much sensitivity. A 200-speed film, for instance, is two times as fast as a 100-speed film. Correspondingly, each arithmetic increase necessitates half the amount of exposure. Since the diameter of a camera's aperture opening is also calibrated arithmetically, each change doubling the amount of light, an increase in film speed enables the photographer

to decrease neatly the necessary amount of exposure. In theory, a 200-speed film needs half the intensity of light of a 100-speed film.

Throughout the history of the medium, photography scientists had worked methodically to make films more sensitive, but during the postwar era the speed of film, and particularly that of color film, increased rather dramatically. In 1950, for instance, Kodacolor film was rated as a 25-speed film. By 1963, however, when Kodachrome-X, Ektachrome-X and Kodacolor-X were introduced for use in the Instamatic cameras, the speed had risen to 64. A little less than ten years later Kodacolor II in the Pocket Instamatic format was designated as an 80-speed film, and by 1977 a 400-speed Kodacolor film was marketed. Other film manufacturers also climbed each step on this ladder of ascending film speeds, sometimes tagging along, sometimes introducing new emulsions concurrently.

As the speed war continued, it was clear that the production of acceptable color photographs was not simply a function of the film's sensitivity. While working on early color processes in the late 1930s, Kodak scientists found themselves formulating a rather odd and surprising axiom. The exact color reproduction of a scene does not, the rule stated, necessarily look like the scene itself. In other words, there were two facets of color, the physical and the psychological, and the two were not always harmonious.

When the spectral color of the sky was accurately captured on film, for example, many observers would remark that the dyes seemed not quite blue enough. Chemists would then adjust the color, in effect correcting nature to meet the demands of viewers. The question of whether this reaction to color was physiological, the response of the human eye to color, or

The palette of color photography, once considered by critics and curators as only suitable for snapshots and advertising work, began to be accepted in the mid-1970s as fitting to fine arts photography. Pete Turner's 1966 Roadsong *(above), for instance, shot on Kodachrome II film, is bright, clean, and deeply saturated with color. Joel Meyerowitz's 1981* Pamela *(opposite), on the other hand, exposed on Vericolor film and printed on resin-coated Ektacolor paper, is more subtle and suggestive, enabling the viewer, as Meyerowitz has said, "to have feeling along the full wavelength of the spectrum, to retrieve emotions that were perhaps bred in you from infancy."*

simply subjective, a wish to see the world in certain hues, has not been adequately answered. In any event, color was manipulated to produce the kind of pictures people considered faithful to their vision of the world.

Color is usually measured by three variables: hue (the color name), value (its brightness), and chroma (its richness or saturation). For many viewers, the more intense the presence of each of these factors, the more pleasing (and accurate) the color photo. A photo of a bright red apple, for example, should be clearly red (its hue unmistakable), should be brilliantly red (its value outstanding), and should be richly red (its chroma fully saturated). If the apple is "in reality" not quite that red, people expect the reproduction of its image to be "that red."

By the mid-1970s the majority of color pictures were taken by amateur photographers, people who preferred their pictures in what Kodak had advertised as "living color." The consumer market thrived on color. After the introduction of the Instamatic system, which simplified and made practically foolproof the exposing of color negatives, this course led toward its inevitable conclusion, and by the 1980s hardly any snapshots were taken on black-and-white film.

The trouble with all this was that to most artistic photographers color photographs seemed, in Edward Steichen's words, too "coloriferous." The pictures were excessively bright, gaudy, and sensational. The usual subtle tonal shifts of black-and-white film were gone, replaced by harsh, contrasty edges of heavily applied color. In fact, until the 1970s, color for most artistic photographers was anathema, despite the fact, or indeed in spite of the fact, that by 1977 three times more color than black-and-white photographs were being printed annually.

By the mid-1960s, however, the resistance to color in other sectors of the photography community began to be relaxed. There were a number of causes for this shift. Mass-market magazines, for example, attempting to compete with television, began to splash their pages with eye-catching color. At first, many photojournalists continued to be uncomfortable with color, particularly with color pictures of war. Color was thought too shapely and alluring. The Vietnam War photographer Eddie Adams said: "I think all war should be done in black and white. It's more primitive; colors tend to make things look too nice. Makes the jungle in Vietnam look lush—which it was, but it wasn't nice."

Others, such as *Life* magazine photographer Larry Burrows, ignored this injunction. Burrows, who had studied and photographed old master paintings, was fascinated by the challenge of color photography, and as early as 1963 covered the breaking story of the Vietnam War in color. *Life* called these pictures the first to present war "thoroughly and satisfactorily photographed in color." Burrows was a master manipulator of film stocks, particularly of Ektachrome film, with which he took many of his most well-known color pictures of the Vietnam War. According to Burrows's son, "The reason for the Ektachrome was that he found that by slightly underexposing it, it produced the greens and the browns which were the hallmark colors of Vietnam. You'll notice in a lot of his pictures that tonally the color is quite deliberate."

Burrows's calculated use of the color film palette was an attempt to tell the story of the Vietnam War in terms so descriptive that viewers would be shocked and moved by the hues of his pictures. Some photographers continued to lodge the perennial timeworn complaints against the use of color film in wartime situations. It would either artificially beautify scenes of horror or, conversely, overstep all reasonable boundaries of good taste, horrifying and disgusting the viewer. Burrows believed that the artful combination of beauty, realism, and shocking drama would accurately depict the conditions of war.

Burrows's most famous color photos were taken during the two months he spent with the crew of the helicopter *Yankee Papa 13*. The series of color photos taken on one particular mission, an attempt to rescue the crew of a downed helicopter, turned out to be emblematic of the entire enterprise. He watched as two *Yankee Papa 13* fliers attempted to care for the wounds of a rescued fellow flier:

A glazed look came into the eyes and he was dead.... I tried to find a way in which to hide the pilot's face when the boys were working on him, feeling that should a photograph be used, it would be hard on the family. Yet it would bring home to many people that this was a war and people were getting killed. It was important to show such a scene and for all to realize that despite the pretty pattern that helicopters made when flying at 1,000 feet, life can be hell.

By the time Burrows's pictures were published in the April 16, 1965, issue of *Life* magazine, color photography had already become the accepted standard in the moving-picture industry. Of all the photographic technologies, motion-picture cinematography had been the least sparing in its use of color. A primarily directorial medium, one that widely skirted the issue of photographic realism, the movies had seized upon color since the introduction of the Technicolor process in the mid-thirties. Though sometimes the phrase was used disparagingly by critics, audiences were enticed into their local theaters by the promise of "Glorious Technicolor." After Eastman color movie stock was introduced, its bright colors were sometimes categorized as "Shocking Eastmancolor."

During the 1950s many critics had complained that wide-screen color was a distraction, that its use was often superfluous and inconsequential. For instance, when reviewing *The Umbrellas of Cherbourg*, Kenneth Tynan wrote, "I have rarely seen such a blaze of irrelevant color." One of the advantages of the Eastman color negative-positive process was that the film could be exposed in a normal black-and-white camera. Freed from the bulky three-strip Technicolor camera, filmmakers were encouraged to shoot more films on location. At first, the color of many of these films was splashy—brilliant but sometimes a little grating. One critic described the cinematography of Alfred Hitchcock's 1954 Eastman color *To Catch a Thief* as "coarse and unpleasing" compared to similar movies filmed in Technicolor.

In spite of such criticism, by the mid-1960s color had become the predominant medium of movie photography. Between 1939 and 1966 two separate Academy Awards had been presented for cinematography, one for black and white, the other for color. In 1967, however, so few films were shot in black and white that only a single award was presented, and from that date until the present all winners in the category of motion-picture cinematography have been color films.

Since the introduction of Eastman color film in 1950, the technology of motion-picture color, like that of still photography, had been continually improved. In 1960 the speed of camera negative film had been doubled and eight years later doubled again. In 1968 a color reversal intermediate film was introduced that made possible the generation of a duplicate negative in a single step. Each of these upgradings of stock gave moviemakers faster, sharper, and finer-grained materials. In 1972 Eastman color negative II film, having an exposure index, or ASA, of 100 was developed, which, along with a new processing system, ECN-2, increased the speed of the stock while at the same time reducing the time necessary for processing.

These new camera, print, and duplicating films, together with the introduction of more sophisticated motion-picture cameras and lenses, signaled a change in the use of color as significant as the initial uses of photographic color in the field of photojournalism. Directors and cinematographers began to utilize color interpretatively. Arthur Penn's period film *Bonnie and Clyde*, for instance, the winner of the 1967 Academy Award for cinematography, recounts the exploits of Clyde Barrow and company, one of the 1930s' most notorious bandit gangs. Penn studied snapshots of Barrow and his girlfriend-in-crime, Bonnie Parker, in order to understand how the two typically dressed, gestured, and indeed posed. In shooting the film, director of photography Burnett Guffey likewise patterned the color of the film on the bleak, sometimes somber tones of Depression era photography. Though, as critic Pauline Kael has written, this is the Depression "of legend," "with faces and poses out of Dorothea Lange and Walker Evans," the film is a prime example of movie photography reflecting upon photography in general. Those seeing the 1967 film were able to recall the era of the 1930s, not simply as a story, but as it had been captured on film.

By the 1970s some of the most skillful cinematographers were able to create even more sophisticated and subtle photographic effects. The 1975 Academy Award winner John Alcott shot Stanley Kubrick's *Barry Lyndon* in colors meant to imitate the style of eighteenth-century British painting. Alcott used a newly introduced camera stock so sensitive that some of the movie's interior scenes were filmed by the light of candles. Even more far ranging in its sources was Terrence Malick's *Days of Heaven*, the 1976 prizewinner. As Nestor Almendros, the film's cinematographer, observed:

Days of Heaven *was a homage to the creators of the silent films, whom I admire for their blessed simplicity and lack of refinement....In this as in my other films, there were a number of influences from painting. In the daytime interiors we used light that came sideways through the windows as in a Vermeer. There were also references to Wyeth, Hopper and other American artists. But as the credits indicate, we were particularly inspired by the great photo-reporters of the turn of the century (like Hine) whose books Malick had a plentiful supply of.*

By 1980, when Vittorio Storaro won the Academy Award for his work on Francis Ford Coppola's epic film about the Vietnam War, *Apocalypse Now*, the use of color photography to

Opposite:
Using Ektachrome 35mm film, Raymond Young won a KINSA prize for this aerial view of a rowboat near the bow of a ship in the Kodak-sponsored 1967 amateur contest.

Ronald Kaufman's portrait of a baboon, shot on 35mm Ektachrome 400 stock, was a prizewinner in the 1980 Kodak-sponsored newspaper contest.

depict war had come full circle. Between Burrows's manipulation of Ektachrome film in 1965 and Storaro's interpretative use of Eastman color stock less than fifteen years later, the use of color film to depict certain truths had become established. Certainly the foundation of those visions was built on different epistemological grounds. Burrows was attempting to capture and interpret what he saw. Storaro was re-creating the specter that remained years later in the minds of all those who remembered the war.

It had not always been assumed that color was capable of such artistry. In his ground-breaking history of photography Beaumont Newhall wrote:

The line between the photographer and the painter is no more clearly drawn than in color photography. Imitation is fatal. By the nature of his medium, the photographer's vision must be rooted in reality; if he attempts to create his own world of color he faces a double dilemma: his results no longer have that unique quality we can only define as "photographic," and he quickly discovers that with only three primary colors, modulated in intensity by three emulsions obeying sensitometric laws, he cannot hope to rival the painter.... The esthetic problem is to define that which is essentially photographic in color photography, to learn what is unique about the process, and to use it to produce pictures which cannot otherwise be obtained.

In 1976 John Szarkowski, Newhall's successor as director of the photography department at The Museum of Modern Art, wrote that photographer William Eggleston had in fact solved this problem and "invented" color photography. Whether Eggleston had actually "invented" the art form or simply legitimized it remains a hotly debated question. In a narrowly technical sense,

however, Eggleston had twined together many of the loose strands of color photography. Though his photographs were printed by the easily manipulated Kodak dye-transfer method, at least in content and framing, the pictures resembled snapshots. And yet at the same time, there was a solid formal symmetry about the work that lifted it above the merely occasional.

Dozens of photographers were working with color during this period. Joel Meyerowitz, for instance, began in the late 1960s shooting Kodachrome slide film of New York Street scenes. At first Meyerowitz could not afford to have dye-transfer images made from the slides, but after 1973, when he began to print his own 8 x 10-inch landscapes and portraits, Meyerowitz began to be known as a photographer able to produce color prints as subtle and immaculately pristine as any of the old masters of black-and-white photography. Another color specialist, William Christenberry, used an old Kodak Brownie camera for his early work, while Jim Dow, who calls himself "a butterfly collector in search of the perfect specimen," began by recording the sometimes tacky and bizarre colors of roadside restaurants, signs, and arcades.

Each of these photographers was drawing the selection of images from a well of individual inspiration. The colors they found in the dyes of individual films. In a very real sense their work was impossible before the introduction of improved color film stocks. As photography historian Jonathan Green wrote of this period, "The Kodak color materials introduced in the seventies were unprecedented in terms of fidelity, range of control and luminosity. The seventies' straight color photograph depends for immediacy and transparency on the new Kodak palette and technology."

By 1980 color was available to photographers in all sectors of the photographic community. After the Instamatic camera's introduction, the average photographer was able to take good-quality 35mm color photos at an affordable price. By the late 1970s, so many snapshots were taken in color that for all intents and purposes amateur black-and-white photography no longer existed. The majority of movies shot were also in color. In the advertising community color was the norm. And even photojournalists were coming to accept the power and subtlety of color.

Nineteen-eighty was also the year when Kodak celebrated its one-hundredth anniversary. Though the word *Kodak* had not been added to the company's name until after the 1888 introduction of the Kodak camera, the 1880 date was correct. That year George Eastman had rented a loft in downtown Rochester and begun selling his first dry plates. Within a very few years film began to replace dry plates as the firm's chief source of revenue and a small hand-held camera was offered for sale. A revolution in the world of photography was underway.

One hundred years later, as the Eastman Kodak Company celebrated its anniversary, making pictures by photochemical means was universally accepted as a fact of life. As the company entered its second hundred years of operation, new image-making systems would begin to challenge that technology. Whether these techniques would also change the world's view of itself would be an open question, one not easily or satisfactorily answered.

Opposite:
Photographers have always been ready to find metaphors wherever they show up, even in fortuitous overlappings of separate and unrelated facts. Whether the split-second vision captured on Tri-X film in Rita McGrath's KINSA-winning Chalk Face on Boy and Girl's Shadows *is a function of resourceful creativity or simply a fluke of crisscrossing visual planes, the picture nonetheless stands as an example of photography's ability to make unlikely but striking comparisons.*

The first high-tech age of photography began one afternoon in the early summer of 1888, when, in what must have been a mood of high anticipation, an unidentified photographer left the Eastman Company's State Street factory in Rochester and headed across town with a brand-new camera under his arm. The photochemical process of image making was just about a year shy of celebrating its fiftieth birthday, though this neat dovetailing of dates probably never entered the man's mind. He was too interested in trying out his new invention. Would it work? How well? How easy would it be to operate? The mechanical device the man carried was the product of a network of insights, chief among which was that photography was just too attractive an undertaking to stay cooped up in the dark rooms and traditions of the nineteenth century.

The day was bright and cloudless, perfect for the making of sharp, clear exposures. All the man needed to do was stop here and there, steady his camera, and take pictures. As he well knew, the act of photographing had not always been so effortless. Fifty years earlier, in 1839, it had been necessary to expose a daguerreotype plate to full sunlight for up to forty minutes in order to capture an acceptable image. (The man's entire walk might not have lasted that long.) Less than twenty years later, in 1856, the introduction of the wet-collodion method of photography reduced exposure time to two minutes (one hundred and twenty slowly counted seconds). In 1880 gelatin dry-plate technology had lowered the length of exposure to about one-twelfth of a minute. Only eight years later, as the photographer walked along the street in Rochester, he had at his service a photographic emulsion capable of shaving this interval down to one-fortieth of second. In relative terms, this means that fewer than fifty years after the official announcement of the invention of photochemical materials their sensitivity had been boosted over five thousand times.

It would be nice to assume that the photographer was George Eastman. The camera was his invention, as was the revolutionary flexible film wound inside its wooden body. Though there is no sure way of knowing who pressed the camera's button (like most photos it lacks a signature), Eastman seems the most plausible candidate. Look at the picture (page 64). Two men in work aprons are standing on the top step of what seems to be a small, freestanding building. Both men are smiling at the photographer, who, ten or twelve yards away, attempted to frame them and building in a single shot. It is not a particularly good photo. Nor is it one likely to elicit much initial interest.

Turn over the copy of the picture as it exists today in the Eastman Kodak Company's archival files, however, and on the back of the print is a simple inscription: "Yawman and Erbe — 1888 — the earliest surviving picture taken with a Kodak camera." Now the story begins to take on at least some slight antiquarian interest. The first of anything, no matter what its quality, usually deserves some historical standing.

It is likely that carrying his first Kodak camera Eastman walked a mile or so north from the factory on State Street and turned left heading toward the Yawman and Erbe metalworking shop on Joy Street. (Turning right he would have crossed the Genesee River and come upon the Bausch & Lomb lens factory.) Arriving at the Yawman and Erbe building he then called the two artisans who had fabricated the metal parts for his camera outside to show them how the thing worked. The picture taken, the two returned to work, and Eastman went on his way.

There seems to be no particular reason why this particular photograph was saved (the camera contained enough film for one hundred exposures). Perhaps it was simply the best of the roll. By today's standards the technology that produced the photo was crude. But, however low-tech the box camera now seems, it fulfilled its mechanical promise with practically unerring efficiency. "You [the human being] press the button," its first slogan pledged, and "we [the technological delivery system] do the rest." Photography was no longer only a nineteenth-century craft; it was a twentieth-century process.

Cameras are time machines. Photographs take one back. When his 1988 portrait was taken on Kodak's T-Max 100 film by Nick Vedros, the bearded Ezekiel Cowell was one hundred years old, though in a curious way he looked much as a man might have looked in 1888, the year of his birth. In Cowell's hands is a picture of himself at age twenty-five, a memory of other, very different times also preserved on film.

During a single five-day work week, often operating in the dark and under extremely exacting conditions, workers at a Kodak film plant are able to coat enough 35mm film to circle the globe. Cellulose acetate, turned the consistency of honey, endlessly flows off thirty-ton, two-story-high coating wheels to create the film's "web," or base. Twelve to sixteen layers formed of gelatin, potassium bromide, and silver nitrate, prepared from 99-percent pure silver and many other chemicals, are spread on this base. Each layer can be as thin as 6/100,000 of an inch. In addition to film, printing papers, cameras, and dozens of specialized photographic supplies are produced daily at Kodak manufacturing plants. Opposite top: rolls of photographic paper. Opposite bottom: film base. Left: bars of pure silver.

When this undistinguished snapshot was taken, Eastman's company had been in existence for less than a decade. Generally, the 1880s had been a pretty good time for Eastman. At the end of 1881, his first year in the photography business, monthly dry-plate orders received from his distributor, the Anthony Company, were just over one thousand dollars. The emulsion debacle of 1881–1882 had brought business to an almost complete halt, but by midsummer 1882, with customers satisfied with the new replacement plates, Eastman and his partner, Henry Strong, were in a position to move their factory from a rented loft in downtown Rochester to a newly constructed four-story building about three-quarters of a mile north of the center of town.

Rochester was in the late nineteenth century no more or less notable than any other medium-sized American city. The next one hundred years would change that completely. In 1980, when the Eastman Kodak Company celebrated its centennial, the original Eastman Dry Plate Company building had been gone sixty-five years, replaced in 1915 by a nineteen-story office structure. The six-story Camera Works factory, which in 1882 had been erected next door to the first Eastman factory, had also been torn down. Since 1967 the manufacture of camera parts was consolidated ten miles away at the Gates, New York, site of the newly organized Kodak Apparatus Division.

In 1891 emulsion making had been shifted three miles north of the State Street location to Kodak Park. By 1980 this industrial complex, which was at first made up of only three buildings, was comprised of nearly two hundred major buildings sitting on some two thousand acres of land. The Kodak Research Laboratories, set up in 1913 in a single three-story building, had by the 1980s moved half a mile away from its original Kodak Park location and occupied three buildings three miles directly north of the Kodak offices. The only turn-of-the-century Eastman Kodak Company buildings still partially recognizable were those across the Genesee River that had since 1907 housed the Hawk-Eye Works.

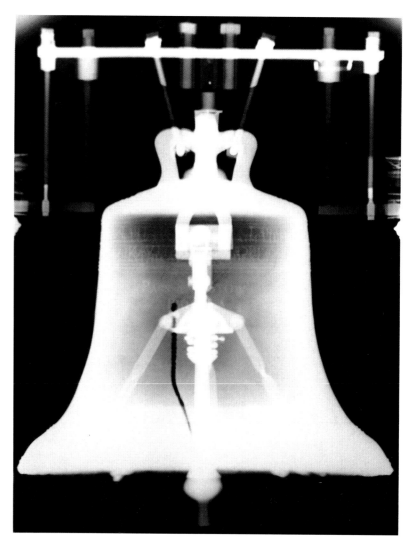

The most well-known use of X-ray "shadow pictures" is for medical and dental diagnoses. Less celebrated, though equally important, is the employment of radiographs in the nondestructive examination of the structural integrity of objects, such as this X-ray portrait of the Liberty Bell, made on a 52x84-inch sheet of Kodak Industrex film.

When a camera is fitted to a microscope, small details, such as the facial features of this fly, are magnified by the microscope, captured on film, further enlarged in the printing stage, and closely studied by natural scientists. In 1971 Kodak introduced a special-order film with ultra-high resolution, Kodak photomicrography film (SO-146), which when used for photomicrography surpassed even Kodachrome film in image quality.

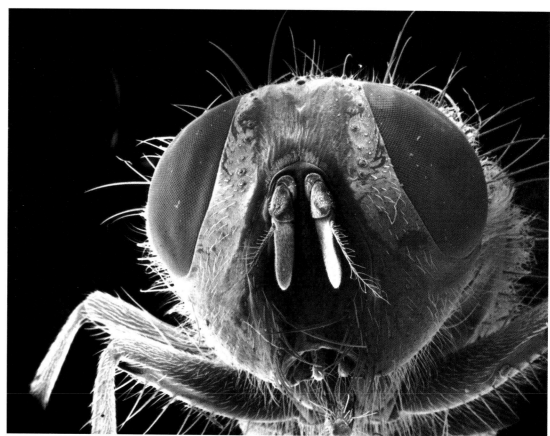

The number of Kodak personnel had increased accordingly. In 1881 sixteen people were on the payroll. During the 1980s there were over one hundred and twenty-five thousand Kodak employees in one hundred and fifty countries. In many ways, however, growth had not signified radical changes in direction. For instance, during the one hundred years since George Eastman and Henry Strong had begun manufacturing photographic supplies, the corporate leadership of the company had been perhaps the slowest-changing and steadiest part of the company's history. When Colby Chandler, the chairman of the board in 1990, became president of the company in 1980, he was only the tenth man to hold that position. Five of those executives preceding Chandler had been with Kodak long enough to have known George Eastman. In fact, when Albert Chapman, Kodak's fifth chairman of the board, retired in 1967, he was the last of the company's leaders to have been born in the nineteenth century.

By 1980 Kodak's base of operations had grown in breadth, volume, and variety. It had become a widely diversified twentieth-century manufacturer. Shortly after Chandler assumed office, Kodak's worldwide sales exceeded 10 billion dollars a year. Only about 8.2 billion of this amount was received from the purchase of photographic goods. Since the 1886 hiring of Henry Reichenbach, its first trained scientist, Kodak had been almost daily involved in the discovery and manufacture of photographic chemicals. In the process Kodak scientists had occasionally come across chemical materials not directly related to the immediate business at hand. These discoveries led to the creation of subsidiary operations not normally associated with photography. Large quantities of the cellulose acetate developed as a base for "safety film" were used to coat the wings of military aircraft during the First World War. In 1930 Kodak's cellulose plant in Kingsport, Tennessee, began producing various sorts of acetate fibers. Kenneth Hickman's work on vacuum distillation in the 1930s led to the creation in 1940 of Distillation Products, Inc., a supplier of vitamin E products. In the 1950s Texas Eastman was formed to provide the petroleum products necessary for the manufacture of some of the company's fiber

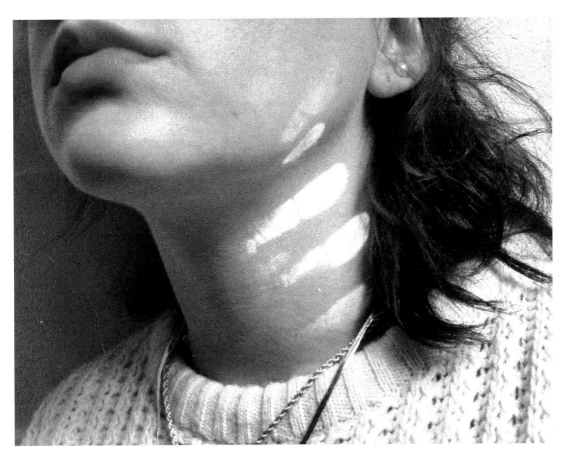

Using Photography to Preserve Evidence, one of Kodak's many specialized professional manuals, provides instruction in crime-scene, fingerprint, footprint, and "dusty-shoe-print" photography as well as in a number of other specialized techniques used by forensic law-enforcement photographers. This Ektapress Gold 400 film laser photo, taken by the Ocean County (New Jersey) Sheriff's office, records as evidence the marks on the neck of an attack victim.

Overleaf:
As color film improved during the 1980s, the Colorama transparency displays viewed in the dim ambient light of New York City's Grand Central Terminal became increasingly spectacular and engaging. Top: Steve Kelly's 1986 photograph of the Taj Mahal (Agra, India). Below: Lee Howick's 1985 view of rice terraces in the Philippines.

and film products. By the late 1970s Arkansas Eastman, an organic chemical subsidiary, and Carolina Eastman, the maker of Kodel polyester yarns and fibers, had joined the Eastman Chemicals Division.

In spite of the increasing importance and profitability of each of these various subsidiaries, the business of photochemical image making remained the commercial operation most closely associated with the Kodak name. But even in this section of the company's business, diversification had been a continuing policy. George Eastman has been rightly called the inventor of popular photography. But neither Eastman nor his company had ever concentrated exclusively on this single sector of the photographic marketplace. Throughout Kodak's one-hundred-year history its cameras, films, and print materials had been used in professional photography, photojournalism, cinematography, science, military planning, and by just about anyone who needed to produce, study, or manipulate photochemical images. Each of these trades and genres lies squarely within what is considered to be the field of traditional photography. At least since the beginning of the twentieth century they have been the benchmarks used by those who have traced the history of photography. But off to the side of these categories, sometimes unnoticed and unacknowledged, sat nontraditional imaging technologies. And by the 1980s even these nontraditional image-making technologies were generating a sizable portion of Kodak's business.

During the 1970s, for instance, new Kodak radiographic films and intensifying screens were introduced, which significantly lowered the amount of radiation necessary to make a readable exposure. By the mid-1980s, a patient undergoing a mammographic examination could expect to receive 99.5 percent fewer "rads" (roentgen-absorbed doses) than one who had been subjected to the same test in 1960.

Microfilming machines, which had been part of the company's business since the 1928 founding of the Recordak Corporation, by the early 1960s had been so simplified that Kodak's Reliant 500 microfilmer was capable of copying up to five hundred checks per minute. A few years later a computer-assisted microfilm retrieval system was introduced, which allowed users to locate any document in a file and make a hard copy in thirty seconds or less. This was followed by Kodak's Oracle and Starvue microfilm products, which provided high-speed, automated retrieval of microfilm images.

Work on an even less established type of image making was begun in the early 1960s when Kodak developed its first electrophotographic copier. For many years Kodak had supplied photographic materials for the Photostat process, which produced copies that resembled negatives with white letters printed on a black background. In 1944 Chester Carlson, the inventor and patentee of the xerographic process, had approached Kodak with a plan to manufacture a machine in which a latent image is formed on an electrically charged surface and reproduced when oppositely charged particles are attracted to copy paper. At the time Kodak was heavily involved in the war effort, and Carlson's proposal was turned down.

In 1952, however, Kodak entered the copying business when it introduced the Verifax copier, which transferred images from an exposed master to paper copies by a version of the traditional silver-halide process. The Verifax copier, however, was not the perfect copying machine. It used water-based activating chemicals, which were messy to handle, and it had a relatively narrow range of exposure. Though the machine survived into the 1960s, superior competing technologies, such as the 3-M Thermofax process and the electrophotographic copier produced by the Haloid Corporation (later named Xerox), who obtained the rights to Carlson's invention, signaled the end of silver-halide copying techniques.

At first some Kodak managers were reluctant to experiment with electrophotography. Before his retirement in the mid-fifties, for instance, Mees reportedly had said to one of the earliest workers in this field, "While I find this work interesting, I hate to see you doing it, since it will only help make it easier for others eventually to displace silver-halide photography." But work continued, and in 1975 the Kodak Ektaprint 100 Copier-Duplicator was introduced. Developed in conjunction with designers at the Kodak Apparatus Division, the Ektaprint copier utilized magnetic brushes and organic photoconductors to produce images of very high quality. During the next few years improved models were manufactured, and by 1982 the Ektaprint 250 was able to make 5,500 copies per hour.

An even more unusual modification of Kodak's standard photographic technology was the development of an automated blood analyzer. As one Kodak scientist described the technique, "Thin layers containing all the necessary reagents for clinical analysis by colorimetry would be coated on a transparent plastic base and dried. When the test fluid was applied to the film, water and other components would diffuse into the reagent layers, initiating the reaction sequence, and the subsequent extent of reaction could be determined by colorimetry." After almost ten years of research, the Kodak Ektachem 400 analyzer was introduced, and three years later a desktop version was manufactured, which allowed physicians to analyze a patient's blood in their offices.

By 1984 the range of these and other Kodak products occasioned the first in a series of company reorganizations. Though the particulars of this reorganization are intricate and involve internal company policies, certain of the changes are a good gauge of the distance photography had come since George Eastman first entered the business. By the mid-1980s about 20 percent of the company's earnings were the result of chemical sales. The balance of the company's revenue came from what was now called the "Photographic and Information Management Division." This division was responsible, of course, for each of the areas into which photography had been traditionally subdivided: consumer products, motion pictures and audio visual, Kodak processing laboratories, photofinishing systems, and professional photography. The information-management side of the division was also divided into recognizable units: business imaging, copy products, graphics, and government systems, which, as its name implies, develops products for government agencies.

In one sense, these structural changes in Kodak's management pattern were mainly a business matter. They were made to streamline the day-to-day operations of the company and, in these terms, were no different than any of the thousands of adjustments made during the company's history. At the same time, a new and ultimately very meaningful word had appeared and begun to take on considerable significance. And that word was *information*.

Chemically generated images had since photography's invention gathered, recorded, and dispersed information. Whatever else photographs have become, they have never been able to stray far from an epistemological relationship with what most people unguardedly consider to be pure fact. Somewhere behind the ability of photosensitive material to capture light lie the data of the world. Furthermore, and even more important, photographs organize that data.

In these admittedly philosophical terms, the 1984 reorganization of Kodak's major businesses into a single Photographic and Information Management Division seems entirely consistent with the company's commercial history. Kodak had always been in the information-management business, the main difference being that by the 1980s the terminology had changed. As one Kodak scientist remarked about the research lab's initial entry into the field of electrophotography, the company "should be exploring all kinds of ways of forming patterns of intelligence."

Would George Eastman have recognized any of this? The answer is yes and no. The need for reliable, easy-to-use, and up-to-date imaging systems has not changed. In that sense, the reach of technology would not have surprised the man whose idea for a "complete system of photography" had initiated a revolution in the business of providing photographic information.

THE FUTURE OF
PHOTOGRAPHY

Some Colorama displays, such as David Muench's 1985 panoramic view of a climber perched atop Mount Sneffels in the San Juan Mountains of Colorado, portrayed the heroic and adventuresome; others, such as Jennifer Carter's 1981 photo of the ceremonial wedding procession of Britain's Prince Charles and Lady Diana Spencer, reprised highly visible public events. Many current-event Colorama displays, such as those dealing with the U.S. space program, were erected within hours after the event had taken place.

The size of the company would also not have been particularly startling to its founder. "The manifest destiny of the Eastman Kodak Company," he had written nearly one hundred years earlier, "is to be the largest manufacturer of photographic materials in the world, or else go pot. As long as we can pay for all our improvements and also some dividends I think we can keep on the upper road. We have never yet started a new department that we have not made it pay for itself very quickly." That these departments included technologies not specifically based on silver-halide chemistry probably would have seemed to Eastman an entirely sensible way "to keep on the upper road."

What would have surprised Eastman least would have been the meteoric growth of photography, still the company's most profitable and important business. The 1880s had been a transitional decade in the history of photography. By the time Eastman's methods of mass production, low pricing, and wide distribution were in place, the course of the medium had been completely altered. As the company entered its second hundred years of operation, however, a new high-tech age seemed about to begin. Electronic methods of transmitting visual information were challenging photochemical technologies, and emulsion makers all over the world were fighting back by producing increasingly higher-quality films. Like all transition times, the high-tech eighties were for Kodak a dramatic and productive yet sometimes disappointing era.

For photography in general the 1980s was among the best of times. Despite the impending revolutionary changes in the world of visual information, the progress of ordinary, everyday conventional photography lost absolutely no momentum. In fact, during this period worldwide

picture taking grew at an estimated annual rate of 5 to 7 percent. In 1988, to pick a single year, forty million cameras were sold worldwide and forty billion color negative exposures were made, and that does not take into account slides or black-and-white exposures, individual motion-picture frames, photos reshot on graphic arts film, microfilm copies, or any of the other uses of the photochemical process. Each of these billions of photographs was the result of individual need, advanced technology, and, perhaps most significantly, the ability of the photo industry to supply picture takers with product.

Early in the century the Eastman Kodak Company annually printed a list of its consumer goods, known simply as *The Catalog*. Each year this enumeration of its current offerings was augmented and updated. Kodak cameras that had been introduced in earlier years were replaced either by mechanically improved models or by entirely new types of cameras. The life span of each of these cameras is instructive, the dates separating introduction and discontinuance reading like historical extracts, short, discrete episodes in the history of popular photography. For example, the following well-known Kodak cameras seem almost perfectly to match the social, historical, and technological forces with a particular photographic era: the No. 1 Kodak camera—1889–1895; the No. 1 Brownie camera—1901–1916; the No. 1A Autographic Kodak camera—1914–1924; the Vanity Kodak camera—1928–1933; the Kodak 35 camera—1938–1948; the Brownie Starflash camera—1957–1965; the Kodak Instamatic 100 camera—1963–1966; the Kodak Pocket Instamatic camera 25—1972–1976. What would be the camera of the 1980s?

In 1976 Kodak entered the instant photography market with cameras and a color film that yielded pictures that developed after exposed film was ejected from the cameras. Polaroid had previously sold instant systems that provided black-and-white and color pictures and had various patents relating to instant photography. Edwin Land had developed a one-step black-and-white photographic process after his daughter complained of the wait required to see

Cute and comic pictures of animals have been a staple of popular (and, indeed, commercial) photography at least since the 1890s, when Kodak camera users discovered that pets and farm animals sometimes could be caught in charming or farcical situations. Francis E. Wood's 1986 KINSA prizewinning photo of a boy named Camden and his dog Nick—one climbing, the other vaulting over a fence in Farmville, Virginia—is nicely representative of the first of these categories. The predicament of the two steers in Scott Theison's 1984 KINSA prizewinning photo (on Tri-X film), both animals rigid with stubbornness as they butt heads over an insignificant white line, is a prime example of the allegorical problems commonly illustrated in Aesopian photographic fables.

THE FUTURE OF
PHOTOGRAPHY

The wonders of nature have traditionally been a favorite subject matter of serious amateur photographers. Christopher Prouty's 1988 KINSA prizewinning winter shot of a stream running under a snow bridge is a prime example of this genre as it is practiced by skilled amateur photographers.

The "smarter" the camera, the more intricate, efficient, and economical its design. Cameras such as the No. 1 Kodak were mechanically quite simple, just a box with a few wood and metal parts. The interior of this 1986 automated Kodak VR 35 is packed with the electronic circuitry necessary for infrared autofocusing and DX film-code readings systems as well as with a maze of precision-made moving parts, including a built-in flash unit and an Ektar aspheric lens.

pictures taken with a conventional camera and film. Kodak independently developed its instant products, and Kodak was told by outside legal counsel that its products did not infringe any valid patent rights.

Polaroid thought otherwise. In 1976 the company filed suit against Kodak, charging that Kodak's instant photography products infringed upon certain Polaroid patents. Nearly ten years later, the U.S. District Court in Boston found in Polaroid's favor on some of these patents and prohibited the sale of Kodak's instant cameras and film in the United States. Kodak appealed, but the District Court decision was upheld, and on January 9, 1986, all Kodak's instant cameras and film were withdrawn from the market. This result came as a shock to Kodak since its legal counsel had advised it that it should prevail in any patent suit brought against it by Polaroid on these products. Owners of the Kodak cameras were offered compensation upon returning them. The litigation continues to determine the damages to be awarded to Polaroid.

Kodak's difficulties in the instant camera sector of the market had in the meantime been paralleled by the curious fate of the disc system of photography it had introduced in 1982. The Kodak disc camera was one of the most technologically sophisticated devices the company had ever manufactured. The camera itself was not much bigger than a cigarette pack, and instead of the usual roll of film it was loaded with a unique rotating disc that contained 8 x 10mm color negatives, the smallest ever put on the market. Even with such a tiny negative size, the camera was designed to make picture taking almost effortless. Exposure control and flash were almost completely automatic, and a specially produced aspheric lens enabled the camera to make very

sharp exposures on the mini-negative. At the time of its introduction the disc seemed destined to join the list of notable Kodak products. It appeared it would be the No. 1 Kodak camera of the 1980s.

Neither of these predictions came true. Though 25 million cameras were sold, it did not match the popularity of the Instamatic camera line it was expected to supersede. Some photofinishers, looking at large investments in new equipment, resisted the change to this new format.

But perhaps most significant was the rapid acceptance of new low-cost, highly automated 35mm "point-and-shoot" cameras. They were about as easy to use as the disc cameras. Improved 35mm films yielded superb results. In 1988 production of the disc camera was discontinued. Disc film is still available for those who own and use the system, but the move toward miniaturization and a new negative format proved to be a dead end.

In an odd turnabout, most photographers continued to prefer what is perhaps the oldest and single most durable of film sizes. When Thomas Edison and W. K. L. Dickson sliced a roll of 70mm No. 1 Kodak camera film in half, they created a width that was to have the longest shelf life of any single film size. Early in the century Edison's 35mm width became the standard gauge of motion-picture film. The high-tech "miniature" cameras first introduced in the late 1920s were built to accept 35mm film. Whatever the make or model, these miniatures were usually nicknamed "35s." By the mid-1980s a large proportion of the photographic world had, it seemed, settled upon 35mm as the format of choice. Kodak had, of course, continued to

The Kodak disc system of photography, introduced in 1982, was a marvel of industrial design. The rolled strip of film common to most snapshot cameras was replaced by individual 8x10mm color negatives attached along the edge of a revolving circular disc. Thin, flat disc film reduced the amount of camera room necessary for a film magazine, enabling Kodak designers to develop the subminiature Kodak disc camera. The print enlargement quality of these disc pictures, however, did not match that produced by 35mm negatives, and by 1988 production of the camera, though not the film, was discontinued.

Skilled amateur photographers who are at the right place at the right time often come up with newsworthy pictures. Merilee K. Thomas, for instance, described the chance to photograph a tornado touching down behind her friend in this 1989 KINSA prizewinning photo (entitled True Nebraska Grit) as a "once in a lifetime opportunity." Similarly, amateur photographer Robert Foor's 1979 photograph (right) of firemen training a high-pressure cloud of water upon an intensely orange yellow wall of gaseous flame proves again, as photojournalist Robert Capa once remarked, "If your pictures aren't good you're not close enough."

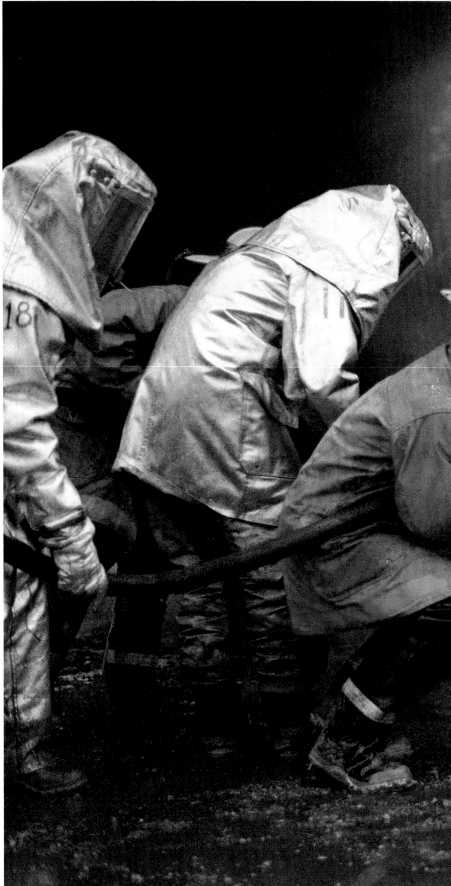

manufacture 35mm film for professional, serious amateur, and movie markets. Indeed, well into the early 1960s, the company had marketed its own brand of reasonably priced precision 35mm cameras. But the Instamatic, a low-price, high-volume camera, sold so well that Kodak ended its involvement in the upper end of this camera market.

In 1986, twenty years after the manufacture of the first Instamatic camera, Kodak reentered the 35mm camera field by introducing its first "VR 35" models. By this time Japanese camera manufacturers such as Nikon and Minolta, who had elected to stay with the 35mm format when Kodak had introduced its disc system, were leading the world in sales of "automatic" cameras. These cameras were sleek, well designed, and relatively inexpensive, and like many other Japanese products marketed during the 1970s and 1980s they took the fancy of a large segment of the buying public. Furthermore Japanese manufacturers had wisely offered products for both the high and low ends of the market. For the average amateur they designed automated "point-and-shoot" 35mm cameras that produced better-quality pictures than either the disc camera or the Pocket Instamatic camera. At the same time, high-quality single-lens-reflex models were manufactured for the serious amateur and professional sectors of the photographic community.

During the 1980s, Japanese photographic companies were also challenging Kodak's long-standing leadership in the film market. Throughout the 1970s, film companies all over the world had played a game of manufacturing leapfrog. One after another each company raised the speed, sharpness, and color saturation of its films. By dint of its reputation for quality and by virtue of its intensive research efforts, Kodak had for the most part managed to stay ahead of its competitors. Two of Kodak's technological breakthroughs became industry standards.

In 1983 Kodak introduced "DX" film coding, a method by which exposure and developing information printed on the film cartridge could be read electronically by both the camera and the film processor. Twelve conductive squares were designed to signal the film's speed, its type, and its number of exposures. Within a year or so of Kodak's introduction of DX coding most

For most of photography's history, individual grains of silver halide included in photographic emulsions were irregularly shaped. Increasing the size of these cubes made them more light sensitive, but there was a drawback. The larger the crystals, the grainier the picture. In 1982 Kodak scientists altered this formula by fabricating tabular grains of silver halide. These flat, platelike crystals have a higher ratio of surface area to volume than the cubic grains, allowing film designers to coat their new stocks with thin, very sensitive multiple layers of silver halide.

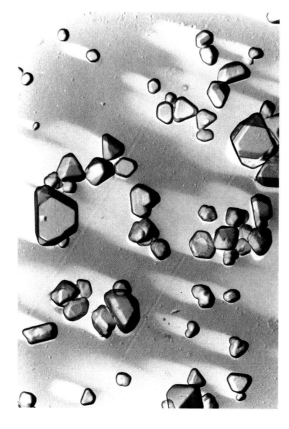 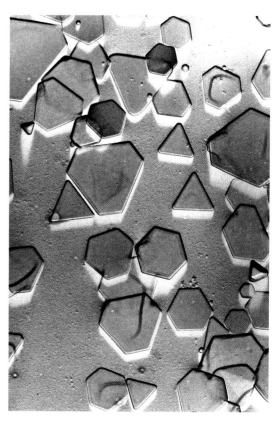

major film and camera manufacturers followed suit by designing their equipment to be DX compatible.

This feature simplified the photographer's task, and it also was at least partially responsible for the explosive growth of the photofinishing industry. In 1954 there had been about 350 labs capable of processing color photographs. By 1986 there were 9,000, many of which were self-contained minilabs, capable of quickly and efficiently processing thousand of pictures each day. Just about one hundred years earlier Kodak had promised its first customers that their photographs could be processed expeditiously. Eastman had in fact replied angrily to an 1890 newspaper report arguing that the company was four weeks behind schedule. At that time there was only a single processing facility available to Kodak's customers, its own plant in Rochester, and ten days was the usual turnaround time for Kodak photoprocessing.

By the late 1980s, after thirty years of growth in the photofinishing industry, there were a number of other options available to photographers. Film could be taken to a minilab and be processed in under an hour. Larger film labs serviced most of the drugstores, supermarkets, and parking-lot kiosks set up as film drop-off points. Some of these outlets advertised the Kodak Colorwatch system, a quality-monitoring program designed by Kodak that had been adopted by some of the world's largest photofinishing concerns. Alternatively, film could be mailed to one of Kodak's former processing laboratories, run as an independent joint venture under the name Qualex, Inc.

Even more potentially significant than developments in the photofinishing industry was Kodak's 1982 introduction of the new T-Grain emulsion. The sensitivity to light of silver-halide grains had always been in part a function of the size of the individual grains. Dyes could be added to the emulsion to increase spectral sensitivity and film speed, but at a certain point the only way to raise sensitivity was to enlarge the grains of silver halide. This procedure, however, automatically increased the graininess of the negative and the print. After much research, Kodak emulsion makers modified this formula by manufacturing each silver-halide crystal in a tabular shape. Having more surface area these tabular grains are able to gather more light, adsorb more dyes, and are thus much "faster."

The sudden leaps in film speeds that followed the introduction of T-Grain emulsions were unprecedented in the history of photography. In 1983 Kodak introduced an amateur color film that was rated by the newly adopted ISO (International Standards Organization) at a speed of 1000. A quick way to measure this increase is to remember that in 1942 the first Kodacolor film to be placed on the market was rated as a 25-speed film. A little over twenty years later, when the 1963 Kodacolor X film was manufactured for the Instamatic camera, the speed had risen to 64. In the late 1970s 100- and 400-rated films were marketed. But the jump to 1000 in 1983 more than doubled the previous highest number.

Following the T-Grain invention, it seemed that a new film was annually added to Kodak's list of emulsion products. This hadn't always been the case. Eastman N. C. film, for instance, was introduced in 1903, and despite occasional increases in sensitivity and a name change to Kodak N. C. film in 1930, the product remained pretty much the same until it was discontinued in 1943. In the 1980s, however, as films began to increase in speed, amateur photographers were presented with more film choices than at any time in the history of the medium.

After color photography replaced black and white as the medium of choice in photography's major markets, new and improved methods of color saturation further expanded the range of film selection. As a general rule, photographers desire bright, lifelike, vivid color. Since color production is a function of grain sensitivity, however, the wish for speed and saturation could not always be satisfied concurrently. For many years the principle governing this issue remained the same: the faster the film, the more grain; and the more grain, the less subtle the color saturation.

Kodak's highly saturated fine-grain Ektar 25 color print film was originally fashioned for the serious amateur sector of the photographic market, those who, with precision-made 35mm cameras, were skilled enough to take shots similar to this Michele Hallen advertising still life—very sharp, highly resolved color photographs soaked with bright, apparently grainless pigment.

By the 1980s there were two major changes in this equation. The first was Kodak's introduction of high-speed color films such as Kodacolor Gold 1000, which incorporated both tabular-grain emulsions and computer-designed dyes to produce acceptable color pictures at high speeds in low levels of light. The second, perhaps equally important, was the introduction of Kodak's highly saturated Ektar line of films. Ektar films were created for the serious amateur market. This group of photo "enthusiasts" used sophisticated single-lens-reflex cameras and could be counted upon to have the knowledge to manipulate whatever photo materials they were offered. Unlike those in the point-and-shoot market, this group did not need a forgiving wide-latitude film. What was most important to them was the best possible color print available.

Given this task, film designers at the Kodak Research Laboratories began to build a new stock. Tabular-grain technology had enabled the makers of film to reduce the grain size and to add more light-absorbing dyes to each crystal. However these highly efficient small grains often tended to scatter light. Ektar film's three color layers thus contain mixtures of tabular and cubic grains: the magenta (green-sensitive) layer is 100-percent tabular grains, the yellow (blue-sensitive) contains a combination of tabular and cubic grains, and the cyan (red-sensitive) layer uses 100-percent cubic grains.

With this amount of sharpness built into the film the designers turned to the problem of chemical development. In the early 1970s it had been discovered that one way to improve image sharpness was to include "developer-inhibitor anchimeric releasing" (DIAR) couplers in the emulsion. The effect of these "time-released" DIAR couplers is that the overall amount of dye produced at the boundaries of an object in the image in all three layers is greater than that produced in the image's center. Edges appear darker, sharper, and more distinct.

At first, two versions of Ektar film were manufactured, the very slow Ektar 25 and the very fast Ektar 1000. Each of these stocks is so complex that the monitoring of factory conditions is critical. Both films are multilayer (25 has nine and 1000 has twelve), and because light-sensitive materials are used, coating has to be carried out in the dark. When manufacturing the slower 25-speed film, workers are guided by a very dim green illumination on the floor, but for 1000-speed film all work must be undertaken in complete darkness, using infrared flashlights only when absolutely necessary.

A year after the introduction of Ektar 25 film to the serious amateur market, a 125-speed version was introduced. Compared with the slower version, this film has two additional emulsion layers (an additional one for blue sensitivity and a newly designed interlayer between the two green-sensitive layers), has new inhibiting couplers, and utilizes tabular grains somewhat more liberally. Most important, since the majority of point-and-shoot cameras are unable to read electronically film speeds lower than 100, the film is fast enough to be used by amateur photographers. In other words, what began as a fairly specialized film designed for serious amateurs made its way, though just barely, into the snapshot sector of the photographic community.

Each of these films are weapons in what *Popular Photography* magazine has called "the cosmic clash of emulsion empires"—the war currently waged between Kodak and its major competitor, the Japanese Fuji company. At least part of this battle has been fought over various international interpretations of what constitutes "correct" color. Traditionally the skin tones produced by Japanese color film have looked to Westerners as unnaturally warm and slightly unrealistic. On the other hand, the "European color" of film manufactured by the German Agfa company seems to some, as the photographic critic Andy Grundberg has written, "too muted and brown, as if the antique flavor of the old world had leaked into the emulsion." In fact, it has been predicted that in the future it is possible that film may be "geography specific," the color of skin tones in particular balanced to fit individual cultures and localities.

Kodak's Professional Photography Division has in recent years set aside significant funding to sponsor exhibitions, publications, and the work of individual photography artists. This support has ranged from the construction of a new gallery for New York City's International Center of Photography to the funding of workshops to assistance given to photographers. (William Clift, Brian Lanker, Josef Koudelka, Marilyn Bridges, James Nachtwey, Sebastiao Salgado, James Balog, Nick Vedros, Lynn Goldsmith, Douglas Kirkland, Will Steeger, and David C. Turnley, among others, have been assisted by the division.)

Clift's 1984 photograph of the St. Louis Arch (opposite) was included in his self-published book Certain Places, *a project supported by Kodak, as Professional Photography Division Vice-President and General Manager Raymond DeMoulin said, "to show what black-and-white products can do when reproduced by the highest quality graphic arts processes."*

THE FUTURE OF
PHOTOGRAPHY

The fine and often debated dividing line between photojournalism and art was crossed with impunity by many press photographers during the 1980s. Color photojournalism, in particular, long thought too painterly and distracting to record documentary truth, was both loaded with critically important content and as carefully formed as the best art-driven pictures. James Nachtwey's shot on Kodachrome 64 film of a child in El Salvador's Chalatenango Province peering through a bomb hole while the menacing shadows of government soldiers materialize on the wall to his right (1984) is a practically seamless blend of informative and evocative photography.

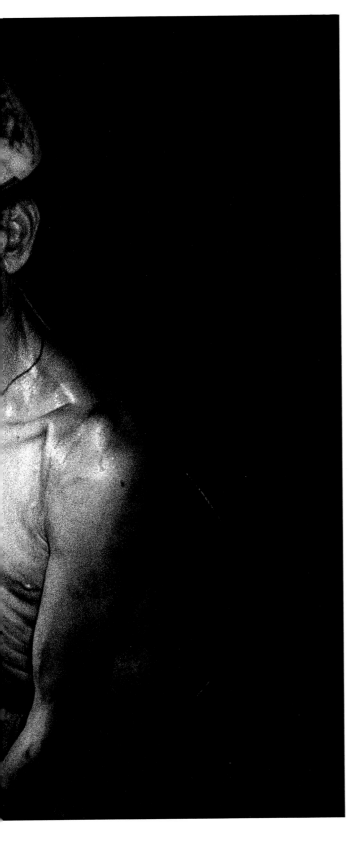

Sebastiao Salgado's ongoing photographic meditation upon the often menial, repetitious life of labor has taken him to work sites around the world. This 1988 photo (left) of two miners in Dhambad, India, was taken without flash, using only the ambient light of the workers' helmet lamps and the high-speed T-Max 3200 film. Eli Reed, a Magnum photo agency photographer, has said of this new tool for photojournalists that "existing light photography will become existing darkness photography." For Salgado's study of workers above ground at the same mine, he used high-speed Tri-X film (pushed one stop) to maximum effect.

Since 1986 James Balog has been compiling a photographic listing of animals under threat of extinction. The Bengal tiger, as seen in this 1989 photograph on Ektachrome 120-Plus Professional film, is one of the "Survivors of Eden," as the title of Balog's book calls these creatures.

At present, however, as reported in the pages of an American magazine such as *Popular Photography*, specific battles between Kodak and Fuji are decided in terms of color reproduction, flesh tones, contrast, image structure, and grain. Ektar 125 film, for instance, is scored as having "excellent" reproduction, vibrant but not overly saturated flesh tones, which "lean slightly toward the yellow," a "very sharp" image structure, and is judged to be "the least contrasty of Kodak fine-grain films."

Perhaps, as Kodak marketers argue, photo equipment in the future will be "market-specific." Following this scenario, photographers will carefully choose from the full palette of films and match skill and situation with film sensitivity and saturation. In 1990 Kodak has on the market twenty-five separate color films for use in general photography. Vernacular photography, for instance, had since the invention of the No. 1 Kodak camera been founded upon ease and reliability. Most casual photographers were interested in good, sharp, detail-filled prints that came out every time. After the mass popularization of color prints in the 1960s, these photographers added lifelike color to their requirements. With one of the four DX-coded Kodacolor print films loaded into a "smart" automated 35mm camera, the average photographer, it is argued, can with very little training take any of the sorts of pictures commonly associated with this genre. One-hundred-speed film is available for portraits, still lifes, or particularly spectacular landscapes. The faster 200 speed is an all-purpose film. It works well in most situations lighted by sunlight or electronic flash. It might be the perfect choice for a backyard birthday party. If the party is indoors and the children animated, 400 might be chosen. And at a sporting event, a child's first ball game, for instance, 1000-speed film will effectively stop the action. Each of these films varies in the amounts of grain, sharpness, and saturation, but if the photographer has the sophistication to fit film to occasion he probably won't mind.

Art photographers, on the other hand, care very much about each of these variables. Since the 1970s boom in color art photography, the stylistic tonal manipulation of images has been the most recognizable of the genre's accomplishments, and the art photographer might single out the film emulsion most suited to the mood he wishes to express. In all likelihood this sort of photographer will select a slide film. Those who prefer high-contrast, highly saturated images might chose a Kodachrome film stock, either the slower 25 and 64 or the faster 200. For quick processing one of the Ektachrome films might be picked. Photojournalists, on the other hand, require speed. The Ektapress line of Kodak color films introduced in 1988, available in 100, 400, and 1600 speeds, allows the working press photographer to take full-color action shots in all but the dimmest available light.

In fact, as Kodak viewed the photographic market of the late 1980s, the company decided, as one executive has written, that the so-called "average photographer is today as mythic as the typical consumer." After its reentry into the 35mm camera market Kodak opted to provide occasion-specific cameras. The Kodak Breeze camera was designed specifically for women in the twenty- to thirty-year-old age bracket; the Kodak Explorer camera for "active outdoor enthusiasts." The moisture-resistant Kodak Weekend 35 camera is aimed at those who might want an inexpensive underwater camera. The disposable Fling camera is marketed for those who need a quick single-use camera. And the returnable Stretch camera is Kodak's first panoramic camera since the discontinuance of the No. 3A Kodak Panoram in 1928.

Smart, user-friendly, market-specific, would these be the catchwords of Kodak's 1990s catalog of photographic supplies? The 1980s had been for Kodak a decade of unusual disruptions and even more striking discoveries. The future of worldwide competition is, of course, uncertain, though there is little doubt that during the second high-tech age of photography, quality will almost certainly remain a major issue, as will price. Battles between producers of photographic goods will in this sense probably not be significantly different than those fought in the past. The commercial history of photography has been predicated upon a steady improvement in the

From the time of Nadar to the present, the monochromatic photographic portrait has interpreted character as a shift of emotional shades, sometimes subtle, often quite graphic and bold. Contemporary work in black and white, such as Nick Vedros's 1983 portrait of Kansas City Royals' infielder George Brett (opposite), and Lynn Goldsmith's 1981 photo of Rolling Stones' guitarist Keith Richards with Patti Hansen (above), continue this tradition, albeit on the highly sensitive contemporary Plus-X portrait film.

Overleaf:

Traditionally, glamour photography has been a collaboration between the skill of a photographer and the ability of his subject to engage the camera with a rich, sometimes ethereal, photogenic presence. (Producer David Selznick, in fact, once wrote that Hedy Lamarr was "established purely by photography.") By the 1980s some of the famous and celebrated, such as singer Michael Jackson (left), here captured by Lynn Goldsmith in 1984 on Kodachrome 64 film, sought to avoid the camera. Others, like Susan Sarandon, seen in Douglas Kirkland's portrait on Ektachrome 100 film (right), sometimes allowed themselves to be presented in distinctly worldly, almost unglamorous terms. "She wasn't afraid," Kirkland wrote, "to let herself be molested, a little, by the camera"—and, indeed, by the capabilities of the film.

caliber of pictures. Whoever produces the best photo materials will sell the most; it is as simple as that.

After a century and a half, the fortunes of photography have piled up in rich, scattered profusion. There are photos everywhere one looks. Newspapers, magazines, museums, family albums, motion-picture theaters, each of these contemporary traders in visual information transmits its messages by means of the language of photographs. Before the invention of photochemical methods of making images, pictures were a wonder. They were a distinctive and special addition to the everyday world. By the late 1980s pictures had become a common coin, bright, plentiful, almost too ubiquitous even to notice.

The Eastman Kodak Company for two-thirds of photography's history has been practically synonymous with this virtually uninhibited spread of photographic images. Few companies have dominated a single industry for so long with such completely all-encompassing commercial strength. Even in the last decade of the twentieth century, when economic conditions are changing the shape of consumer habits, the familiar yellow and red Kodak logo continues to symbolize long-held standards of quality, reliability, and technological achievement. That, of course, had been precisely Eastman's idea. High-quality products manufactured by mass production and sold in high volume would inevitably, he thought, pay back investors in the form of substantial revenues. None of these rewards would have been so fruitful, however, if all of Kodak's individual commercial and technological decisions had not satisfied basic and deeply felt consumer needs.

Shortly after its invention photography began almost spontaneously to divide itself into genres, more or less distinct classes of pictures that responded to society's repeated requests for new sorts of photographic data. What George Eastman had recognized in the 1880s was that another genre could be added to the established list of portrait, documentary, and art photography. He saw no reason why the average man, given sophisticated but easy-to-use equipment, could not also make pictures. With this idea in mind, he invented "popular

photography." Though the result of this insight altered the medium more dramatically than any of its previous permutations, Eastman's company did not limit itself to this single market. Even in its first decade the Eastman Company moved laterally into other photographic fields. By the early twentieth century the Kodak *Grand Exhibition* displayed pictures representative of every conceivable photographic genre: art, photojournalism, portraits, documentary, vernacular snapshots, landscape, advertisements, even pictures that seemed to move. In that sense, "popular photography" is a misnomer. After Eastman's company distributed its expertise to other of the medium's clients and customers, almost all photography became popular.

If a similar photographic show were mounted in 1990, there would be no good reason to develop new categories. Certainly, some of these photos must cut across generic lines in ways that might have surprised even Eastman. What would separate great contemporary photojournalism, for instance, from great art? A lucky snapshot of an important world event from a piece of professional photojournalism? A telling portrait from an advertising shot? A panoramic landscape from a sweeping film scene? A perfectly exposed photograph taken with a single-use camera from one that was made with the most expensive piece of equipment?

The satisfactions of photography, its emotional modes and traditional genres, have remained deeply embedded in its history. As the photographer Henri Cartier-Bresson has written, "Photography since its origins has not changed, except in its technical aspects." Cartier-Bresson's clever aphorism might well stand as a short description of the history of the Eastman Kodak Company's one-hundred-and-ten-year involvement with photography. Kodak's chief strength has been its ability to understand that improved technology merely increases the pleasures of photography; it does not fundamentally change them. More than any other visual medium, photography is a commercial enterprise, a vendor of images, and as such its continued success depends upon both the wide range of its emotional appeal and the superiority of its standing as a carrier of visual information.

The story of Kodak's second century in this highly competitive marketplace is, of course, as yet untold. In the late 1980s the company continued its trend toward diversification when it purchased Sterling Drug, Inc. Kodak had from its earliest days researched and manufactured chemical compounds, and the acquisition of this pharmaceutical firm was a natural outgrowth of that sort of expertise. In the related field of the health sciences Kodak upgraded its Ektachem blood analyzers and continued to investigate and market a variety of other biotechnical products. Similar nonphotographic merchandise such as Kodakpak PET, a polymer used for making food and beverage packaging, came out of the Eastman Chemicals Division. Kodak Diversified Technologies Division also manufactured optical discs, computer diskettes, Ektaprint copiers, computer-assisted microfilm systems, acetate yarns, and even batteries. Though many would be surprised to discover the Kodak name on some of these products, each contributed to the company's total revenues. Annual sales in Eastman Chemicals Division alone, for instance, equaled those of firms listed in *Fortune* magazine's top two hundred American companies.

In spite of all this activity in the spheres of chemistry, electronics, and nontraditional image making, conventional silver-halide photography remained the field with which Kodak was principally affiliated. Even during the 1980s, when foreign competition and the introduction of electronic methods of image making were forcing it to confront a new economic order, the Eastman Kodak Company was the bellwether of the photographic world. Analysts of the medium, whether their primary interests were artistic, technological, or financial, looked to Kodak for signs of change in the business of picture taking, and the link between its business decisions and the future of photography was impossible to ignore, particularly in the flourishing area of consumer photography.

By the late 1980s almost all amateur photographers in the world's most technologically advanced countries were taking color negative pictures. In a few, most notably Russia and

Seen from the air, the earth's surface often seems to have been hammered out of a soft modeling substance. Marilyn Bridges spe- *cializes in aerial views such as this 1983 photograph of Monument Valley on Tri-X pan professional film. In her photographs,* *Bridges "reinforces the emotion of the landscape" by "maintaining a relation-ship between tone, shape, and texture."*

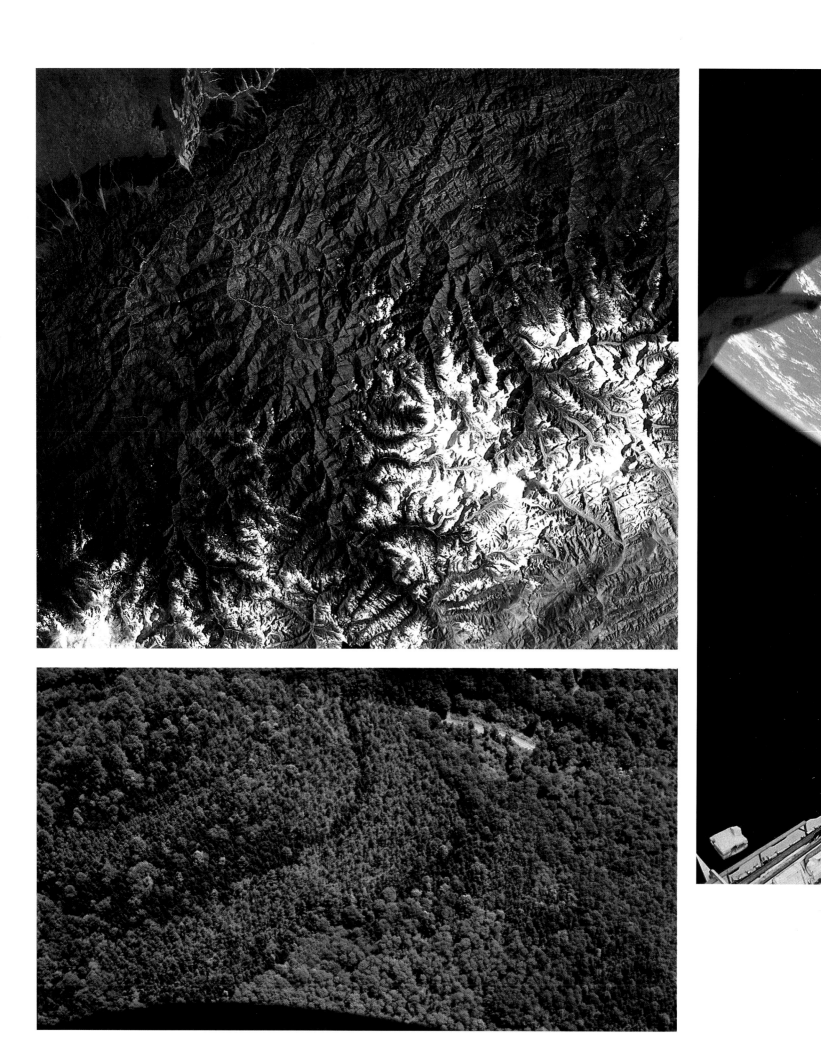

High-altitude aerial photography of various specialized (and spectacular) varieties continued to be produced throughout the 1980s. The infrared view of Mount Everest (top left), for instance, one half of a mapping stereo taken from the Columbia space shuttle in December 1983, encompassed the mountain and the surrounding 185 square kilometers of Himalayan landscape.

"False color" infrared film, which usually renders normally invisible infrared rays as colors of the visible spectrum, can be used, as in this U.S. Bureau of Mines infrared photograph on Ektachrome infrared film (lower left), to detect subtle changes in the health of vegetation. (continued)

China, black and white was still the standard, but even in these places a change was beginning to be seen as they opened their markets to Western products. In China, for instance, Kodak had sold film-manufacturing technology to Xiamen Photographic, and in Russia, Kodak and six other companies had formed a trading consortium. It seems inevitable that at some point the entire world will see itself in color.

For the most part, color pictures would be conventionally printed in the popular 3½ x 5-inch size either by minilabs or by larger facilities such as those linked to the Kodak Colorwatch system. There would be a change, however, in the availability of enlargements. The Kodak Create-a-Print 35mm print-enlargement center was introduced in 1989 to give amateurs the opportunity to enlarge favorite photos themselves. With this machine a film image is copied electronically and displayed on a video screen. The customer is then able to zoom in on an important section of the scene, crop out unwanted parts of the picture, and within five minutes have the edited photograph printed.

The question inevitably posed by such systems seems obvious. Why not produce pictures by purely electronic means and dispense with the film altogether? By the early 1980s three Japanese camera manufacturers were marketing electronic still video cameras that captured images on floppy disks. Though these filmless cameras continue at present to be very expensive, there is little doubt that they will come down in price, and even now their attractions are obvious. Each 2-inch disk is capable of containing either twenty-five high-resolution pictures or fifty images with half the resolving power. What's more, with proper interactive equipment images can easily be displayed on a video monitor for "soft viewing."

As technically far reaching as each of these still video cameras is, however, none is able to match film in the amount of information captured on a single photographic negative. The resolving powers of electronic sensors on which video stills are viewed are measured by picture elements, or pixels. Kodak's latest version of this electronic sensor can provide 4 million pixels of image information at a time. By contrast, a typical 35mm color negative frame contains the equivalent of 15 million pixels, and a transparency on Kodachrome 64-speed professional film holds about that of 60 million pixels. With the almost yearly introduction of finer-grain, more highly resolved films, there seems no way this gap can be closed in the immediate future.

But what about the less immediate future? Most people, after all, watch thousands of hours of television each year without complaint, and it seems likely that video technology will vastly improve. The experts polled by Kodak disagree about the outlook for video. Benedict Fernandez, chairman of the photography department at the Parsons School of Design in New York City, has written:

Electronics definitely will have a big impact on amateur photography. By the early 21st century, the majority of people will be using still video cameras. They want its rapid capability and they love to project pictures on their home television. Eventually everyone will have the technology to produce hard copies from their still video cameras.

Others, such as the fine-art photographer Larry Fink, think the differences between the two media too significant to allow anyone to make such a pat prophecy:

Television didn't replace radio, still images won't replace silver-halide photography, and Life *magazine came back.*

More and more people are buying cameras and taking pictures. The reason may be that the nature of a cold fact, imprisoned on film, gives birth to intense nostalgia. It allows people to relive the meaning of a factual moment.

There is something indelible about a moment that is photographed well. When you freeze it beautifully it gives birth in the mind to a fluid sense of associations. In video, associations are flooded away by the on-going currency of linear movement. A still photograph is like a novel. It allows you to think. Photography is an illusion. It frees your memory and makes your brain a more active element.

People are drawn to photography because luck can produce a good photograph, while luck seldom produces a good piece of any other kind of art. A photograph can be discovered. A snapshot can be an incredible document. Photographing is a gamble. While most pictures are bland and banal, people keep snapping those frames, pulling down that lever to see if the strawberries are coming across the board.

Between these two positions lies the question of whether Kodak should aggressively enter the business of electronic image making. Simply put, will video render silver-halide photography a quaint, antique way of making pictures? Kodak analysts think not. By all accounts film remains and will continue to remain the preferred medium for picture taking. In 1986, however, Kodak made its first forays into the electronic field when it announced the formation of an Electronic Photography Division. Most of the products produced by this division, such as video recorder/players, a video thermal printer, and a video transceiver for sending electronic images over telephone lines, are intended for professional and commercial use. A prototypical still video camera was also announced, but even its initial effect upon the market remains unclear. One Kodak executive has speculated that electronic imaging is currently about where the video-cassette recording industry was ten years ago, and that it will take at least that long for its impact to be felt.

For amateurs, then, despite the imminent arrival of electronics, the chemically produced photograph is still the established and favored way to make visual records. The same is true of many of photography's other traditional genres. Indeed, even with the accelerated growth of televised news, the demand for silver-halide pictures shows no signs of decreasing. Perhaps the most significant shift in this genre was the move toward color. Traditionally photojournalists, unlike their counterparts in the amateur sector of the photo community, took few color photos. Black-and-white film, lacking the complex layering of color stock, was usually faster and easier to manipulate. By the late 1980s, in fact, Kodak T-Max P3200 film not only could capture scenes under extremely low levels of light but it stopped even the most rapid action. Photojournalists covering sporting events, nighttime disasters, or any of the many typically difficult assignments calling for on-the-spot pictures were returning with easily processed and reliable records.

By the mid-1980s, however, with more news publications utilizing color printing, photojournalists were increasingly required to use color stock. In 1988, Kodak introduced its Ektapress Gold series of films in 100, 400, and 1600 speeds. The last stock in particular enabled press photographers to expose color negative film when only low ambient light, such as at a nighttime football game, was available. In brighter situations, a golf tournament, for instance, Ektar 1000 film could be used to produce highly saturated, high-speed photos.

Though many predicted its imminent arrival on the photojournalistic scene, electronics has most often been used for the transmittal of photochemical images. At the 1988 summer Olympics in Seoul, for example, slides and negatives were scanned on a Kodak Eikonix 1435 digital scanner and transmitted via satellite to Kodak's Designmaster 800 systems in London and New York City, where they were enhanced, retouched, printed as color separations, and then sent to U.S. and British newspapers.

Like their counterparts in the fine arts and educational worlds, press photographers were divided about the place of purely electronic imaging in their business. For instance, Magnum agency's photojournalist Eli Reed observed:

Opposite:

Ed Webster took this shot on film provided by Kodak as his climbing partner Robert Anderson rappeled down a Mount Everest crevasse after their successful 1988 unaided ascent up the mountain. Determined to get a picture of the sunrise one bitter cold morning, Webster took off his gloves, in the process suffering frostbite on the ends of eight of his fingers.

Left above:

Taking photographs in weather conditions as extreme as those encountered by Will Steeger's 1989 Trans Antarctica expedition puts incredible strains on photographic equipment. Shutters stiffen, lens elements separate, and the film itself can become brittle and break. If adequate precautions are taken (chemical hand warmers attached to the camera body, for instance), photographs such as this shot on professional Kodachrome 64 film of a dogsled on an Antarctic plain can bring back, as they have since the days of Peary's drive to the Pole, visual journal entries made during record-breaking expeditions.

Left below:

In the summer of 1980, as the runner carrying the Olympic torch through the darkened streets of Seoul, South Korea, approached the Olympic stadium, Maja Moritz of Bongarts Sportspressphoto took this color shot on high-speed Kodak Ektapress 1600 color film using only the ambient light of the runner's torch and a few stray incandescent lights.

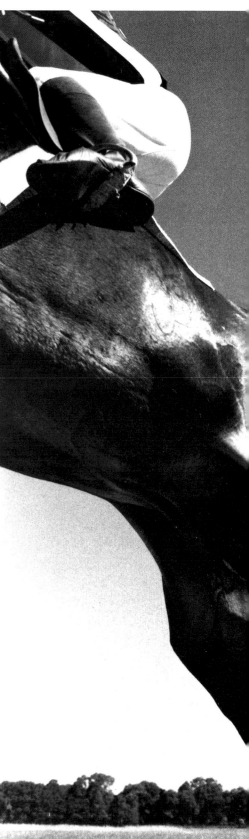

When Eadweard Muybridge performed his famous photographic experiment in 1878 to capture a horse's movements, he claimed to have invented a shutter that operated at 1/1,000 of a second. Muybridge's pictures, as historian Naomi Rosenblum has written, were "not remarkably clear," but they proved the point. These photographs taken by the East German Rudi Schaefer in 1989 were exposed at 1/8,000 of a second using Kodak's high-speed T-Max P3200 professional film. In Schaefer's study, motion is caught suspended in photographs distinctly remarkable for their sharpness and depth of detail.

Contemporary cinematographers usually refer to film stocks by the last two digits of a four-digit Eastman Kodak Company film number. For instance, "47" is the short-hand version of Eastman color-negative film 5247. Each of Kodak's movie stocks is created for specific lighting situations and is used, as cinematographer Vittorio Storaro has said, to "write with light and motion, using shade and color to punctuate one important part of the vocabulary of cinema." The overall look of Steven Spielberg's Shanghai-based World War II drama Empire of the Sun, cinematographer Alan Daviau has explained, was intended to give a "feeling as much as possible of the darkness and doom over Shanghai...to get some feel of the corruption and yet the color of the city, the strange hothouse atmosphere." To create this effect Daviau used "94 for all the night interiors and night exteriors, basically all night scenes. The 47 was for day and all day exteriors."

I wonder, though, if it will be possible to make video images work in a form as successful as a traditional still photograph. I think people will always want the printed image. Everyone remembers that Pulitzer Prize-winning photograph that Eddie Adams took of the Vietnamese officer shooting the prisoner in the head. Most people don't realize that they also saw the same image on television. We simply don't remember it.

Bill Pierce, a U.S. News & World Report contract photographer, has speculated otherwise:

Film and electronics will coexist because they each offer advantages. Electronics offers speed. Film is portable and cheap and provides an incredible "pixel" count.... There will be very good film photography and very good electronic photography. The question will be when do I use what.

For many analysts, including those at Kodak, the film/electronics issue will not be posed as an either/or question. Rather than choosing one or the other of these media, many photographers, it is thought, will employ hybrid systems that combine the best of both worlds. When it was introduced in the fall of 1989, for instance, Kodak's Premier system was able to read a piece of film, display it electronically on an imaging work station, and after enhancement "output" second-generation original images onto an 8 x 10-inch color transparency or color negative film. Similarly the Kodak Prism system captures a photographic image on a still-video floppy disc for electronic previewing. It was expected that portrait photographers would use this

system to allow customers to select poses immediately, without waiting for the film to be processed. However, the final product, a high-quality photochemical image, remains the same.

The hybridization of film/electronics is also becoming a fixture in the movie industry. While the debate continues over the future of high-definition television, moviemakers were by early 1990 able to take advantage of two new extended-range color negative films, the 500-speed EXR 5296 for use in low-light situations and 50-speed EXR 5245 for use in real or artificial daylight. Like the Ektar still stock, these films make use of the new tabular-grain and DIAR technology and are sharper and more highly resolved than any previous movie film. When Kodak scientists compared these films with the resolving power of the proposed 1125-line digital HDTV system currently under study, they discovered that each frame of exposed EXR stock contains three times the amount of visual information.

Hybridization also seems to be the answer in this section of the photographic world. Like the Premier and Prism systems, Kodaks's high-resolution electronic intermediate system for use in the movie industry begins with film and ends with film. Thirty-five millimeter film is electronically scanned, manipulated at an image-computing station, and finally put back on film by a laser film recorder. With this technology motion-picture makers are allowed to use digital image-processing technologies to create special effects without compromising image quality.

And image quality has for little over one hundred years been the most noticeable figure in the carpet of the Eastman Kodak Company's technological history. Not the only shape woven into the tableau, but the easiest to see at a glance. During each discrete era of the company's

The 1988 Who Framed Roger Rabbit? *(above left), many scenes of which are composites featuring two or more separate images, used "97" and "94" "for normal daylight and night exteriors, respectively, but switched to "47" for scenes that would be optically pieced together by George Lucas's ILM (Industrial Light and Magic) laboratories to create the integrated shots of human and animated characters. For much of the 1990 film* Blaze *(above), cinematographer Haskell Wexler loaded his cameras with 45 and 96, the newly introduced sharp, wide-latitude, fine-grained Eastman EXR (extended-range) 5245 and 5296 films. As Wexler has said of one of these stocks, "If you are shooting a film in bright daylight, and you want the look to have an aura of reality, the 45 film, combined with a crisp, sharp lens, will yield brilliant, truer-than-life images without filtration."*

The power of black-and-white photography to sum up certain symbolic truths is still unmistakable, as in this James Nachtwey photograph taken at the Berlin Wall on Tri-X film in 1989.

history it developed, manufactured, and merchandised equipment designed to enable masses of people to more accurately and more pleasurably view images. The Kodak camera, roll film, 35mm movie stock, panchromatic emulsions, color film, each of these products fundamentally transformed the manner in which the world viewed itself. But image quality alone does not fully account for the legacy left after one hundred and ten years of technological progress. It is the artifacts, the photos, that finally tell the story.

Will any of photography's traditional modes or genres change? Probably not. Pictures will be made by anonymous amateurs that are powerful but ultimately very private. The press of events will continue to be shaped by photojournalists. These still images seem more compelling than any other sort of visual record. It is also likely that the artistry of the medium will rise along with the level of information contained in a single piece of film. Fine-art photographers may, in fact, manipulate form and color with the confidence of other plastic artists. The appeal and glamour of motion-picture illusion seem too deeply satisfying to be outmoded by the newest video technology. The world may be linked by electronic images, but the act of sitting in a darkened theater and watching events unfold on the silver screen seems too special to be replaced by more private forms of entertainment.

Will the technical nature of each of these genres change? Indeed, almost certainly. But that's another story, one of Kodak and another century.

In 1989 Kodak manufactured its first panoramic camera since the discontinuance of the No. 3-A Kodak Panoram camera in 1928. This new single-use camera, called the "Stretch 35," encompasses a 75-degree field of view and, like the original Kodak camera, is returned to company labs, where it is taken apart and the film removed and processed. This 3½x10-inch picture was taken in Blue Pearl Bay, Whitsunday Islands, Australia, in 1989.

John Green. Yosemite. 1986. Ektachrome 64 film.

CREDITS

Numbers refer to page numbers.

TEXT CREDITS

20, 38, & 40: extracts from Carl Ackerman, *George Eastman*, Riverside Press, 1932.

48, 55, 59–60, 62, 63–64, 65, 70–71, 72–73, & 81: extracts from Ackerman, *George Eastman*, op. cit.

49: *American Journal of Photography*, Spring 1886.

73: Gilbert & Sullivan, *Utopia Ltd.*

99 & 107–8: extracts from Ackerman, *George Eastman*, op. cit.

123: Jacques Saloman, *Vuillard and His Kodak*, Lefevre Gallery, London, 1964.

141, 147–48, 148–49, 149, & 156: extracts from Ackerman, *George Eastman*, op. cit.

143: Peter Bogdanovitch, *Allan Dwan: The Last Pioneer*, © 1971 Praeger Publishers, Inc.

151: Kevin Brownlow, *The War, the West, the Wilderness*, © Kevin Brownlow 1978, Alfred A. Knopf, Inc.

163–64: courtesy Eastman Kodak Company.

167: Excerpts from *I Married Adventure* by Osa Johnson. Revised edition © 1989 by The Martin and Osa Johnson Safari Museum, Chanute, Kansas. Reprinted by William Morrow & Company, Inc.

185–86, 187, & 189: courtesy Eastman Kodak Company.

192: The New York Times Company © 1930.

195, 204, & 208: quotations from T. H. James, *A Biography-Autobiography of Charles Edward Kenneth Mees* (unpublished manuscript).

215: quotation from *Journey: 75 Years of Kodak Research*, Eastman Kodak Company.

218: *Life* magazine © Time Warner. Reprinted with Permission.

220: *The New York Herald Tribune*, 1937.

226: courtesy Eastman Kodak Company.

233: quotation courtesy Kodak AG (West Germany).

239: John Kobal, *The Art of the Great Hollywood Portrait Photographers*, © 1980 Alfred A. Knopf, Inc.

253 top & bottom: *Life* magazine © Time Warner. Reprinted with Permission.

254: Frank Capra, *The Name above the Title*, © Frank Capra 1971, Macmillan

259–61, 261, 263, 267, & 268: quotations from *Journey*, op. cit.

275 & 285: courtesy Eastman Kodak Company.

293: Letter from Edward Steichen to Ivan Dmitri, Eastman Kodak Company Archives, courtesy Joanna Steichen.

294: Letter from Beaumont Newhall to Ivan Dmitri, Eastman Kodak Company Archives, courtesy the Estate of Beaumont Newhall.

298: Reprinted from *The Saturday Evening Post*, © 1947.

304, 304–5, & 315: courtesy NASA.

314 top: Reprinted by permission from *Winogrand: Figments from the Real World* by John Szarkowski, © The Museum of Modern Art, New York 1988.

314 bottom: Susan D. Moeller, *Shooting War*, © 1989 Susan D. Moeller, Basic Books, Inc.

326: Quote reprinted from transcript of tape *Da Nang*, April 4, 1965, p. 10, Time Life Archives.

327: Excerpt from *A Man with a Camera* by Nestor Almendros. Translation © 1984 by Farrar, Straus and Giroux, Inc. Reprinted by permission of Farrar, Straus and Giroux, Inc.

329: Reprinted by permission from *The History of Photography* by Beaumont Newhall, © The Museum of Modern Art, New York 1982.

374–75, 375, & 375–80: courtesy Eastman Kodak Company.

INDEX